INSIGHTS FOR MARKETING MANAGEMENT

INSIGHTS FOR MARKETING MANAGEMENT

Gabriel M. Gelb
Certified Management Consultant
Gelb Consulting Group, Houston

Betsy D. Gelb, Ph.D.
Assistant Professor of Marketing
University of Houston

Goodyear Publishing Company, Inc.
Santa Monica, California

024412

Library of Congress Cataloging in Publication Data

Gelb, Gabriel M   1929-   comp.
     Insights for marketing management.

     Includes bibliographical references.
     1. Marketing management—Addresses, essays, lectures.
I. Gelb, Betsy D., 1935-   joint comp.   II. Title.

HF5415.13.G39 1977   658.8   76-53773
ISBN: 0-87620-474-4

Copyright © 1977 by Goodyear Publishing Company, Inc.
Santa Monica, California

Current printing (last digit):

10 9 8 7 6 5 4 3   2   1

ISBN: 0-87620-474-4
Library of Congress Catalog Card Number: 76-53773

Y-4744-2

Printed in the United States of America

CONTENTS

3 INSIGHTS INTO:
THE ANALYTICAL/STRATEGIC APPROACH

4 INSIGHTS INTO:
MANAGING THE MARKETING ACTIVITY

5 INSIGHTS INTO:
THE CHALLENGE TO MARKETING

PREFACE

This book of readings is designed for those who are involved in communication and persuasion—in other words, virtually every person in our society.

More narrowly, it is designed for marketing managers, present and future.

We have selected 34 articles by a diversified group of authors who, we believe, shed considerable light on the managing of marketing activities. Furthermore, our choices indicate a belief that the range of those activities grows daily, offering ideas of relevance in fields that we used to call public relations, government relations, and non-profit agency management, to name just a few. As a result, the area of marketing today is much more complex than the subject matter taught even five years ago in most colleges of business administration.

Although this book can stand by itself, it is also planned as a companion volume to a new textbook, *Marketing Principles: The Management Process*, second edition (Santa Monica: Goodyear Publishing Co., 1977), written by our friend Ben M. Enis. Like Dr. Enis' book, our selection of reading is divided into five parts, which we have labeled:

One: The Real Face of Marketing
Two: The New Marketplace

Three: The Analytical/Strategic Approach
Four: Managing the Marketing Activity
Five: The Challenge to Marketing

Students and marketing practitioners alike will find both practical and theoretical concepts expressed in these readings. There are ideas about market segmentation and positioning that can be put into use today, as well as explorations into the "why" of marketing.

Useful marketing literature comes from a variety of sources, not just from marketing professors. Therefore, we have combed many publications for articles which are both helpful and well written. Included in this volume are contributors representing such occupations as advertising agency executives, two futurists, an economist, two marketing research managers, an official of the Federal Trade Commission, and several consultants. The usual galaxy of business and marketing professors will also be found in these pages.

Four Canadians and two British writers also contribute to the multinational interplay of ideas.

To all of these authors, our thanks, not only for permission to reprint their articles, but principally for their cogent and stimulating thoughts.

INSIGHTS INTO: THE REAL FACE OF MARKETIN

Marketing, we are now beginning to realize, is not merely a course taught in colleges of business—it is a basic human activity.

Like many other basic concepts such as communications, marketing's real face is difficult to see. Difficult to define in words, marketing's features are perceived differently by different people.

The "manager of marketing" at one business firm might be in charge of sales. At another firm, he might be in charge of sales and promotion. At a third firm, he might direct new product planning, physical distribution, sales, advertising, and public relations.

In its broadest sense, however, marketing encompasses all of these activities and more, since it represents the exchange of value for value for the purpose of satisfying human wants.

In business, the *management* of marketing is the process of increasing the effectiveness of the firm's marketing activities. In simplest terms, the marketing manager is involved in matching his organization's products and/or services to the present and future needs of customers within the constraints imposed by society

This process can also be considered in relation to a company, a nonprofit group, a church, a police department, a medical society, a political party, and a host of other nonbusiness activities. Marketing is marketing whether we are selecti a school to attend or we are trading our money at a checkout counter for a bagful of groceries.

The four authors in this section explore these key concepts as they search fo the real face of marketing.

1
A GENERIC CONCEPT OF MARKETING

Philip Kotler
Harold T. Martin Professor of Marketing
Northwestern University

In this opening reading, Dr. Kotler offers an important vision of marketing. A very basic definition is outlined: marketing is seen as the disciplined task of creating and offering values to others for the purpose of achieving a desired response.

One of the signs of the health of a discipline is its willingness to reexamine its focus, techniques, and goals as the surrounding society changes and new problems require attention. Marketing has

From Philip Kotler, "A Generic Concept of Marketing," Journal of Marketing, *April 1972, pp. 46-54. Published by the American Marketing Association. Reprinted by permission of the author and publisher.*

shown this aptitude in the past. It was originally founded as a branch of *applied economics* devoted to the study of distribution channels. Later marketing became a *management discipline* devoted to engineering increases in sales. More recently, it has taken on the character of an *applied behavioral science* that is concerned with understanding buyer and seller systems involved in the marketing of goods and services.

The focus of marketing has correspondingly shifted over the years. Marketing evolved through a *commodity focus* (farm products, minerals, manufactured goods, services); an *institutional focus* (producers, wholesalers, retailers, agents); a *functional focus* (buying, selling, promoting, transporting, storing, pricing); a *managerial focus* (analysis, planning, organization, control); and a *social focus* (market efficiency, product quality, and social impact). Each new focus had its advocates and its critics. Marketing emerged each time with a refreshed and expanded self-concept.

Today marketing is facing a new challenge concerning whether its concepts apply in the non-business as well as the business area. In 1969, this author and Professor Levy advanced the view that *marketing is a relevant discipline for all organizations insofar as all organizations can be said to have customers and products.*[1] This "broadening of the concept of marketing" proposal received much attention, and the 1970 Fall Conference of the American Marketing Association was devoted to this theme.

Critics soon appeared who warned that the broadening concept could divert marketing from its true purposes and dilute its content. One critic did not deny that marketing concepts and tools could be useful in fund raising, museum membership drives, and presidential campaigns, but he felt that these were extracurricular applications of an intrinsical business technology.[2]

Several articles have been published which describe applications of marketing ideas to non-business areas such as health services, population control, recycling of solid wastes, and fund raising.[3] Therefore, the underlying issues should be reexamined to see whether a more generic concept of marketing can be established. This author concludes that the traditional conception of marketing would relegate this discipline to an increasingly narrow and pedestrian role in a society that is growing increasingly postindustrial. In fact, this article will argue that the broadening proposal's main weakness was not that it went too far but that it did not go far enough.

This article is organized into five parts. The first distinguishes three stages of consciousness regarding the scope of marketing. The second presents an axiomatic treatment of the generic concept of marketing. The third suggests three useful marketing typologies that are implied by the generic concept of marketing. The fourth describes the basic analytical, planning, organization, and control tasks that make up the logic of marketing management. The fifth discusses some interesting questions raised about the generic concept of marketing.

THREE STAGES OF MARKETING CONSCIOUSNESS

Three different levels of consciousness can be distinguished regarding the boundaries of marketing. The present framework utilizes Reich's consciousness categories without his specific meanings.[4] The traditional consciousness, that marketing is essentially a business subject, will be called *consciousness one.* Consciousness one is the most widely held view in the mind of practitioners and the public. In the last few years, a marketing *consciousness two* has appeared among some marketers holding that marketing is appropriate for all organizations that have customers. This is the thrust of the original broadening proposal and seems to be gaining adherents. Now it can be argued that even consciousness two expresses a limited concept of marketing. One can propose *consciousness three* that holds that marketing is a relevant subject for all organizations in their relations with all their publics, not only customers. The future character of marketing will depend on the particular consciousness that most marketers adopt regarding the nature of their field.

Consciousness One

Consciousness one is the conception that marketing is essentially a business subject. It maintains that marketing is concerned with *sellers, buyers,* and *"economic" product and services.* The sellers offer goods and services, the buyers have purchasing power and other resources, and the objective is an exchange of goods for money or other resources.

The core concept defining marketing consciousness one is that of *market transactions.* A market transaction involves the transfer of ownership or use of an economic good or service from one party to another in return for a payment of some kind. For market transactions to occur in a society, six conditions are necessary:

1. Two or more parties
2. A scarcity of goods
3. Concept of private property
4. One party must want a good held by another
5. The "wanting" party must be able to offer some kind of payment for it
6. The "owning" party must be willing to forego the good for the payment.

These conditions underlie the notion of a market transaction, or more loosely, economic exchange.

Market transactions can be contrasted with nonmarket transactions. Nonmarket transactions also involve a transfer of resources from one party to another, *but without clear payment by the other*. Giving gifts, paying taxes, receiving free services are all examples of nonmarket transactions. If a housekeeper is paid for domestic services, this is a market transaction; if she is one's wife, this is a nonmarket transaction. Consciousness one marketers pay little or no attention to nonmarket transactions because they lack the element of explicit payment.

Consciousness Two

Consciousness two marketers do not see *payment* as a necessary condition to define the domain of marketing phenomena. Marketing analysis and planning are relevant in all organizations producing products and services for an intended consuming group, whether or not payment is required.

Table 1 lists several nonbusiness organizations and their "products" and "customer groups." All of these products, in principle, can be priced and sold. A price can be charged for museum attendance, safe driving lessons, birth control information, and education. The fact that many of these services are offered "free" should not detract from their character as products. A product is something that has value to someone. Whether a charge is made for its consumption is an incidental rather than essential feature defining value. In fact, most of these social goods are "priced," although often not in the normal fashion. Police services are paid for by taxes, and religious services are paid for by donations.

Each of these organizations faces marketing problems with respect to its product and customer group. They must study the size and composition of their market and consumer wants, attitudes, and habits. They must design their products to appeal to their target markets. They must develop distribution and communication programs that facilitate "purchase" and satisfaction. They must develop customer feedback systems to ascertain market satisfaction and needs.

Table 1. Some Organizations and Their Products and Customer Groups.

Organization	Product	Customer Group
Museum	Cultural appreciation	General public
National Safety Council	Safer driving	Driving public
Political candidate	Honest government	Voting public
Family Planning Foundation	Birth control	Fertile public
Police department	Safety	General public
Church	Religious experience	Church members
University	Education	Students

Thus consciousness two replaces the core concept of *market transactions* with the broader concept of *organization-client transactions.* Marketing is no longer restricted only to transactions involving parties in a two-way exchange of economic resources. Marketing is a useful perspective for any organization producing products for intended consumption by others. *Marketing consciousness two states that marketing is relevant in all situations where one can identify an organization, a client group, and products broadly defined.*

Consciousness Three

The emergence of a marketing consciousness three is barely visible. Consciousness three marketers do not see why marketing technology should be confined only to an organization's transactions with its client group. An organization —or more properly its management—may engage in marketing activity not only with its customers but also with all other publics in its environment. A management group has to market to the organization's supporters, suppliers, employees, government, the general public, agents and other key publics. *Marketing consciousness three states that marketing applies to an organization's attempts to relate to all of its publics, not just its consuming public.* Marketing can be used in

multiple institutional contexts to effect transactions with multiple targets.

Marketing consciousness three is often
expressed in real situations. One often hears a
marketer say that his real problem is not *outside
marketing* but *inside marketing*; for example,
getting others in his organization to accept his
ideas. Companies seeking a preferred position
with suppliers or dealers see this as a problem
of marketing themselves. In addition, companies
try to market their viewpoint to congressmen in
Washington. These and many other examples
suggest that marketers see the marketing problem
as extending far beyond customer groups.

The concept of defining marketing in terms
of *function* rather than *structure* underlies consciousness three. To define a field in terms of
function is to see it as a process or set of activities.
To define a field in terms of structure is to identify
it with some phenomena such as a set of institutions. Bliss pointed out that many sciences are
facing this choice.[5] In the field of political science,
for example, there are those who adopt a structural
view and define political science in terms of political institutions such as legislatures, government
agencies, judicial courts, and political parties.
There are others who adopt a functional view and
define political science as the study of *power*
wherever it is found. The latter political scientists
study power in the family, in labor-management
relations, and in corporate organizations.

Similarly, marketing can be defined in
terms of functional rather than structural considerations. Marketing takes place in a great number
of situations, including executive recruiting, political campaigning, church membership drives, and
lobbying. Examining the marketing aspects of
these situations can yield new insights into the
generic nature of marketing. The payoff may be
higher than from continued concentration in one
type of structural setting, that of business.

It is generally a mistake to equate a science
with a certain phenomenon. For example, the
subject of *matter* does not belong exclusively to
physics, chemistry, or biology. Rather physics,
chemistry, and biology are logical systems that
pose different questions about matter. Nor does
human nature belong exclusively to psychology,
sociology, social psychology, or anthropology.
These sciences simply raise different questions

about the same phenomena. Similarly, traditional
business subjects should not be defined by institutional characteristics. This would mean that
finance deals with banks, production with factories
and marketing with distribution channels. Yet
each of these subjects has a set of core ideas that
are applicable in multiple institutional contexts.
An important means of achieving progress in a
science is to try to increase the generality of its
concepts.

Consider the case of a hospital as an institution. A production-minded person will want to
know about the locations of the various facilities,
the jobs of the various personnel, and in general
the arrangement of the elements to produce the
product known as health care. A financial-minded
person will want to know the hospital's sources
and applications of funds and its income and
expenses. A marketing-minded person will want
to know where the patients come from, why
they appeared at this particular hospital, and how
they feel about the hospital care and services.
Thus the phenomena do not create the questions
to be asked; rather the questions are suggested by
the disciplined view brought to the phenomena.

What then is the disciplinary focus of
marketing? The core concept of marketing is the
*transaction. A transaction is the exchange of
values between two parties.* The things-of-values
need not be limited to goods, services, and money
they include other resources such as time, energy,
and feelings. Transactions occur not only between
buyers and sellers, and organizations and clients,
but also between any two parties. A transaction
takes place, for example, when a person decides
to watch a television program; he is exchanging
his time for entertainment. A transaction takes
place when a person votes for a particular candidate; he is exchanging his time and support for
expectations of better government. A transaction
takes place when a person gives money to a charity
he is exchanging money for a good conscience.
*Marketing is specifically concerned with how trans-
actions are created, stimulated, facilitated, and
valued.* This is the generic concept of marketing.

THE AXIOMS OF MARKETING

The generic concept of marketing will now
be more rigorously developed. Marketing can be

viewed as a *category of human action* distinguishable from other categories of human action such as voting, loving, consuming, or fighting. As a category of human action, it has certain characteristics which can be stated in the form of axioms. A sufficient set of axioms about marketing would provide unambiguous criteria about what marketing is, and what it is not. Four axioms, along with corollaries, are proposed in the following section.

Axiom 1. *Marketing involves two or more social units, each consisting of one or more human actors.*

    Corollary 1.1. The social units may be individuals, groups, organizations, communities, or nations.

Two important things follow from this axiom. First, marketing is not an activity found outside of the human species. Animals, for example, engage in production and consumption, but do not engage in marketing. They do not exchange goods, set up distribution systems, and engage in persuasive activity. Marketing is a peculiarly human activity.

Second, the referent of marketing activity is another social unit. Marketing does not apply when a person is engaged in an activity in reference to a *thing* or *himself*. Eating, driving, and manufacturing are not marketing activities, as they involve the person in an interactive relationship primarily with things. Jogging, sleeping, and daydreaming are not marketing activities, as they involve the person in an interactive relationship primarily with himself. An interesting question does arise as to whether a person can be conceived of marketing something to himself, as when he undertakes effort to change his own behavior. Normally, however, marketing involves actions by a person directed toward one or more other persons.

Axiom 2. *At least one of the social units is seeking a specific response from one or more other units concerning some social object.*

    Corollary 2.1. The social unit seeking the response is called the *marketer*, and the social unit whose response is sought is called the *market*.

    Corollary 2.2. The social object may be a product, service, organization, person, place, or idea.

    Corollary 2.3. The response sought from the market is some behavior toward the social object, usually acceptance but conceivably avoidance. (More specific descriptions of responses sought are purchase, adoption, usage, consumption, or their negatives. Those who do or may respond are called buyers, adopters, users, consumers, clients, or supporters.)

    Corollary 2.4. The marketer is normally aware that he is seeking the specific response.

    Corollary 2.5. The response sought may be expected in the short or long run.

    Corollary 2.6. The response has value to the marketer.

    Corollary 2.7. *Mutual marketing* describes the case where two social units simultaneously seek a response from each other. Mutual marketing is the core situation underlying bargaining relationships.

Marketing consists of actions undertaken by persons to bring about a response in other persons concerning some specific social object. A social object is any entity or artifact found in society, such as a product, service, organization, person, place, or idea. The marketer normally seeks to influence the market to accept this social object. The notion of marketing also covers attempts to influence persons to avoid the object, as in a business effort to discourage excess demand or in a social campaign designed to influence people to stop smoking or overeating.[6] *The marketer is basically trying to shape the level and composition of demand for his product.* The marketer undertakes these influence actions because he values their consequences. The market may also value the consequences, but this is not a necessary condition for defining the occurrence of marketing activity. The marketer is normally conscious that he is attempting to influence a market, but it is also possible to interpret as marketing activity cases where the marketer is not fully conscious of his ends and means.

Axiom 2 implies that "selling" activity rather than "buying" activity is closer to the core meaning of marketing. The merchant who assembles goods for the purpose of selling them is engaging in marketing, insofar as he is seeking a purchase response from others. The buyer who comes into his store and pays the quoted price is engaging in buying, not marketing, in that he does not seek to produce a specific response in the seller, who has already put the goods up for sale. If the buyer decides to bargain with the seller over the terms, he too is involved in marketing, or if the seller had been reluctant to sell, the buyer has to market himself as an attractive buyer. The terms "buyer" and "seller" are not perfectly indicative of whether one, or both, of the parties are engaged in marketing activity.

Axiom 3. *The market's response probability is not fixed.*

> Corollary 3.1. The probability that the market will produce the desired response is called the *market's response probability.*
>
> Corollary 3.2. The market's response probability is greater than zero; that is, the market is capable of producing the desired response.
>
> Corollary 3.3. The market's response probability is less than one; that is, the market is not internally compelled to produce the desired response.
>
> Corollary 3.4. The market's response probability can be altered by marketer actions.

Marketing activity makes sense in the context of a market that is free and capable of yielding the desired response. If the target social unit *cannot respond* to the social object, as in the case of no interest or no resources, it is not a market. If the target social unit *must respond* to the social object, as in the case of addiction or perfect brand loyalty, that unit is a market but there is little need for marketing activity. In cases where the market's response probability is fixed in the short run but variable in the long run, the marketer may undertake marketing activity to prevent or reduce the erosion in the response probability. Normally, marketing activity is most relevant where the market's response probability is less than one and highly influenced by marketer actions.

Axiom 4. *Marketing is the attempt to produce the desired response by creating and offering values to the market.*

> Corollary 4.1. The marketer assumes that the market's response will be voluntary.
>
> Corollary 4.2. The essential activity of marketing is the creation and offering of value.

Value is defined subjectively from the market's point of view.

> Corollary 4.3. The marketer creates and offers value mainly through configuration, valuation, symbolization, and facilitation. (Configuration is the act of designing the social object. Valuation is concerned with placing terms of exchange on the object. Symbolization is the association of meanings with the object. Facilitation consists of altering the accessibility of the object.)
>
> Corollary 4.4. *Effective marketing* means the choice of marketer actions that are calculated to produce the desired response in the market. *Efficient marketing* means the choice of *least cost* marketer actions that will produce the desired response.

Marketing is an approach to producing desired responses in another party that lies midway between *coercion* on the one hand and *brainwashing* on the other.

Coercion involves the attempt to produce a response in another by forcing or threatening him with agent-inflicted pain. Agent-inflicted pain should be distinguished from object-inflicted pain in that the latter may be used by a marketer as when he symbolizes something such as cigarettes as potentially harmful to the smoker. The use of agent-inflicted pain is normally not a marketing solution to a response problem. That is not to deny that marketers occasionally resort to arranging a "package of threats" to get or keep a customer. For example, a company may threaten to discontinue purchasing from another company if the latter failed to behave in a certain way. But normally, marketing consists of noncoercive actions to induce a response in another.

Brainwashing lies at the other extreme and involves the attempt to produce a response in another by profoundly altering his basic beliefs and values. Instead of trying to persuade a person to see the social object as serving his existing values and interests, the agent tries to shift the subject's values in the direction of the social object. Brainwashing, fortunately, is a very difficult feat to accomplish. It requires a monopoly of communication channels, operant conditioning, and much patience. Short of pure brainwashing efforts are attempts by various agents to change people's basic values in connection with such issues as racial prejudice, birth control, and private property. Marketing has some useful insights to offer to agents seeking to produce basic changes in people, although its main focus is on creating products and messages attuned to existing attitudes and values. It places more emphasis on preference engineering than attitude conditioning, although the latter is not excluded.

The core concern of marketing is that of producing desired responses in free individuals by the judicious creation and offering of values. The marketer is attempting to get value from the market through offering value to it. The marketer's problem is to create attractive values. Value is completely subjective and exists in the eyes of the beholding market. Marketers must understand the market in order to be effective in creating value. This is the essential meaning of the marketing concept.

The marketer seeks to create value in four ways. He can try to design the social object more attractively (configuration); he can put an attractive term on the social object (valuation); he can add symbolic significance in the social object (symbolization); and he can make it easier for the market to obtain the social object (facilitation). He may use these activities in reverse if he wants the social object to be avoided. These four activities have a rough correspondence to more conventional statements of marketing purpose, such as the use of product, price, promotion, and place to stimulate exchange.

The layman who thinks about marketing often overidentifies it with one or two major component activities, such as facilitation or symbolization. In *scarcity economies*, marketing is often identified with the facilitation function. Marketing is the problem of getting scarce goods to a marketplace. There is little concern with configuration and symbolization. In *affluent economies*, marketing is often identified with the symbolization function. In the popular mind, marketing is seen as the task of encoding persuasive messages to get people to buy more goods. Since most people resent persuasion attempts, marketing has picked up a negative image in the minds of many people. They forget or overlook the marketing work involved in creating values through configuration, valuation, and facilitation. In the future post-industrial society concern over the quality of life becomes paramount, and the public understanding of marketing is likely to undergo further change, hopefully toward an appreciation of all of its functions to create and offer value.

TYPOLOGIES OF MARKETING

The new levels of marketing consciousness make it desirable to reexamine traditional classifications of marketing activity. Marketing practitioners normally describe their type of marketing according to the *target market or product.* A *target-market classification* of marketing activity consists of consumer marketing, industrial marketing, government marketing, and international marketing.

A *product* classification consists of durable goods marketing, nondurable goods marketing, and service marketing.

With the broadening of marketing, the preceeding classifications no longer express the full range of marketing application. They pertain to business marketing, which is only one type of marketing. More comprehensive classifications of marketing activity can be formulated according to the *target market*, *product*, or *marketer.*

Target Market Typology

A *target-market classification* of marketing activity distinguishes the various *publics* toward which an organization can direct its marketing activity. *A public is any group with potential interest and impact on an organization.* Every organization has up to nine distinguishable publics (Figure 1). There are three *input publics* (supporters, employees, suppliers), two *output publics* (agents, consumers), and four *sanctioning publics* (government, competitors, special publics, and general public). The organization is viewed as a resource conversion machine which takes the resources of supporters (e.g., stockholders, directors), employees, and suppliers and converts these into products that go directly to consumers or through agents. The organization's basic input-output activities are subject to the watchful eye of sanctioning publics such as government, competitors, special publics,

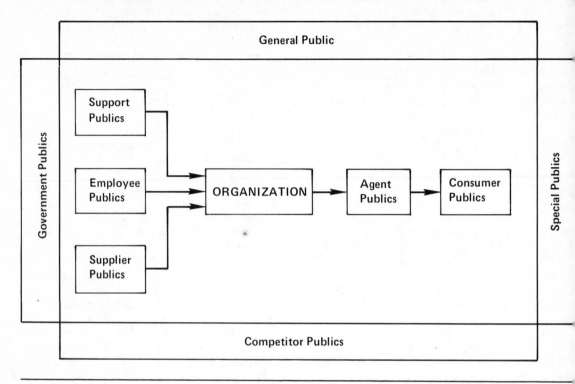

Figure 1. An organization's publics.

and the general public. All of these publics are targets for organizational marketing activity because of their potential impact on the resource converting efficiency of the organization. Therefore, a *target-market classification* of marketing activity consists of supporter-directed marketing, employee-directed marketing, supplier-directed marketing, agent-directed marketing, consumer-directed marketing, general-public-directed marketing, special-public-directed marketing, government-directed marketing, and competitor-directed marketing.

Product Typology

A typology of marketing activity can also be constructed on the basis of the *product* marketed. Under the broadened concept of marketing, the product is no longer restricted to commercial goods and services. An organization can try to market to a public up to six types of products or social objects.

A product classification of marketing consists of goods marketing, service marketing, organization marketing, person marketing, place marketing, and idea marketing.

Goods and service marketing, which made up the whole of traditional marketing, reappear in this classification. In addition, marketers can specialize in the marketing of organizations (e.g., governments, corporations, or universities), persons (e.g., political candidates, celebrities), places (e.g., real estate developments, resort areas, states, cities and ideas (e.g., family planning, Medicare, anti-smoking, safe driving).

Marketer Typology

A typology can also be constructed on the basis of the *marketer*, that is, the organization that is carrying on the marketing. A first approximation would call for distinguishing between business and nonbusiness organization marketing. Since there are several types of nonbusiness organizations with quite different products and marketing tasks, it would be desirable to build a marketer classification that recognizes the different types of organizations. This leads to the following classifications: Business organization marketing, political organization marketing, social organization marketing, religious organization marketing, cultural organization marketing, and knowledge organization marketing.

Organizations are classified according to their primary or formal character. Political organizations would include political parties, government agencies, trade unions, and cause groups. Social organizations would include service clubs, fraternal organizations, and private welfare agencies. Religious organizations would include churches and evangelical movements. Cultural organizations would include museums, symphonies, and art leagues. Knowledge organizations would include public schools, universities, and research organizations. Some organizations are not easy to classify. Is a nonprofit hospital a business or a social organization? Is an employee credit union a political or a social organization? The purpose of the classification is primarily to guide students of marketing to look for regularities that might characterize the activities of certain basic types of organizations.

In general, the purpose of the three classifications of marketing activity is to facilitate the accumulation of marketing knowledge and its transfer from one marketing domain to another. Thus political and social organizations often engage in marketing ideas, and it is desirable to build up generic knowledge about idea marketing. Similarly, many organizations try to communicate a program to government authorities, and they could benefit from the accumulation of knowledge concerning idea marketing and government-directed marketing.

BASIC TASKS OF MARKETING MANAGEMENT

Virtually all persons and organizations engage in marketing activity at various times. They do not all engage in marketing, however, with equal skill. A distinction can be drawn between *marketing* and *marketing management. Marketing* is a descriptive science involving the study of how transactions are created, stimulated, facilitated, and valued. *Marketing management* is a normative science involving the efficient creation and offering of values to stimulate desired transactions. Marketing management is essentially a disciplined view of the task of achieving specific responses in others through the creation and offering of values.

Marketing management is not a set of answers so much as an orderly set of questions by which the marketer determines what is best to do in each situation. Effective marketing consists of intelligently analyzing, planning, organizing, and controlling marketing effort.

The marketer must be skilled at two basic analytical tasks. The first is *marketing analysis.* He must be able to identify the market, its size and location, needs and wants, perceptions and values. The second analytical skill is *product analysis.* The marketer must determine what products are currently available to the target, and how the target feels about each of them.

Effective marketing also calls for four major planning skills. The first is *product development,* i.e., configuration. The marketer should know where to look for appropriate ideas, how to choose and refine the product concept, how to stylize and package the product, and how to test it. The second is *pricing,* i.e., valuation. He must develop an attractive set of terms for the product. The third is *distribution,* i.e., facilitation. The marketer should determine how to get the product into circulation and make it accessible to its target market. The fourth is *promotion,* i.e., symbolization. The marketer must be capable of stimulating market interest in the product.

Effective marketing also requires three organizational skills. The first is *organizational design.* The marketer should understand the advantages and disadvantages of organizing market activity along functional, product, and market lines. The second is *organizational staffing.* He should know how to find, train, and assign effective comarketers. The third is *organizational motivation.* He must determine how to stimulate the best marketing effort by his staff.

Finally, effective marketing also calls for two control skills. The first is *market results measurement,* whereby the marketer keeps informed of the attitudinal and behavioral responses he is achieving in the marketplace. The second is *marketing cost measurement,* whereby the marketer keeps informed of his costs and efficiency in carrying out his marketing plans.

SOME QUESTIONS ABOUT GENERIC MARKETING

The robustness of the particular conception of marketing advocated in this article will be known in time through testing the ideas in various situations. The question is whether the logic called marketing really helps individuals such as educational administrators, public officials, museum directors, or church leaders to better interpret their problems and construct their strategies. If these ideas are validated in the marketplace, they will be accepted and adopted.

However, academic debate does contribute substantially to the sharpening of the issues and conceptions. Several interesting questions have arisen in the course of efforts by this author to expound the generic concept of marketing. Three of these questions are raised and discussed below.

1. *Isn't generic marketing really using influence as the core concept rather than exchange?*

It is tempting to think that the three levels of consciousness of marketing move from *market transactions* to *exchange* to *influence* as the succeeding core concepts. The concept of influence undeniably plays an important role in marketing thought. Personal selling and advertising are essentially influence efforts. Product design, pricing, packaging, and distribution planning make extensive use of influence considerations. It would be too general to say, however, that marketing is synonymous with interpersonal, intergroup, or interorganizational influence processes.

Marketing is a particular way of looking at the problem of achieving a valued response from a target market. It essentially holds that exchange values must be identified, and the marketing program must be based on these exchange values. Thus the anticigarette marketer analyzes what the market is being asked to give up and what inducements might be offered. The marketer recognizes that every action by a person has an opportunity cost. The marketer attempts to find ways to increase the person's perceived rate of exchange between what he would receive and what he would give up in *freely* adopting the behavior. The marketer is a specialist at understanding human wants and values and knows what it takes for someone to act.

2. *How would one distinguish between marketing and a host of related activities such as lobbying, propagandizing, publicizing, and negotiating?*

Marketing and other influence activities and tools share some common characteristics as well as exhibit some unique features. Each influence activity has to be examined separately in relation to marketing. *Lobbying,* for example, is one aspect of government-directed marketing. The lobbyist attempts to evoke support from a legislator through offering values to the legislator (e.g., information, votes, friendship, and favors). A lobbyist thinks through the problem of marketing his legislation as carefully as the business marketer thinks through the problem of marketing his product or service. *Propagandizing* is the marketing of a political or social idea to a mass audience. The propagandist attempts to package the ideas in such a way as to constitute values to the target audience in exchange for support. *Publicizing* is the effort to create attention and interest in a target audience. As such it is a tool of marketing. *Negotiation* is a face-to-face mutual marketing process. In general, the broadened concept of marketing underscores the kinship of marketing with a large number of other activities and suggests that marketing is a more endemic process in society than business marketing alone suggests.

3. *Doesn't generic marketing imply that a marketer would be more capable of managing political or charitable campaigns than professionals in these businesses?*

A distinction should be drawn between marketing as a *logic* and marketing as a *competence.* Anyone who is seeking a response in another would benefit from applying marketing logic to the problem. Thus a company treasurer seeking a loan, a company recruiter seeking a talented executive, a conservationist seeking an antipollution law, would all benefit in conceptualizing their problem in marketing terms. In these instances, they would be donning a marketer's hat although they would not be performing as professional marketers. A professional marketer is someone who (1) regularly works with marketing problems in a specific area and (2) has a specialized knowledge of this area. The political strategist, to the extent he is effective, is a professional marketer. He has learned how to effectively design, package, price, advertise, and distribute his type of product in his type of market. A professional marketer who suddenly decides to handle political candidates would need to develop competence and knowledge in this area just as he would if he suddenly decided to handle soap or steel. Being a marketer only means that a person has mastered the logic of marketing. To master the particular market requires additional learning and experience.

SUMMARY AND CONCLUSION

This article has examined the current debate in marketing concerning whether its substance belongs in the business area, or whether it is applicable to all areas in which organizations attempt to relate to customers and other publics. Specifically, *consciousness one marketing* holds that marketing's core idea is *market transactions*, and therefore marketing applies to buyers, sellers, and commercial products and services. *Consciousness two marketing* holds that marketing's core idea is *organization-client transactions*, and therefore marketing applies in any organization that can recognize a group called customers. *Consciousness three marketing* holds that marketing's core area is *transactions*, and therefore marketing applies to any social unit seeking to exchange values with other social units.

This broadest conception of marketing can be called *generic marketing*. Generic marketing takes a functional rather than a structural view of marketing. Four axioms define generic marketing.

Axiom 1. *Marketing involves two or more social units.*

Axiom 2. *At least one of the social units is seeking a specific response from one or more other units concerning some social object.*

Axiom 3. *The market's response probability is not fixed.*

Axiom 4. *Marketing is the attempt to produce the desired response by creating and offering values to the market.*

These four axioms and their corollaries are intended to provide unambiguous criteria for determining what constitutes a marketing process.

Generic marketing further implies that marketing activity can be classed according to the *target market* (marketing directed to supporters, employees, suppliers, agents, consumers, general public, special publics, government, and competitors); the *product* (goods, services, organizations, persons, places, and ideas); and the *marketer* (business, political, social, religious, cultural, and knowledge organizations).

Marketers face the same tasks in all types of marketing. Their major analytical tasks are *market analysis* and *product analysis*. Their major planning tasks are *product development*, *pricing*, *distribution*, and *promotion*. Their major organizational tasks are *design*, *staffing*, and *motivation*. Their major control tasks are *marketing results measurement* and *marketing cost measurement*.

Generic marketing is a logic available to all organizations facing problems of market response. A distinction should be drawn between applying a marketing point of view to a specific problem and being a marketing professional. Marketing logic alone does not make a marketing professional. The professional also acquires competence, which along with the logic, allows him to interpret his problems and construct his marketing strategies in an effective way.

Notes

1. Philip Kotler and Sidney J. Levy, "Broadening the Concept of Marketing," *Journal of Marketing*, Vol. 33 (January, 1969), pp. 10-15.
2. David Luck, "Broadening the Concept of Marketing—Too Far," *Journal of Marketing*, Vol. 33 (July, 1969), pp. 53-54.
3. *Journal of Marketing*, Vol. 35 (July, 1971).
4. Charles A. Reich, *The Greening of America* (New York: Random House, 1970).
5. Perry Bliss, *Marketing Management and the Behavioral Environment* (Englewood Cliffs, N.J.: Prentice-Hall, Inc., 1970), pp. 106-108, 119-120.
6. See Philip Kotler and Sidney J. Levy, "Demarketing, Yes, Demarketing," *Harvard Business Review*, Vol. 49 (November-December, 1971), pp. 71-80.

2
MARKETING
MYOPIA

Theodore Levitt
Professor of Business Administration
Harvard University

This is perhaps the best-known article on marketing ever written. We believe it should be read once a year by every marketing manager. Read it and learn why "there is no such thing as a growth industry."

Every major industry was once a growth industry. But some that are now riding a wave of growth enthusiasm are very much in the shadow of decline. Others which are thought of as seasoned growth industries have actually stopped growing. In every case the reason growth is threatened, slowed, or stopped is *not* because the market is saturated. It is because there has been a failure of management.

FATEFUL PURPOSES

The failure is at the top. The executives responsible for it, in the last analysis, are those who deal with broad aims and policies. Thus:

The railroads did not stop growing because the need for passenger and freight transportation declined. That grew. The railroads are in trouble today not because the need was filled by others (cars, trucks, airplanes, even telephones), but because it was *not* filled by the railroads themselves. They let others

Reprinted by permission of the publishers from Edward C. Bursk and John F. Chapman, eds., Modern Marketing Strategy, *Cambridge, Mass.: Harvard University Press, Copyright, 1960, 1964, by the President and Fellows of Harvard College.*

take customers away from them because they assumed themselves to be in the railroad business rather than in the transportation business. The reason they defined their industry wrong was because they were railroad-oriented instead of transportation-oriented; they were product-oriented instead of customer-oriented.

Hollywood barely escaped being totally ravished by television. Actually, all the established film companies went through drastic reorganizations. Some simply disappeared. All of them got into trouble not because of TV's inroads but because of their own myopia. As with the railroads, Hollywood defined its business incorrectly. It thought it was in the movie business when it was actually in the entertainment business. "Movies" implied a specific, limited product. This produced a fatuous contentment which from the beginning led producers to view TV as a threat. Hollywood scorned and rejected TV when it should have welcomed it as an opportunity—an opportunity to expand the entertainment business.

Today TV is a bigger business than the old narrowly defined movie business ever was. Had Hollywood been customer-oriented (providing entertainment), rather than product-oriented (making movies), would it have gone through the fiscal purgatory that it did? I doubt it. What ultimately saved Hollywood and accounted for its recent resurgence was the wave of new young writers, producers, and directors whose previous successes in television had decimated the old movie companies and toppled the big movie moguls.

There are other less obvious examples of industries that have been and are now endangering their futures by improperly defining their purposes. I shall discuss some in detail later and analyze the kind of policies that lead to trouble. Right now it may help to show what a thoroughly customer-oriented management *can* do to keep a growth industry growing, even after the obvious opportunities have been exhausted; and here there are two examples that have been around for a long time. They are nylon and glass—specifically E. I. duPont de Nemours & Company and Corning Glass Works:

Both companies have great technical competence. Their product orientation is unquestioned. But this alone does not explain their success. After all, who was more pridefully product-oriented and product-conscious than the erstwhile New England textile companies that have been so thoroughly massacred? The DuPonts and the Cornings have succeeded not primarily because of their product or research orientation but because they have been thoroughly customer-oriented also. It is constant watchfulness for opportunities to apply their technical know-how to the creation of customer-satisfying uses which accounts for their prodigious output of successful new products. Without a very sophisticated eye on the customer, most of their new products might have been wrong, their sales methods useless.

Aluminum has also continued to be a growth industry, thanks to the efforts of two wartime-created companies which deliberately set about creating new customer-satisfying uses. Without Kaiser Aluminum & Chemical Corporation and Reynolds Metals Company, the total demand for aluminum today would be vastly less than it is.

Error of Analysis

Some may argue that it is foolish to set the railroads off against aluminum or the movies off against glass. Are not aluminum and glass naturally so versatile that the industries are bound to have more growth opportunities than the railroads and movies? This view commits precisely the error I have been talking about. It defines an industry, or a product, or a cluster of know-how so narrowly as to guarantee its premature senescence. When we mention "railroads," we should make sure we mean "transportation." As transporters, the railroads still have a good chance for very considerable growth. They are not limited to the railroad business as such (though in my opinion rail transportation is potentially a much stronger transportation medium than is generally believed).

What the railroads lack is not opportunity, but some of the same managerial imaginativeness and audacity that made them great. Even an amateur like Jacques Barzun can see what is lacking when he says:

"I grieve to see the most advanced physical and social organization of the last century go down in shabby disgrace for lack of the same comprehensive imagination that built it up. [What is lacking is] the will of the companies to survive and to satisfy the public by inventiveness and skill."[1]

SHADOW OF OBSOLESCENCE

It is impossible to mention a single major industry that did not at one time qualify for the magic appellation of "growth industry." In each case its assumed strength lay in the apparently unchallenged superiority of its product. There appeared to be no effective substitute for it. It was itself a runaway substitute for the product it so triumphantly replaced. Yet one after another of these celebrated industries has come under a shadow. Let us look briefly at a few more of them, this time taking examples that have so far received a little less attention:

Dry cleaning—This was once a growth industry with lavish prospects. In an age of wool garments, imagine being finally able to get them safely and easily clean. The boom was on.

Yet here we are 30 years after the boom started and the industry is in trouble. Where has the competition come from? From a better way of cleaning? No. It has come from synthetic fibers and chemical additives that have cut the need for dry cleaning. But this is only the beginning. Lurking in the wings and ready to make chemical dry cleaning totally obsolescent is that powerful magician, ultrasonics.

Electric utilities—This is another one of those supposedly "no-substitute" products that has been enthroned on a pedestal of invincible growth. When the incandescent lamp came along, kerosene lights were finished. Later the water wheel and the steam engine were cut to ribbons by the flexibility, reliability, simplicity, and just plain easy availability of electric motors. The prosperity of electric utilities continues to wax extravagant as the home is converted into a museum of electric gadgetry. How can anybody miss by investing in utilities, with no competition, nothing but growth ahead?

But a second look is not quite so comforting. A score of nonutility companies are well advanced toward developing a powerful chemical fuel cell which could sit in some hidden closet of every home silently ticking off electric power. The electric lines that vulgarize so many neighborhoods will be eliminated. So will the endless demolition of streets and service interruptions during storms. Also on the horizon is solar energy, again pioneered by non-utility companies.

Who says that the utilities have no competition? They may be natural monopolies now, but tomorrow they may be natural deaths. To avoid this prospect, they too will have to develop fuel cells, solar energy, and other power sources. To survive, they themselves will have to plot the obsolescence of what now produces their livelihood.

Grocery stores—Many people find it hard to realize that there ever was a thriving establishment known as the "corner grocery store." The supermarket has taken over with a powerful effectiveness. Yet the big food chains of the 1930s narrowly escaped being completely wiped out by the aggressive expansion of independent supermarkets. The first genuine supermarket was opened in 1930, in Jamaica, Long Island. By 1933 supermarkets were thriving in California, Ohio, Pennsylvania, and elsewhere. Yet the established chains pompously ignored them. When they chose to notice them, it was with such derisive descriptions as "cheapy," "horse-and-buggy," "cracker-barrel storekeeping," and "unethical opportunists."

The executive of one big chain announced at the time that he found it "hard to believe that people will drive for miles to shop for foods and sacrifice the personal service chains have perfected and to which Mrs. Consumer is accustomed."[2] As late as 1936, the National Wholesale Grocers convention and the New Jersey Retail Grocers Association said there was nothing to fear. They said that the supers' narrow appeal to the price buyer limited the size of their market. They had to draw from miles around. When imitators came, there would be wholesale liquidations as volume fell. The current high sales of the supers was said to be partly due to their novelty. Basically people wanted convenient neighborhood grocers. If the neighborhood stores "cooperate

with their suppliers, pay attention to their costs, and improve their service," they would be able to weather the competition until it blew over.[3]

It never blew over. The chains discovered that survival required going into the supermarket business. This meant the wholesale destruction of their huge investments in corner store sites and in established distribution and merchandising methods. The companies with "the courage of their convictions" resolutely stuck to the corner store philosophy. They kept their pride but lost their shirts.

Self-Deceiving Cycle

But memories are short. For example, it is hard for people who today confidently hail the twin messiahs of electronics and chemicals to see how things could possibly go wrong with these galloping industries. They probably also cannot see how a reasonably sensible businessman could have been as myopic as the famous Boston millionaire who 50 years ago unintentionally sentenced his heirs to poverty by stipulating that his entire estate be forever invested exclusively in electric streetcar securities. His posthumous declaration, "There will always be a big demand for efficient urban transportation," is no consolation to his heirs who sustain life by pumping gasoline at automobile filling stations.

Yet, in a casual survey I recently took among a group of intelligent business executives, nearly half agreed that it would be hard to hurt their heirs by tying their estates forever to the electronics industry. When I then confronted them with the Boston streetcar example, they chorused unanimously, "That's different!" But is it? Is not the basic situation identical?

In truth, *there is no such thing* as a growth industry, I believe. There are only companies organized and operated to create and capitalize on growth opportunities. Industries that assume themselves to be riding some automatic growth escalator invariably descend into stagnation. The history of every dead and dying "growth" industry shows a self-deceiving cycle of bountiful expansion and undetected decay. There are four conditions which usually guarantee this cycle:

1. The belief that growth is assured by an expanding and more affluent population.
2. The belief that there is no competitive substitute for the industry's major product.
3. Too much faith in mass production and in the advantages of rapidly declining unit costs as output rises.
4. Preoccupation with a product that lends itself to carefully controlled scientific experimentation, improvement, and manufacturing cost reduction.

I should like now to begin examining each of these conditions in some detail. To build my case as boldly as possible, I shall illustrate the points with reference to three industries—petroleum, automobiles, and electronics—particularly petroleum, because it spans more years and more vicissitudes. Not only do these three have excellent reputations with the general public and also enjoy the confidence of sophisticated investors, but their managements have become known for progressive thinking in areas like financial control, product research, and management training. If obsolescence can cripple even these industries, it can happen anywhere.

POPULATION MYTH

The belief that profits are assured by an expanding and more affluent population is dear to the heart of every industry. It takes the edge off the apprehensions everybody understandably feels about the future. If consumers are multiplying and also buying more of your product or service, you can face the future with considerably more comfort than if the market is shrinking. An expanding market keeps the manufacturer from having to think very hard or imaginatively. If thinking is an intellectual response to a problem, then the absence of a problem leads to the absence of thinking. If your product has an automatically expanding market, then you will not give much thought to how to expand it.

One of the most interesting examples of this is provided by the petroleum industry. Probably our oldest growth industry, it has an enviable record. While there are some current apprehensions about its growth rate, the industry itself tends to

be optimistic. But I believe it can be demonstrated that it is undergoing a fundamental yet typical change. It is not only ceasing to be a growth industry, but may actually be a declining one, relative to other business. Although there is widespread unawareness of it, I believe that within 25 years the oil industry may find itself in much the same position of retrospective glory that the railroads are now in. Despite its pioneering work in developing and applying the present-value method of investment evaluation, in employee relations, and in working with backward countries, the petroleum business is a distressing example of how complacency and wrongheadedness can stubbornly convert opportunity into near disaster.

One of the characteristics of this and other industries that have believed very strongly in the beneficial consequences of an expanding population, while at the same time being industries with a generic product for which there has appeared to be no competitive substitute, is that the individual companies have sought to outdo their competitors by improving on what they are already doing. This makes sense, of course, if one assumes that sales are tied to the country's population strings, because the customer can compare products only on a feature-by-feature basis. I believe it is significant, for example, that not since John D. Rockefeller sent free kerosene lamps to China has the oil industry done anything really outstanding to create a demand for its product. Not even in product improvement has it showered itself with eminence. The greatest single improvement, namely, the development of tetraethyl lead, came from outside the industry, specifically from General Motors and DuPont. The big contributions made by the industry itself are confined to the technology of oil exploration, production, and refining.

Asking for Trouble

In other words, the industry's efforts have focused on improving the *efficiency* of getting and making its product, not really on improving the generic product or its marketing. Moreover, its chief product has continuously been defined in the narrowest possible terms, namely, gasoline, not energy, fuel, or transportation. This attitude has helped assure that:

Major improvements in gasoline quality tend not to originate in the oil industry. Also, the development of superior alternative fuels comes from outside the oil industry, as will be shown later.

Major innovations in automobile fuel marketing are originated by small new oil companies that are not primarily preoccupied with production or refining. These are the companies that have been responsible for the rapidly expanding multipump gasoline stations, with their successful emphasis on large and clean layouts, rapid and efficient driveway service, and quality gasoline at low prices.

Thus, the oil industry is asking for trouble from outsiders. Sooner or later, in this land of hungry inventors and entrepreneurs, a threat is sure to come. The possibilities of this will become more apparent when we turn to the next dangerous belief of many managements. For the sake of continuity, because this second belief is tied closely to the first, I shall continue with the same example.

Idea of Indispensability

The petroleum industry is pretty much persuaded that there is no competitive substitute for its major product, gasoline—or if there is, that it will continue to be a derivative of crude oil, such as diesel fuel or kerosene jet fuel.

There is a lot of automatic wishful thinking in this assumption. The trouble is that most refining companies own huge amounts of crude oil reserves. These have value only if there is a market for products into which oil can be converted—hence the tenacious belief in the continuing competitive superiority of automobile fuels made from crude oil.

This idea persists despite all historic evidence against it. The evidence not only shows that oil has never been a superior product for any purpose for very long, but it also shows that the oil industry has never really been a growth industry. It has been a succession of different businesses that have gone through the usual historic cycles of growth, maturity, and decay. Its overall survival is owed to a series of miraculous escapes from total obsolescence, of last-minute and unexpected reprieves from total disaster reminiscent of the Perils of Pauline.

Perils of Petroleum

I shall sketch in only the main episodes:

First, crude oil was largely a patent medicine. But even before that fad ran out, demand was greatly expanded by the use of oil in kerosene lamps. The prospect of lighting the world's lamps gave rise to an extravagant promise of growth. The prospects were similar to those the industry now holds for gasoline in other parts of the world. It can hardly wait for the underdeveloped nations to get a car in every garage.

In the days of the kerosene lamp, the oil companies competed with each other and against gaslight by trying to improve the illuminating characteristics of kerosene. Then suddenly the impossible happened. Edison invented a light which was totally nondependent on crude oil. Had it not been for the growing use of kerosene in space heaters, the incandescent lamp would have completely finished oil as a growth industry at that time. Oil would have been good for little else than axle grease.

Then disaster and reprieve struck again. Two great innovations occurred, neither originating in the oil industry. The successful development of coal-burning domestic central heating systems made the space heater obsolescent. While the industry reeled, along came its most magnificent boost yet—the internal combustion engine, also invented by outsiders. Then when the prodigious expansion for gasoline finally began to level off in the 1920s, along came the miraculous escape of a central oil heater. Once again, the escape was provided by an outsider's invention and development. And when that market weakened, wartime demand for aviation fuel came to the rescue. After the war the expansion of civilian aviation, the dieselization of railroads and the explosive demand for cars and trucks kept the industry's growth in high gear.

Meanwhile centralized oil heating—whose boom potential had only recently been proclaimed—ran into severe competition from natural gas. While the oil companies themselves owned the gas that now competed with their oil, the industry did not originate the natural gas revolution, nor has it to this day greatly profited from its gas ownership. The gas revolution was made by newly formed transmission companies that marketed the product with an aggressive ardor. They started a magnificent new industry, first against the advice and then against the resistance of the oil companies.

By all the logic of the situation, the oil companies themselves should have made the gas revolution. They not only owned the gas; they also were the only people experienced in handling, scrubbing, and using it, the only people experienced in pipeline technology and transmission, and they understood heating problems. But, partly because they knew that natural gas would compete with their own sale of heating oil, the oil companies pooh-poohed the potentials of gas.

The revolution was finally started by oil pipeline executives who, unable to persuade their own companies to go into gas, quit and organized the spectacularly successful gas transmission companies. Even after their success became painfully evident to the oil companies, the latter did not go into gas transmission. The multibillion dollar business which should have been theirs went to others. As in the past, the industry was blinded by its narrow preoccupation with a specific product and the value of its reserves. It paid little or no attention to its customers' basic needs and preferences.

The postwar years have not witnessed any change. Immediately after World War II the oil industry was greatly encouraged about its future by the rapid expansion of demand for its traditional line of products. In 1950 most companies projected annual rates of domestic expansion of around 6 per cent through at least 1975. Though the ratio of crude oil reserves to demand in the free world was about 20 to 1, with 10 to 1 being usually considered a reasonable working ratio in the United States, booming demand sent oil men searching for more without sufficient regard to what the future really promised. In 1952 they "hit" in the Middle East; the ratio skyrocketed to 42 to 1. If gross additions to reserves continue at the average rate of the past five years (37 billion barrels annually), then by 1970 the reserve ratio will be up to 45 to 1. This abundance of oil has weakened crude and product prices all over the world.

Uncertain Future

Management cannot find much consolation today in the rapidly expanding petrochemical industry, another oil-using idea that did not originate in the leading firms. The total United States production of petrochemicals is equivalent to about 2 per cent (by volume) of the demand for all petroleum products. Although the petrochemical industry is now expected to grow by about 10 per cent per year, this will not offset other drains on the growth of crude oil consumption. Furthermore, while petrochemical products are many and growing, it is well to remember that there are nonpetroleum sources of the basic raw material, such as coal. Besides, a lot of plastics can be produced with relatively little oil. A 50,000-barrel-per-day oil refinery is now considered the absolute minimum size for efficiency. But a 5,000-barrel-per-day chemical plant is a giant operation.

Oil has never been a continuously strong growth industry. It has grown by fits and starts, always miraculously saved by innovations and developments not of its own making. The reason it has not grown in a smooth progression is that each time it thought it had a superior product safe from the possibility of competitive substitutes, the product turned out to be inferior and notoriously subject to obsolescence. Until now gasoline (for motor fuel, anyhow) has escaped this fate. But, as we shall see later, it too may be on its last legs.

The point of all this is that there is no guarantee against product obsolescence. If a company's own research does not make it obsolete, another's will. Unless an industry is especially lucky, as oil has been until now, it can easily go down in a sea of red figures—just as the railroads have, as the buggy whip manufacturers have, as the corner grocery chains have, as most of the big movie companies have, and indeed as many other industries have.

The best way for a firm to be lucky is to make its own luck. That requires knowing what makes a business successful. One of the greatest enemies of this knowledge is mass production.

PRODUCTION PRESSURES

Mass-production industries are impelled by a great drive to produce all they can. The prospect of steeply declining unit costs as output rises is more than most companies can usually resist. The profit possibilities look spectacular. All effort focuses on production. The result is that marketing gets neglected.

John Kenneth Galbraith contends that just the opposite occurs.[4] Output is so prodigious that all effort concentrates on trying to get rid of it. He says this accounts for singing commercials, desecration of the countryside with advertising signs, and other wasteful and vulgar practices. Galbraith has a finger on something real, but he misses the strategic point. Mass production does indeed generate great pressure to "move" the product. But what usually gets emphasized is selling, not marketing. Marketing, being a more sophisticated and complex process, gets ignored.

The difference between marketing and selling is more than semantic. Selling focuses on the needs of the seller, marketing on the needs of the buyer. Selling is preoccupied with the seller's need to convert his product into cash; marketing with the idea of satisfying the needs of the customer by means of the product and the whole cluster of things associated with creating, delivering, and finally consuming it.

In some industries the enticements of full mass production have been so powerful that for many years top management in effect has told the sales departments, "You get rid of it; we'll worry about profits." By contrast, a truly marketing-minded firm tries to create value-satisfying goods and services that consumers will want to buy. What it offers for sale includes not only the generic product or service, but also how it is made available to the customer, in what form, when, under what conditions, and at what terms of trade. Most important, what it offers for sale is determined not by the seller but by the buyer. The seller takes his cues from the buyer in such a way that the product becomes a consequence of the marketing effort, not vice versa.

Lag in Detroit

This may sound like an elementary rule of business, but that does not keep it from being violated wholesale. It is certainly more violated than honored. Take the automobile industry:

Here mass production is most famous, most honored, and has the greatest impact on the entire society. The industry has hitched its fortune to the relentless requirements of the annual model change, a policy that makes customer orientation an especially urgent necessity. Consequently the auto companies annually spend millions of dollars on consumer research. But the fact that the new compact cars are selling so well in their first year indicates that Detroit's vast researches have for a long time failed to reveal what the customer really wanted. Detroit was not persuaded that he wanted anything different from what he had been getting until it lost millions of customers to other small car manufacturers.

How could this unbelievable lag behind consumer wants have been perpetuated so long? Why did not research reveal consumer preferences before consumers' buying decisions themselves revealed the facts? Is that not what consumer research is for—to find out before the fact what is going to happen? The answer is that Detroit never really researched the customer's wants. It only researched his preferences between the kinds of things which it had already decided to offer him. For Detroit is mainly product-oriented, not customer-oriented. To the extent that the customer is recognized as having needs that the manufacturer should try to satisfy, Detroit usually acts as if the job can be done entirely by product changes. Occasionally attention gets paid to financing, too, but that is done more in order to sell than to enable the customer to buy.

As for taking care of other customer needs, there is not enough being done to write about. The areas of the greatest unsatisfied needs are ignored, or at best get stepchild attention. These are at the point of sale and on the matter of automotive repair and maintenance. Detroit views these problem areas as being of secondary importance. That is underscored by the fact that the retailing and servicing ends of this industry are neither owned and operated nor controlled by the manufacturers. Once the car is produced, things are pretty much in the dealer's inadequate hands. Illustrative of Detroit's arm's-length attitude is the fact that, while servicing holds enormous sales-stimulating, profit-building opportunities, only 57 of Chevrolet's 7,000 dealers provide night maintenance service.

Motorists repeatedly express their dissatisfaction with servicing and their apprehensions about buying cars under the present selling setup. The anxieties and problems they encounter during the auto buying and maintenance processes are probably more intense and widespread today than 30 years ago. Yet the automobile companies do not *seem* to listen to or take their cues from the anguished consumer. If they do listen, it must be through the filter of their own preoccupation with production. The marketing effort is still viewed as a necessary consequence of the product, not vice versa, as it should be. That is the legacy of mass production, with its parochial view that profit resides essentially in low-cost full production.

What Ford Put First

The profit lure of mass production obviously has a place in the plans and strategy of business management, but it must always *follow* hard thinking about the customer. This is one of the most important lessons that we can learn from the contradictory behavior of Henry Ford. In a sense Ford was both the most brilliant and the most senseless marketer in American history. He was senseless because he refused to give the customer anything but a black car. He was brilliant because he fashioned a production system designed to fit market needs. We habitually celebrate him for the wrong reason, his production genius. His real genius was marketing. We think he was able to cut his selling price and therefore sell millions of $500 cars because his invention of the assembly line had reduced the costs. Actually he invented the assembly line because he had concluded that at $500 he could sell millions of cars. Mass production was the *result* not the cause of his low prices.

Ford repeatedly emphasized this point, but a nation of production-oriented business managers refused to hear the great lesson he taught. Here is his operating philosophy as he expressed it succinctly:

"Our policy is to reduce the price, extend the operations, and improve the article. You will notice that the reduction of price comes first. We have never considered any costs as fixed. Therefore we first reduce the price to the point where we believe more sales will result. Then we go ahead and try to make the prices. We do not bother about the costs. The new price forces the costs down. The more usual way is to take the costs and then determine the price, and although that method may be scientific in the narrow sense, it is not scientific in the broad sense, because what earthly use is it to know the cost if it tells you that you cannot manufacture at a price at which the article can be sold? But more to the point is the fact that, although one may calculate what a cost is, and of course all of our costs are carefully calculated, no one knows what a cost ought to be. One of the ways of discovering . . . is to name a price so low as to force everybody in the place to the highest point of efficiency. The low price makes everybody dig for profits. We make more discoveries concerning manufacturing and selling under this forced method than by any method of leisurely investigation."[5]

Product Provincialism

The tantalizing profit possibilities of low unit production costs may be the most seriously self-deceiving attitude that can afflict a company, particularly a "growth" company where an apparently assured expansion of demand already tends to undermine a proper concern for the importance of marketing and the customer.

The usual result of this narrow preoccupation with so-called concrete matters is that instead of growing, the industry declines. It usually means that the product fails to adapt to the constantly changing patterns of consumer needs and tastes, to new and modified marketing institutions and practices, or to product developments in competing or complementary industries. The industry has its eyes so firmly on its own specific product that it does not see how it is being made obsolete.

The classical example of this is the buggy whip industry. No amount of product improvement could stave off its death sentence. But had the industry defined itself as being in the transportation business rather than the buggy whip business, it might have survived. It would have done what survival always entails, that is, changing. Even if it had only defined its business as providing a stimulant or catalyst to an energy source, it might have survived by becoming a manufacturer of, say, fanbelts or air cleaners.

What may some day be a still more classical example is, again, the oil industry. Having let others steal marvelous opportunities from it (e.g., natural gas, as already mentioned, missile fuels, and jet engine lubricants), one would expect it to have taken steps never to let that happen again. But this is not the case. We are now getting extraordinary new developments in fuel systems specifically designed to power automobiles. Not only are these developments concentrated in firms outside the petroleum industry, but petroleum is almost systematically ignoring them, securely content in its wedded bliss to oil. It is the story of the kerosene lamp versus the incandescent lamp all over again. Oil is trying to improve hydrocarbon fuels rather than to develop *any* fuels best suited to the needs of their users, whether or not made in different ways and with different raw materials from oil.

Here are some of the things which nonpetroleum companies are working on:

> Over a dozen such firms now have advanced working models of energy systems which, when perfected, will replace the internal combustion engine and eliminate the demand for gasoline. The superior merit of each of these systems is their elimination of frequent, time-consuming, and irritating refueling stops. Most of these systems are fuel cells designed to create electrical energy directly from chemicals without combustion. Most of them use chemicals that are not derived from oil, generally hydrogen and oxygen.
>
> Several other companies have advanced models of electric storage batteries designed to power automobiles. One of these is an aircraft producer that is working jointly with several electric utility companies. The latter hope to use off-peak generating capacity to supply overnight plug-in battery regeneration. Another company, also using the battery approach, is a medium-size electronics firm with extensive small-battery experience that it developed in connection with its work on hearing aids. It is collab-

orating with an automobile manufacturer. Recent improvements arising from the need for high-powered miniature power storage plants in rockets have put us within reach of a relatively small battery capable of withstanding great overloads or surges of power. Germanium diode applications and batteries using sintered-plate and nickel-cadmium techniques promise to make a revolution in our energy sources.

> Solar energy conversion systems are also getting increasing attention. One usually cautious Detroit auto executive recently ventured that solar-powered cars might be common by 1980.

As for the oil companies, they are more or less "watching developments," as one research director put it to me. A few are doing a bit of research on fuel cells, but almost always confined to developing cells powered by hydrocarbon chemicals. None of them are enthusiastically researching fuel cells, batteries, or solar power plants. None of them are spending a fraction as much on research in these profoundly important areas as they are on the usual run-of-the-mill things like reducing combustion chamber deposit in gasoline engines. One major integrated petroleum company recently took a tentative look at the fuel cell and concluded that although "the companies actively working on it indicate a belief in ultimate success . . . the timing and magnitude of its impact are too remote to warrant recognition in our forecasts."

One might, of course, ask: Why should the oil companies do anything different? Would not chemical fuel cells, batteries, or solar energy kill the present product lines? The answer is that they would indeed, and that is precisely the reason for the oil firms having to develop these power units before their competitors, so they will not be companies without an industry.

Management might be more likely to do what is needed for its own preservation if it thought of itself as being in the energy business. But even that would not be enough if it persists in imprisoning itself in the narrow grip of its tight product orientation. It has to think of itself as taking care of customer needs, not finding, refining, or even selling oil. Once it genuinely thinks of its business as taking care of people's transportation needs, nothing can stop it from creating its own extravagantly profitable growth.

"Creative Destruction"

Since words are cheap and deeds are dear, it may be appropriate to indicate what this kind of thinking involves and leads to. Let us start at the beginning—the customer. It can be shown that motorists strongly dislike the bother, delay, and experience of buying gasoline. People actually do not buy gasoline. They cannot see it, taste it, feel it, appreciate it, or really test it. What they buy is the right to continue driving their cars. The gas station is like a tax collector to whom people are compelled to pay a periodic toll as the price of using their cars. This makes the gas station a basically unpopular institution. It can never be made popular or pleasant, only less unpopular, less unpleasant.

To reduce its unpopularity completely means eliminating it. Nobody likes a tax collector, not even a pleasantly cheerful one. Nobody likes to interrupt a trip to buy a phantom product, not even from a handsome Adonis or a seductive Venus. Hence, companies that are working on exotic fuel substitutes which will eliminate the need for frequent refueling are heading directly into the outstretched arms of the irritated motorist. They are riding a wave of inevitability, not because, they are creating something which is technologically superior or more sophisticated, but because they are satisfying a powerful customer need. They are also eliminating noxious odors and air pollution.

Once the petroleum companies recognize the customer-satisfying logic of what another power system can do, they will see that they have no more choice about working on an efficient, long-lasting fuel (or some way of delivering present fuel without bothering the motorist) than the big food chains had a choice about going into the supermarket business, or the vacuum tube companies had a choice about making semiconductors. For their own good the oil firms will have to destroy their own highly profitable assets. No amount of wishful thinking can save them from the necessity of engaging in this form of "creative destruction."

I phrase the need as strongly as this because I think management must make quite an effort to break itself loose from conventional ways. It is all too easy in this day and age for a company or industry to let its sense of purpose become dominated by the economies of full production and to develop a dangerously lopsided product orientation. In short, if management lets itself drift, it invariably drifts in the direction of thinking of itself as producing goods and services, not customer satisfactions. While it probably will not descend to the depths of telling its salesmen, "You get rid of it; we'll worry about profits," it can, without knowing it, be practicing precisely that formula for withering decay. The historic fate of one growth industry after another has been its suicidal product provincialism.

DANGERS OF R & D

Another big danger to a firm's continued growth arises when top management is wholly transfixed by the profit possibilities of technical research and development. To illustrate I shall turn first to a new industry—electronics—and then return once more to the oil companies. By comparing a fresh example with a familiar one, I hope to emphasize the prevalence and insidiousness of a hazardous way of thinking.

Marketing Shortchanged

In the case of electronics, the greatest danger which faces the glamorous new companies in this field is not that they do not pay enough attention to research and development, but that they pay *too much* attention to it. And the fact that the fastest growing electronics firms owe their eminence to their heavy emphasis on technical research is completely beside the point. They have vaulted to affluence on a sudden crest of unusually strong general receptiveness to new technical ideas. Also, their success has been shaped in the virtually guaranteed market of military subsidies and by military orders that in many cases actually preceded the existence of facilities to make the products. Their expansion has, in other words, been almost totally devoid of marketing effort.

Thus, they are growing up under conditions that come dangerously close to creating the illusion that a superior product will sell itself. Having created a successful company by making a superior product, it is not surprising that management continues to be oriented toward the product rather than the people who consume it. It develops the philosophy that continued growth is a matter of continued product innovation and improvement.

A number of other factors tend to strengthen and sustain this belief:

1. Because electronic products are highly complex and sophisticated, managements become topheavy with engineers and scientists. This creates a selective bias in favor of research and production at the expense of marketing. The organization tends to view itself as making things rather than satisfying customer needs. Marketing gets treated as a residual activity, "something else" that must be done once the vital job of product creation and production is completed.

2. To this bias in favor of product research, development, and production is added the bias in favor of dealing with controllable variables. Engineers and scientists are at home in the world of concrete things like machines, test tubes, production lines, and even balance sheets. The abstractions to which they feel kindly are those which are testable or manipulatable in the laboratory, or, if not testable, then functional, such as Euclid's axioms. In short, the managements of the new glamour-growth companies tend to favor those business activities which lend themselves to careful study, experimentation, and control—the hard, practical, realities of the lab, the shop, the books.

What gets shortchanged are the realities of the *market*. Consumers are unpredictable, varied, fickle, stupid, shortsighted, stubborn, and generally bothersome. This is not what the engineer-managers say, but deep down in their consciousness it is what they believe. And this accounts for their concentrating on what they know and what they can control, namely, product research, engineering, and production. The emphasis on production becomes particularly attractive when the product can be made at declining unit costs. There is no more inviting way of making money than by running the plant full blast.

Today the top-heavy science-engineering-production orientation of so many electronics companies works reasonably well because they are pushing into new frontiers in which the armed services have pioneered virtually assured markets. The companies are in the felicitous position of having to fill, not find markets; of not having to discover what the customer needs and wants, but of having the customer voluntarily come forward with specific new product demands. If a team of consultants had been assigned specifically to design a business situation calculated to prevent the emergence and development of a customer-oriented marketing viewpoint, it could not have produced anything better than the conditions just described.

Stepchild Treatment

The oil industry is a stunning example of how science, technology, and mass production can divert an entire group of companies from the main task. To the extent the consumer is studied at all (which is not much), the focus is forever on getting information which is designed to help the oil companies improve what they are now doing. They try to discover more convincing advertising themes, more effective sales promotional drives, what the market shares of the various companies are, what people like or dislike about service station dealers and oil companies, and so forth. Nobody seems as interested in probing deeply into the basic human needs that the industry might be trying to satisfy as in probing into the basic properties of the raw material that the companies work with in trying to deliver customer satisfaction.

Basic questions about customers and markets seldom get asked. The latter occupy a stepchild status. They are recognized as existing, as having to be taken care of, but not worth very much real thought or dedicated attention. Nobody gets as excited about the customers in his own backyard as about the oil in the Sahara Desert. Nothing illustrates better the neglect of marketing than its treatment in the industry press:

> The centennial issue of the *American Petroleum Institute Quarterly*, published in 1959 to celebrate the discovery of oil in Titusville, Pennsylvania, contained 21 feature articles proclaiming the industry's greatness. Only one of these talked about its achievements in marketing, and that was

only a pictorial record of how service station architecture has changed. The issue also contained a special section on "New Horizons," which was devoted to showing the magnificent role oil would play in America's future. Every reference was ebulliently optimistic, never implying once that oil might have some hard competition. Even the reference to atomic energy was a cheerful catalogue of how oil would help make atomic energy a success. There was not a single apprehension that the oil industry's affluence might be threatened or a suggestion that one "new horizon" might include new and better ways of serving oil's present customers.

But the most revealing example of the stepchild treatment that marketing gets was still another special series of short articles on "The Revolutionary Potential of Electronics." Under that heading this list of articles appeared in the table of contents:

"In the Search for Oil"

"In Production Operations"

"In Refinery Processes"

"In Pipeline Operations"

Significantly, every one of the industry's major functional areas is listed, *except* marketing. Why? Either it is believed that electronics holds no revolutionary potential for petroleum marketing (which is palpably wrong), or the editors forgot to discuss marketing (which is more likely, and illustrates its stepchild status).

The order in which the four functional areas are listed also betrays the alientation of the oil industry from the consumer. The industry is implicitly defined as beginning with the search for oil and ending with its distribution from the refinery. But the truth is, it seems to me, that the industry begins with the needs of the customer for its products. From that primal position its definition moves steadily backstream to areas of progressively lesser importance, until it finally comes to rest at the "search for oil."

Beginning and End

The view that an industry is a customer-satisfying process, not a goods-producing process, is vital for all businessmen to understand. An industry begins with the customer and his needs, not with a patent, a raw material, or a selling skill. Given the customer's needs, the industry develops backwards, first concerning itself with the physical *delivery* of customer satisfactions. Then it moves back further to *creating* the things by which these satisfactions are in part achieved. How these materials are created is a matter of indifference to the customer, hence the particular form of manufacturing, processing, or what-have-you cannot be considered as a vital aspect of the industry. Finally, the industry moves back still further to *finding* the raw materials necessary for making its products.

The irony of some industries oriented toward technical research and development is that the scientists who occupy the high executive positions are totally unscientific when it comes to defining their companies' overall needs and purposes. They violate the first two rules of the scientific method—being aware of and defining their companies' problems, and then developing testable hypotheses about solving them. They are scientific only about the convenient things, such as laboratory and product experiments. The reason that the customer (and the satisfaction of his deepest needs) is not considered as being "the problem" is not because there is any certain belief that no such problem exists, but because an organizational lifetime has conditioned management to look in the opposite direction. Marketing is a stepchild.

I do not mean that selling is ignored. Far from it. But selling, again, is not marketing. As already pointed out, selling concerns itself with the tricks and techniques of getting people to exchange their cash for your product. It is not concerned with the values that the exchange is all about. And it does not, as marketing invariably does, view the entire business process as consisting of a tightly integrated effort to discover, create, arouse, and satisfy customer needs. The customer is somebody "out there" who, with proper cunning, can be separated from his loose change.

Actually not even selling gets much attention in some technologically minded firms. Because there is a virtually guaranteed market for the abundant flow of their new products, they do not actually know what a real market is. It is as if they lived in a planned economy, moving their products routinely from factory to retail outlet. Their successful concentration on products tends to convince them of the soundness of what they have been doing, and they fail to see the gathering clouds over the market.

CONCLUSION

Less than 75 years ago American railroads enjoyed a fierce loyalty among astute Wall Streeters. European monarchs invested in them heavily. Eternal wealth was thought to be the benediction for anybody who could scrape a few thousand dollars together to put into rail stocks. No other form of transportation could compete with the railroads in speed, flexibility, durability, economy, and growth potentials. As Jacques Barzun put it, "By the turn of the century it was an institution, an image of man, a tradition, a code of honor, a source of poetry, a nursery of boyhood desires, a sublimest of toys, and the most solemn machine—next to the funeral hearse—that marks the epochs in man's life."[6]

Even after the advent of automobiles, trucks, and airplanes, the railroad tycoons remained imperturbably self-confident. If you had told them 60 years ago that in 30 years they would be flat on their backs, broke, and pleading for government subsidies, they would have thought you totally demented. Such a future was simply not considered possible. It was not even a discussable subject, or an askable question, or a matter which any sane person would consider worth speculating about. The very thought was insane. Yet a lot of insane notions now have matter-of-fact acceptance —for example, the idea of 100-ton tubes of metal moving smoothly through the air 20,000 feet above the earth, loaded with 100 sane and solid citizens casually drinking martinis—and they have dealt cruel blows to the railroads.

What specifically must other companies do to avoid this fate? What does customer orientation involve? These questions have in part been answered by the preceding examples and analysis. It would take another article to show in detail what is required for specific industries. In any case, it should be obvious that building an effective customer-oriented company involves far more than good intentions or promotional tricks; it involves profound matters of human organization and leadership. For the present, let me merely suggest what appear to be some general requirements.

Visceral Feel of Greatness

Obviously the company has to do what survival demands. It has to adapt to the requirements of the market, and it has to do it sooner rather than later. But mere survival is a so-so aspiration. Anybody can survive in some way or other, even the skid-row bum. The trick is to survive gallantly to feel the surging impulse of commercial mastery not just to experience the sweet smell of success, but to have the visceral feel of entrepreneurial greatness.

No organization can achieve greatness without a vigorous leader who is driven onward by his own pulsating *will to succeed*. He has to have a vision of grandeur, a vision that can produce eager followers in vast numbers. In business, the followers are the customers. To produce these customers, the entire corporation must be viewed as a customer-creating and customer-satisfying organism. Management must think of itself not as producing products but as providing customer creating value satisfactions. It must push this idea (and everything it means and requires) into every nook and cranny of the organization. It has to do this continuously and with the kind of flair that excites and stimulates the people in it. Otherwise, the company will be merely a series of pigeonholed parts, with no consolidating sense of purpose or direction.

In short, the organization must learn to think of itself not as producing goods or services but as *buying customers*, as doing the things that will make people *want* to do business with it. And the chief executive himself has the inescapable responsibility for creating this environment, this viewpoint, this attitude, this aspiration. He himself must set the company's style, its direction, and its goals. This means he has to know precisely where he himself wants to go, and to make sure the whole organization is enthusiastically aware of where that is. This is a first requisite of leadership, for *unless he knows where he is going, any road will take him there.*

If any road is okay, the chief executive might as well pack his attache' case and go fishing. If an organization does not know or care where it s going, it does not need to advertise that fact with a ceremonial figurehead. Everybody will notice it soon enough.

Notes

1. Jacques Barzun, "Trains and the Mind of Man," *Holiday,* February 1960, p. 21.
2. For more details see M. M. Zimmerman, *The Super Market: A Revolution in Distribution* (New York, McGraw-Hill Book Company, Inc., 1955), p. 48.
3. Ibid., pp. 45-47.
4. *The Affluent Society* (Boston, Houghton Mifflin Company, 1958), pp. 152-160.
5. Henry Ford, *My Life and Work* (New York, Doubleday, Page & Company, 1923), pp. 146-147.
6. Op. cit., p. 20.

③ THE MANAGEMENT OF SPECIFIC DEMAND

John Kenneth Galbraith
Professor of Economics
Harvard University

A noted economist maintains that marketing management is so powerful that it is able to control demand and prices. This is a highly controversial and pessimistic view of marketing if you believe, as we do, that marketing should satisfy human wants, not control them.

"Bristol-Meyers does not, in general, develop products in its labs and then determine how they might be marketed. It ordinarily *begins* with extensive consumer testing and other market research, proceeds from there to develop some concepts of a marketing opportunity, including even some notions about advertising campaigns; and only then does it turn to the labs for products that might meet these specifications."
            Fortune, February, 1967

For all planning, that of the United States as well as of other industrial societies, the control of prices is strategic. These must be subject to the authority of the planning unit; otherwise there is risk of loss from uncontrolled price movements and there is no reliable number by which units of product and input can be multiplied to get projected income and outlay. If these estimates

From The New Industrial State, *pp. 198-210. Copyright © 1967, 1971 by John Kenneth Galbraith. Reprinted by permission of Houghton Mifflin Company.*

are not available in reliable form, there is a large random element in decisions as to what to produce, and with what and by what means, and there is total uncertainty as to the outcome—whether there will be profit or loss and in what dimension. Such error is the antithesis of effective planning. A moment's thought will suggest not only how nearly impossible it would make modern industrial performance but how remote, in practice, such uncontrolled prices are from real life.

The control of prices in the industrial system is not perfect, and the fact of this imperfection is important not only in itself but also for economic polemics. It is a well-established technique of argument, on encountering something which cannot easily be reconciled with preconception, to point to the exceptions. What does not invariably exist is held not to exist. Economics is committed by ancient faith to the control of the firm by the market. Some, accordingly, will be tempted to argue that since the control of prices by the mature corporation is not complete, it can be dismissed. This mode of argument need not detain us; once recognized as a polemical device, it becomes unpersuasive. It is worth noting that until comparatively recently trade unions were held by some to be relatively unimportant in wage-setting because their sway was incomplete or their powers circumscribed.[1] And even the large corporation was ignored because it had not completely replaced the proprietary firm. Though imperfect, control of prices in the industrial system is organic—it serves its most fundamental goals. And the fact of such control, fortunately for anyone who urges the reality, is admirably visible.

Control of prices is for a purpose—for the security of the technostructure and to allow it to plan. But price control does little to advance these goals unless there is also control over the amounts that are bought or sold at these prices. Security, growth and effective planning would be jeopardized by erratic or unpredictable price behavior. But these would equally be frustrated by a decision by the public not to buy at the controlled prices. It would be quixotic for the mature corporation to seek control over its prices and then leave purchases at these prices to the random fate of taste and accident. Such fluctuations in the amounts taken would be no less damaging to planning and the goals that it serves than fluctuations in prices.

Moreover, the fluctuations in amounts taken are accentuated by price control; a fall in prices (through elasticity of demand) no longer acts to arrest a fall in purchases and vice versa. So, intimately intertwined with the need to control prices is the need to control what is sold at those prices.

The control or management of demand is, in fact, a vast and rapidly growing industry in itself. It embraces a huge network of communications, a great array of merchandising and selling organizations, nearly the entire advertising industry, numerous ancillary research, training and other related services and much more. In everyday parlance this great machine, and the demanding and varied talents that it employs, are said to be engaged in selling goods. In less ambiguous language it means that it is engaged in the management of those who buy goods.

The key to the management of demand is effective management of the purchases of final consumers—of individuals and the state. If these are under effective control, there will then be a comparatively reliable demand for raw materials, parts machinery and other items going into the ultimate product. If the demand for its automobiles is reliable, General Motors can accord its suppliers the security of long-term contracts. And, in the absence of such contracts, there will still be a reliable and predictable flow of orders which allows of planning. Although the techniques for managing government purchases are different from those employed for consumer demand they make the same contribution to planning by prime and subcontractors.

The effective management of consumer behavior does not embrace the whole task of controlling demand. An automobile company must insure that consumers devote a dependable share of their outlays to automobiles in general and to its cars in particular. But its sales will still be highly irregular if, though they spend a constant share of their income on its vehicles, there is a radical fluctuation from year to year in what they have to spend. It follows that effective control of consumer demand requires management not only of how income is spent but also of the amount of income that is available for spending. There must be management of demand both for the specific product and for products in general. Measures to maintain a desired level of aggregate demand are part and parcel of the task of industrial planning.[2] We are here concerned with the management of demand for the specific product.

As so often, change in the industrial system has made possible what change requires. The need to control consumer behavior is a requirement of planning. Planning, in turn, is made necessary by extensive use of advanced technology and capital and by the related scale and complexity of organization. These produce goods efficiently; the result is a very large volume of production. As a further consequence, goods that are related only to elementary physical sensation—that merely prevent hunger, protect against cold, provide shelter, suppress pain— have come to comprise a small and diminishing part of all production. Most goods serve needs that are discovered to the individual not by the palpable discomfort that accompanies deprivation, but by some psychic response to their possession. They give him a sense of personal achievement, accord him a feeling of equality with his neighbors, divert his mind from thought, serve sexual aspiration, promise social acceptability, enhance his subjective feeling of health, well-being or orderly peristalsis, contribute by conventional canons to personal beauty, or are otherwise psychologically rewarding.

Thus it comes about that, as the industrial system develops to the point where it has need for planning and the management of the consumer that this requires, it is also serving wants which are psychological in origin and hence admirably subject to management by appeal to the psyche.

Hunger and other physical pain have an objective and compelling quality. No one whose stomach is totally empty can be persuaded that his need is not for food but for entertainment. A man who is very cold will have a high preference for what makes him warm. But psychic reactions have no such internal anchor; since they exist in the mind they are subject to what influences the mind. Though a hungry man cannot be persuaded as between bread and a circus, a well-nourished man can. And he can be persuaded as between different circuses and different foods. The further a man is removed from physical need the more open he is to persuasion—or management—as to what he buys. This is, perhaps, the most impor-

tant consequence for economics of increasing affluence.[3]

Along with the opportunity for managing consumer demand, there must also be a mechanism for managing it. Authority is not well regarded here. By giving him a ration card or distributing to him the specific commodities he is to use, the individual can be required to consume in accordance with plan. But this is an onerous form of control, ill-adapted to differences in personality. Save under conditions of great stress as during war or for the very poor, it is not thought acceptable in advanced industrial societies. Even the formally planned economies—the Soviet Union and the Eastern European states—regard rationing as a manifestation of failure. It is easier and, if less precise, still sufficient to manage demand by persuasion rather than by fiat.

Although advertising will be thought the central feature of this management, and is certainly important, much more is involved. Included among the managers are those who sell goods and design the strategies by which they are sold. And so are many who are thought of as engaged in the production of goods. The management of demand consists in devising a sales strategy for a particular product. It also consists in devising a product, or features of a product, around which a sales strategy can be built. Product design, model change, packaging and even performance reflect the need to provide what are called strong selling points. They are thus as much a part of the process of demand management as an advertising campaign.[4]

The purpose of demand management is to insure that people buy what is produced—that plans as to the amounts to be sold at the controlled prices are fulfilled in practice. Not all advertising and selling activity is directed to this end. This fact has polemical importance for it is readily possible to cite forms of advertising or sales effort which are unrelated to the purposes of demand management and industrial planning.

Thus a certain amount of advertising, that of the classified ads and the department store displays, has no great purpose beyond that of conveying information—of advising the public that a particular person or enterprise has a particular item for sale and at what price. Such advertising is seized upon to show that the function of advertising is merely to convey information although, as I have noted on other occasions, only a gravely retarded citizen can need to be told that the American Tobacco Company has cigarettes for sale.

Economic theory, under the cachet of monopolistic competition, has also long featured the case of the seller, one among many, who seeks by advertising to associate particular qualities with his product and thus reduce the chances for substitution by another. He then has liberty to charge a higher price and, at least in the short run, reward himself with monopoly profits. This too is a possible case although its requirements as imposed by the textbooks—*numerous* sellers who have comparative ease of entry into the industry—make it of small practical importance. The accounts of the monopolistically competitive sellers are not those that are cherished by J. Walter Thompson, McCann-Erickson or Ogilvy, Benson and Mather.

Finally, conventional economic theory associates advertising and related arts with oligopoly. Here the characteristic firm of the industrial system eschews price competition as too dangerous and channels its rivalry into ever-changing strategies for winning customers away from another.

> "In lieu of [price competition] oligopolists rely on . . . competition through advertising and other merchandising efforts, and competition through style changes and product improvement . . . These large advertising budgets, like heavy armaments, largely cancel each other out. Not even the oligopolists benefit from them."[5]

If it be assumed that the consumer is sovereign, save that he is in doubt as to whose product he will buy, this conclusion—that such advertising and by implication many other expenditures including that for model and design changes[6] are self-cancelling and functionless—is inescapable. Firms spend money to take business away from each other; all cannot succeed so the result is a standoff. The only consequence is that prices are higher and profits are lower than if by some act of government or industrial statesmanship the struggle were curbed.

But such a notion of limited sovereignty is nonsense. If advertising affects the distribution of demand between sellers of a particular product it

must also be supposed that it affects the distribution as between products. This is not functionless; rather it increases the flow of revenue to all who advertise. And in the context of planning it does much more. For, along with the other arts of demand management, it allows the firm a decisive influence over the revenue it receives. What seems to the traditional market economists a sense-deadening struggle between the detergent-makers leading only to stalemate serves a deeper and highly important purpose.

There will be confort in this conclusion. The present disposition of conventional economic theory to write off annual outlays of tens of billions of dollars of advertising and similar sales costs by the industrial system as without purpose or consequence is, to say the least, drastic. No other legal economic activity is subject to similar rejection. The discovery that sales and advertising expenditures have an organic role in the system will not, accordingly, seem wholly implausible.

The general effect of sales effort, defined in the broadest terms, is to shift the locus of decision in the purchase of goods from the consumer where it is beyond control to the firm where it is subject to control. This transfer, like the control of prices, is by no means complete. But again what is imperfect is not unimportant. The "general rule with fewer exceptions than we would like to think, is that if they make it we will buy it."[7]

The specific strategy, though it varies somewhat between industries and over time, consists first in recruiting a loyal or automatic corps of customers. This is variously known as building customer loyalty or brand recognition. To the extent that it is successful, it means that the firm has a stable body of custom which is secure against the mass defection which might follow from freely exercised consumer choice. This is the initial contribution to the firm's planning.

A purely defensive strategy will not, however, suffice. Given the goals of the technostructure all firms will seek to expand sales. Each, accordingly, must seek to do so if it is not to lose out to others. Out of this effort, from firms that are fully able to play the game, comes a crude equilibrating process which accords to each participant a reasonably reliable share of the market. It works, very roughly, as follows.

When a firm is enjoying steady patronage

by its existing customers and recruiting new ones, the existing sales strategy, broadly defined, will usually be considered satisfactory. The firm will not quarrel with success. If sales are stationary or slipping, a change in selling methods, advertising strategy, product design or even in the product itself is called for. Testing and experiment are possible. Sooner or later, a new formula that wins a suitable response is obtained. This brings a countering action by the firms that are then failing to make gains.

This process of action and response, which belongs to the field of knowledge known as game theory, leads to a rough equilibrium between the participating firms. Each may win for a time or lose for a time, but the game is played within a narrow range of such gain or loss. As in the case of Packard or Studebaker (as a producer of cars), firms that do not have the resources to play— particularly to stand the very large costs of product design and redesign—will lose out and disappear. And the firms that can play the game will, on occasion, find customers adamant in their resistance to a particular product; no response can be obtained at tolerable cost by any strategy that can be devised.[8] The size and product diversification of the mature corporation allow the firm to accept an occasional such failure without undue hazard. But it is the everyday assumption of the industrial system that, if sales are slipping, a new selling formula can be found that will correct the situation. By and large this assumption is justified, which is to say that means can almost always be found to keep exercise of consumer discretion within workable limits.

Were there but one manufacturer of automobiles in the United States, it would still be essential that it enter extensively on the management of its demand. Otherwise consumers, exercising the sovereignty that would be inconsistent with the company's planning, might resort to other forms of transportation and other ways of spending their income. (This is the answer to the orthodox contention that advertising is principally induced by market oligopoly.) And under present circumstances a slippage in automobile sales as a whole sets in motion by all the firms the sales strategies (including always the product redesign) by which it is offset. This, in turn, stabilizes the expenditures accruing to the industry.

Persuasion on the scale just outlined requires that there be comprehensive, repetitive and compelling communication by the managers of demand with the managed. It should be capable of holding the attention of the consumer for considerable periods of time and in a comparatively effortless manner. It should reach people in all spectrums of intelligence. None should be barred by illiteracy or unwillingness to read. Such a means of mass communication was not necessary when the wants of the masses were anchored primarily in physical need. The masses could not then be persuaded as to their spending—this went for basic foods and shelter. The wants of a well-to-do minority could be managed. But since this minority was generally literate, or sought to seem so, it could be reached selectively by newspapers and magazines, the circulation of which was confined to the literate community. With mass affluence, and therewith the possibility of mass management of demand, these media no longer served.

Technology, once again, solved the problems that it created. Coincidentally with rising mass incomes came first radio and then television. These, in their capacity to hold effortless interest and their accessibility over the entire cultural spectrum, and their independence of any educational qualification, were admirably suited to mass persuasion. Radio and more especially television have, in consequence, become the prime instruments for the management of consumer demand. There is an insistent tendency among solemn social scientists to think of any institution which features rhymed and singing commercials, intense and lachrymose voices urging highly improbable enjoyments, caricatures of the human esophagus in normal or impaired operation, and which hints implausibly at opportunities for antiseptic seduction, as inherently trivial. This is a great mistake. The industrial system is profoundly dependent on commercial television and could not exist in its present form without it. Economists who eschew discussion of its economic significance, or dismiss it as a wicked waste, are protecting their reputation and that of their subject for Calvinist austerity. But they are not adding to their reputation for relevance.

The management of demand, as here to be seen, is in all respects an admirably subtle arrangement in social design. It works not on the individual but on the mass. Any individual of will and determination can contract out from its influence. This being so, no case for individual compulsion in the purchase of any product can be established. To all who object there is a natural answer: You are at liberty to leave! Yet there is slight danger that enough people will ever assert their individuality to impair the management of mass behavior.

This management performs yet another service. For, along with bringing demand under substantial control, it provides in the aggregate, a relentless propaganda on behalf of goods in general. From early morning until late at night, people are informed of the services rendered by goods—of their profound indispensability. Every feature and facet of every product having been studied for selling points, these are then described with talent, gravity and an aspect of profound concern as the source of health, happiness, social achievement, or improved community standing. Even minor qualities of unimportant commodities are enlarged upon with a solemnity which would not be unbecoming in an announcement of the combined return of Christ and all the apostles. More important services, such as the advantages of whiter laundry, are treated with proportionately greater gravity.

The consequence is that while goods become ever more abundant they do not seem to be any less important. On the contrary it requires an act of will to imagine that anything else is so important. Morally, we agree that the supply of goods is not a measure of human achievement; in fact, we take for granted that it will be so regarded.

Yet it might not have been. In the absence of the massive and artful persuasion that accompanies the management of demand, increasing abundance might well have reduced the interest of people in acquiring more goods. They would not have felt the need for multiplying the artifacts—autos, appliances, detergents, cosmetics—by which they were surrounded. No one would have pressed upon them the advantages of new packages, new forms of processed foods, newly devised dentifrices, new pain-killers or other new variants on older products. Being not pressed by the need for these things, they would have spent less reliably of their income and worked less reliably to get

more. The consequence—a lower and less reliable propensity to consume—would have been awkward for the industrial system. That system requires that people will work without any limiting horizon to procure more goods. Were they to cease to work after acquiring a certain sufficiency, there would be limits on the expansion of the system. Growth could not then remain a goal. Advertising and its related arts thus help develop the kind of man the goals of the industrial system require—one that reliably spends his income and works reliably because he is always in need of more.

This effort has the further effect of sustaining the prestige of the industrial system. Goods are what the industrial system supplies. Advertising by making goods important makes the industrial system important. And therewith it helps to sustain the social importance and prestige that attach to the technostructure. As the landowner and the capitalist lost prestige when land and capital ceased to be socially decisive, so the technostructure would soon sink into the background were the supply of industrial products to become routine in the manner of water from a waterworks in a year of adequate rainfall. This would have happened long since had not advertising, with its unremitting emphasis on the importance of goods, kept people persuaded to the contrary.

When viewed not in the absolute context but in the relevant context of industrial planning, it will be evident that advertising and its related arts have a large social function. This extends on from the management of demand, the necessary counterpart of the control of prices, to the conditioning of attitudes necessary for the operation and prestige of the industrial system. For advertising men it has long been a sore point that economists dismissed them as so much social waste. They have not quite known how to answer. Some have doubtless sensed that, in a society where wants are psychologically grounded, the instruments of access to the mind cannot be unimportant. They were right. The functions here identified may well be less exalted than the more demanding philosophers of the advertising industry might wish. But none can doubt their importance for the industrial system, given always the standards by which that system measures achievement and success.

Notes

1. "[The] weak unions are probably more numerous than the strong . . . statistical studies
find little relationship between unionization
and long-term wage movements." George J.
Stigler, *The Theory of Price*, Revised Edition
(New York: Macmillan, 1952), pp. 256-257.
Cf. also "Addendum on Economic Method
and the Nature of Social Argument" later in
this volume.
2. A circumstance, as previously noted, which
greatly diminishes the significance of one of
the common distinctions in economics—that
between microeconomics or the theory of
prices and the market, and macroeconomics
or the theory which concerns itself with
national aggregates. Both prices and aggregate
demand are ultimately accommodated to
the planning needs of the technostructure.
I return to this problem in Chapter XX. Chapters XXVI and XXVII take up the special
problem of managing the state as a consumer.
3. I have dealt with this tendency on two earlier
occasions (*American Capitalism, The Concept
of Countervailing Power* [Boston: Houghton,
1956], Chapter VIII; and *The Affluent
Society* [Boston: Houghton, 1958], Chapter
11). Accordingly, I am confining myself
here to the barest essentials. These notions,
particularly the distinction between physical
and psychologically based wants, together
with a declining marginal utility of income,
though they will seem eminently sensible
to the reader, are not widely accepted by
economists. There are certain methodological
excuses but the reason has, alas, more to do
with the instinct for professional self-
preservation than with science. As elsewhere
noted, a central problem of economics,
and long *the* central problem, was the allocation of resources between uses, that is to say,
between products. If this choice is not terribly
important and becomes increasingly less
important, with increasing income, the economic problem also diminishes in importance
and so, unhappily, do the scholars who dwell
on it.
4. In a culture which places high value on technological change, there will be a natural presumption that any "new" product is inherently
superior to an old one. This attitude will be
exploited by those who devise sales strategy
with the result that a great many changes in
product and packaging will be merely for the
sake of having something that can be called
new. We have here the explanation of the
repetitious claims in virtually all advertising
that products are new.

5. Robert Dorfman, *The Price System* (New
York: Prentice-Hall, Inc., 1964), p. 102.
Samuelson agrees but in much more circum-
spect language. See Paul A. Samuelson,
Economics, Sixth Edition (New York: McGraw,
1964), pp. 485, 500-501.
6. Franklin M. Fisher, Zvi Griliches and Carl Kay-
sen, "The Costs of Automobile Model Changes
Since 1949," *The Journal of Political Economy*,
Vol. LXX, No. 5 (October, 1962).
7. Andrew Hacker, "A Country Called Corporate
America," *The New York Times Magazine*,
July 3, 1966.
8. As in the case of the Edsel. I mention this again
for, to a quite remarkable extent, this disaster
is cited (by those who are made unhappy
by these ideas) to prove that planning will
not work. It proves what I unhesitatingly
concede, which is that it doesn't work
perfectly. Its notoriety owes much to its
being exceptional.

4
SYSTEMS APPROACH TO MARKETING

Lee Adler
Director of Marketing Research
RCA Corp.

There seems to be little doubt that managers are moving toward more formalized procedures for making marketing decisions. While, practically speaking, there are many barriers to a systems approach to marketing, the successes that the author describes contain lessons for all companies which seek to control their destinies.

More and more businessmen today recognize that corporate success is, in most cases, synonymous with marketing success and with the coming of age of a new breed of professional managers. They find it increasingly important not only to pay lip service to the marketing concept but to do something about it in terms of (a) customer orientation, rather than navel-gazing in the factory, (b) organizational revisions to implement the marketing concept, and (c) a more orderly approach to problem solving.

In an increasing number of companies we see more conscious and formal efforts to apply rational, fact-based methods for solving marketing problems, and greater recognition of the benefits these methods offer. While these benefits may be newly realized, there is nothing new about the underlying philosophy; in the parlance of military men and engineers, it is the systems approach. For, whether we like it or not, marketing is, by definition, a system, if we accept Webster's definition of system as "an assemblage of objects united by some form of regular interaction or interde-

From Lee Adler, "Systems Approach to Marketing," Harvard Business Review, *May-June 1967, pp. 105-118.*

pendence." Certainly, the interaction of such "objects" as product, pricing, promotion, sales calls, distribution, and so on fits the definition.

There is an expanding list of sophisticated applications of systems theory—and not in one but in many sectors of the marketing front. The construction of mathematical and/or logical model to describe, quantify, and evaluate alternate marketing strategies and mixes is an obvious case in point. So, too, is the formulation of management information systems[1] and of marketing plans with built-in performance measurements of predetermined goals. But no less vital is the role of the systems approach in the design and sale of product and services. When J. P. Stevens Company color-harmonizes linens and bedspreads, and towels and bath mats, it is creating a product system. An when Avco Corporation sells systems management to the space exploration field, involving the marriage of many scientific disciplines as well as adherence to budgetary constraints, on-time performance, and quality control, it is creating a *service* system.

In this article I shall discuss the utilization of the systems concept in marketing in both quantitative and qualitative ways with case histories drawn from various industries. In doing so, my focus will be more managerial and philosophical than technical, and I will seek to dissipate some of the hocus-pocus, glamor, mystery, and fear which pervade the field. The systems concept is not esoteric or "science fiction" in nature (although it sometimes *sounds* that way in promotional descriptions). Its advantages are not subtle or indirect; as we shall see, they are as real and immediate as decision making itself. The limitations are also real, and these, too, will be discussed.

(Readers interested in a brief summary of the background and the conceptual development of the systems approach may wish to turn to page 41.)

PROMISING APPLICATIONS

Now let us look at some examples of corp rate application of the systems approach. Here will deal with specific parts or "subsystems" of total marketing system. Exhibit 1 is a schematic portrayal of these relationships.

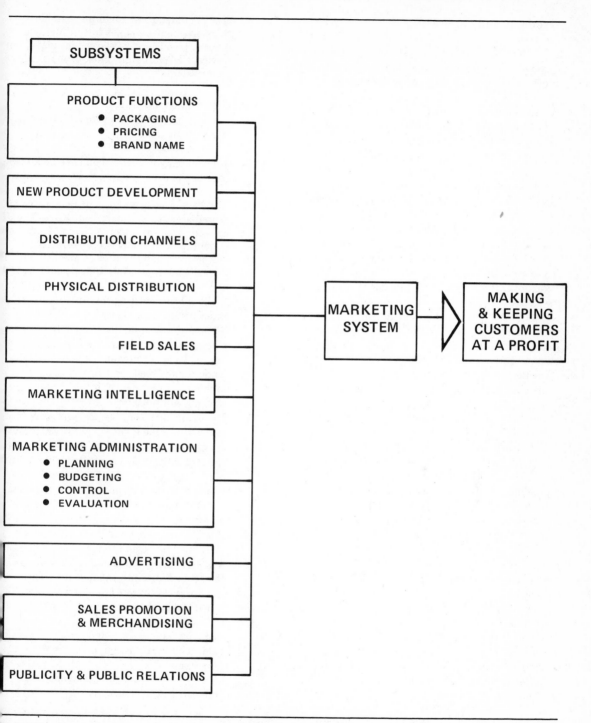

Exhibit 1. *Marketing Subsystems and the Total System.*

Products and Services

The objective of the systems approach in product management is to provide a complete "offering" to the market rather than merely a product. If the purpose of business is to create a customer at a profit, then the needs of the customer must be carefully attended to; we must, in short, study what the customer is buying or wants to buy, rather than what we are trying to sell.

In the consumer products field we have forged ahead in understanding that the customer buys nutrition (not bread), beauty (not cosmetics), warmth (not fuel oil). But in industrial products this concept has been slower in gaining a foothold. Where it has gained a foothold, it expresses itself in two ways: the creation of a complete product system sold (1) as a unit, or (2) as a component or components which are part of a larger consumption system.

Perhaps the most eloquent testimony to the workability and value of the systems approach comes from companies that have actually used it. For a good example let us turn to the case of The Carborundum Company. This experience is especially noteworthy because it comes from industrial marketing, where, as just indicated, progress with the systems concept has generally been slow.

Birth of the Concept Founded in 1894, the company was content for many years to sell abrasives. It offered an extremely broad line of grinding wheels, coated abrasives, and abrasive grain, with a reputed capacity for 200,000 different products of varying type, grade, and formulation. But the focus was on the product.

In the mid-1950s, Carborundum perceived that the market for abrasives could be broadened considerably if—looking at abrasives through customers' eyes—it would see the product as fitting into *metal polishing, cleaning,* or *removal systems.* Now Carborundum is concerned with all aspects of abrading—the machine, the contact wheel, the workpiece, the labor cost, the overhead rate, the abrasive, and, above all, the customer's objective. In the words of Carborundum's president, W. H. Wendel:

"That objective is never the abrasive per se, but rather the creation of a certain dimension, a type of finish, or a required shape, always related to a minimum cost. Since there are many variables to consider, just one can be misleading. To render maximum service, Carborundum (must offer) a complete system."[2]

Organizational Overhaul To offer such a system, management had to overhaul important parts of the organization:

1. The company needed to enhance its knowledge of the total system. As Wendel explains

   "We felt we had excellent knowledge of coated abrasive products, but that we didn't have the application and machine know-how in depth. To be really successful in the business, we had to know as much about the machine tools as we did the abrasives."[3]

   To fill this need, Carborundum made three acquisitions—The Tysaman Machine Company, which builds heavy-duty snagging, billet grinding, and abrasive cut-off machine; Curtis Machine Company, a maker of belt sanders; and Pangborn Corporation, which supplied systems capability in abrasive blast cleaning and finishing.

2. The company's abrasive divisions were reorganized, and the management of them was realigned to accommodate the new philosophy and its application. The company found that *centering responsibility for the full system in one profit center* proved to be the most effective method of coordinating approaches in application engineering, choice of distribution channels, brand identification, field sales operations, and so forth. This method was particularly valuable for integrating the acquisitions into the new program.

3. An Abrasives Systems Center was established to handle development work and to solve customer problems.

4. Technical conferences and seminars were held to educate customers on the new developments.

5. Salesmen were trained in machine and application knowledge.

Planning A key tool in the systems approach is planning—in particular, the use of what I like to call "total business plans." (This term emphasizes the contrast with company plans that cover only limited functions.) At Carborundum, total business plans are developed with extreme care by the operating companies and divisions. Very specific objectives are established, and then detailed action programs are outlined to achieve these objectives. The action programs extend throughout the organization, including the manufacturing and development branches of the operating unit. Management sets specific dates for the completion of action steps and defines who is responsible for them. Also, it carefully measures results against established objectives. This is done both in the financial reporting system and in various marketing committees.

Quantitative Methods Carborundum has utilized various operations research techniques, like decision tree analysis and PERT, to aid in molding plans and strategies. For example, one analysis, which concerned itself with determining the necessity for plant expansion, was based on different possible levels of success for the marketing plan. In addition, the computer has been used for inventory management, evaluation of alternate pricing strategies for systems selling, and the measurement of marketing achievements against goals.

It should be noted, though, that these quantitative techniques are management tools only and that much of the application of systems thinking to the redeployment of Carborundum's business is qualitative in nature.

Gains Achieved As a consequence of these developments, the company has opened up vast new markets. To quote Carborundum's president again:

> "Customers don't want a grinding wheel, they want metal removed . . . The U.S. and Canadian market for abrasives amounts to $700 million a year. But what companies spend on stock removal—to bore, grind, cut, shape, and finish metal—amounts to $30 billion a year."[4]

Illustrating this market expansion in the steel industry is Carborundum's commercial success with three new developments—hot grinding, an arborless wheel to speed metal removal and cut grinding costs, and high-speed conditioning of carbon steel billets. All represent conversions from nonabrasive methods. Carborundum now also finds that the close relationship with customers gives it a competitive edge, opens top customer management doors, gains entree for salesmen with prospects they had never been able to "crack" before. Perhaps the ultimate accolade is the company's report that customers even come to the organization itself, regarding it as a consultant as well as a supplier.

Profitable Innovation

The intense pressure to originate successful new products cannot be met without methodologies calculated to enhance the probabilities of profitable innovation. The systems approach has a bearing here, too. Exhibit 2 shows a model for "tracking" products through the many stages of ideation, development, and testing to ultimate full-scale commercialization. This diagram is in effect a larger version of the "New Product Development" box in Exhibit 1.

Observe that this is a logical (specifically, sequential), rather than numerical, model. While some elements of the total system (e.g., alternate distribution channels and various media mixes) can be analyzed by means of operations research techniques, the model has not been cast in mathematical terms. Rather, the flow diagram as a whole is used as a checklist to make sure "all bases are covered" and to help organize the chronological sequence of steps in new product development. It also serves as a conceptual foundation for formal PERT application, should management desire such a step, and for the gradual development of a series of equations linking together elements in the diagrams, should it seem useful to experiment with mathematical models.

Marketing Intelligence

The traditional notion of marketing research is fast becoming antiquated. For it leads to dreary chronicles of the past rather than focusing on the present and shedding light on the future. It is particularistic, tending to concentrate on the study of tiny fractions of a marketing problem rather

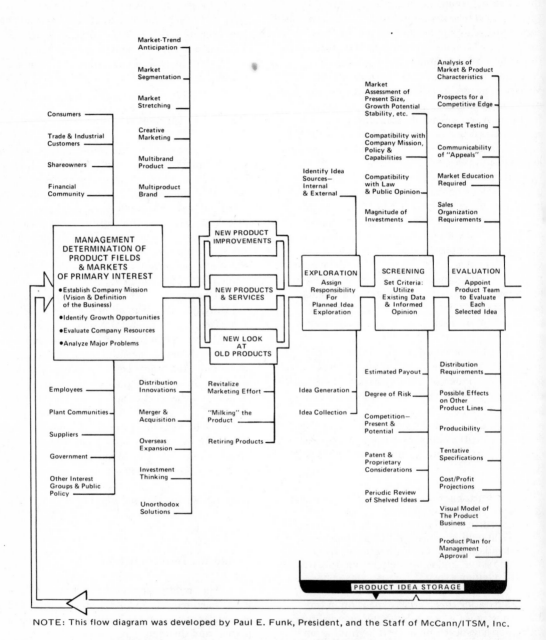

NOTE: This flow diagram was developed by Paul E. Funk, President, and the Staff of McCann/ITSM, Inc.

Exhibit 2. Work Flow and Systems Chart for Management of New Products.

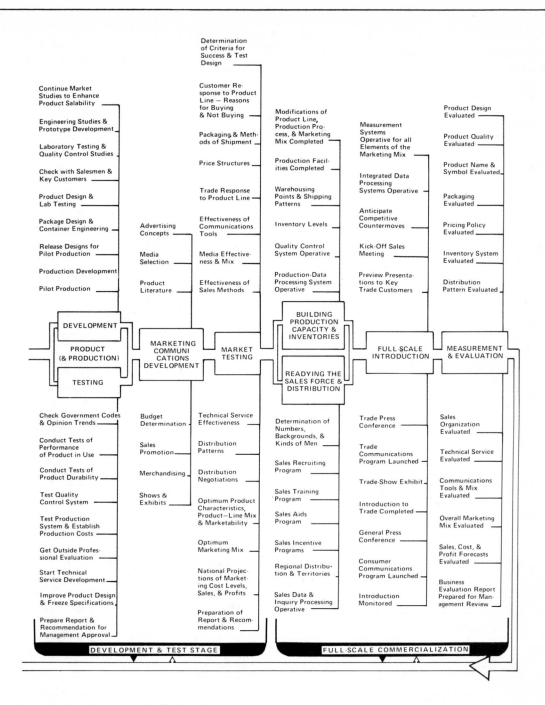

than on the problem as a whole. It lends itself to assuaging the curiosity of the moment, to fire-fighting, to resolving internecine disputes. It is a slave to technique. I shall not, therefore, relate the term *marketing research* to the systems approach—although I recognize, of course, that some leading businessmen and writers are breathing new life and scope into the ideas referred to by that term.

The role of the systems approach is to help evolve a *marketing intelligence* system tailored to the needs of each marketer. Such a system would serve as the ever-alert nerve center of the marketing operation. It would have these major characteristics:

Continuous surveillance of the market.

A team of research techniques used in tandem.

A network of data sources.

Integrated analysis of data from the various sources.

Effective utilization of automatic data-processing equipment to distill mountains of raw information speedily.

Strong concentration not just on reporting findings but also on practical, action-oriented recommendations.

Concept in Use A practical instance of the use of such an intelligence system is supplied by Mead Johnson Nutritionals (division of Mead Johnson & Company), manufacturers of Metrecal, Pablum, Bib, Nutrament, and other nutritional specialties. As Exhibit 3 shows, the company's Marketing Intelligence Department has provided information from these sources:

A continuing large-scale consumer market study covering attitudinal and behavioral data dealing with weight control.

Nielsen store audit data, on a bimonthly basis.

A monthly sales audit conducted among a panel of 100 high-volume food stores in 20 markets to provide advance indications of brand share shifts.

Supermarket warehouse withdrawal figures, from Time, Inc.'s new service, Selling Areas-Marketing, Inc.

Salesmen's weekly reports (which, in addition to serving the purposes of sales management control, call for reconnaissance on competitive promotions, new product launches, price changes, and so forth).

Advertising expenditure data, by media class, from the company's accounting department.

Figures on sales and related topics from company factories.

Competitive advertising expenditure and exposure data, supplied by the division's advertising agencies at periodic intervals.

A panel of weight-conscious women.

To exemplify the type of outputs possible from this system, Mead Johnson will be able, with the help of analyses of factory sales data, warehouse withdrawal information, and consumer purchases from Nielsen, to monitor transactions at each stage of the flow of goods through the distribution channel and to detect accumulations or developing shortages. Management will also be able to spot sources of potential problems in time to deal with them effectively. For example, if factory sales exceed consumer purchases, more promotional pressure is required. By contrast, if factory sales lag behind consumer purchases, sales effort must be further stimulated.

Similarly, the company has been able to devise a practical measurement of advertising's effectiveness in stimulating sales—a measurement that is particularly appropriate to fast-moving packaged goods. By relating advertising outlays and exposure data to the number of prospects trying out a product during a campaign (the number is obtained from the continuing consumer survey), it is possible to calculate the advertising cost of recruiting such a prospect. By persisting in such analyses during several campaigns, the relative value of alternative advertising approaches can be weighed. Since measurement of the sales, as opposed to the communications, effects of promotion is a horrendously difficult, costly, and chancy process, the full significance of this achievement is difficult to exaggerate.

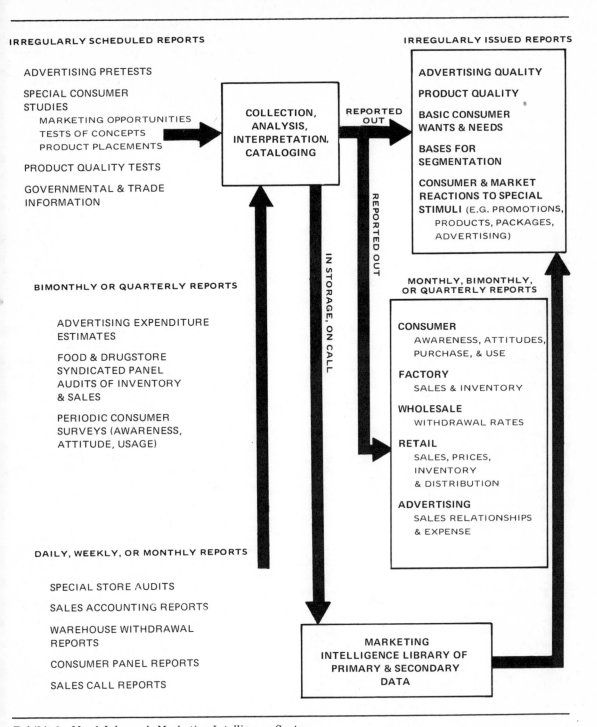

IRREGULARLY SCHEDULED REPORTS

ADVERTISING PRETESTS

SPECIAL CONSUMER
STUDIES
- MARKETING OPPORTUNITIES
- TESTS OF CONCEPTS
- PRODUCT PLACEMENTS

PRODUCT QUALITY TESTS

GOVERNMENTAL & TRADE
INFORMATION

BIMONTHLY OR QUARTERLY REPORTS

ADVERTISING EXPENDITURE
ESTIMATES

FOOD & DRUGSTORE
SYNDICATED PANEL
AUDITS OF INVENTORY
& SALES

PERIODIC CONSUMER
SURVEYS (AWARENESS,
ATTITUDE, USAGE)

DAILY, WEEKLY, OR MONTHLY REPORTS

SPECIAL STORE AUDITS

SALES ACCOUNTING REPORTS

WAREHOUSE WITHDRAWAL
REPORTS

CONSUMER PANEL REPORTS

SALES CALL REPORTS

COLLECTION,
ANALYSIS,
INTERPRETATION,
CATALOGING

REPORTED
OUT

REPORTED OUT

IN STORAGE, ON CALL

IRREGULARLY ISSUED REPORTS

ADVERTISING QUALITY

PRODUCT QUALITY

BASIC CONSUMER
WANTS & NEEDS

BASES FOR
SEGMENTATION

CONSUMER & MARKET
REACTIONS TO SPECIAL
STIMULI (E.G. PROMOTIONS,
PRODUCTS, PACKAGES,
ADVERTISING)

MONTHLY, BIMONTHLY,
OR QUARTERLY REPORTS

CONSUMER
AWARENESS, ATTITUDES,
PURCHASE, & USE

FACTORY
SALES & INVENTORY

WHOLESALE
WITHDRAWAL RATES

RETAIL
SALES, PRICES,
INVENTORY
& DISTRIBUTION

ADVERTISING
SALES RELATIONSHIPS
& EXPENSE

MARKETING
INTELLIGENCE LIBRARY OF
PRIMARY & SECONDARY
DATA

Exhibit 3. Mead Johnson's Marketing Intelligence System.

Benefits Realized Mead Johnson's marketing intelligence system has been helpful to management in a number of ways. In addition to giving executives early warning of new trends and problems, and valuable insights into future conditions, it is leading to a systematic *body* of knowledge about company markets rather than to isolated scraps of information. This knowledge in turn should lead ultimately to a theory of marketing in each field that will explain the mysteries that baffle marketers today. What is more, the company expects that the system will help to free its marketing intelligence people from fire-fighting projects so that they can concentrate on long-term factors and eventually be more consistently creative.

Despite these gains, it is important to note that Mead Johnson feels it has a long road still to travel. More work is needed in linking individual data banks. Conceptual schemes must be proved out in practice; ways must still be found to reduce an awesome volume of data, swelled periodically by new information from improved sources, so as to make intelligence more immediately accessible to decision makers. And perhaps the biggest problem of the moment, one underlying some of the others, is the difficulty in finding qualified marketing-oriented programmers.

Physical Distribution

A veritable revolution is now taking place in physical distribution. Total systems are being evolved out of the former hodgepodge of separate responsibilities, which were typically scattered among different departments of the same company. These systems include traffic and transportation, warehousing, materials handling, protective packaging, order processing, production planning, inventory control, customer service, market forecasting, and plant and warehouse site selection. Motivating this revolution are the computer, company drives to reduce distribution costs, and innovations in transportation, such as jet air freight, container ships, the interstate highway network, and larger and more versatile freight cars.

Distribution is one area of marketing where the "bread-and-butter" uses of the computer are relatively easily deployed for such functions as order processing, real-time inventory level reports, and tracking the movements of goods. Further into

the future lie mathematical models which will include every factor bearing on distribution. Not only will packaging, materials handling, transportation and warehouse, order processing, and related costs be considered in such models; also included will be sales forecasts by product, production rates by factory, warehouse locations and capacities, speeds of different carriers, etc. In short, a complete picture will be developed for management.

Program in Action The experiences of the Norge Division of Borg-Warner Corporation point up the values of the systems approach in physical distribution. The firm was confronted externally with complaints from its dealers and distributors, who were trying to cope with swollen inventories and the pressures of "loading deals." Internally, because coordination of effort between the six departments involved in distribution was at a minimum, distribution costs and accounts receivable were mounting persistently.

To grapple with this situation, Norge undertook a comprehensive analysis of its distribution system. Out of this grew a new philosophy. A company executive has described the philosophy to me as follows:

"An effective system of physical distribution cannot begin at the end of the production line. It must also apply at the very beginning of the production process—at the planning, scheduling, and forecasting stages. Logistics, in short, is part of a larger marketing system, not just an evaluation of freight rates. We must worry not only about finished refrigerators, but also about the motors coming from another manufacturer, and even about where the copper that goes into those motors will come from. We must be concerned with *total flow.*"

To implement this philosophy, the appliance manufacturer took the following steps:

1. It reorganized the forecasting, production scheduling, warehousing, order processing, and shipping functions into *one* department headed by a director of physical distribution

2. The management information system was improved with the help of EDP equipment tied into the communications network. This

WHAT IS THE SYSTEMS APPROACH?

There seems to be agreement that the systems approach sprang to life as a semantically identifiable term sometime during World War II. It was associated with the problem of how to bomb targets deep in Germany more effectively from British bases, with the Manhattan Project, and with studies of optimum search patterns for destroyers to use in locating U-boats during the Battle of the North Atlantic.* Subsequently, it was utilized in the defeat of the Berlin blockade. It has reached its present culmination in the success of great military systems such as Polaris and Minuteman.

Not surprisingly, the parallels between military and marketing strategies being what they are, the definition of the systems approach propounded by the RAND Corporation for the U.S. Air Force is perfectly apt for marketers:

> "An inquiry to aid a decision-maker choose a course of action by systematically investigating his proper objectives, comparing quantitatively where possible the costs, effectiveness, and risks associated with the alternative policies or strategies for achieving them, and *formulating additional alternatives if those examined are found wanting.*"†

The systems approach is thus an orderly, "architectural" discipline for dealing with complex problems of choice under uncertainty.

Typically, in such problems, multiple and possibly conflicting objectives exist. The task of the systems analyst is to specify a closed operating network in which the components will work together so as to yield the optimum balance of economy, efficiency, and risk minimization. Put more broadly, the systems approach attempts to apply the "scientific method" to complex marketing problems studied *as a whole*; it seeks to discipline marketing.

But disciplining marketing is no easy matter. Marketing must be perceived as a *process* rather than as a series of isolated, discrete actions; competitors must be viewed as components of each marketer's own system. The process must also be comprehended as involving a flow and counterflow of information and behavior between marketers and customers. Some years ago, Marion Harper, Jr., now chairman of the Interpublic Group of Companies, Inc., referred to the flow of information in marketing communications as the cycle of "listen (i.e., marketing research), publish (messages, media), listen (more marketing research), revise, publish, listen. . . ." More recently, Raymond A. Bauer referred to the "transactional" nature of communications as a factor in the motivations, frames of reference, needs, and so forth of recipients of messages. The desires of the communicator alone are but part of the picture.‡

Pushing this new awareness of the intricacies of marketing communications still further, Theodore Levitt identified the interactions between five different forces—source effect (i.e., the reputation or credibility of the sponsor of the message), sleeper effect (the declining influence of source credibility with the passage of time), message effect (the character and quality of the message), communicator effect (the impact of the transmitter—e.g., a salesman), and audience effect (the competence and responsibility of the audience).§ Casting a still broader net are efforts to model the entire purchasing process, and perhaps the ultimate application of the systems concept in attempts to make mathematical models of the entire marketing process.

Mounting recognition of the almost countless elements involved in marketing and of the mind-boggling complexity of their interactions is a wholesome (though painful) experience. Nevertheless, I believe we must not ignore other ramifications of the systems approach which are qualitative in nature. For the world of marketing offers a vast panorama of non- or part-mathematical systems and opportunities to apply systems thinking. We must not become so bedazzled by the brouhaha of the operations research experts as to lose sight of the larger picture.

* See Glen McDaniel, "The Meaning of The Systems Movement to the Acceleration and Direction of the American Economy," in *Proceedings of the 1964 Systems Engineering Conference* (New York, Clapp & Poliak, Inc., 1964), p. 1; see also E. S. Quade, editor, *Analysis for Military Decisions* (Santa Monica, California, The RAND Corporation, 1964), p. 6.

† Quade, op. cit., p. 4.

‡ "Communications as a Transaction." *Public Opinion Quarterly*, Spring 1963, p. 83.

§ See Theodore Levitt, *Industrial Purchasing Behavior* (Boston, Division of Research, Harvard Business School, 1965), p. 25ff.

step made it possible to process and report data more speedily on orders received, inventory levels, and the actual movement of goods.

3. Management used a combination of computer and manual techniques to weigh tradeoffs among increased costs of multiple warehousing, reduced long-haul freight and local drayage costs, reduced inventory pipeline, and the sales value of an improved "total" product offering. Also assessed were tradeoffs between shorter production runs and higher inventory levels, thereby challenging the traditional "wisdom" of production-oriented managers that the longer the run, the better.

4. The company is setting up new regional warehouses.

As a result of these moves, Norge has been able to lower inventories throughout its sales channels and to reduce accounts receivable. These gains have led, in turn, to a reduction of the company's overall investment and a concomitant increase in profitability.

It is essential to note that even though Norge has used operations research as part of its systems approach, many aspects of the program are qualitative. Thus far, the company has found that the development of an all-encompassing model is not warranted because of

a.   the time and cost involved,
b.   the probability that the situation will change before the model is completed,
c.   a concern that such a model would be so complex as to be unworkable, and
d.   the difficulty of testing many of the assumptions used.

In addition, management has not tried to quantify the impact of its actions on distributor and retailer attitudes and behavior, possible competitive countermoves, and numerous other factors contributing to results.

Toward Total Integration

The integration of systems developed for product management, product innovation, market-

ing intelligence, physical distribution, and the other functions or "subsystems" embraced by the term *marketing* creates a total marketing system. Thus, marketing plans composed according to a step-by-step outline, ranging from enunciation of objectives and implementational steps to audit and adjustment to environmental changes, constitute a complete application of systems theory. Further, as the various subsystems of the overall system are linked quantitatively, so that the effect of modifications in one element can be detected in other elements, and as the influences of competitive moves on each element are analyzed numerically, then the total scheme becomes truly sophisticated.

PLUSES AND MINUSES

Two elements underlie the use and benefits of systems theory—order and knowledge. The first is a homely virtue, the second a lofty goal. Marketing is obviously not alone among all human pursuits in needing them; but, compared with its business neighbors, production and finance, marketing's need is acute indeed. The application of the systems concept can bring considerable advantages. It offers:

A methodical problem-solving orientation—with a broader frame of reference so that all aspects of a problem are examined.

Coordinated deployment of all appropriate tools of marketing.

Greater efficiency and economy of marketing operations.

Quicker recognition of impending problems, made possible by better understanding of the complex interplay of many trends and forces.

A stimulus to innovation.

A means of quantitatively verifying results.

These functional benefits in turn yield rich rewards in the marketplace. The most important gains are:

A deeper penetration of existing markets — As an illustration, the Advanced Data Division of Litton Industries has become a leader in the automatic revenue control business by designing systems meshing together "hardware" and "software."

A broadening of markets — For example, the tourist industry has attracted millions of additional travelers by creating packaged tours that are really product-service systems. These systems are far more convenient and economical than anything the consumer could assemble himself.

An extension of product lines — Systems management makes it more feasible to seek out compatibilities among independently developed systems. Evidence of this idea is the work of automatic control system specialists since the early 1950s.[5] Now similar signs are apparent in marketing. For example, Acme Visible Records is currently dovetailing the design and sale of its record-keeping systems with data-processing machines and forms.

A lessening of competition or a strengthened capacity to cope with competition — The systems approach tends to make a company's product line more unique and attractive. Carborundum's innovation in metal-removal systems is a perfect illustration of this.

Problems in Practice

Having just enumerated in glowing terms the benefits of the systems approach, realism demands that I give "equal time" to the awesome difficulties its utilization presents. There is no better evidence of this than the gulf between the elegant and sophisticated models with which recent marketing literature abounds and the actual number of situations in which those models really work. For the truth of the matter is that we are still in the foothills of this development, despite the advances of a few leaders. Let us consider some of the obstacles.

Time and Manpower Costs First of all, the systems approach requires considerable time to implement; it took one company over a year to portray its physical distribution system in a mathe-matical model before it could even begin to solve its problems. RCA's Electronic Data Processing Division reports models taking three to five years to build, after which holes in the data network have to be filled and the model tested against history. Add to this the need for manpower of exceptional intellectual ability, conceptual skills, and specialized education—manpower that is in exceedingly short supply. Because the problems are complex and involve all elements of the business, one man alone cannot solve them. He lacks the knowledge, tools, and controls. And so many people must be involved. It follows that the activation of systems theory can be very costly.

Absence of "Canned" Solutions Unlike other business functions where standardized approaches to problem solving are available, systems must be tailored to the individual situation of each firm. Even the same problem in different companies in the same industry will frequently lead to different solutions because of the impact of other inputs, unique perceptions of the environment, and varying corporate missions. These factors, too, compound time and expense demands.

"Net Uncertainties" Even after exhaustive analysis, full optimization of a total problem cannot be obtained. Some uncertainty will always remain and must be dealt with on the basis of judgment and experience.

Lack of Hard Data In the world of engineering, the systems evolved to date have consisted all or mostly of machines. Systems engineers have been wise enough to avoid the irrationalities of man until they master control of machines. Marketing model-builders, however, have not been able to choose, for the distributor, salesman, customer, and competitor are central to marketing. We must, therefore, incorporate not only quantitative measures of the dimensions of things and processes (e.g., market potential, media outlays, and shipping rates), but also psychological measures of comprehension, attitudes, motivations, intentions, needs—yes, even psychological measures of physical behavior. What is needed is a marriage of the physical and behavioral sciences—and we are about as advanced in this blending of disciplines as astronomy was in the Middle Ages.

Consider the advertising media fields as an instance of the problem:

A number of advertising agencies have evolved linear programming or simulation techniques to assess alternate media schedules. One of the key sets of data used covers the probabilities of exposure to all or part of the audience of a TV program, magazine, or radio station. But what is exposure, and how do you measure it? What is optimum frequency of exposure, and how do you measure it? How does advertising prevail on the predispositions and perceptions of a potential customer? Is it better to judge advertising effects on the basis of exposure opportunity, "impact" (whatever that is), messages retained, message comprehension, or attitude shifts or uptrends in purchase intentions? We do not have these answers yet.

Even assuming precise knowledge of market dimensions, product performance, competitive standing, weights of marketing pressure exerted by direct selling, advertising and promotion, and so on, most marketers do not yet know, except in isolated cases, how one force will affect another. For instance, how does a company "image" affect the setting in which its salesmen work? How does a company's reputation for service affect customer buying behavior?

Nature of Marketing Men Man is an actor on this stage in another role. A good many marketing executives, in the deepest recesses of their psyches, are artists, not analysts. For them, marketing is an art form, and, in my opinion, they really do not want it to be any other way. Their temperament is antipathetic to system, order, knowledge. They enjoy flying by the seat of their pants—though you will never get them to admit it. They revel in chaos, abhor facts, and fear research. They hate to be trammeled by written plans. And they love to spend, but are loathe to assess the results of their spending.

Obviously, such men cannot be sold readily on the value and practicality of the systems approach! It takes time, experience, and many facts to influence their thinking.

Surmounting the Barriers

All is not gloom, however. The barriers described are being overcome in various ways. While operations research techniques have not yet made much headway in evolving total marketing systems and in areas where man is emotionally engaged, their accomplishments in solving inventory control problems, in sales analysis, in site selection, and in other areas have made many businessmen more sympathetic and open-minded to them.

Also, mathematical models—even the ones that do not work well yet—serve to bolster comprehension of the need for system as well as to clarify the intricacies among subsystems. Many models are in this sense learning models; they teach us how to ask more insightful questions. Moreover, they pinpoint data gaps and invite a more systematized method for reaching judgments where complete information does not exist. Because the computer abhors vague generalities, it forces managers to analyze their roles, objectives, and criteria more concretely. Paradoxically, it demands more, not less, of its human masters.

Of course, resistance to mathematical models by no means makes resistance to the systems approach necessary. There are many cases where no need may ever arise to use mathematics or computers. For the essence of the systems approach is not its techniques, but the enumeration of options and their implications. A simple checklist may be the only tool needed. I would even argue that some hard thinking in a quiet room may be enough. This being the case, the whole trend to more analysis and logic in management thinking, as reflected in business periodicals, business schools, and the practices of many companies, will work in favor of the development of the systems approach.

It is important to note at this juncture that not all marketers need the systems approach in its formal, elaborate sense. The success of some companies is rooted in other than marketing talents; their expertise may lie in finance, technology, administration, or even in personnel— as in the case of holding companies having an almost uncanny ability to hire brilliant operating managers and the self-control to leave them alone. In addition, a very simple marketing operation—for example, a company marketing one product through one distribution channel— may have no use for the systems concept.

APPLYING THE APPROACH

Not illogically, there is a system for applying the systems approach. It may be outlined as a sequence of steps:

1. *Define the problem and clarify objectives.* Care must be exercised not to accept the view of the propounder of the problem lest the analyst be defeated at the outset.

2. *Test the definition of the problem.* Expand its parameters to the limit. For example, to solve physical distribution problems it is necessary to study the marketplace (customer preferences, usage rates, market size, and so forth), as well as the production process (which plants produce which items most efficiently, what the interplant movements of raw materials are, and so forth). Delineate the extremes of these factors, their changeability, and the limitations on management's ability to work with them.

3. *Build a model.* Portray all factors graphically, indicating logical and chronological sequences—the dynamic flow of information, decisions, and events. "Closed circuits" should be used where there is information feedback or go, no-go and recycle signals (see Exhibit 2).

4. *Set concrete objectives.* For example, if a firm wants to make daily deliveries to every customer, prohibitive as the cost may be, manipulation of the model will yield one set of answers. But if the desire is to optimize service at lowest cost, then another set of answers will be needed. The more crisply and precisely targets are stated, the more specific the results will be.

5. *Develop alternative solutions.* It is crucial to be as open-minded as possible at this stage. The analyst must seek to expand the list of options rather than merely assess those given to him, then reduce the list to a smaller number of practical or relevant ones.

6. *Set up criteria or tests of relative value.*

7. *Quantify some or all of the factors or "variables."* The extent to which this is done depends, of course, on management's inclinations and the "state of the art."

8. *Manipulate the model.* That is, weigh the costs, effectiveness, profitability, and risks of each alternative.

9. *Interpret the results, and choose one or more courses of action.*

10. *Verify the results.* Do they make sense when viewed against the world as executives know it? Can their validity be tested by experiments and investigations?

Forethought and Perspective

Successful systems do not blossom overnight. From primitive beginnings, they evolve over a period of time as managers and systems specialists learn to understand each other better, and learn how to structure problems and how to push out the frontiers of the "universe" with which they are dealing. Companies must be prepared to invest time, money, and energy in making systems management feasible. This entails a solid foundation of historical data even before the conceptual framework for the system can be constructed. Accordingly, considerable time should be invested at the outset in *thinking* about the problem, its appropriate scope, options, and criteria of choice before plunging into analysis.

Not only technicians, but most of us have a way of falling in love with techniques. We hail each one that comes along—*deus ex machina.* Historically, commercial research has wallowed in several such passions (e.g., probability sampling, motivation research, and semantic scaling), and now operations research appears to be doing the same thing. Significantly, each technique has come, in the fullness of time, to take its place as one, but only one, instrument in the research tool chest. We must therefore have a broad and dispassionate perspective on the systems approach at this juncture. We must recognize that the computer does not possess greater magical properties than the abacus. It, too, is a tool, albeit a brilliant one.

Put another way, executives must continue to exercise their judgment and experience. Systems analysis is no substitute for common sense. The computer must adapt itself to their styles, personalities, and modes of problem solving. It is an aid to management, not a surrogate. Businessmen may be slow, but the good ones are bright; the electronic monster, by contrast, is a speedy idiot.

It demands great acuity of wit from its human managers lest they be deluged in an avalanche of useless paper. (The story is told of a sales manager who had just found out about the impressive capabilities of his company's computer and called for a detailed sales analysis of all products. The report was duly prepared and wheeled into his office on a dolly.)

Systems users must be prepared to revise continually. There are two reasons for this. First, the boundaries of systems keep changing; constraints are modified; competition makes fresh incursions; variables, being what they are, vary, and new ones crop up. Second, the analytical process is iterative. Usually, one "pass" at problem formulation and searches for solutions will not suffice, and it will be necessary to "recycle" as early hypotheses are challenged and new, more fruitful insights are stimulated by the inquiry. Moreover, it is impossible to select objectives without knowledge of their effects and costs. That knowledge can come only from analysis, and it frequently requires review and revision.

Despite all the efforts at quantification, systems analysis is still largely an art. It relies frequently on inputs based on human judgment; even when the inputs are numerical, they are determined, at least in part, by judgment. Similarly, the outputs must pass through the sieve of human interpretation. Hence, there is a positive correlation between the payoff from a system and the managerial level involved in its design. The higher the level, the more rewarding the results.

Finally, let me observe that marketing people merit their own access to computers as well as programmers who understand marketing. Left in the hands of accountants, the timing, content, and format of output are often out of phase with marketing needs.

CONCLUSION

Nearly 800 years ago a monk wrote the following about St. Godric, a merchant later turned hermit:

"He laboured not only as a merchant but also as a shipman . . . to Denmark, Flanders, and Scotland; in which lands he found cer-

tain rare, and therefore more precious, wares, which he carried to other parts wherein he knew them to be least familiar, and coveted by the inhabitants beyond the price of gold itself, wherefore he exchanged these wares for others coveted by men of other lands. . . ."[6]

How St. Godric "knew" about his markets we are not told, marketing having been in a primitive state in 1170. How some of us marketers today "know" is, in my opinion, sometimes no less mysterious than it was eight centuries ago. But we are trying to change that, and I will hazard the not very venturesome forecast that the era of "by guess and by gosh" marketing is drawing to a close. One evidence of this trend is marketers' intensified search for knowledge that will improve their command over their destinies. This search is being spurred on by a number of powerful developments. To describe them briefly:

The growing complexity of technology and the accelerating pace of technological innovation.

The advent of the computer, inspiring and making possible analysis of the relationships between systems components.

The intensification of competition, lent impetus by the extraordinary velocity of new product development and the tendency of diversification to thrust everybody into everybody else's business.

The preference of buyers for purchasing from as few sources as possible, thereby avoiding the problems of assembling bits and pieces themselves and achieving greater reliability, economy, and administrative convenience. (Mrs. Jones would rather buy a complete vacuum cleaner from one source than the housing from one manufacturer, the hose from another, and the attachments from still another. And industrial buyers are not much different from Mrs. Jones. They would rather buy an automated machine tool from one manufacturer than design and assemble the components themselves. Not to be overlooked, in this connection, is the tremendous influence of the U.S government in buying systems for its military and aerospace programs.)

The further development and application of the systems approach to marketing represents, in my judgment, the leading edge in both marketing theory and practice. At the moment, we are still much closer to St. Godric than to the millenium, and the road will be rocky and tortuous. But if we are ever to convert marketing into a more scientific pursuit, this is the road we must travel. The systems concept can teach us how our businesses really behave in the marketing.arena, thereby extending managerial leverage and control. It can help us to confront more intelligently the awesome complexity of marketing, to deal with the hazards and opportunities of technological change, and to cope with the intensification of competition. And in the process, the concept will help us to feed the hungry maws of our expensive computers with more satisfying fare.

Notes

1. See, for example, Donald F. Cox and Robert E. Good, "How to Build a Marketing Information System." *Harvard Business Review,* May-June 1967, p. 145.
2. "Abrasive Maker's Systems Approach Opens New Market," *Steel,* December 27, 1965, p. 38.
3. Ibid.
4. "Carborundum Grinds at Faster Clip," *Business Week,* July 23, 1966, pp. 58, 60.
5. See *Automatic and Manual Control: Papers Contributed to the Conference at Cranford, 1951,* edited by A. Tustin (London, Butterworth's Scientific Publications, 1952)
6. *Life of St. Godric,* by Reginald, a monk of Durham, c. 1170.

2 INSIGHTS INTO: THE NEW MARKETPLACE

Traditionally, the exchange process takes place in a marketplace, where buyer meets seller.

During the past decade—the late sixties and early seventies—the marketplace has been beset by dramatic upheavals. In brief, the framework within which buyer and seller function has been transformed by the social, economic, and legal forces which surround it.

With an enlarged responsibility placed on marketing managers to comprehend the New Marketplace, there is a great need for broader understanding of the long-range implications of the dislocations taking place.

The authors in this section bring us up-to-date in such significant areas as: demographic movement, a shortages economy, consumerism, antitrust, advertising regulation, multinational marketing— and positioning, and marketing information systems to keep track of it all.

It is clear that the New Marketplace will never be as fixed as was the marketplace of the past. These eight articles show why the marketing practitioner must constantly anticipate the changes wrought by the various elements at work within society.

5 THE SECOND HALF OF THE SEVENTIES

Fabian Linden
Consumer Research
The Conference Board

Although the recent recession slowed the growth of the affluent society, a business researcher predicts that by 1980 about 45% of all families will be in the $15,000-and-over income bracket. Marketers will also be interested in his prediction as to whether the migration to the suburbs will continue.

The first half of the seventies was, by almost any measure, the most trying period for the U.S. consumer since the end of World War II. The decline in real spending power was larger and lasted longer than in any prior economic turndown in the past three decades.

From Fabian Linden, "The Second Half of the Seventies," The Conference Board Record, *Vol. XII, No. 12, December, 1975, pp. 2-5. Reprinted by permission of the publisher.*

But in actual fact, there are in process a number of important demographic and social changes which are especially auspicious for economic growth and an improvement in living standards. For instance, in the past five years the labor force expanded at a rate of 2.1% a year but the U.S. population grew by less than 1.0%. This arithmetic suggests we would have experienced a significant improvement in real per capita consumption if the economic environment had been more favorable.

Beyond that, there has also been a significant increase in the number of persons reaching family formation age. This development, under more favorable circumstances, would have accelerated the demand for housing and a wide range of durable goods, among other things. But these potentials were at best only partially realized.

In very recent months, however, the economic readings have become increasingly heartening. This, then, is a particularly appropriate juncture to appraise the various currents of change and look ahead at what might be anticipated for the second half of the seventies.

THE POPULATION BULGE

For some years now the babies born in the great boom following World War II have been coming of age. The sixties was the decade of the teenager: it was a period of social and cultural upheaval accompanied by a precipitous upsurge in demand for a wide range of goods—from pop records to blue jeans—having special appeal for the young.

We are now in the era of the young adult. In the past five years the 25–34 age group expanded by some 22%, which is some five times faster than the growth of the population. The full impact of this demographic development has, to some extent, been muted by the recent economic turndown. But in the next five years we will continue to experience a significant expansion in the size of that age bracket. This, in conjunction with the release of demand pent up in the last year or two, suggests that the outlook for industries related to the home—residential construction, furnishings, appliances—is most promising.

In the second half of the seventies there will also be an appreciable increase in the number of persons aged 35 to 44. This bracket actually decreased in size during the first half of the decade, if only moderately. The expansion scheduled for the coming period is also of importance to marketers. For at this period in the life cycle a large number of persons have achieved the experience and the stature to fetch well-above-average pay. This means that discretionary spending power is likely to grow a bit faster than in the recent past.

The 45–64 age category expanded only moderately in the first half of the seventies, and it will not grow at all in the second half. Persons 65 and over, however, will become some 10% more numerous.

All told, the nation's adult population will increase by 12.5 million persons, slightly under 9%, in the next five years. Most of this growth—some two-thirds of it—will be accounted for by the 25–44 age bracket. This will be the principal growth area in the immediate future.

HOUSEHOLDS AND FAMILIES

Because of the rapid growth of young adults, there has been and will continue to be for some time ahead, an acceleration in the rate of net household and family formation. In the second half of the sixties the population of households expanded at an average annual rate of about 1.2 million, and by 1.5 million in the past five years; the next five should see further, if somewhat slower, growth.

To no small degree the past high level of household formation was accounted for by young people leaving home and moving to places of their own. Since 1970, for instance, the number of single-person households rose by more than 20%. In the coming years these independent young people will marry, with the probable result that two households will be dissolved for the formation of one family. Thus, in the past five years we experienced a sharp rise in the household population, but only a modest increase in families. In the next five years there will be a significant rise in the family count. Recently the total number of families rose by 825,000 annually, but between now and the end of the decade the figure will be close to 1.0 million.

BIRTHS

Forecasting births is one of the more precarious branches of demography. The record of professional statisticians in recent years has been only slightly better than that of meteorologists. But for all that, the data available suggest that the long decline in births—a decline which has persisted since 1960—will turn around shortly. According to the latest figures on hand, we are likely to have a slightly larger baby crop this year than last. Again, of course, this is the result of our abruptly changing age mix.

Based on the demographic schedule, it now seems highly probable that, in the next five years at least, the annual number of births will be increasing. The precise dimensions and duration of this expected trend is still difficult to assess. However, it is quite certain that we will have more "low order" births (the family's first or second child), in the next few years than in the

Selected Measures of Growth, 1965-1980 (Dollar figures in 1975 prices)

	1965	1970	1975	1980
Gross National Product	$1,142.9	$1,336.8	$1,475.0	$1,930.0
Disposable Personal Income	$ 762.6	$ 937.5	$1,085.0	$1,390.0
Per Capita Disposable Income[a]	$3,925.0	$4,575.0	$5,080.0	$6,240.0
Supernumerary Income (After Taxes)	$ 45.5	$ 77.0	$ 90.0	$ 170.5
Supernumerary as % of D.P.I.	6.0%	8.0%	8.5%	12.5%
U.S. Population	194.3	204.9	213.6	222.8
Persons by Age				
Under 18	69.7	69.7	66.3	63.3
18-24	20.3	24.7	27.6	29.4
25-34	22;5	25.3	30.9	36.2
35-44	24.4	23.1	22.8	25.7
45-54	21.8	23.3	23.8	22.6
55-64	17.1	18.7	19.8	21.0
65 and over	18.5	20.1	22.3	24.5
Marriages	1.8	2.2	2.3	2.5
Births	3.8	3.7	3.2	3.9
Families	48.0	51.6	55.7	61.1
Households	57.4	63.4	71.1	78.2
Educational Attainment[b]				
Elementary or less	34.0	30.3	27.0	23.5
Some high school	18.6	18.7	19.9	20.9
High school graduate	31.7	37.1	42.8	48.7
Some college	9.1	11.2	13.3	16.1
College graduates	9.7	12.1	15.1	19.3
Total Employment[c]	71.1	78.6	84.9	96.1
White-collar workers	31.9	37.2	42.1	49.2
Blue-collar workers	26.2	28.0	28.2	31.7
Service workers	8.9	10.4	11.6	12.7
Other	4.1	3.1	2.9	2.5
Working Women				
As % of women 16 years and over	38.8%	42.8%	46.2%	48.5%
Place of Residence[d]				
Metropolitan areas	128.6	137.1	143.3	150.4
Central cities	61.8	62.9	61.4	59.8
Outside central cities	66.9	74.2	81.9	90.6
Nonmetropolitan areas	61.0	62.8	66.6	70.8
Families by Income Class				
Under $5,000	8.6	7.5	7.8	7.3
$5,000-10,000	13.4	12.4	12.5	12.5
10,000-15,000	12.9	13.2	14.2	14.5
15,000 and over	12.9	18.6	21.2	26.9

Note: Dollar figures in billions; all other figures in millions, unless otherwise indicated.

[a] Figures are in actual dollars.

[b] Based on persons 25 and over.

[c] 1965 figures not strictly comparable with figures for later years.

[d] Based on the civilian noninstitutional population.

Sources: U.S. Departments of Commerce and Labor; The Conference Board.

peak birth year, 1960. Such "low order" births are of special importance to marketers, for it is these children that generate the most spending. Many of the needs of subsequent babies are fulfilled through hand-me-downs.

This year a total of 3.2 million babies will be born, a figure which is some 25% lower than in 1960. However, almost all of the difference is accounted for by "high order" births, by women who have three or more offspring. The number of "high order" births is, in fact, currently off by some 60%, as compared with 15 years ago. Large families are evidently out of fashion.

First births, on the other hand, are actually now running almost 15% higher, second births are off by about 10%. In the years ahead we are likely to experience a continuation of a fairly high level of first births, and probably a significant increase in second babies.

About 65% of all "low order" births are accounted for by women aged 20–29. In the first half of the seventies the size of this group rose by 17%, but there was no corresponding increment in early births. In some measure this may be attributed to the fact that more women are now disinclined to have children, but there is also evidence indicating that the average age of marriage is rising, and that the time interval between marriage and children is also increasing. At some point, of course, this "delay factor" will level off. At that time we should begin to experience a fairly significant rise in at least "low order" births.

It is estimated that in 1980 births will total 3.9 million, for an increment of more than 20%, as compared with now. This latter figure assumes a completed fertility rate of 2.1 which, of course, is the zero population growth (ZPG) ratio. We have recently been running marginally below that level, but this may be attributed to the delay factor noted above, and to some small extent to the economic turndown, which tends to have a dampening effect on marriages and births.

LABOR FORCE, OCCUPATION, EDUCATION

For some years now we have been experiencing a quickening in the growth rate of the nation's labor force. In the past five years the number of persons working or looking for jobs expanded at the impressive annual rate of 2.1%. This extraordinarily high figure reflects the maturation of persons born in the initial explosive phase of the birth boom. By the mid-fifties, while births were still rising, the rate was slower than in the immediately preceding years. Accordingly, in the second half of this decade the labor force will also expand somewhat more slowly. Exactly how much more slowly is difficult to assess, since much has to do with the labor force participation rate—that is, the proportion of all adults that works.

Currently the participation ratio is about 62%, which represents a gain of about 0.6 points since the start of the seventies. If a similar increment is experienced in the years ahead, the labor force will grow by an estimated 1.6% a year between now and 1980. This represents a relatively modest expectation, since the rise in the labor force participation rate in the past five years was appreciably less than in the immediately preceding period—a development which might, in part at least, be explained by the general slowdown in economic activity.

Because 1975 is in many respects an atypical year, it is also difficult to anticipate the likely changes in the nation's occupational mix between now and the end of the decade. However, throughout the postwar period the number of service workers expanded at a well-above-average rate, and there was also a relatively sizable increment in white-collar employment. The growth in the blue-collar category, however, was relatively small. The evidence suggests that we will continue to experience a similar configuration in the years ahead.

The sizable influx of young persons into the adult population is also affecting the educational profile. Each new generation secures more schooling than the one preceding. Among those who are now of retirement age, only about 15% have had any exposure to college, but some 35% of all young people today enter college—although only about half earn a degree. In the past five years the number of adults with at least some college exposure increased by some 22%; an increment of similar magnitude is expected over the next five. In 1970 about 11% of our adult population held a college degree, today the ratio is close to 13%, and by 1980 it will reach 15%.

Those with relatively modest schooling, on

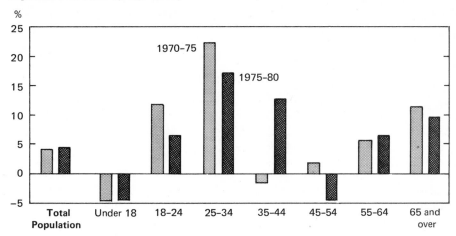

Population Growth by Age Groups

Sources: U.S. Department of Commerce; The Conference Board.

the other hand, are decreasing, and at a rather rapid rate. A mere five years ago some 28% of all adults had failed to enter high school, but the proportion is now only 23%, and by 1980 it will be down to almost 18%.

PLACE OF RESIDENCE

The movement of population from city to suburb is still very much an ongoing process. While the trek is less hectic than in the years immediately following World War II, it is nevertheless continuing at a steady pace. Over the past five years, for example, while the U.S. population grew by about 4%, the number of persons living in the suburbs expanded by more than 10%. Less than half of this latter figure, of course, is attributable to natural growth, but the other half is a net gain from migration. In the same time interval the population of the nation's central cities actually declined by 2.5%. Moreover, this figure tends to understate the situation since, had there been no out-migration, the population of the cities would have risen by the nation's natural growth rate.

In looking ahead, we can expect a continuation of these broad trends, at least over the next five years. The evidence urging this conclusion is formidable—on the one hand, the continuing deterioration of the cities and their worsening financial fortunes; on the other, the nation's changing age mix and the related, expected turnaround in the birth level. At the start of the present decade the suburbs accounted for 54% of the total metropolitan population. The present ratio is 57%, and between now and 1980 it is projected to exceed 60%.

SPENDING POWER

The recent economic turndown was especially traumatic for the U.S. consumer: it was not only the most severe experience in decades but it followed a period of almost unparalleled growth. During the sixties disposable personal income expanded at an exceptionally rapid rate. Between 1960 and 1973 (the last good business year), real per capita disposable income—that is, the consumer's capacity to buy—increased at an annual rate of 3.5%. In the first half of this decade, however, the figure dropped below 2.2%, and in the past year or so real spending power actually declined. This year, even after adjusting for a turnaround in the economy in the months ahead, real per capita disposable income will average out some 1.5% below 1973.

What can be expected in the next five years? At this still-troublesome juncture of the business cycle there continues to be broad speculation within the economic fraternity. Plainly, there are a number of problems that will remain with us for some time. The unemployment level is disconcertingly high and stubborn, and while the rate of inflation has subsided, this problem is apparently a long way from being under control. But there are increasing signs that the U.S. economy is beginning to grow again. Many crucial, if not all, statistical indicators have been turning up in recent months.

Given the exceptionally sharp decline of the recent recession, the business rebound should be vigorous. It is estimated that between now and 1980 real gross national product will expand at an average annual rate of about 5.5%. This, of course, is appreciably better than the historical experience, but we will be making up for considerable ground lost over the last year and a half. Based on the indicated growth assumption we can, therefore, expect a substantial improvement in consumer buying power. Real per capita disposable income in the next five years is projected to increase by over 4% annually—faster in the early phase of the recovery, slower in the final years of the decade.

Once disposable income begins to rise again, we can anticipate a significant expansion in the size of the upper-income bracket. Perhaps the single most significant development for marketers in the past three decades has been the rapid expansion in the size of the top earning brackets. But in the past five years the process slowed down considerably. Back in 1965, for example, about 25% of all families had earnings in excess of $15,000 a year (in today's dollars), but by 1970 the ratio had risen to 36%. This year the proportion will average out at about 38%, which is almost no problem at all in terms of our past experience. By 1980, however, an estimated 45% of all families will be in the $15,000-and-over bracket.

This, of course, means that supernumerary income—the money available for discretionary spending—should begin to increase again, and at a substantial rate. In the past two years or so there was no growth in the consumer's discretionary buying power, a situation which explains in considerable measure the particularly sharp contraction in the demand for the many goods and services generally associated with affluence. But with the expected turnaround in the economy top-of-the-line and carriage-trade oriented industries should begin to prosper again.

It may take some time before the consumer regains sufficient confidence to spend lavishly once more, but the arithmetic of the future strongly suggests that the prevailing prediction—that America's era of affluence is a thing of the past—is at least grossly exaggerated.

6 BUYER BEHAVIOR IN A STAGFLATION/ SHORTAGES ECONOMY

Eugene J. Kelley
Dean, College of Business Administration
Pennsylvania State University

L. Rusty Scheewe
Doctoral Student in Business
Pennsylvania State University

What happens to marketing when the economy is "down" is discussed in this article. The authors maintain that buyer behavior can be explained, in part, by probing into buyer *expectations*.

We are rapidly approaching an economic crisis of unprecedented proportions . . . we will never again return to the "normalcy" we knew in earlier periods because the continuing and growing energy problems will make that impossible . . . The problem is worldwide, encompassing developed and underdeveloped nations alike, because of the interdependency that has developed between nations as both sources of materials and markets for goods . . . we owe it to ourselves and succeeding generations and to people all over the world to manage our problems and opportunities as best we can, even in a rapidly changing and worsening economic environment.[1]

This note of urgency struck by John T. Connor, chairman of Allied Chemical Corporation,

From Eugene J. Kelly and L. Rusty Scheewe, "Buyer Behavior in a Stagflation/Shortages Economy," Journal of Marketing, April 1975, pp. 44-50. Reprinted by permission of the publisher.

was maintained by others at the Washington, D.C., Summit Conference on Inflation.[2] The current stagflation was found to be a multidimensional problem. (Inflation + recession = stagflation: a stagnant economy in some industries in a time of accelerated inflationary pressures.) The solutions discussed at the summit were eclectic in composition, with both economic and political trade-offs considered necessary.

The environment for marketing will be radically changed by the problems resulting from a stagflation and shortages economy and the attempts to find solutions to them. Marketers will have to adapt to this change. Marketing managers and others will undergo a most searching and critical examination. They will be measured by the standards of a society concerned with stagflation, shortages, and vested political interests.

Marketers will have to reeducate themselves and adjust to the rapid changes in the complex economic environment. Marketing professionals may become "order takers" unless the new environmental realities are assimilated into the everyday repertoire of marketing decisions. Just as "stagflation reminds economics professors how little they know,"[3] marketing managers cannot depend on past education and experience alone in making decisions under current economic conditions.

HOW ARE CHANGING ECONOMIC CONDITIONS INFLUENCING YOUR CUSTOMERS' DECISIONS

The current stagflation/shortages economy alters life-style patterns and expectations. The normal patterns of behavior regarding consumer spending and saving, which appeared to be relatively consistent between 1952 and 1972, do not generally apply today.[4] Buyers are modifying their behavior in view of their expectations about an uncertain future. Marketers are aware of this shift in expectations at the macro level, but a formal evaluation of specific segments of the population is slow in developing.

Until recently, government action and policy determination have followed a "wait and see" strategy, and yet buyer expectations are continuing to change with the shift in economic conditions. It may be two to three years before expectations are altered substantially in response to effective policy programs. Whatever outlook of future economic conditions individuals choose to act upon (or buyers select as their forecast), the fact remains that expectations have been so ground into the economic thinking of all our citizens that they will be slow in changing. The widespread tendency to assume that stagflation is inevitable makes its correction more difficult. This has been further compounded by the distrust in government at all levels because of "Watergate-type" incidents. On some points it may not be as much a matter of distrust as it is the doubts that exist about the government's ability to implement effective anti-inflationary policy. This lack of confidence is caused by a combination of perceived

1. Ineffective appraisals of causes and cures of inflation and recession
2. Political concessions as a result of pressure group dynamics
3. Inability to overcome structural impediments such as the Oil Cartel (OPEC)
4. Numerous "sacred cows" protecting various interest groups
5. Natural disasters such as flood and drought
6. International political and military commitments that have extended and complex interactive effects on the economy

Management's reaction to the current situation must not be a "wait and see" policy. Businesses are still concerned with marketing to their customers, but now the "new" economic environment has forced a modification of expectations and a possible shift (temporarily or permanently) in life-style patterns.[5]

THE "NEW" ECONOMIC REALITY

The extent to which monetary and fiscal policies have contributed to the current inflation and recession will be debated for some time. Expectations of rising costs, wages, and prices lead to an inflationary bias that makes the implementation of effective anti-inflationary policy difficult. Many participants in the summit conference felt that "the old-time religion" of

monetary and fiscal policy would no longer be effective in fighting inflation. The problem is not that monetary and/or fiscal policy will not work, but because of the social pressures applied to government policy makers, support for anti-inflationary policy is more difficult to generate. These social pressures are based on interest group reactions to adverse economic conditions, as well as on the consumer-citizens' expectations that the government will return the economy to a state of "normalcy." In addition to the internal interaction of production, wages, and prices, certain unexpected external "shocks" have had an effect on the economy. Some examples are:

1. The relative decline in the value of the dollar, following abandonment of the system of fixed exchange rates
2. Crop failures in the Soviet Union and the subsequent sale of large amounts of U.S. grain
3. Failure of the Peruvian anchovy catch and subsequent higher prices for feedstocks

Interaction of these unforeseen events complicates the economic formula for stabilizing the economy.

The "new" economic reality is characterized by pressure group politics on both a national and international scale, as the world struggles to allocate and develop its resources. The impact of personal expectations directly affects the decision making processes on an individual or family level, as well as at strategic levels in business and government.

Following is a discussion of an existing discipline—behavioral economics—and the means by which expectations are taken into account in economic decision making. Guidelines for research are suggested, and some practitioner implications are set forth.

BEHAVIORAL ECONOMICS

Behavioral economics is a rapidly evolving and important discipline that traditionally has focused on the role of the private household in economic affairs. It embodies the application of research techniques from the behavioral sciences, primarily psychology and sociology, to specific human problem areas. Research in this area is likely to broaden in the next few years to include other buying groups and segments. This field, as an approach to the study of economics, can no longer be neglected in developing marketing theories and policies.[6]

Research on all buyer segments will be necessary to ascertain the impact of changing economic conditions on expectations. Little information is available on how the current stagflation/shortages environment and the forthcoming prescriptive government policies will affect the behavior of the firm's viable market segments.

The General Nature of Expectations

". . . A period of high demand and rising prices molds attitudes, and even institutions in such a way as to bias the future in favor of further inflation."[7]

The nature of the complex relationship that influences this phenomenon is not well understood. The bias referred to above is caused by the expectations of consumers who buy goods and services produced by the economic system.

Katona states that:

People's time perspective extends both backward and forward: expectations constitute the forward-looking subclass of attitudes of particular importance for economic behavior. Just as other attitudes, expectations have an affective component in addition to their cognitive and predictive content.[8]

Expectations must have an object, and they are formed about the object. Objects may be events, economic conditions, persons, products, life styles, and the like. An expectation is the relationship between a class of behavior and the object. An individual's *expectancy* is a psychological state, while *expectations* refer more to the content of what is expected. The expectancy may be stated as a probability that defines the relationship between a behavior and the object, that is, the *probability* that a particular behavior will lead to the confirmation of a person's expectation about the object. Persons use expectations in an

attempt to forecast and anticipate the future state of affairs.

Expectations are concerned with either covert or overt behavior. An example of covert behavior would be an attitudinal change or the formation of a behavioral intention. Expectations are formed in t_0 and behavior is measured during some subsequent time interval, t_1. Expectancy theory postulates that persons select the behavior that, given a certain probability, will lead to the preferred outcome. The process is to select from a larger set of possible behavior patterns the one that promises to fulfill expectations about the object. "The motivational force experienced by an individual to select one behavior from a larger set is some function of the attainment of various outcomes to the person."[9]

Expectancy theory is concerned with cognitive expectancies regarding the outcomes of behavior and the subsequent actual behavior, either covert or overt.

A General Typology of Expectations

The three most important classes of expectations governing economic behavior are social/life style, product and service, and price and wage expectations. Although the occurrence of expectations is a *psychological phenomenon*, social psychological, sociological, and cultural factors can and do influence their formation. The following discussion refers to these three types of expectations.

Type 1: Social/Life-Style Expectations Certain expectations grow from the American dream of an open and classless society. The social class system in the United States has been undergoing radical changes during the past fifteen years. Farmers, blue-collar workers, immigrants, blacks, women, and youths are moving into the mainstream of economic life. Their expectations are that they can and will improve their status relative to other groups and individuals. These citizens are seeking equality, a better life style, and/or higher social status. Modern economic systems in both the industrialized and developing nations are operating in an atmosphere of economic revolution which fosters an explosion of expectations. This atmosphere carries demands for social benefits and programs that exceed the ability of technology to produce them. Also, political institutions have promised social equity and well-being for all members of society; although, in many cases, these promises are unrealistic given the time frame necessary to develop and support required programs.

The U.S. government has used deficit spending to partially finance its programs to fulfill the expectations that have been fostered. Government borrowing and government-guaranteed borrowing to pay for these programs have dominated the long-term capital markets. Turner sums up the effect of social expectations as follows:

> It is obvious that everyone cannot improve his economic position relative to everyone else. The obvious consequence of the attempt is a strong, virtually inevitable tendency for money, wages and other money incomes to rise—and rise across the board. There are two sides to every counter; money income to one person is a cost to someone else. Therefore, a broad rise in money incomes, if it exceeds the rise in productivity, inevitably means a rise in final product prices—inflation.[10]

Thus, the pursuit of social equality leads to inflationary expectations. This inflationary bias has been built into consumer-citizen thinking; the implications of attempting to alter this bias have yet to be probed. In this case, a mode of behavior is selected that will lead to the outcome that is expected to occur, for example, a better future life style.

Type 2: Product and Service Expectations
Product and service expectations for the most part are concerned with brand choice, product choice, or choice predictions based on opinion interviewing. Cardozo, Olshavsky and Miller, Anderson, and Carlsmith and Aronson have attempted to predict possible purchase evaluations or other behavioral outcomes as they are related to intentions, attitudes, beliefs, and like psychological constructs.[11] Product and service expectations deal with evaluation in t_0 and then a reevaluation in a later time, t_1. Certain expectations are formed in t_0 (hypothesized), and in t_1 these expectations are either confirmed or disconfirmed. An evaluation of products or brands in t_1 is usually made to deter-

mine the effects of expectancies. The object of the expectations is the product or service. The consumer will theoretically select the product or brand that promises to fulfill the expected benefits he/she is seeking. Thus, the customer is not buying a physical product, only a bundle of expected benefits.

During the current crisis, when inflation tends to erode purchasing power, recession threatens job security, and shortages restrict the availability of "common" goods, the consumer attempts to adapt traditional buying patterns to these new circumstances. His consumption choices will be consistent with the ability to purchase, the availability of goods, and the means to support their extended use. For example, the ability to operate and repair a large car or a foreign car; the ability to feed all the electric appliances in modern homes; and the ability to fuel motor homes, recreational vehicles, or to travel to distant recreational areas all affect customers' expectations concerning their ability to receive benefits from these items in the future. Expected benefits that goods and services may be able to provide must be reevaluated as new priorities for the use of available resources are developed.

Type 3: Price and Wage Expectations
Price and wage expectations have received the most attention from economists in relation to inflation in particular and consumer economics in general. The individual's personal forecast of certain events or conditions, over which he/she has little or no control, influences these expectations.

Expectations of Buyers Concerning Prices:
Buyers know that inflation adversely affects personal finances and the economy in general. When prices of individual items or prices in a general sense are preceived as being at a higher level than they were at some earlier time, buyers identify this as inflation, irrespective of any change in the level of wages. Actual price increases and consumers' expectations of further price increases create misgivings and uncertainties about the ability to purchase in the future. When prices are expected to be higher on necessities, the resources to pay for them are seen as being proportionately smaller relative to these items. Inflationary expectations may lead many buyers to postpone discretionary expenditures. The result is a reduction

rather than an increase in the quantity of discretionary goods and services demanded. On the other hand, as was evident in 1973 and 1974, many people react to price increases by buying in advance and in excess of their needs to beat inflation or expected shortages (e.g., on items such as toilet paper, sugar, small cars, freezers).

In response to the escalation of expectations concerning prices, buyers modify their economic behavior to protect themselves against a perceived loss in purchasing power. This modified behavior can take such forms as demands for higher wages, altered consumption patterns, or purchases reflecting a "hedging" strategy.

Expectations of Buyers Concerning Wages: Buyers believe that inflation adversely affects personal finances and the ability to purchase perceived necessities in the future. These inflationary expectations lead many workers to seek cost-of-living or escalation clauses in contract and wage agreements. The determination of all workers to improve their standards of living through substantial pay increases each year, disregarding a rise in productivity, has been built into the system. Income or wage expectations are a real, though elusive, economic factor that has to be confronted.

Real-income consciousness is a powerful force. Since workers are concerned with the purchasing power of their wages (real wages), they will want inflation accounted for in wage agreements. "If an hour's work earned them a steak yesterday, they will not settle for hamburger for an hour's work today,"[12] is one economist's interpretation of this force. During inflationary periods, pressure on the sale of high-priced goods will be partly relieved by the expectation of rising prices as long as interest rates in the capital market fail to keep pace. The same expectations will induce many consumers to devise ways to protect their real incomes from erosion by higher prices. To the extent that they succeed, their real demands will be unimpaired.

These are the major categories of expectations influencing the consumer-citizen's economic behavior. Although this typology is, to a large extent, arbitrary, it can be useful in analyzing the buyer behavior of selected population segments. The primary emphasis has been on the final consumer but, as was mentioned previously, all buyer (and seller) markets are important links in the market system that require further investigation.

RESEARCH DIRECTIONS

In a recent article, Tucker indicated that marketing theory should move in several directions. He proposed research concentrating on two important markets: money and labor.[13] The authors endorse this idea and propose a new orientation in marketing theory development. Research on the money markets is not altogether lacking, but it definitely requires refinement in methodology. Expectations are deemed important in the money markets as a variable that, in conjunction with liquidity and income, affects interest rates.[14] However, in economics generally, there is a lack of reliable data on expectations.

Research needs to be conducted on the buyer's income consciousness, long- vs. short-term expectations, interest rate and credit cost awareness (important today in light of the large percentage of credit card and installment purchases), and the knowledge and use of "hedging strategies."

A proper analysis of expectations requires theories. There is a dearth of theoretical constructs describing or explaining the relationship between buyer expectations and specific behaviors in a stagflation/shortages environment. Even with a theory in hand, it would be a complex task to test it against available data. Outside the field of economics, little research has been conducted on the effects of expectations. Within the field of economics, econometric studies have treated this subject mostly in an aggregated post hoc manner. Demand theory in any discipline stresses many significant variables. Expenditure data reflect the results of the separate impacts of all of these variables. Analysis requires that their individual effects be traced, and new methods of measuring buyer expectations are viewed as a necessary first step in theory development.

The authors agree with Katona that both the research methods and the level of analysis must be altered if more meaningful buyer behavior theories are to be developed.[15] Katona observed that:

Econometric studies are still commonly restricted to an analysis of interrelations among aggregate data that reflect past activities such as consumer expenditures, business investments, incomes, and profits. Correlations among data on results of behavior are deemed preferable to a consideration of the allegedly elusive psychological factors which behavioral economics postulates between stimuli, such as changes in the environment or information transmitted, and spending or saving decisions.[16]

Evaluations of buyer expectations are currently in a general state of confusion because recent past trends are used as indicators of expectations. This extrapolation process is not a reliable technique regardless of what is being forecast. Economists usually have little empirical data on expectations, so they frequently use past variables as proxies for expectations of the future. The relevant criterion variables, however, are current expectations of the future.[17]

In times of widely held inflationary expectations, the relationships that were constant under very low rates of inflation, as studied by Gibson, Sargent and Katona, are not accurate. With either double-digit or high inflation rates, the expectations generated require a new analysis. When double-digit inflation is accompanied by a recession and shortages, the problem is complicated further.

IMPLICATIONS FOR PRACTITIONERS

The development and testing of theories of expectations will be useful to marketers and public policy makers alike. Disaggregated data on individual buyers are needed to develop a microanalytic basis for a theory. These micro-data can be aggregated to produce macro-data, which is the form more useful to marketing and economics policy makers. The segmentation approach to analysis must be followed, however, if meaningful theory is to be developed. This procedure applies to marketers using various consumer segments based on traditional or more meaningful new methods of market segmentation.

Some important questions that can be answered through survey methods are posed in Table 1. Answers to these questions will, when aggregated, provide data on important population segments.

Table 1. Questions Pertinent to Marketing Strategy Planning.

Do you know what your customers (publics) are thinking—are doing with their money?

Are they using "hedging" strategies that affect your sales? How?

Are your customers or are your market segments saving their money? Investing money—where—what ROI?

Are your customers hoarding? How will this affect your present and future plans?

Are customers postponing purchase of your products—for how long: 6-12-24 months?

Are your customers product switching—substitutable goods? Yours or another firm's products?

Are your customers brand switching? Are you getting new clients because of switching?

Are your customers trading down—cheaper—simpler?

Are your customers altering their life styles to adapt to new conditions? How? Will it last?

What percentage of sales are on credit compared to last year?

How will your customers react to changes in government policy?

How will your customers react to changes in the elements of your marketing mix: product, price, place, and promotion?

CONCLUDING REMARKS

This article has emphasized the use of behavioral economics as a means of understanding buyer behavior. The central concept of *expectations* has been used to illustrate the relevance and usefulness of behavioral economics in a time of rapidly changing economic conditions.

In the current worldwide economic crisis, the authors charge marketing leaders with the task of finding new and innovative solutions to the problems confronting practitioners. The answers do not lie in a "business as usual" philosophy. Now more than ever, research is needed to provide more accurate input to the decision makers who will direct the policies of business and government.

Notes

1. *Transcripts for The Business and Industry Conference on Inflation,* Pittsburgh (September 16, 1974) and Detroit (September 19, 1974), U.S. Department of Commerce, pp. 20-21.
2. *The Conference on Inflation,* September 27-28, 1974 (Washington, D.C.: U.S. Government Printing Office, 1974).
3. *The Wall Street Journal,* September 6, 1974, p. 1.
4. The benchmark for research in consumer economics is that conducted by Katona and his associates. Recent significant reports begin with George Katona, *The Powerful Consumer* (New York: McGraw-Hill Book Co., 1960); and will be capped off by a new and important book in the field, also by Katona, *Psychological Economics* (New York: Elsevier Scientific Publishing Co., forthcoming).
5. Introductory materials discussing the role and importance of life-style patterns are found in Eugene J. Kelley and William Lazer, *Managerial Marketing: Policies, Strategies and Decisions* (Homewood, Ill.: Richard D. Irwin, 1973), readings 10-13, pp. 113-142.
6. For a state-of-the-art reference, see Burkhard Strumpel, James N. Morgan, and Ernest Zahn, eds., *Human Behavior in Economic Affairs* (San Francisco: Jossey-Bass, 1972).
7. Paul A. Samuelson and Robert M. Solow, "Analytical Aspects of Anti-inflation Policy," *American Economic Review,* Vol. 50 (May 1960), pp. 177-194.
8. George Katona, "Theory of Expectations," in *Human Behavior in Economic Affairs,* Burkhard Strumpel, James N. Morgan, and Ernest Zahn, eds. (San Francisco: Jossey-Bass, 1972), pp. 549-582.
9. Richard L. Oliver, "Expectancy Theory Predictions of Salesmen's Performance," *Journal of Marketing Research,* Vol. 11 (August 1974), pp. 243-253.
10. Robert G. Turner, "ZPG, ZEG and Zero Inflation," *Business Horizons,* Vol. 16 (December 1973), p. 11, as quoted in "Marketing Memo," *Journal of Marketing,* Vol. 38 (July 1974), p. 19.
11. Richard N. Cardozo, "An Experimental Study of Customer Effort, Expectation and Satisfaction," *Journal of Marketing Research,* Vol. 2 (August 1965), pp. 244-249; Richard

W. Olshavsky and John A. Miller, "Consumer Expectations, Product Performance, and Perceived Product Quality," *Journal of Marketing Research,* Vol. 8 (February 1972), pp. 19-21; Rolph E. Anderson, "Consumer Dissatisfaction: The Effect of Disconfirmed Expectancy on Perceived Product Performance," *Journal of Marketing Research,* Vol. 8 (February 1972), pp. 38-44; and J. Merrill Carlsmith and Elliot Aronson, "Some Hedonic Consequences of the Confirmation and Disconfirmation of Expectancies," *Journal of Abnormal and Social Psychology,* Vol. 66 (February 1963), pp. 151-156.
12. James M. O'Brien, "Inflation and Unemployment: the Great Debate," *Business Review,* Federal Reserve Bank of Philadelphia, January 1973, pp. 13-18.
13. W. T. Tucker, "Future Directions in Marketing Theory," *Journal of Marketing,* Vol. 38 (April 1974), pp. 30-35.
14. William E. Gibson, "Price Expectations Effects on Interest Rates," *Journal of Finance,* Vol. 25 (March 1970) pp. 19-34; and "Interest Rates and Monetary Policy," *The Journal of Political Economy,* Vol. 78 (May/June 1970), pp. 431-455.
15. George Katona, "Psychology and Consumer Economics," *Journal of Consumer Research,* Vol. 1 (June 1974), pp. 1-8.
16. Same reference as footnote 15, p. 1.
17. Robert Eisner, "Factors Affecting the Level of Interest Rates," in *Savings and Residential Financing, 1968 Conference Proceedings,* Donald Jacobs and Richard Pratt, eds. (Chicago: U.S. Savings and Loan League, 1968), pp. 29-40; Katona, same reference as footnote 11; and Thomas J. Sargent, "Commodity Price Expectations and the Interest Rate," *Quarterly Journal of Economics,* Vol. 83 (February 1969), pp. 127-140.

7
HIGH-PRESSURE CONSUMERISM AT THE SALESMAN'S DOOR

Gilbert Burck
Associate Editor
Fortune

After many years of abuses by business, the government has stepped in to provide better protection from unfair and deceptive selling tactics. However, the author contends, the trend to strong regulation may eventually be self-defeating.

The most successful door-to-door salesman of all time, according to legend, was an ingratiating drummer named Percy Beemish, representing an outfit called Cremo Cosmetics. Beemish's approach was simple. He rang the doorbell, politely doffed his hat, and paused. Then he won over the lady of the house, no matter what her age, with five plain but powerful words: "Girlie, is your mother home?" Today we live in sterner times. The Beemish approach has been sentenced to death by the New Consumerism, which not only frowns darkly on arguments *ad hominem* and *ad feminam*, but prosecutes them as unfair and deceptive.

The art of salesmanship, particularly in its more persuasive and high-pressure forms, is up against the greatest challenge in its long history. Legislators and bureaucrats, citizens and councilmen, academicians and students, working in more than 500 active consumer organizations, are putting the pressure on a new-model, superpowered Fed-

From Gilbert Burck, "High-Pressure Consumerism at the Salesman's Door," *Fortune, July 1972, pp. 224-29.* Reprinted by permission of the publisher.

eral Trade Commission, and together they are out to scourge and abolish the abuses of persuasion.

"What's the New Consumerism doing to us?" asks the head of a book company that sells door to door. "Why, it's just grinding us out of business, that's what." His distress is exaggerated but pardonable. Thanks to the New Consumerism, his sales are off sharply. The less aggressive forms of person selling are also feeling the heat. Auto dealers are touting fewer "executive," "predriven," and other used cars palmed off as practically new. Appliance salesmen are actually being given short courses in the fundamentals of consumerism.

Even more than personal selling, advertising is being forced to mend its ways. Calculated, controlled, and tested, advertising is, of course, in some ways the most persuasive of all forms of salesmanship. Now its functional puissance sometimes seems a handicap. Companies that rely on persuasive advertising to move their goods suddenly find themselves denounced as purveyors of unfair and deceptive information, and ordered to repent their sins in public. Even some businessmen who cheerily describe the New Consumerism as a good thing are disturbed and apprehensive. Testifying before the Federal Trade Commission last fall, Donald M. Kendall, chairman of PepsiCo, remarked that "the distrust [of advertising and free enterprise] is taught . . . taught often and all too well by men whose intentions for our country are either curious or unknown to me . . . I think the ultimate target is free enterprise itself." What *is* behind it all?

One of the things behind it all is a new awareness that the consumer is the most important person in a free economy. The late Professor Henry Simons of the University of Chicago, an eloquent prophet of the free market, used to argue that the greatest economic mistakes of the West result from considering the interests of people as producers rather than as consumers. "One gets the right answers," he said, "by regarding simply the interests of consumers, since we are all consumers. From that point of view, the deceptions practiced on consumers these days, if not so bald as they once were or so numerous as they are often made out to be, are a proper target for reform.

Yet the misgivings of some businessmen have a certain justification. The New Consumerism comes in all shapes and intensities, and includes

extreme zealots as well as sensible people. It sometimes seems dominated by activists to the point
where it resembles a religious movement. Too
often it is narrow, single-minded, and evangelical,
selling its ideas with the same high pressure it
abhors in commercial salesmen. Too often it lacks
a sense of humor and the sense of proportion that
goes with it (a lot of Americans these days seem
to have no sense of humor), and so fails to distinguish between good and bad. Most important,
its only cure for unfairness and deception seems
to lie in the toils of government regulation.

THE FTC REACHES FOR POWER

Consumerism's flight into regulation has
taken on the character of a mass movement. City
and state agencies, harassed by politicians and
reformers, strive to outdo one another in their
rules and regulations. By far the most important
and powerful of all regulatory bodies, however, is
the FTC, with its 11 regional offices and their 120
consumer-protection specialists and advisory
boards, representing hundreds of consumer groups.

Inoculated with the New Consumerism, the
57-year-old commission is prancing around like an
adolescent. It was set up to prevent unfair competition, but found its mandate confusing and frus-
trating, since the process of preventing unfair
competition, unless conducted with great sagacity,
itself results in stifling competition. Although the
commission was empowered in 1938 to prevent and
prosecute deceptive selling practices, it confined its
activities mainly to wrongs done by business to
business.

Then, in 1968, Ralph Nader and his raiders
swooped down on the FTC and took it apart on
paper. Their report was biased and narrow, but it
contained enough sensational information to
generate a more professional study. That one was
made by the American Bar Association and written
by Miles W. Kirkpatrick, chief of the A.B.A.'s antitrust section. Kirkpatrick accused the FTC of being
awash in trivia, bogged down in red tape, and
devoid of reason to exist unless it reformed. By
then, however, the commission was beginning
to be more interested in consumers, and in 1970,
after President Nixon asked Kirkpatrick himself
to become its chairman, it began to make up for

lost time. Kirkpatrick revitalized the commission
with bright young lawyers. He appointed Robert
Pitofsky, a 42-year-old New York University law
professor, to head the new Bureau of Consumer
Protection, which accounts for 22 per cent of the
commission's 1,360 employees. Kirkpatrick and
Pitofsky let it be known that their aim was to
explore the limits of FTC power to deal with unfair
and deceptive selling and advertising.

A HIGH-OCTANE ISSUE

So the commission issued "trade regulation
rules" intended to bind whole industries. But it
ran into trouble when it ordered oil refiners to
post octane ratings of their various grades of gasoline. One staff member unofficially estimated
that motorists were unwittingly paying $50 to
$75 per car more a year for motor fuel than they
would pay if they knew the ratings. Thirty-two
refiners and two trade associations promptly
challenged the FTC's right to issue orders of this
kind, and last April the federal district court in
Washington upheld the challenge. Since the case
probably will wind up in the Supreme Court, it
may be a long time before it is resolved. But two
bills have been introduced in Congress that would
give the FTC the authority it craves.

Meantime, although it can take action only
against individual companies, the FTC is able to
throw its weight around with remarkable effectiveness. After a preliminary investigation, it issues
a "proposed" complaint against what it considers
an unfair or deceptive practice. A proposed or
preliminary complaint is not a decision, and each
press release announcing a complaint is careful
to note that the commission only "has reason to
believe that the law has been violated." If the
company consents to the complaint, a settlement
is usually negotiated. If the company does not
consent, the FTC issues a formal complaint,
and may resort to litigation. The process can be
long, but it sounds fair, and technically it may be.
Since July 1, 1970, the commission has issued
more than 450 complaints involving consumer
issues. Only about 40 have been contested,
which suggests that there was real substance to
many of the complaints.

But this system is open to much criticism.

An ordinary prosecutor gets an indictment by
bringing a case before a grand jury. The proceedings are secret, and remain secret until the jury
is convinced there is a case; and even then the
prosecutor is not supposed to try his case in the
papers before the trial. The FTC, by contrast,
has installed a new high-powered public-relations
department that issues a "hot line" news release
of every proposed complaint. If the case is complex, the FTC announces the proposed complaint
beforehand, at a formal press conference, with
members of the FTC staff there to answer questions.
Representatives of the accused company are also
invited. Almost invariably, and naturally enough,
the news stories emanating from such gatherings
are written in such a way that the company seems
to have no case at all.

"These releases may be just proposed complaints," says one company lawyer. "But right
away you're in some trouble, and maybe hurt.
Unless you consent to the proposed complaint,
you're in real trouble. You can dicker for years
and years, really spending hours educating FTC
staff members. By this time your top executives
are all involved, and more and more dependent
on us lawyers. It's a colossal waste of executive
talent."

Many lawyers and executives are worried
that the FTC will be one more illustration of the
truism that every venture in government regulation
creates the "need" for more regulation. Given its
mandate to proceed against unfair or deceptive
acts or practices, add its resolve to test its powers
to the limit—and just where will the commission
stop?

Last March, Kirkpatrick told a meeting of
the American Association of Advertising Agencies
that unfairness and deception are not static concepts: "As our understanding of such techniques
develops or changes, so too must the application
of the words 'unfair' or 'deceptive' change in the
interests of sound public policy." Everything,
in other words, depends on the judiciousness of
the commissioners.

Among those who have shaken their heads
over the prospects is Lee Loevinger, a Washington
attorney who was Assistant Attorney General for
Antitrust during the Kennedy Administration and
then spent five years on the Federal Communications Commission. Loevinger can envision a state
of affairs where the FTC, its bureaucratic apparatu
enormously expanded, would end up not only
prescribing closely what it considered proper sales
techniques, but defining quality and even advising
consumers on which brand to buy. As a few
examples of the FTC's recent strictures on selling
and advertising suggest, Loevinger's projection
is far from fanciful.

THE ITINERANT PEDDLERS

One of the early targets of the FTC's Bureau of Consumer Protection was door-to-door
selling. This occupation is looked upon with
great disfavor by some consumer groups, who
would like to regulate it closely and in some circumstances abolish it altogether. Actually . . .
door-to-door selling plays a useful and substantial part in the economy and is relied upon by
some of the nation's least unfair and deceitful
companies. The big objection to it, ever since the
first itinerant peddler took to the road, was that
it confronted the salesman with a sometimes
irresistible temptation to practice unfair and
deceptive salesmanship.

One major deception is the old trick of
getting into a house by informing the housewife
that she has won a special free gift, or by pretendi
to be making a survey, or by telling her that her
parson or her son's schoolteacher suggested the
call. Another abuse is the custom of high-pressur-
ing the housewife into signing what turns out to b
an ironclad contract. To remedy this, the FTC
proposed a cooling-off rule that compelled the
salesman to present the housewife with self-
addressed forms enabling her to cancel the sale
within, say, three days. The rule also contained
some restrictions on door-opening techniques,
such as making the salesman present his credentia
at the door.

The Direct Selling Association, which repre
sents about 100 leading companies in the field,
has meantime undertaken some self-regulation,
and has drawn up what it calls a "very tough"
code of ethics that among other things forbids
door-opening ruses. It is also experimenting with

popular education. In Wisconsin, for example, it is distributing thousands of copies of the code, and telling people about it on TV, radio, and in the press. The FTC seems to think well of these activities; last February it published a revised proposed rule that softened the door-opening provision temporarily ("pending the development of more information"). Given a few very minor changes, says D.S.A. President J. Robert Brouse, he will go along with the rule.

There are, however, two big catches. One is that no fewer than 33 states and 10 cities have beaten the FTC to the gun and adopted cooling-off and door-opening laws of their own. What makes these a problem is that they differ widely. Most of the laws embody different provisions for the cancellation period. Some regulate only credit sales, others cash sales of more than $25. Two prescribe just how the salesman must approach the prospect. The Direct Selling Association thus finds itself in an ironical position. A year and a half ago it was fighting for less federal regulation, but now it is obliged to lobby for more. To end the confusion, it wants Congress to preempt state and local laws and ordinances dealing with direct selling.

The other big catch is that the FTC is "developing more information" by testing stricter controls on door-opening procedures company by company, and any agreement it makes with one company will probably apply to all. About a year ago, for instance, it cracked down hard on Grolier Inc., which sells annually about $145 million worth of reference books and encyclopedias. The commission's complaint got worldwide attention. "But we didn't hear about it until the next day, when a newsman called," says President William J. Murphy. "I guess you can call that trial by press."

The FTC's preliminary complaint accused Grolier of just about everything a direct-selling organization can do "wrong," from its hiring practices to door-opening ruses and deceptions in drawing up contracts. Murphy expects that it will take a half dozen years of litigation to settle all the issues. But Grolier is losing salesmen to companies that haven't yet been hit by FTC, and its domestic book sales are 45 per cent lower than they were three years ago.

IS CHARM DECEPTIVE?

Many companies in the direct-selling field have taken pains to keep their operations tolerably free of abuses, and they worry little about the New Consumerism. An especially good example is Avon Products, the great growth company, whose methods could hardly be more forthright. Avon's nearly 400,000 American representatives are mostly housewives who make the rounds of friends and neighbors and on the average sell about $2,000 worth of cosmetics a year. Backed by conservative national advertising, Avon's representatives simply call on their clients, display their lines, take orders, deliver, and collect for orders given last time around. Two or so weeks later they repeat the routine. So Avon is unconcerned, even complacent.

But nobody else can afford to be that carefree. Some ardent consumerists, taking their cue from a Columbia University study entitled *Debtors in Default*, contend that door-to-door selling of expensive merchandise on credit should be abolished. Another complaint is that it is impossible to control a salesman once he is in the house. Just take a look, the critics say, at manuals and training courses for salesmen. They are taught how to greet the customer in a positive way, how to find out what she is thinking about, how to ask her for advice, how to induce her to say something that the salesman can later use to his advantage, how to anticipate her objections, and how to ask for the order without seeming to ask for it. Anyone who knows how to get along with people, of course, behaves this way almost instinctively. In the last analysis, politeness, charm, and good looks themselves can be deceptive.

Nevertheless, the extremists want to police personal selling "more effectively." What many sales managers fear is that consumerists will pressure the FTC into adopting detailed, national rules or codes, compelling salesmen (and copywriters) to assume that customers are not reasonable but credulous.

Few if any sales practices, thanks to consumer groups, are escaping the FTC's attention. It is, for example, a long-standing and widespread practice of manufacturers of everything from shoes to big-ticket appliances and automobiles to get rid of excessive inventories by offering retail salesmen a special premium—known as push money or "spiff"—for selling them. In December, 1970, Consumers Union described the spiff as a bribe that keeps a salesman from tendering impartial advice and often induces him to push inferior goods, and it asked the FTC to ban the practice. Ever since, the FTC has been considering doing something about spiffs—just what is not yet clear. Pitofsky himself allows that push-money allowances might be considered price competition, which they surely are. Moreover, a rule prohibiting them would probably be unenforceable, since there is no law (as yet) forbidding manufacturers to discount certain goods to all retailers, or any law forbidding retailers to pay their salesmen bonuses.

PERSUASION AND COERCION

The FTC is discharging its biggest guns against what it calls unfair and deceptive advertising. To say that the advertising industry is worried is putting it mildly. "The danger to advertising," says Gilbert H. Weil, counsel to the Association of National Advertisers, "has reached a point critical to its continued existence." Even when discounted generously, Weil's lament cannot be laughed out of court. Pitofsky and other staff members of the FTC have been fairly candid about their conceptions of what advertising should be. As a result of a petition filed by Ralph Nader and his Center for Study of Responsive Law, the FTC in June, 1971, adopted a resolution requiring all advertisers to be able to document any claim about a product's safety, performance, effectiveness, quality, or comparative price.

This was only the beginning. More than a year ago, in a talk before a convention of the American Association of Advertising Agencies, Pitofsky granted that the vast majority of advertising is truthful, relevant, and relatively straightforward. But he also implied that advertising's prime if not only function is to provide useful information, and not to carry a "persuasive" or "coercive" message. Other commission staffers have expressed similar views. Because advertising exploits emotions, in other words, the FTC should not confine itself to monitoring truthfulness in advertising; it should prohibit appeals to

emotions and compel advertising to contain enough information for a consumer to judge a product or service accurately. "If the FTC carries on like this," Lee Loevinger remarks, "an advertisement would read like an SEC prospectus, and the FTC itself would become an officially sponsored Consumers Union."

Many others who have thought a lot about the subject of persuasion do not agree with Pitofsky and his colleagues. Professor Stephen A. Greyser of the Harvard Business School says, "the myth of the defenseless consumer is one of the most enduring outputs of the social critics of advertising." He maintains that the persuasive aspects of advertising cannot be separated from its informative aspects, for the objective of all advertising is to influence thinking or buying. Persuasion, Greyser reminds us, is deeply ingrained in U.S. society.

And in a much quoted article in the *Harvard Business Review* in July-August, 1970, Professor Theodore Levitt argued that legitimate or non-mendacious distortion (not deception) is as much a part of advertising as it is of poetry or music. "Commerce," Levitt wrote, "takes essentially the same liberties with reality and literality as the artist. The purpose is to influence the audience by creating illusions, symbols, and implications that promise more than pure functionality. . . . The consumer suffers from an old dilemma. He wants 'truth' but he also wants and needs the alleviating imagery and tantalizing promises of the advertiser and designer. Business is caught in the middle. There is hardly a company that would not go down in ruin if it refused to provide fluff, because nobody will buy pure functionality. Yet if it uses too much fluff and little else, business invites possibly ruinous legislation. The problem is to find a middle way."

ADVERTISERS IN THE SOUP

About two years ago, after a George Washington University student group known as SOUP ("Students Opposed to Unfair Practices") petitioned the FTC to require erring companies to disclose past deception in future advertisements, the commission adopted the idea and called it "corrective advertising." A company that publishes very deceptive advertising, it decided, must not merely promise to refrain from publishing more of the same, but must show or print a specified amount of new advertising confessing its sin. To make this corrective advertising palatable to the courts, they described it as remedial rather than punitive.

The first advertiser to repent in public was Profile Bread, a Continental Baking product, which the FTC charged was deceptively advertised as a sure way to control weight. Rather than fight, Profile gave in and printed corrective ads. Another important case was that of Wonder Bread, also a Continental product, which the FTC attacked on the ground that its advertising implied it was nutritionally unique. (See "How Big Does the FTC Want to Be?" *Fortune*, February, 1972, page 107.) This case centers on the question of whether advertisers possess the right to promote the qualities their products have in common with others. FTC argues that Wonder Bread was promoting those qualities as if they were unique to its product. The case is being fought by Continental, and will probably go to the Supreme Court.

The uniqueness principle was raised again by the FTC's recent blast against analgesics: Anacin, Bufferin, Excedrin, Cope, Vanquish, Midol, and Bayer aspirin. In a well-attended press conference last April 19, the commission charged that the claims of significant differences between these brands were unproved, and that advertising based on purporteded differences is therefore deceptive and unfair. Bristol-Myers, the maker of Bufferin and Excedrin, promptly issued a strong disclaimer. The burden of the press reports on the FTC's preliminary complaint, however, sounded as if they were all guilty. Whether they are remains to be established in court.

The FTC's new zeal has already resulted in at least one big blunder. Late in November, 1970, it challenged an award-winning television commercial (prepared by B.B.D.O.) calculated to demonstrate the antileak properties of Zerex, Du Pont's antifreeze. The commercial showed a can of Zerex being stabbed, but even as the streams of the fluid spouted from the can, they began to coagulate. The commission denounced the demonstration as false and misleading because it did not prove that Zerex can stop radiator leaks under ordinary driving conditions, and because the product might damage a car's cooling system. It

called upon Du Pont to discontinue this advertisement, and to warn people in future advertisements that the fluid might damage a cooling system. If Du Pont did not agree, the FTC warned, it would consider banning Zerex from the market. Just what effect this widely publicized exchange had on Zerex sales, Du Pont does not care to say. But it appears to have been substantial, for a survey showed that nearly half of all U.S. car owners were aware of the charge, and about half of *them* accepted the charge as wholly or partly true.

WHO DOESN'T MAKE MISTAKES?

Last November the FTC quietly dropped the charge. Because it coupled this action with a complaint that Du Pont had not adequately tested Zerex before 1969, its change of mind went almost unnoticed. What had happened, according to B.B.D.O., was that the demonstration had represented accurately the action of Zerex in a radiator, and that its commercial, far from overstating or misrepresenting the product's sealing properties, deliberately understated them. What is more, the script of the demonstration had been submitted to the FTC in 1969 before the commercial was run. But commission investigators made no effort to witness an actual demonstration until six weeks after the charge was released to the press. When they finally did, they discovered the charges were unfounded. Du Pont, incidentally, cannot sue for damages.

The episode drew an understandably angry reaction from *Advertising Age*, which argued that business should be allowed to sue the government for inadequate investigations and careless statements. The magazine further suggested "only half facetiously" that the FTC apply the corrective-advertising remedy to its own operations—say by publicizing the error in 25 per cent of its press releases dealing with B.B.D.O. and Du Pont.

Replying to such criticism, Chairman Kirkpatrick said that any harmful impact on the product sales and the reputation of the manufacturer "is an unfortunate but unavoidable incident of this nation's commitment to an open judicial system, in which all enforcement actions are subject to public scrutiny. The commission has made 'mistakes.' What prosecutor (or plaintiff)

has not? I can only say that the commission is
bending every effort to avoid such events." As its
critics have pointed out, however, the FTC's
approach does not, but perhaps *should*, resemble
judicial proceedings. Just recently Pitofsky took a
step in that direction by deciding to invite plain-
tiffs to discuss the case before a complaint is
issued.

OPEN AVENUES OF PERSUASION

One of the most important tenets in the
FTC's "philosophy" is that advertising is a means
of monopolizing a market and keeping profits
and prices high. This at best is only a theory,
and more and more eminent scholars are dis-
puting it. Last fall, in a closely reasoned talk to
the FTC itself, Professor Harold Demsetz of the
University of Chicago (who is now teaching at
U.C.L.A.) threw cold water on the contention that
oligopolies rely on advertising to crush competition
and pass along the cost in higher prices. Advertising
outlays are small, he explained, when customers
are few. But as industries specialize, advertising
inexorably takes a small but increasing percentage
of G.N.P. This is as it should be. Without advertising, the cost of commerce is significantly higher
than it otherwise would be and the penalties for
irresponsible behavior significantly lower. The
so-called problems of advertising, indeed, are
probably a small price to pay for the benefit it
confers.

Quoting from the most important of many
recent economic studies on the function and
cost of advertising, Demsetz avowed that the use
of advertising is no more a source of monopoly
than the use of labor. Much criticism of advertising, he pointed out, rests on the notions that
commodities possess intrinsic values and that
persuasion through advertising is undesirable,
if not unethical. Neither assertion, he said, can
be justified. "Freedom surely consists of more
than the right to exercise only some foolish
person's notion of simple, inborn, natural wants,"
Demsetz concluded. "The free society keeps open
the avenues of persuasion . . . and what threatens
the free society most is the blocking of those
avenues. . . . The vast sums spent by rivals to present their products and air their suggestions are

our best guarantee against successful misrepresentation. . . . There is little more that the FTC can do
that does not risk costing society more than the
results are worth."

NO BARRIER TO ENTRY

The commission was not moved. Staff members held that breakfast-cereal prices were 15 to
25 per cent higher than they should have been,
presumably because exorbitant advertising outlay
running about 20 per cent of sales, enabled the
manufacturers to realize monopoly profits. Last
April, at all events, the FTC issued a formal complaint against the four largest cereal makers—
Kellogg, General Mills, General Foods, and Quaker
Oats—of sharing a monopoly of more than 80 per
cent of the industry volume. What is more, it
threatened to begin action to break the cereal
makers up into smaller and more competitive
companies.

The four companies denied the charge.
Kellogg noted that breakfast cereals account for
only 20 per cent of all main breakfast dishes. Both
General Mills and General Foods asserted that
advertising alone enabled them to maintain their
competitive position. And Quaker Oats, which
increased its share of the market from 3 to 9 per
cent during the past 10 years, said reasonably
enough it was "particularly conscious of how
extremely competitive this entire business is."

Competition in the breakfast-cereal business
has been investigated by University of Chicago
economists, who found that, between 1954 and
1970, cereal advertising outlays decreased from
11.3 to 10.9 per cent of sales. The allegation that
cereal prices would be 20 to 25 per cent lower if
the Big Four were busted up is based on the
assumption that retailers are allowed markups
averaging 20 per cent. The actual average, however,
is 14 per cent. Moreover, before cereals were
heavily advertised, their sales fluctuated because
people ate less cereal in winter; hence, without
advertising, cereals were more costly to produce,
distribute and sell. Cereal selling and distribution
cost, up to 1940, averaged 35 per cent of sales.
With the rise of advertising, these costs dropped,
in the 1960s, to 26 per cent. In general, the
Chicago economists argue, advertising is a means

of entering a business—not a barrier to entry. It is a means of competing, not of monopolizing.

Whatever lies in store for advertisers, it must be admitted that some good has come out of the conflict. Many advertisers are finding that candor pays, and are even developing a partiality for stark truth. Dayton Hudson's Minneapolis store recently ran a series of how-to-buy advertisements that outdid even Consumer Reports. General Electric's advertising campaign for its new line of heavy appliances is chock-full of genuine information. Extravagant claims, even when supported by facts, are being toned down. The Encyclopaedia Britannica is running ads promoting not its books but the character of the handsome young men selling them. Grolier is telling people that after you've said yes to the salesman you can still say no to the company—i.e., you can call up and cancel your order.

A few advertising men take a rather gloomy view of their future. But William Bernbach, chairman of Doyle Dane Bernbach (whose clients include Volkswagen, Levy's rye, Heinz's ketchup), who has made an art out of imparting information dramatically, believes that the restrictions will stimulate creativity and so make advertising more effective than ever. "Artistry," he says, "is the most important selling tool." Provided, of course, that the FTC doesn't denounce artistry as deceptive.

THE CONSUMER'S REAL PROBLEM

Too much regulation of advertising and selling, over the long run, can only be self-defeating and do the consumer more harm than good. To tackle the problem of so-called trivial product differentiation, for example, the FTC would end up dictating product specifications, or even end up eliminating some products. What is more, says Dr. Lewis Mandell of the University of Michigan's Institute for Social Research, regulation cannot solve the really *important* problem consumers face. That problem is the result of what he calls galloping consumerism, or the enormous recent increase in consumers' discretionary income and in the choices available to them. The problem is how to choose between a good product and another one, or how to choose from many products the one best suited for his family's needs.

The consumer needs to be protected against fraudulence. But to solve his big problem he needs education, not regulation.

To illustrate his point, Mandell cites a study he made of the failure of the Truth in Lending Law. The law requires the lender to publicize the true cost of his loan, both in percentage rate and in dollars, so that the borrower can shop around for the best rate. Mandell's study showed that most consumers didn't understand or take the trouble to understand the meaning of the percentage; they forgot it almost as soon as it was told to them, and did not shop around.

One of the reasons for this ignorance, Mandell points out, is that neither high schools nor colleges condescend to teach such practical subjects as how to spend money intelligently. College students who have counted all the commas in Hamlet and harangue their parents on the tragedy of Vietnam don't know the difference between interest rates of 8 and 18 per cent. This is deplorable and unnecessary, says Mandell. His studies show that educated and high-income adults eventually develop into intelligent, skeptical buyers; and he argues that it would take very little education to improve the bargaining capacity of most consumers.

"If the government has any responsibility to our economy," Mandell concludes, "It must be in the area of increasing the consumer's economic knowledge, and increasing his ability to make the decisions that are in the aggregate so important to our society." Given such knowledge and ability, the problems of misleading and deceptive selling and advertising would largely take care of themselves.

8
IS
JOHN SHERMAN'S
ANTITRUST
OBSOLETE?

by the Editors of Business Week

Despite complaints by managers about the vagueness of antitrust laws, there is mounting political pressure to strengthen antitrust enforcement. The alternatives to present antitrust policy are outlined in this article.

The head of the major U.S. corporation spoke feelingly: "I would be very glad if we knew exactly where we stand, if we could be free from danger, trouble, and criticism." His plea could have been made yesterday, by executives at IBM, Xerox, GTE, General Motors, AT&T, Exxon, Standard Brands, Chrysler, or dozens of other large companies that have recently stood in the dock, accused of violating the nation's antitrust laws.

It was, in fact, said back in 1912 by Elbert H. Gary, chairman of U.S. Steel Corp. He was giving a congressional committee his views on the need for updating the country's first antitrust law, the Sherman Act, to which Ohio Senator John Sherman gave his name in 1890. Echoing the sentiments of many executives, Gary complained bitterly of the restraints imposed by the antitrust law on his company's ability to compete in world markets. Business had grown too big and complex, Gary maintained, to be shoehorned into laws

drawn from Adam Smith's economic model of many small companies competing in local markets.

Two years later Congress gave Gary an unwelcome answer to his plea. It passed an even more restrictive antitrust measure, the Clayton Act, and set up the Federal Trade Commission to police business practices and methods of competition even more closely.

Today business faces much the same danger, trouble, and criticism that disturbed Gary, and is raising much the same complaints against antitrust. The International Telephone & Telegraph Corp. scandal and corporate participation in Watergate has stirred up deep public distrust of national institutions, including business. In response, as in Gary's day, the antitrust wind is rising, blown up currently by the oil crisis and fanned by consumerists, such as Ralph Nader, who argue that antitrust weapons have been used like peashooters against dinosaurs. Business almost certainly faces even tougher antitrust enforcement and possibly even a new antitrust law aimed at breaking up the corporate giants in the country's basic industries.

This prospect points up the underlying question businessmen ask about antitrust: Are laws framed more than three-quarters of a century ago appropriate legal weapons in a market system grown increasingly large, complex, and multinational? In raising this basic issue, businessmen can point to a far-reaching, intricate web of laws and rules that has made the government the regulator, watchdog, and even partner of business. Wage and price controls, health and safety regulations, and disclosure laws, are all a far cry from the economy of Sherman's or Gary's day.

Businessmen complain of the unsettling vagueness of the antitrust laws, which permits antitrusters to attack many long-standing business practices in their effort to root out restraints of trade and monopoly. The FTC, for example, is now suing Kellogg, General Foods, General Mills, and Quaker Oats, alleging that such procedures as having route men arrange their breakfast cereals on supermarket shelves are anticompetitive. The Justice Dept. has a similar suit against tire makers Goodyear and Firestone.

Executives of International Business Machines Corp., caught by both government and private antitrust suits attacking pricing and promotion policies, privately declare that they are baffled over what they can legally do. Bertram C. Dedman, vice-president and general counsel for INA Corp., echoes a widely held view: "We never really know precisely what antitrust means. It's frequently strictly a matter of opinion."

Enormous economic stakes are involved in antitrust enforcement. Such current cases as those against IBM, Xerox Corp., and other giants involve billions of dollars' worth of capital investment and stockholder interests. Executives fear that such suits give broad power to courts not schooled in business, economics, or industrial technology. This power was dramatically illustrated last fall when U.S. District Judge A. Sherman Christensen announced a $352-million judgment against IBM and then confessed error, sending IBM's stock into wild gyrations.

Many businessmen wonder whether their companies are often targets of antitrust prosecution simply because they are big and successful. Philadelphia lawyer Edward D. Slevin sums up this attitude: "If the free market is pushed to its fullest extent, somebody wins. But the Justice Dept. seems to say: 'Now that you've won, you've cornered the market. We're going to break you up and start over.'"

All this, say many executives, makes it increasingly difficult for American business to compete internationally. Douglas Grymes, president of Koppers Co., argues that "big corporations are the only ones that can compete with big corporations in world markets." He says that the antitrust laws seem to equate bigness itself with monopoly and thus hinder American corporations from reaching the size necessary for world competition.

TOUGHER ENFORCEMENT LIKELY

Despite all these deeply felt concerns, the antitrust laws are likely to become even tougher and more restrictive. Starting with the Sherman Act, antitrust has been a product more of politics than of economics. Today's rising populist sentiment has led to demands for tighter antitrust enforcement. Only a decade ago historian Richard Hofstadter wrote, "The antitrust movement is one of the faded passions of American reform." Today it is the darling of reform. As James T. Halverson, director of the FTC's Bureau of Competition, sums up: "The political atmosphere is very favorable to antitrust right now."

The many signs of stepped-up antitrust activity in the last one or two years make an impressively lengthy list. They include:

New Investigations Last week three federal agencies—Justice, the FTC, and the SEC—as well as some congressmen, revealed that they are turning to a little-used section of the Clayton Act to investigate the complex of interlocking directorships among major oil companies.

New Legislation The industrial reorganization bill that Senator Philip A. Hart (D-Mich.) introduced in Congress last year would provide a new legal basis for breaking up leading companies in the nation's most basic industries: autos, iron and steel, nonferrous metals, chemicals and drugs, electrical machinery and equipment, electronic computing and communications equipment, and energy. It is given no immediate chance to pass, but its ideas could find their way into future legislation. Another bill introduced by Senator John V. Tunney (D-Calif.), already approved by the Senate and taking a back seat to impeachment considerations in the House, would increase the current maximum criminal antitrust fine from $50,000 to $500,000 for corporations and $100,000 for executives. It would also require the Justice Dept. to explain publicly its reasons for accepting a consent decree instead of preparing a case and actually going to trial.

Bigger Enforcement Budgets The Administration is seeking large increases, by usually puny antitrust standards, in the fiscal 1975 budgets of both the Justice Dept. and the FTC for their antitrust departments. If Congress approves, Justice's Antitrust Div. will pick up 83 additional staff slots, more than half lawyers and economists. At the last big increase, fiscal 1970, the division got only 20. The FTC is due for an additional $3 million, or a 20% increase in its present antitrust budget.

Growing Muscle at FTC After a long hibernation, the FTC is stepping out as a feisty agency with a new esprit, a highly professional staff, and a taste for going after bigness. It filed the monopoly suits against Xerox Corp. and the four biggest cereal makers. It has a special unit with an extra $1-million appropriation to litigate its case to break up the eight leading oil companies. And it got important new powers from Congress last year, including the right to demand otherwise unavailable product-line sales and profit figures from companies without first clearing with the Office of Management & Budget.

Reorganizing Justice   If the Justice Dept.'s monopoly case against IBM, filed more than five years ago, is successful, it would give new spirit to the Antitrust Div., which at least until recently has been demoralized by the successive shocks of ITT and Watergate. Even so, the division reorganized and beefed up its economics staff last fall to enable it to undertake investigations and prosecutions with a sharper eye to the economic impact of its actions.

More and tougher antitrust enforcement is foreshadowed by more subtle changes in mood and belief as well as by these specific developments. One such change is a growing recognition that the government itself creates monopoly power. Several weeks ago Columbia Law School called together many of the nation's leading industrial economists and antitrust lawyers for a conference on industrial concentration. The participants examined what business concentration means both for the economy and for antitrust policy. About the only thing generally agreed on was that governmental attempts to regulate an industry often result in preserving the monopoly power of those being regulated. In line with this belief, insiders say that the Antitrust Div. will step up its policy of intervening in other government proceedings to shape regulatory policy consistent with antitrust principles. Last January, for example, the division formally intervened in FCC proceedings in an attempt to deny renewal of the broadcasting license of Cowles Communications, Inc., in Des Moines, and those of Pulitzer Publishing Co. and Newhouse Broadcasting Corp. in St. Louis. All these companies also own newspapers.

Another change has been the dramatic multiplication of private antitrust suits—those brought by one company against another. These include the 40-odd private business suits against IBM, ITT's suit to split up General Telephone & Electronics Corp., and the large class actions against plumbing and wallboard manufacturers. In fiscal 1973

the government filed 45 antitrust suits. By comparison, businessmen and other private parties filed 1,152, making the business community itself a significant factor in antitrust enforcement.

All this is leading to an antitrust Congress. Victor H. Kramer, director of Washington's Institute for Public Interest Representation and a leading antitrust lawyer, expects that "more supporters of an effective antimonopoly program are going to be elected to the 94th Congress than to any previous Congress in many years."

THE ALTERNATIVES

But as antitrust action steps up, so do the conflicts over the direction antitrust policy should take. The populists contend that antitrust enforcement in the past has been spineless. Businessmen complain that current policy paralyzes corporations because they are uncertain what practices are lawful and that they are being punished for being successfully competitive. Who is right?

The conflicts lead many businessmen to push for an updating of the antitrust laws. Richard L. Kattel, president of Atlanta's Citizens & Southern National Bank, which has been sparring with the Justice Dept. over the bank's expansion plans, feels that the antitrust laws "need complete revamping."

Major revamping, though, will not come because there is no general agreement on what form it should take. Most of the Columbia conference participants believe that the economic evidence for a change in policy is scanty and inconclusive. Suggestions ranged from doing nothing to pushing the tough Hart bill through Congress.

In approaching antitrust policy, there are alternatives:

1. *Abolish the laws altogether.* A very few economists, such as Yale Brozen of the University of Chicago, talk as though antitrust laws are largely unnecessary. But as Robert L. Werner, executive vice-president and general counsel of RCA Corp., told a Conference Board antitrust seminar earlier this month: "There should be little disagreement by industry over the basic validity of the doctrine of antitrust. Certainly no businessman would seriously suggest that we

scuttle that doctrine and return to a pre-Shermanite jungle." The courts have ruled that such practices as fixing prices, dividing markets, boycotting, some mergers, and predatory pricing designed to destroy competitors unlawfully impose restraints on the market.

2. *Clarify the laws by specifying precisely what business practices are unlawful.* If various practices can be identified and prohibited through case-by-case litigation, why not draft a detailed code of conduct?

But the very difficulty of identifying such practices when business conditions are constantly changing led to the broad wording of the Sherman Act originally. No one has ever produced an all-inclusive list of anticompetitive conduct. No one can possibly delineate all the circumstances that amount to price fixing and other illegal practices. If publication of future prices by members of a trade association is unlawful, as the Supreme Court held in 1921, is dissemination of past inventory figures and prices equally unlawful? (No, said the Court in 1925. For other such cases, see Table 1.) Moreover, as Thomas M. Scanlon, chairman of the American Bar Assn.'s 8,500-member antitrust section points out: "There's uncertainty in any kind of litigation. Laws intended to bring more certainty often bring less."

3. *Replace antitrust laws with direct regulation.* U.S. Steel's Gary favored and Koppers' Grymes favors a business-government partnership with this approval. Its advocates agree with John Kenneth Galbraith that antitrust is a "charade," that it has not and cannot produce a competitive economy in the face of the technological imperatives of large corporations. University of Chicago's George J. Stigler concludes that antitrust has not been "a major force" on the economy to date. "The government has won most of its 1,800 cases," he points out, "and there has been no important secular decline in concentration." On the other hand, many economists and lawyers would argue that Stigler has drawn the wrong conclusion. As Almarin Phillips, professor of economics and law at the Wharton School of Finance & Commerce, puts it: "The success of antitrust can only be measured by the hundreds of mergers and price-fixing situations that never happened."

Moreover, in the view of an increasing number of observers, regulation that is designed to mitigate the effects of "natural" monopolies, such as telephone service, often winds up fostering them instead. Civil Aeronautics Board regulations, for example, have compelled higher airline rates than prevail on federally nonregulated intrastate flights. Wesley James Liebler, recently named director of policy planning at the FTC, says: "What the airline industry needs is a little competition. In the long run we should get rid of the CAB and let in some free competition." Liebler also wants to abolish fixed commission rates for stockbrokers.

Much of the energy of regulatory commissions seems to be devoted to anticompetitive ends. The Federal Communications Commission promulgated rules several years ago designed to stifle the growth of pay-cable television. Sports events, for example, may not be broadcast on pay-cable TV if similar events have been shown on commercial television any time during the previous five years.

Walter Adams, a Michigan State University economist, notes that regulatory commissions can exclude competitors through licensing power, maintain price supports by regulating rates, create concentration through merger surveillance, and harass the weak by supervising practices that the strong do not like. To combat this kind of government behavior, the Antitrust Div. itself has, for the past several years, been intervening or attempting to intervene in such agencies as the ICC, CAB, and SEC to force decisions that spur competition in industry.

In support of their position, reformers make a further point: Large corporations have the political muscle to force the government to support their anticompetitive goals. Adams charges that the government has established an industry-wide cartel for the oil companies through publishing monthly estimates of demand; through establishing quotas for each state pursuant to the Interstate Oil Compact, which Congress approved at behest of the oil companies; and through "prorationing devices" that dictate how much each well can produce. It is illegal to ship excess production in interstate commerce. Tariffs and import quotas protect only the producers, Adams says.

What this all amounts to is maintenance of shared monopoly power with the active cooperation of government. Only when the power of large companies is reduced, argue the populists, will the government be able to guide a competitive economy rather than serve as a prop for large interests. This was one of the original arguments for the Sherman Act in the 1880s.

4. *Move toward tougher enforcement.* Populist critics of antitrust, such as Nader and Senator Hart, agree with Galbraith that antitrust has been all too ineffectual, but they move in the opposite policy direction. Since they believe that government regulation usually entrenches the power of big firms and concentrated industries, they favor a get-tough antitrust approach. They argue for two related tactics: extending existing law through the courts to curtail many practices of large firms in concentrated industries and getting congressional legislation such as the Hart bill to attack the structure of these industries.

The Hart bill would permit the prosecution of companies because of their size alone. The history of antitrust has largely been to define and prosecute practices that courts would rule were restraints of trade, such as price fixing by agreement among competitors. But with increasing fervor, "structuralists" argue that size itself can be harmful.

HISTORICAL DEFICIENCIES

Before the Civil War, Americans felt uncomfortable with corporate bigness. The image of the yeoman farmer and the small, fiercely competitive businessman largely reflected economic reality. But the growth of railroads, with their "pools" carving up markets, changed all that. By 1871, Charles Francis Adams, grandson and great-grandson of presidents, was writing that corporations "have declared war, negotiated peace, reduced courts, legislatures, and sovereign states to an unqualified obedience to their will."

Populist politics, such as the formation of the Grange movement, picked up steam, but at the same time, in 1882, the first big trust, Standard Oil of Ohio, was born, followed by the Whiskey Trust, the Sugar Trust, the Lead Trust, and the

Cotton Oil Trust. Senator Sherman warned that without federal action the country would confront "a trust for every production and a master to fix the price for every necessity of life." The upshot was his Sherman Act.

But federal prosecutions were limited, aimed mostly at fledgling labor unions, and the Sherman Act failed to curb bigness. Corporate mergers speeded up. U.S. Steel, Standard Oil (New Jersey), American Tobacco, American Can, International Harvester, and United Shoe Machinery were all put together at this time. As a result, antitrusters increased pressure for even tougher laws and an independent agency, which could develop industrial expertise, to enforce them.

These efforts came to fruition in 1914, with the passage of the Clayton and Federal Trade Commission Acts. The Clayton Act specifically banned anticompetitive mergers, while the FTC Act set up an agency to police "unfair competition" in the marketplace but not to regulate prices and output.

Like the Sherman Act, the Clayton Act proved ineffectual for many years, largely because of the way courts interpreted the law. As recently as 1948 the court permitted U.S. Steel to acquire one of its own customers.

Partly in response to this decision, Congress passed the Celler-Kefauver Act in 1950, amending the Clayton Act to prohibit mergers through acquisition of assets or stock as well as those that would tend to foreclose competition in any market in the country. This effectively closed the door on many mergers. But the merger wave of the late 1960s comprised so-called conglomerate get-togethers of companies in different, often unrelated, industries. The case intended to settle this issue—ITT—never got to the Supreme Court because it was settled by a consent decree.

Mergers became the target of antitrusters because they mean the disappearance of independent competitors and lead to concentrations of industrial power. And, argue antitrusters, a few large companies may "share" monopoly power simply by dominating a given market. But unless collusion among competitors can be proved, there is no way under conventional enforcement to prosecute them.

Table 1. The Supreme Court's Tougher Stance.

Although there have been hundreds of antitrust decisions, the following Supreme Court cases would be on any list as landmarks on the road to tougher antitrust.

Standard Oil Co. of N.J. v. U.S. (1911)
Only "unreasonable" restraints of trade are prohibited. To be guilty of monopolization, a company must have "purpose or intent" to exercise monopoly power.

American Column & Lumber Co. v. U.S. (1921)
Control of competition through a trade association that distributes current price and inventory information and company-by-company forecasts, is unlawful.

Maple Flooring Manufacturers Assn. v. U.S. (1925)
Mere dissemination of cost and past price and inventory statistics through a trade association is not unlawful.

U.S. v. Trenton Potteries Co. (1927)
Price-fixing is inherently unreasonable, and any such agreement is a per se violation of the Sherman Act.

Interstate Circuit, Inc., v. U.S. (1939)
Consciously parallel behavior, where each competitor knew, even without direct communication with the others, how to act in order to control the market, is unlawful.

U.S. v. Socony Vacuum Oil Co. (1940)
Program by a group of oil companies to purchase surplus gasoline on spot market from independent refiners in order to stabilize price violates the Sherman Act.

Fashion Originators Guild v. FTC (1941)
Group boycotts are per se unlawful.

U.S. v. Aluminum Co. (1945)
It is not a defense to a charge of monopolization that the company was not morally derelict or predatory in its abuse of monopoly power. Even though monopoly may have been "thrust upon" the company because of its superior foresight, actions designed to prevent competition from arising constitute unlawful monopolization.

International Salt Co. v. U.S. (1947)
Tying agreements are unlawful per se.

Theatre Enterprises v. Paramount Film Distributing Corp. (1954)
Parallel behavior in the absence of any collusive activity is not unlawful per se.

U.S. v. United Shoe Machinery Corp. (1954)
Business practices that "further the dominance of a particular firm" are unlawful where the company has monopoly power.

Du Pont–GM Case (1956)
The government may move to undo a merger not only immediately after stock is acquired but whenever the requisite lessening of competition is likely to occur, even if that is decades after the merger.

Brown Shoe Co. v. U.S. (1962)
For purposes of determining a merger's effects on competition, there may be broad markets "determined by the reasonable interchangeability" of products and also "well-defined submarkets," whose boundaries may be determined by examining industrial customs and practices.

U.S. v. Philadelphia National Bank (1963)
"A merger which produces a firm controlling an undue percentage share of the relevant market and results in a significant increase in the concentration of firms in that market, is so inherently likely to lessen competition substantially that it must be enjoined in the absence of evidence clearly showing that the merger is not likely to have such anticompetitive effects."

El Paso Natural Gas Co. v. U.S. (1964)
A merger that eliminates substantial potential competition violates the Clayton Act.

U.S. v. Penn-Olin Chemical Co. (1964)
A joint venture by two competitors may violate the Clayton Act.

U.S. v. Pabst Brewing Co. (1966)
A merger with "substantial anticompetitive effect somewhere in the U.S." is unlawful.

U.S. v. Arnold, Schwinn & Co. (1967)
It is unlawful per se for a manufacturer to limit its wholesalers' rights to sell goods purchased from the manufacturer.

U.S. v. Topco Associates (1972)
All territorial allocations among distributors are unlawful, even if they might foster competition against others.

CONFLICTING VIEWS

To remedy this supposed defect, Senator Hart's new law would create a presumption of monopoly power whenever:

> A company's average rate of return is greater than 15% of its net worth for each of five consecutive years.

> There has been no substantial price competition for three consecutive years among two or more corporations within an industry.

> Four or fewer companies account for half or more of an industry's sales in a single year.

Clearly, these criteria create a net that would sweep up hundreds of large corporations. Hart's staff estimates, for example, that a quarter to a third of all U.S. manufacturing concerns meet the third condition.

A company that met any of these criteria would not automatically have to divest. Its defense before the special agency and court the bill would create could be either that its position rests on legally acquired patents or that divesting would deprive it of "substantial economies." (At present economies are not a defense.)

Howard O'Leary, chief counsel to Hart's antitrust subcommittee, argues that without "some mandate" from Congress, the Justice Dept. would be unlikely to embark "on an antitrust crusade." The bill would provide that mandate.

Senator Hart asserts that statistics can be misleading. He cites concentration ratios which according to economists show competition in the oil industry. But, says Hart, "Look at the evidence of joint ventures, banking interlocks, vertical integration, joint ownership of facilities, joint production, absence of real price competition, and lockstep decision-making, and one must wonder."

Economist Walter Adams agrees. He points out that between 1956 and 1968, 20 major oil companies were involved in 226 mergers and thereby gained control over a variety of substitute fuels, such as coal and atomic energy. The oil companies also moved into allied businesses, such as fertilizers, plastics, and chemicals, through vertical integration. Adams believes that a new law is necessary to fragment the power of the companies in the oil and other industries.

The only businessmen to come forward so far in support of at least the thrust of what Senator Hart is trying to do, says O'Leary, are some in communications and data processing. Through a series of hearings the subcommittee hopes, says O'Leary, "to persuade politicians and to some extent the public that it is feasible to come up with more firms than now exist, that the market won't crash, and that jobs won't be lost."

Most other businessmen see little good in the Hart bill. Carl H. Madden, chief economist for the U.S. Chamber of Commerce, brands its basic thrust as "faulty." He told Senate hearings last spring that the bill would thwart competition, not aid it, "by changing the legally permitted goal and cutting back the prizes."

Legal experts have many other objections. Richard Posner, of the University of Chicago Law School, feels that the Hart bill is symptomatic of "antitrust off on a tangent." Antitrust chief Thomas E. Kauper is not "satisfied with the economic evidence favoring broad deconcentration statutes." Kellogg Co. vice-president and corporate counsel J. Robert O'Brien says: "There is no reason whatever to assume that a 'concentrated' industry will necessarily be any less competitive than a fractionated industry. A course of antitrust enforcement that seeks to break up companies and restructure industries by looking at little more than concentration levels is misguided, to say the least."

Many have pointed out that among the defects in Hart's approach is the difficulty of measuring and the ease of manipulating rates of return. Further, even Ralph Nader, a supporter of the bill, says that deconcentrating an industry "is a 15-year job, at least."

OTHER TACTICS

Antitrusters are not holding their breath waiting for legislation. In a series of cases initiated during the past five years, they are using existing laws prohibiting monopolization and unfair methods of competition to check alleged anti-competitive conditions in concentrated industries.

The FTC's suit against Xerox and the Justice Dept.'s against IBM represent marked change from the past. The government has brought very few cases against single companies for alleged monopoly, partly because of limited prosecution budgets, partly because of political pressure from business, and partly because officials thought them unnecessary. These two recent suits single out a variety of practices—pricing policies, for example, and such things as announcing products embodying new technology far in advance of actual availability—that are alleged ways the two companies exercise monopoly power. The antitrust subcommittee's O'Leary says, "The IBM case is potentially very significant, if it is won and a remedy can be found. It is the first such case in 25 years."

The Justice Dept. also brought suit last August against Goodyear and Firestone, charging them with monopolizing the replacement tire market through a combination of practices, including acquisitions, periods of uneconomically low prices designed to drive out competitive products, service station tie-ins, and reciprocity deals. The two companies are charged with acting independently to maintain their dominant positions; they are not charged with collusion.

Perhaps the most innovative case is the FTC's suit against the four leading breakfast food makers, charging them with a variety of unfair methods of competition. The Commission is not claiming any conspiracy among the companies. It is trying to prove, instead, that a lengthy list of long-standing industry practices are anticompetitive and permit the companies, whose market shares have gone from 68% in 1940 to 90% today, to "share" monopoly power in their respective industries. If successful, this suit would strengthen the commission's ability to use its statute to go after many heavily concentrated industries.

The FTC's current prosecution against the eight major oil companies also attempts to break new ground. The key allegation is that the majors have been "pursuing a common course" in using control of crude oil and shipping facilities to stall the development of independent refineries. This includes eliminating retail competition by keeping prices low at the refinery and marketing end and high at the production end of the business. The FTC also charges the companies with such practices as using barter and exchange agreements to keep crude oil in their own hands and reluctance to sell to independent marketers. Unlike the cereal suits, the FTC charges that some of the oil practices are collusive.

CAN WE COMPETE?

In the face of government attack, some businessmen wonder whether such antitrust action aimed at cutting down corporate size might not handicap U.S. companies in keeping pace with the growing number of multinational corporations around the world. Koppers Co.'s Grymes, who argues for permitting mergers, would prefer to see the government "adopt a whole new philosophy of life." He would like to see 26 steel companies, for example, merged into five or six. "Let them get together, produce together, sell together," he says. He concedes that to make up for the absence of competition, the government would have to levy an excess-profits tax or put limitations on investments. He vigorously opposes the Hart bill.

So does J. Fred Weston, a professor at the University of California at Los Angeles' Graduate School of Management, and for similar reasons. "The world market requires increasingly large firms," he argues. "If we hold on to the 18th century idea of a nation of small shopkeepers and small farms, we will become a small nation." Unlike Grymes, Weston would not encourage mergers. Rather, he is against "fighting a rearguard battle to prevent deconcentration based on invalid premises." Corporate size, he insists, should be judged in relation to the world market. "If there are firms of increasing size abroad and there are economies of scale, U.S. firms have to be able to compete."

Supporters of deconcentration policy do not quarrel with the premise that U.S. companies must be able to compete, but they do argue that existing levels of concentration in many industries are more than adequate. They believe that size alone is not a guarantee of economies of scale or of efficiencies. And they point to industrial studies indicating that economies of scale relate primarily to plant size but not necessarily to the numbers of plants that any one manufacturer controls.

Frederic M. Scherer, the FTC's incoming economics bureau chief, believes that economic studies show that many industries are more concentrated than efficiency requires. Nader argues that the best evidence is "clinical, not statistical." He says that studies of industries that have become less concentrated would show consumer gains without loss of efficiency. The arrival of a new supermarket chain in the Washington metropolitan area several years ago, he says, forced prices down, and he cites the aluminum industry after Aluminum Co. of America had to face competition. It was still able to compete.

Moreover, the fact that a company can be efficient does not mean that it will be. On the contrary, absence of competition may make the company fat and lazy—capable of efficiency but acting inefficiently because it is not spurred by the need to compete.

In the 1950 congressional hearings on monopoly power, Benjamin Fairless, president of U.S. Steel, admitted that his company had less efficient production processes than its competitors, including much smaller foreign companies. Studies have demonstrated that American steel producers lagged woefully in innovation. Between 1940 and 1955, 13 major inventions came from abroad, yet American steel boasted the largest companies in the world.

The basic oxygen process, which Avery C. Adams, chairman and president of Jones & Laughlin Steel Corp., described in 1959 as "the only major technological breakthrough at the ingot level in the steel industry since before the turn of the century," was perfected by a tiny Austrian steel company in 1950. It was introduced into the U.S. in 1954 by McLouth Steel Corp., which then had less than 1% of American ingot capacity. Jones & Laughlin waited until 1957, and U.S. Steel and Bethlehem Steel Corp. waited until 1964 to adopt the process, resulting in lost profits to the steel industry, according to one study, of some $216-million after taxes by 1960 alone.

As for ability to compete abroad, there is practically no evidence that the Justice Dept. has impaired the competitive posture of U.S. companies in world markets. In the past few years the Justice, Commerce, and Treasury depts., as well as congressional committees, have practically pleaded for businessmen to come forward with examples of how Americans have been hurt, with minimal results. The Antitrust Div.'s recent release of business review letters from 1968 through 1972 indicates not a single turndown of joint export ventures.

David H. Baker, director of the Commerce Dept.'s Office of Export Development, made an intense search for examples of antitrust harm. A large food company wanted to enter a joint venture with another big U.S. outfit to bid on a plant an Eastern European government planned to build. The Justice Dept. indicated it might refuse to approve the deal, and the food company pulled out. A small U.S. company then bid for the contract on its own and won.

A NEW APPROACH

Some experts believe that the government cannot deal with business complaints adequately unless it develops a comprehensive approach to competition generally. Victor Kramer suggests the creation of an "office of antimonopoly affairs within the Executive Office of the President. The function of this office, Kramer says, would be to implement a new executive order he would like to see promulgated, directing all federal agencies to act to promote a "free competitive enterprise system." It would require the federal departments and bureaus to prepare antitrust impact statements whenever they suggest action that would "significantly affect competition in the private sector."

Professor Neil H. Jacoby, of UCLA's Graduate School of Management, agrees with the general thrust of Kramer's suggestion. Jacoby, who believes that oligopoly is here to stay, proposes the creation of a Federal Competition Agency, either as an independent commission or within the White House. He would have it submit a "competition impact report" for "all proposed federal legislation."

Kramer concludes that his policy would have compelled the State Dept. to evaluate public the competitive impact of the voluntary steel import agreements with Japan and European nations. The Pentagon would have been called on to explain how the public benefits from the awarding of nonbid contracts. The Internal Revenue Service and the White House, he believes, would have to consider the competitive effects of proposed changes in tax laws.

This broadened approach to competition could come closer to resolving the conflicts between the tendency of companies to exert control over their markets and the public requirement that monopoly be held in check. Short of this, the evidence suggests that antitrust is the best we have.

9 MARKETING RESEARCH AND THE LEGAL REQUIREMENTS OF ADVERTISING

J. Thomas Rosch
Director, Bureau of Consumer Protection
Federal Trade Commission

When is an advertisement deceptive? Who is to decide? Marketing research surveys, especially if data are developed before litigation is considered, help the FTC resolve whether the public has been deceived.

The purpose of this article is to discuss four areas of Federal Trade Commission law in which marketing research is, or can be, relevant. In this discussion, it is important to remember that I am expressing my own views and that these views are not necessarily shared by the FTC or by individual commissioners.

The first two areas of the law derive from the bedrock provision of the Commission's law enforcement mandate—Section 5 of the Federal Trade Commission Act—which prohibits all acts or practices in or affecting commerce that are either *deceptive* or *unfair*. A third area in which marketing research is useful is that of *corrective* advertising. Finally, there appears to be an untapped potential for the effective use of marketing research in *rule-making proceedings*, particularly in the implementation of the product information disclosure program.

From J. Thomas Rosch, "Marketing Research and the Legal Requirements of Advertising," Journal of Marketing, *July 1975, pp. 69-79. Reprinted by permission of the publisher.*

DECEPTION AND UNFAIRNESS IN ADVERTISING

The development of the concepts of deception and unfairness at the FTC and in the courts seems to have some distinct implications for marketing research. These implications are particularly relevant in light of the misperceptions about the need for marketing research data in Federal Trade Commission litigation.

Deception

There have been two major developments with respect to deception. First, the Commission has held—and the courts have agreed—that the FTC does not need to find that an ad has actually deceived the public to find that it is deceptive within the meaning of Section 5.[1] It is enough if the ad has the "tendency or capacity" to deceive. Second, the Commission has held—again with the blessing of the courts—that tendency or capacity to deceive need not be proved by marketing research or other data.[2] The Commission can find such a tendency or capacity on the basis of its own expertise as a judicial body dealing constantly with advertising.

What this means, in practical terms, is that an ad can be found to be deceptive within the meaning of Section 5 without any evidence as to how it was actually interpreted by the public. What is does not mean, however, is that the Commission will reject evidence as to actual effect. On the contrary, in several recent cases the Commission has accepted and used marketing research data offered in evidence by respondents to make a determination as to whether the ads in question had the tendency or capacity to deceive.[3] In some of these cases—*Wonder Bread* and *Hi-C*, for example—this kind of research was apparently important to the Commission.[4]

In other words, there is some risk in *not* having marketing research data to demonstrate the actual effect of an ad. The advertiser or agency cannot just sit back and rely on a failure of proof arising from the lack of such evidence from the Commission staff, because that evidence is not needed to prove a violation. And there may be substantial benefits to providing this evidence,

for it may influence the Commission in its determination.

It is important, however, to keep two caveats in mind. The first relates to the timing of the research. In most litigation the results of tests conducted before the litigation are much more probative than the results of tests conducted afterwards—when there is a different set of incentives. The situation does not seem to be any different in the FTC setting; consequently, it is reasonable to expect that postlitigation data are, as they should be, much less probative than pretesting data.

The second caveat relates to representations about the state of the art. Marketing experts have apparently convinced the Commission that the state of the art is very advanced. Thus, in *Wonder Bread* the Commission described the advertising agency as an "expert in determining what representations are made in a given advertisement."[5] This image may have distinct advantages in a deception case, but it may create certain hazards when the Commission is applying a second legal concept—Section 5 unfairness.

Unfairness

Section 5 also prohibits acts or practices that are "unfair." The Supreme Court, in the landmark S&H case, decided in 1973 that the FTC had great latitude in fleshing out the meaning of unfairness in various business settings.[6] One of the areas in which the Commission has defined unfairness has to do with advertising substantiation.

The FTC's current ad substantiation program is generally regarded as an outgrowth of its opinion in the Pfizer case.[7] In fact, the program predated the Pfizer decision and was the product of Commission thinking expressed as early as 1963, in the Kirchner case.[8] In that case, as in *Pfizer*, the FTC suggested that it was unfair within the meaning of Section 5 for the advertiser to make a claim without a reasonable basis in fact for the claim.

In 1974, I suggested to the Dallas Advertising League that this conceptual approach might also be used to treat a recurring problem in national advertising—the use of ambiguous words and phrases which the public could interpret in a number of ways.[9] The word *energy*, for example, is understood by different people to mean different things. The sophisticated nutritionist would understand that energy is simply a reflection of calories. The layman would almost certainly consider it to connote strength and vigor. Similarly, to some people the words *natural food* simply suggest the absence of artificial coloring or other additives; to others they carry certain implications as to how the food was grown.

These are not isolated examples. Pursuant to the Commission's ad substantiation program, the staff periodically sends out questionnaires to advertisers asking them to substantiate the claims that the staff sees in their advertising. In virtually every round the staff receives at least one response contesting the staff's interpretation of the advertisement.

I suggested in Dallas that the FTC might not always take "we don't know" or "we never said that" for an answer. Where the staff's interpretation was plausible, the ad agency making the claim might be obliged to back it up. Its failure to do so might, by analogy to *Kirchner* and *Pfizer*, be considered unfair. This is not to suggest that its obligation would be the same in all cases. As the Commission's decision in *Pfizer* made clear, the duty to substantiate varies depending on a number of factors, including the extent of dissemination and whether the claim involved health or safety.[10] It did not then—and does not now—seem unreasonable that an advertising agency that makes health or safety claims must be certain that false inferences are not being drawn by any substantial part of the public.

After I made that suggestion, I received several letters from the advertising community asserting that the state of the art of marketing research simply was not far enough advanced to hold advertising agencies responsible for such "meaning substantiation." That comes as something of a surprise to those of us at the Commission who have read the record in recent deception cases. It also has some disturbing consequences. It may mean that words and phrases that have a potential for misinterpretation simply cannot be used because of that potential. There is plenty of Commission case law that says that when a claim can be interpreted several ways, none of them can be false or the claim is deceptive.[11] So, in the

long run, it may be that the latitude that advertisers and their agencies have in making claims will depend on the state of the art in consumer research.

CORRECTIVE ADVERTISING

Another matter to which marketing research is relevant is that of FTC remedies and, specifically, corrective advertising. The Commission has stated several times—in *Firestone* in 1972 and more recently in *Wonder Bread*—that it has the power to impose corrective advertising as a remedy.[12] In the recent Heater case, the Ninth Circuit Court of Appeals indicated in a note to its opinion that it agreed.[13] The Commission has also indicated, however, that the remedy is appropriate only when it is necessary to correct continuing consumer misperceptions created by a deceptive claim.[14]

What these decisions mean for marketing researchers is not entirely clear. It may be that the Commission will be willing to infer continuing consumer misperception where a deceptive claim has been made repeatedly over a long period of time. But I suspect that in detecting continuing consumer misperception, as in detecting deception, the Commission will welcome marketing research. The fact is that marketing research has played a decisive role in virtually all cases decided to date involving corrective advertising.

RULE-MAKING PROCEEDINGS

The preceding sections primarily dealt with the role marketing research can or may play in a litigation setting. Let me turn finally to another kind of proceedings—rule-making proceedings—and, specifically, to rule-making proceedings that implement the Commission's product information disclosure program.

The law has long recognized that silence, as well as affirmative representation, can create deception. If your house is built on fill land in an earthquake area and you do not tell a prospective buyer about it, you are engaging in misrepresentation just as surely as if you tell him the house is sitting on rock. However, it has also long been the law that not every fact needs to be disclosed to avoid deception; only the material facts need to be revealed. These are facts that, if disclosed, would be likely to influence a significant number of buying decisions. This concept of "material" fact is at the heart of the product information disclosure program.

Under that program, the FTC proposes to require, by rules, that material information about products be disclosed. The proposed food nutrition rule is a variant of this program. The gasoline mileage rule-making proceeding is another. Both look to the disclosure of *material* product information—material in the sense that a significant number of consumers want, and will use, the information disclosed.

Marketing research appears to have two roles in this program. The first is to identify what information is *material*, in the sense that I have just described it. If consumers don't care what mileage their cars are getting, that is something that goes to the legal roots of the program and that can be determined with the aid of marketing research.

There is another, more constructive, role for marketing research in these proceedings: to determine the most effective way of communicating material information. Several surveys, for example, have established that a significant number of consumers want, and will use, information about the nutritional value of the foods they are buying, that such information can influence buying habits. Experience has shown that it is extremely difficult to develop an effective way of conveying that message. But it is by no means impossible. With the help of creative communicators using all of the tools of their trade, including pretesting alternative messages, I think the key can be found.

CONCLUSIONS

My hope is not only that the state of the art of marketing research is very far advanced but also that it will take quantum leaps in the future. For whatever hazards that poses in terms of a "meaning substantiation" requirement, I think the hazards are greater if it does *not* happen. I am convinced that the development of reliable marketing data is in the best interests of the advertiser, the FTC, and, ultimately, the American public.

Notes

1. *FTC v. Algoma Lumber Co.*, 291 U.S. 67, 81 (1934); *FTC v. Raladam Co.*, 316 U.S. 149, 151 (1942); *Charles of the Ritz Distributors Corp. v. FTC*, 143 F.2d 676, 680 (2d Cir. 1944); *U.S. Retail Credit Association, Inc. v. FTC*, 300 F.2d 212, 221 (4th Cir. 1962).
2. *FTC v. Colgate Palmolive Co.*, 380 U.S. 374, 391-392 (1965); *J. B. Williams Co. v. FTC*, 381 F.2d 884, 890 (6th Cir. 1967).
3. In re Firestone Tire & Rubber Co., 81 F.T.C. 398 (1972), *aff'd*, 481 F.2d 246 (6th Cir.), *cert. denied*, 414 U.S. 1112 (1973); In re Benrus Watch Co., Inc., 64 F.T.C. 1018, *aff'd*, 352 F.2d 313 (8th Cir. 1965), *cert. denied*, 384 U.S. 939 (1966); In re Coca-Cola Co., 3 Trade Reg. Rep ¶ 20,470 at 20,391 (1973); In re ITT Continental Baking Co., Inc., 3 Trade Reg. Rep. ¶ 20,464 at 20,372 (1973).
4. In re ITT Continental Baking Co., Inc., and In re Coca-Cola Co., same references as footnote 3.
5. In re ITT Continental Baking Co., Inc., 3 Trade Reg. Rep. ¶ 20,384.
6. *FTC v. Sperry & Hutchinson Co.*, 405 U.S. 233 (1972).
7. In re Pfizer, Inc., 81 F.T.C. 23 (1972).
8. In re Universe Co., 63 F.T.C. 1282 (1963), *aff'd sub nom.*, *Kirchner v. FTC*, 337 F.2d 751 (9th Cir. 1964).
9. Address by J. Thomas Rosch, Dallas Advertising League, February 26, 1974.
10. 81 F.T.C. at 64.
11. See, for example, *Murray Space Shoe Corp. v. FTC*, 304 F.2d 270, 272 (2d Cir. 1962); and *Continental Wax Corp. v. FTC*, 330 F.2d 475, 477 (2d Cir. 1965).
12. In re Firestone Tire & Rubber Co., 81 F.T.C. at 471; and In re ITT Continental Baking Co., Inc., 3 Trade Reg. Rep. at ¶ 20,386.
13. *Heater v. FTC*, 503 F.2d 321, 325 n.13 (9th Cir. 1974).
14. In re ITT Continental Baking Co., Inc., 3 Trade Reg. Rep. at ¶ 20,386.

10 MULTINATIONAL MARKETING STRATEGY AND ORGANIZATION

Warren J. Keegan
Associate Professor of Business Administration
Columbia University

Virtually all major American companies have gone "multinational." Some have been successful while others have badly stubbed their toes. What does the question of international marketing strategy have to do with a $10 plastic washing "machine"?

One of the most striking business developments in recent years has been the emergence of the multinational manufacturing corporation as an important factor in the international economy. Natural resource extraction, transportation, utility, and financial companies have been operating directly in foreign countries for many decades; so have a limited number of manufacturing companies. But for the most part, it has only been since World War II that large numbers of manufacturing companies have extended the scope of their international operations to anything more extensive than a domestically based export operation selling through a network of independent agents and distributors. Today, increasing numbers of United States corporations look abroad for substantial proportions of their profits and sales, and indeed, it is not uncommon to find companies whose sales and profits from abroad exceed those

From Warren Keegan, "Multinational Marketing Strategy and Organization: An Overview," Changing Marketing Systems, American Marketing Association Proceedings, 1967, published by the American Marketing Association, by permission of the author and the publisher.

from the United States. The investments of United States companies abroad are now six times greater than at the end of World War II. Increasingly, they include not only manufacturing facilities, but research facilities as well as extensive marketing organizations.

A small but growing number of U.S. companies have substantial proportions of assets and sales outside the United States. To reflect this foreign involvement, and the change it has brought about, the terms "international," "worldwide," and "multinational" corporation have appeared and are now frequently used to describe the company whose scope of operations encompasses many countries and regions, and whose management considers the entire world as the company's potential area of operations.

THE PROBLEM

One of the most important challenges to a headquarters executive of a multinational firm is the formulation of an effective world marketing strategy. This objective is by no means an accepted goal. There is a widespread view current among international executives that it is impossible to plan the marketing function at the headquarters level in a multinational corporation. Advocates of this position argue that the variations in local markets are so great in so many different dimensions—economic, social and political—that it is imperative that the marketing function be handled entirely at the local level.

In this article, we shall show that in a multinational corporation, important elements of marketing strategy must be formulated at the headquarters level. In a multinational company, the organizational framework and extent of decision-making decentralization will vary from company to company, but at a minimum, the headquarters executive group is responsible for formulating company strategy, that is, for the determination of overall objectives and the allocation of financial and manpower resources to achieve these objectives. Marketing strategy at the headquarters level includes the identification of areas of operation, both in geographic and product terms, the formulation of strategy regarding marketing communications (advertising, sales promotion, direct mail) which will be prepared for the areas of operation, the formulation of a strategic pricing policy to set limits upon pricing tactics employed by subsidiary companies, and the allocation of corporate resources to support formulated programs.

A CONCEPTUAL FRAMEWORK FOR MULTINATIONAL MARKETING STRATEGY FORMULATION

The strategic marketing task of the headquarters based international executive is formidable. He must identify worldwide opportunities and risks in both geographic and product dimensions. He must appraise the company's internal resources, competence, and response capability. In the light of these factors, he must adjust the mix of controllable marketing factors to formulate a marketing program designed to achieve the maximum level of profitable product adoption in the world marketplace. Conceptually, this strategic process can be represented as a hexagon within a hexagon within a pentagon (Exhibit 1). The sides of the hexagon represent the controllable elements of a marketing program, or the marketing mix. These elements are the product, price, marketing communications, channels of distribution, the marketing information system, which includes feedback from marketing operations as well as marketing intelligence operations designed to gather environmental information, and marketing organization.

The marketing executive, as he adjusts the controllable elements of the marketing mix, responds to relevant observable and measurable independent variables which together form the environment for marketing decisions. These directly relevant variables are shown as the sides of the hexagon enclosing the hexagon in Exhibit 1. These variables include prescriptions, or any ruling affecting a company from "guidelines" to decisions of administrative tribunals, to laws or decrees. Prescriptions may originate with voluntary associations, national or regional governmental or para-governmental institutions, or with legal authority. These are the "rules of the game" which provide the parameters of the marketing decision framework.

The other sides of the pentagon include the distribution system, customers, competition, technology and cost. These relevant independent variables are themselves manifestations of underlying basic forces which are represented in Exhibit 1 as the sides of the outer pentagon. The underlying basic macro-forces (economic, social, political, geographi and scientific) are more important in the context of long-range planning than in the formulation of current programs.

MULTINATIONAL MARKETING: STRATEGIC ALTERNATIVES

Given this conceptual framework in the product and communications policy areas there are two broad strategic marketing alternatives open to the manufacturing company in internationa markets: extension or adjustment. The extension approach takes the home marketing mix as given and extends it without adjustment to foreign markets. The product is unchanged, marketing communications are unchanged except for translation, and factory selling price is unchanged. This strategy is frequently employed by companies which are entering foreign markets for the first time. It is also employed by companies which have been involved in international operations for many years and which fail to appreciate the marketing opportunities they have foregone by not pursuing a strategy of adjustment in international markets. The extension strategy in world markets assumes th the need satisfied by a product is the same in all cultures and that the appeals to this need are universal. Perhaps the most notable example of the successful application of this strategy are the soft-drink franchisers. Pepsico's Vice President for Research has expressed this position as follows:

"We do not believe that each country requires an individual advertising and product approach. Our experience and our relative success tell us otherwise. Each one of our 530 bottlers in the U.S. will claim at one time or another that their franchise is different. Yet we do not set up an advertising department in Shreveport, Louisiana, to set up a separate plan or campaign for that market. No, we develop our plans and

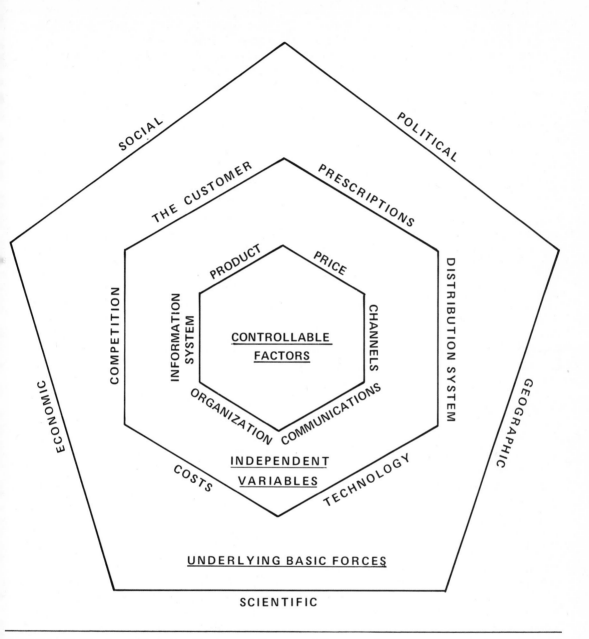

Exhibit 1. Multinational Marketing Strategy: A Conceptual Framework.

general strategy for all 50 states from a central headquarters.

In developing our international marketing strategy, we believe in the basic psychological truth that there are greater differences within groups than between groups. It is the sameness in all human beings on which we believe we must base our selling appeals."[1]

Another Pepsi Cola official described that company's international marketing strategy as "one product, one image, and one sound, worldwide."

There are other products for which the extension approach has been applied with apparent success in international markets. American-blend cigarettes and U.S. bourbon are examples of products which have succeeded abroad because foreign consumers have adopted U.S. tastes. Still another application of this strategy is the case of clothing companies which have extended U.S. styles to foreign markets. A notable example is Levi-Strauss, which has sold the famous Levi blue jean without adapting to foreign markets. Indeed, the appeal of the Levi jean has been its close identification with the U.S. market and the far west.

Unfortunately, however, there are even more examples of the unsuccessful application of the extension strategy to international marketing. The failure of the extension strategy can be traced to basic differences in foreign markets which may be reflected in different needs, or in different characteristics in foreign consumers and customers which require different marketing appeals. Food products extended from the U.S. to the British market provide a sobering record of market failure for the U.S. executive who believes that the British market is no different from the U.S. market. Campbell's found, for example, that its fabulously successful U.S. tomato soup formulation was not accepted in Britain, where consumers prefer a less sweet taste. Another U.S. company spent several million dollars in an unsuccessful effort to introduce U.S.-style cake mixes to the British market. Closer to home is Philip-Morris' experience in attempting to take advantage of U.S. television advertising campaigns which have a sizeable Canadian audience in border areas. The Canadian cigarette market is a Virginia or straight

tobacco market in contrast to the U.S. market, which is a blended tobacco market. Philip-Morris officials decided that they would ignore market research evidence which indicated that Canadians would not accept a blended cigarette and went ahead with programs which achieved retail distribution of U.S. blended brands in the Canadian border areas served by U.S. television. Unfortunately, the Canadian preference for the straight cigarette remained unchanged. American-style cigarettes sold right up to the border but no further. Philip-Morris was forced to withdraw its U.S. brands.

One of the major strengths of the extension strategy is its lower cost. There are two sources of cost savings which follow from this approach. One, manufacturing economies of scale, is well known and understood. Less well known are the substantial economies associated with the standardization of marketing communications. For a company with worldwide operations, the cost of preparing separate print and TV-cinema films for each market would be enormous. Pepsi Co., International marketers have estimated, for example, that production costs for specially prepared advertising for foreign market would cost them eight million dollars per annum, which is considerably more than the amounts now spent by Pepsi Co., International for advertising production. Although these cost savings are important, they should not distract executives from the more important objective of maximum profit performance, which may require the use of an adjustment strategy.

However, the many failures of the extension strategy in international marketing support the utility of considering a second strategic approach to international markets which is extension with adjustment. This approach takes the U.S. or home marketing mix as the base, and makes adjustments to this mix where it is believed desirable to do so. The adjustments may be in the product or marketing communications or in both. The decision of whether or not to adjust is based upon a comparison of estimates of market response to specified adjustments and of estimates of cost that would be involved in making such adjustments. (The argument that international marketers should adjust both product and communications to the different environmental conditions which exist around the world is clearly superficial, for it does not take into account the cost of adjusting or adapting a product or a communication program.)

The adjustment strategy in international marketing assumes that a product will either:

1. Serve the same function in foreign markets under different use conditions, or
2. serve a new function or fill a different need under the same use conditions, or
3. serve a different function or fill a different need under different environmental conditions.

These market conditions and indicated adjustment responses are illustrated in Table 1.

The international marketer pursuing the adjustment strategy adjusts his marketing mix abroad to fit the conditions which exist in foreign markets. For example, in markets where a product serves the same function under different conditions (Situation A), the international marketer will change or adjust the product while maintaining the same program of marketing communications. Gasoline refiners, for example, adjust their formulations to meet the weather conditions prevailing in market areas, but make no adjustments in marketing communications. Thus, Esso has successfully extended its U.S. "tiger in your tank" campaign to markets around the world. International soap and detergent manufacturers have adjusted their product formulations to meet local water conditions and the characteristics of washing equipment. Marketing communications, again, have remained unchanged. Other examples of products which have been adjusted to perform the same function internationally under different environmental conditions are agricultural chemicals, which have been adjusted to meet different soil conditions and different types and levels of insect resistance, household appliances which have been scaled to sizes appropriate to different use environments, and clothing, which is adjusted to meet fashion criteria.

When a product fills a different need or serves a different function under the same use conditions, (Situation B), the adjustment indicated is in marketing communications. There are many illustrations of market conditions which suggest this approach. Bicycles and motorscooters, for example, satisfy needs for basic transportation in many foreign countries and for recreation in the United States. Outboard motors are sold mainly to a recreation market in the United States, while the same motors in many foreign countries are sold

Table 1. Alternative Adjustment Situations in Multinational Marketing.

Adjustment Situation	Market Conditions		Adjustment Response
	Function or Need Satisfied	Use Conditions	
A	Same	Different	Change product
B	Different	Same	Change communications
C	Different	Different	Change both product and communications

mainly to fishing and transportation fleets. There are many examples of food products which serve entirely different needs in different markets. Many dry soup powders, for example, are sold mainly as soups in Europe and as sauces or cocktail dips in the United States. The products are identical; the only change is in marketing communications. In this case, the main communications adjustment is in the labeling of the powder. In Europe, the label illustrates and describes how to make soup out of the powder. In the United States, the label illustrates and describes how to make sauce and dip as well as soup. The appeal of the same product/different communication strategy is its cost of implementation. Since the product in this strategy is unchanged, there is no cost for product research and development or product adjustment. The only costs of the strategy are in identifying different product functions and reformulating marketing communications (advertising, sales promotion, point of sale material, etc.) around the newly identified function.

A third market condition indicating an adjustment strategy occurs when there are differences in environmental conditions of use and in the function which the product serves (Situation C). U.S. greeting card manufacturers have faced this set of circumstances in Europe, where the function of a greeting card is to provide a space for the sender to write his own message in contrast to the U.S. card, which contains a prepared message, or what is known in the greeting card industry as "sentiment." The conditions under which greeting cards are purchased in Europe are also different than in the United States. Cards are handled frequently by customers, a practice which makes it necessary to package the greeting card in European markets in cellophane. American manufacturers pursuing an adjustment strategy have changed both their product and their marketing communications in response to this set of environmental differences.

SOURCES OF STRATEGIC INFORMATION

When a headquarters executive in a multinational corporation decides to formulate an international marketing strategy, he requires information to answer two basic questions. First, should I make an adjustment in the marketing mix for product x in international markets? And second, if I should adjust, what should be adjusted, and in what direction? The headquarters executive wishing to answer such questions must keep informed about the complex and changing world market environment by acquiring information from other people, both inside and outside his company, from publications and other documentary sources, and by directly observing the world in which he operates. Research we have recently conducted indicates the relative importance to high-level headquarters executives in U.S. based multinational corporations of different sources of strategic information about the world environment.

In our study, we classified all sources of information utilized by executives into three basic types: human, documentary and physical phenomena. Human sources, we found, are clearly more important than documentary and physical sources combined. Three important factors explain the commanding relative importance of human sources. The first is the opportunity to interact with a person. Interaction with an information source results in a focusing of the message flow upon the recipient's information needs, a process which is impossible with a single documentary source, and cumbersome with a collection of documents. The more focused a message, the more likely it is to be information, as opposed to meaningless data.

A second characteristic of human sources is that they can, like documentary sources, be checked over a period of time for accuracy and reliability. One executive, in talking about company representatives as a source of information, identified this factor in these words:

> You learn to evaluate the company's representative in an area. If he is good, you rely on him for all your information. If he is not good, say, for example, he has a history of misinterpreting or holding back information, you double-check, and use additional or even alternative sources.

Another and very important characteristic of human in contrast to documentary sources is the "off the record" nature of word-of-mouth communication. The same source may be less candid in print than in conversation for perfectly justifiable and understandable reasons. Bank newsletters, for example, when commenting on the situation in a particular country, must be somewhat guarded in their observations to avoid backlash against the sponsoring bank.

The single most important source of external information for executives are company executives based abroad in company subsidiaries, affiliates, and branches. The importance of executives abroad as a source of information about the world environment is one of the most striking features of the modern multinational corporation. When a headquarters executive in an international corporation with operations abroad acquires external information, the most likely single source of this information is the company's own staff abroad. The general view of headquarters executives is that company executives overseas are the people who know best what is going on in their areas.

For the most part, we found, company executives abroad are in the same functional area as the headquarters executive acquiring information. The international division head tends to get information from the head of operating companies abroad, the headquarters marketing executive from the overseas company's top marketing execu and so on. There is a notable absence of informati gained from lower level employees such as salesme whose work brings them into everyday contact wit the environment. (This pattern is by no means unique to international operations. In most domes tic business operations, there is little or no direct information flow from lower level field sales people to headquarters executives and product engineers.)

The presence of an information network abroad in the form of company people is a major strength of the international company. It may also, paradoxically, be a weakness in the scanning posture of a company that has only partially extended the limits of its geographical operations because inside sources abroad tend to scan only information about their own countries, or at best their own region. Even though there may be more attractive opportunities outside of existing areas of operation, the chances of their being picked up by inside sources abroad is very low for their horizons tend to end at their national borders.

Competitors are an important human source of information for international executives. There is a much greater willingness and openess about exchanging information with competitors among international U.S. executives than among domestic executives, particularly those representing other U.S. international companies. There is a feeling among international executives that "we are all in this boat together" and indeed, there is some truth in this view. Overseas, U.S. executives often face well-developed patterns of "cooperation" among established national firms. At home, many international executives are still, or have been until very recently, engaged in a struggle to gain recognition, support, and understanding of international operations from corporate management. In addition, international U.S. companies that are intensely competitive in the United States are often less competitive abroad, particularly in the lower and middle income areas of the globe.

All of these factors, plus of course the social factor of common experiences, language, and attitudes, serve to create a climate of relatively free information exchange among U.S. international executives.

DOCUMENTARY SOURCES

Documentary information sources, we found, are secondary to humans as sources of strategic information. Publications are the single most important source of documentary information. The second most important outside documentary source is information services. If these two outside documentary categories are combined, they are of equal relative importance to international division executives abroad.

Inside the company, letters and reports, mainly from executives abroad, are the most important documentary sources of information. Together, they are the source of as much important information as publications. Another documentary source category inside a company is information storage, which we conceive of as broadly inclusive of any kind of documentary, mechanical, or electrical storage of information outside of the human mind. We found this source to be of almost negligible importance. This finding underlines the difficulties of external information storage and transfer outside of the human memory, yet it suggests an opportunity for development of a major new source of external information. This finding is also a reminder that in spite of the broad label "comprehensive" which is applied to computer-based information systems in many companies, these systems are today almost exclusively concerned with internal information and are thus irrelevant to the task of keeping informed about the outside environment.

Many executives express frustration at the difficulty in trying to keep up with the outpouring of publications. Executives have responded in different ways to the publications explosion. In our investigation, a standard technique encountered was intensive use of the proverbial circular file. A few companies rely upon an internal routing arrangement for publications which permit readers to flag articles of particular interest for subsequent readers. Of far greater importance are the informal systems of cooperative publications scanning. Executives pass things on to other executives who they feel might be interested. These arrangements are reciprocal when executives are at the same level. In superior-subordinate cooperative scanning, however, the flow is mainly upward.

None of the management groups we studied employed a formal system for monitoring published information. This absence of formalized publications surveillance is somewhat surprising in light of the size of the larger companies in our sample. When questioned about the absence of such a system, executives were split between those who expressed some interest in the possibilities of such a system, and those who felt that an expenditure on such an effort would not be worth the gain.

The absence of a formal publications monitoring system has resulted in a considerable amount of reading duplication in many of the companies we studied. For example, in three companies, the high proportions of executives reading information services were *all* reading the same service. If only one executive in each of these companies would read a different service, the scope of the information service scanning in each company would be considerably extended.

PHYSICAL PHENOMENA

The direct perception of physical phenomena is a relatively limited but important source of strategic information acquired by executives. Thus, a major independent variable in the utilization of this source is travel. The instances cited are of two types—one is where the information gained by the executive was easily available from other sources but which required sensory perception of the actual phenomena to register the information in the executive's mind. An example of such an instance was the case of the executive who recalled his astonishment when he realized that his flight from Australia to New Zealand had taken three hours. This observation caused him to realize that the distance from Australia to New Zealand is much greater than he had thought. His image of the relative closeness of the two countries (based upon looking at maps and globes) had led him to suggest that New Zealand be placed under the operating control of the Australian manager. The direct perception of the physical distance led him to recommend that authority for New Zealand be transferred from Australia to New Zealand.

The other type of physical phenomena instances were those where the information gained was *not* readily available from alternative sources. An example of such an instance was the

information that a company was erecting a plant in a country that was capable of producing directly competitive product x. Local executives in the country in question drove by the new plant every day on their way to their offices, but were unaware of the product x potential of the plant under construction. The company erecting the plant had announced that it was for product y, and local executives had accepted this announcement. The headquarters executive realized immediately as he was driven by the plant in question that it was potentially capable of producing product x. He possessed technical knowledge which enabled him to perceive information in a physical object— the plant—which his local executives, because they lacked this knowledge, were unable to perceive.

SOURCE LOCATION

Although for organizations as a whole, all external information comes originally from outside, this is not the case for the individual executive within an organization who gets much of his external information from sources located inside his company. The *relative* importance of inside sources, however, is frequently exaggerated. For our overall sample, *two-thirds* of the important external information acquired came from sources located outside the executive's company. This overall reliance upon outside sources is one of the important findings of our study. For some executives, the reliance upon outside sources is a deliberate strategy.

For many executives and students of organizations, the finding of heavy reliance upon outside sources will come as a surprise. For example, one writer, after emphasizing that the executive is within an organization, maintains that:[2]

> What goes on outside is usually not even known firsthand. It is received through an organizational filter of reports, that is, in an already predigested and highly abstract form that imposes organizational criteria of relevance on the outside reality.

An explanation for the tendency of observers and practitioners alike to overestimate the relative importance of sources inside the company might be the result of a failure to distinguish between external and internal information. The sheer volume of internal data and information contained in regularly presented reports that make up a management information system far exceed the very limited amount of external information contained in such reports. Many executives have erronously assumed that because inside sources are the most important sources of internal information that they are also the most important sources of external information. As we have shown, this is a serious error.

ORGANIZATION AND MULTINATIONAL MARKETING STRATEGY

Organizations should be structured to respond to the most important dimensions of the environment. In the international operations area, the most important dimension has been distance or geography. Thus, the typical international organization today is structured around geography. Europe, Africa and the Middle East; Japan, Australia and Southeast Asia; and all of Latin America are frequently combined in the same regional group. This structure, we submit, is more related to the era of steamboat surface travel and carrier pigeon communications than it is to the contemporary world of countries at vastly different stages of economic and market development. When it took weeks to travel, or send a letter, from one continent to the next, the geographic organization structure made sense. The cost, in time and money, of attempting any other grouping, given the need for face to face contact between local and headquarters executives, would have been prohibitive. Today, with 600 m.p.h. jet aircraft and instant worldwide communications, geography is no longer the barrier it once was. Moreover, future developments in travel and communications are expected to continue to raise speeds and lower costs.

Today, the crucial factor in international markets is their socioeconomic and not their geographic distance from each other. Japan has less in common with Malaysia than with the U.K. and EEC countries. South Africa has more in common with Australia than with Tanzania. The emergence

of countries at vastly different stages of market development in the same geographic region is a development which calls for a new organizational approach by companies whose international operations are spread over markets at different socioeconomic stages of development on many continents.

One approach which may prove to be viable is organization by stages of market development. A stages-of-market-development organization would assemble the countries in its system into groups which reflected similar market conditions. An example of the categories and country assignments that a multinational company might utilize is shown in Table 2.

The advantage of the stage of market development organization is its ability to focus the efforts of executives at the headquarters and subheadquarters level upon strategic problems and opportunities associated with the most significant dimensions of today's international environment.

The weakness of the geographic organizational structure is its failure to focus company skills and efforts on markets in underdeveloped or intermediate stages of development. This failure to perform is most evident in the product dimension. For example, there are an estimated 600 million women in the world who still scrub their clothes by hand. These women have been served by multinational soap and detergent companies for decades, yet until this year, none of these companies had attempted to develop an inexpensive manual washing device.

Table 2. Stages of Market Development Hypothetical Grouping.

Underdeveloped	Intermediate	Advanced
Tanzania	Southern Italy	U.S.A.
Malaysia	Portugal	U.K.
Tunisia	Ghana	France
Laos	Philippines	Germany
Gabon	Venezuela	No. Italy
Peru	Argentina	Japan, etc.

Colgate Palmolive has shown what can be done when product development efforts are focused upon market needs. A vice president of Colgate asked the leading inventor of modern mechanical washing processes to consider "inventing backwards"; to apply his knowledge not to a better mechanical washing device, but to a much better manual device. The device developed by the inventory is an inexpensive (selling price: under $10), all plastic, hand powered washer that has the tumbling action of a modern automatic machine. The response to this device in less-developed country markets has been enthusiastic.

Organization by stages of market development would, by focusing organizational efforts on market needs, encourage not only product development but pricing and communications strategies tailored to market needs. The important question for a company considering a market stages organizational structure is whether or not the scale of company operations in markets at different stages of development is, or is expected to be, sufficient to justify the creation of separate organizational units.

The cost in time and money of travel and communications has dramatically fallen in recent years, but it is still significant. In companies where organizational adjustments are expected to justify themselves on an immediate payback basis, there is a certain minimum size which must be achieved in order to cover the additional travel and communications expenditures of the stages of market development type of organization. Only larger companies can justify this type of organization on an immediate payback basis. However, companies which view organizational structure as a capital investment may decide to move to a stages-of-market-development organization as part of a strategic plan to develop business in middle and lower income markets.

CONCLUSION

Marketing strategy and organizational structure in the multinational company are closely interrelated. Decisions regarding market goals and objectives, product, price, and communication strategies, and resource commitments to implement these strategies are the basic elements of the strategic process. These decisions are a function of the information available to executives, and information flows are directly related to the job relationships and direct perception experiences of executives. Since these relationships and perception experiences are a function of organizational structure, strategic decisions and adjustments will be, in our judgment, more market-oriented when markets are grouped according to stages of socio-economic development. This structure will mass the organization's marketing and technical resources around environmental differences. These differences are essential dimensions of response for companies whose products (1) serve a different function, (2) fill a different need or (3) are used under significantly different conditions in foreign markets.

*

Notes

1. Norman Heller, "How Pepsi Cola Does It in 110 Countries," Address delivered at the 1966 World Congress, American Marketing Association, Chicago, page 11, 13 (duplicated).
2. Peter F. Drucker, *The Effective Executive* (New York: Harper and Row, 1966), page 13.

11 MULTINATIONAL POSITIONING STRATEGY

David R. McIntyre
Advertising Manager
Seven-Up International, Inc.

Positioning your product in the minds of consumers is a concept developed by American advertisers. An international practitioner demonstrates, with specific examples, how positioning strategy works overseas as well.

The 1970s have been heralded as the "Age of Positioning." That is, positioning your product, which can be either a brand or service, in the minds of prospective consumers by taking into consideration the strengths and weaknesses of not only your brand but those of your competitors as well. We have seen this positioning concept, which emphasizes market strategy rather than creativity, work in quite a few instances in North America, i.e., Avis Rental Car System "We're Number 2" campaign and "7UP, The Uncola" campaign to name two classic examples.

The concept, however, although used in some individual European countries, has not been used extensively on a multinational basis. Admittedly, the possibilities for multinational positioning are limited because fewer brands are marketed on a worldwide basis, language barriers exist and local regulations prohibit any reference, implied or otherwise, to competitors. Nevertheless, a multinational positioning strategy can be just as effective as it has been in North America because

From David R. McIntyre, "Multinational Positioning Strategy," Columbia Journal of World Business, Fall 1975, pp. 106-10. Reprinted by permission of the publisher.

of the important similarities which exist in the world marketplace. To support this statement, let me back up somewhat by explaining the positioning concept and how it evolved in the United States. The case will then be made for a more effective use of the positioning strategy on a multinational basis by using 7Up as an example.

To correctly position a product, an "outward" examination of the market must be made to accurately determine what is happening there. It is imperative to know first what consumers think of the product, and, secondly, how it is perceived vis-à-vis major competitors. If a company's marketing department has not gone through this soul searching process recently, the results may be surprising. What seems to have been a sound strategy three or even two years ago, could actually be detrimental to the brand's growth in today's economic climate of retrenchment.

This outward approach is a considerable departure from the 1950s in North America when a company's strategy was to simply look "inward" at their own product in terms of how many units could be sold. These were the days when only a few brands competed in most product categories and a little hard sell TV advertising would generally result in a sales increase. A case in point is the cigarette industry. Twenty years ago there were only six brands on the U.S. market. Camels, Chesterfields, Lucky Strike, Old Gold, Philip Morris and Pall Mall. Today, there are literally scores with more being introduced each year.

The devastating effects of World War II plus lack of commercial television retarded the development of most consumer products in Europe. However, by the early 1960s, our European marketing counterparts had caught up. As more and more products were being introduced through TV advertising on both sides of the Atlantic, hard sell competition for a smaller share of each market caused the advertising industry to seek new methods of getting their message across to consumers. Each brand had to have an image. Remember the successful worldwide Esso gasoline campaign "Put a Tiger in Your Tank." Here was an ingenious strategy which used an animated tiger to build an image for an unromantic product like gasoline. Most of us can also recall the one-eyed man in Hathaway Shirt ads and Commander Whitehead of Schweppes.

Just as the "Me Too" brands killed the hard sell era of the 1950s, the "Me Too" brands crowded in and eventually brought an end to the image era of the 1960s. In overseas markets where commercial television advertising exists without rigid government controls, the same situation prevails. By 1968 the noise level of television advertising became so loud with this type of image advertising, that some companies realized that by looking "outward" into the marketplace through consumer research studies, they would find that consumers subconsciously related some brands to others according to the position it holds in their minds.

We all know that the human mind is a very complex organ . . . yet in some ways it is rather limited. One of these limiting characteristics is its peculiar inability to readily recall more than one major event related to a particular subject. For example, most of us can easily recall the first time we drove a car alone. We can also probably remember the first airplane ride we took and the first boy/girl we kissed. These recollections are fairly easy, but now try remembering the second or third time you drove a car alone, flew in an airplane or the boy/girl you kissed. If these events come to mind as quickly as the first, then your recall facilities are better than average.

Let me carry this train of thought one step further by asking you to again recall certain things which related to these first happenings . . . such as the year and make of the first car you drove alone, the destination of that first airplane ride or your exact location when that first kiss was experienced. If you're like most people, the answers will come to mind almost immediately because they directly relate to something which occupies a strong "first" position in your mind. This same principle applies to the position a particular brand occupies in the consumers' minds.

Let me illustrate this point by using 7UP as a case study. In 1967 when The Seven-Up Company's product-oriented "Wet & Wild" campaign failed to stop the brand's declining market share, a focus group study revealed that even though consumers knew 7UP was a soft drink, they did not think of it as such. With the cola segment of the market, led by Coke and Pepsi, accounting for a whopping 60% share and both major brands spending over $50 million to promote a similar

image for two products which look and taste somewhat alike, it was no wonder that the word "cola" became generic to mean soft drink. The problem for 7UP was clear . . . it had to convince consumers that it was a soft drink just like cola but different. This could not be accomplished by attacking cola's strong position directly with cola-type advertising like the Wet & Wild campaign. Since cola occupied the leading soft drink position in consumers' minds, 7UP had to relate to this strong position in terms they would readily understand . . . by positioning itself as an alternative to cola, or as "The Uncola."

This, of course, has been a tremendous success story for The Seven-Up Company but let's relate it to the brand's overseas position. Although there are many differences between the New York Metro market and the large Southern California area most U.S. product managers will look for the similarities, or common denominators, in planning strategy for a national advertising campaign. The same principal also works in international markets. There are more similarities among worldwide consumers than dissimilarities. In addition to the basic human physiological need for food, shelter, etc., most people have similar psychological needs such as achievement, status, recognition within peer groups, etc. The human mind seems to work in much the same manner for Malaysians and Nigerians as it does for Americans and Europeans.

Another universal factor which strengthens the argument for an international positioning strategy is the "noise level" on commercial media. Most overseas markets have commercial television, radio, newspapers, etc., which accept advertising. Many countries, even in developing regions, have also experienced a rapid increase in the number of consumer products being introduced during the past ten years . . . an explosion similar to that experienced in the industrial nations. In observing the rapid, universal increase in television advertising rates, we strongly suspect that the "noise level," or number of products being aimed at consumers via television, is also approaching U.S. and European saturation levels. Because of these two major similarities, I believe that the concept of positioning is just as usable in Manila, Johannesburg or Cairo as it is in New York.

Let's look more closely at 7UP's international position vis-à-vis major cola competitors. In 1973 we re-examined our market position by analyzing the annual bottler marketing plans. These individual market plans serve as the cornerstone for the entire corporate planning procedure: while marketing programs vary from country to country, the planning process, i.e., updating existing market conditions, identifying opportunities and formulating action plans, is highly standardized.

The first step was to segment these markets according to existing brand strength and potential development to redefine where our major markets were. In doing so, we clearly saw that 80% of the total overseas business came from only 18 of the 79 countries where 7UP is marketed.

By eliminating the top three markets which have well-staffed subsidiary offices that produce their own national advertising campaigns, and therefore do not rely on St. Louis headquarters for TV commercials, fifteen major markets remain which account for 30% of the total business. Although thought was given to adding three or four additional markets to this list where the brand is presently weak but the potential is great, it was decided not to because a solid brand base is needed to successfully launch a new advertising campaign in this particular instance.

Once it was determined where the major markets were, the next step was to analyze them to find where the opportunities lay. In this endo-market analysis, we found three interesting common denominators:

12 of these 15 markets were dominated by either Coke or Pepsi or both to the extent that 10 of these markets showed cola share of market exceeding 40%.

The 7UP bottler in most of these markets had developed the brand over the years into a leading competitive position.

Most of these 7UP bottlers had extensively used previous series of multinational film commercials and the brand has a positive image on which a new campaign can be built. The 1973 image in these major markets probably equaled 7UP's domestic image prior to the introduction of the Uncola campaign in 1968.

In addition to these endo-market similarities there were two other extra-market factors which presented additional opportunities for 7UP:

Coke, Pepsi and 7UP have universal package designs and trademarks. Additionally, the flavor category into which both cola products belong is a part of their brand names. This allows both competitors to be collectively referred to as "Cola."

Both cola competitors market products which are similar in taste, similar in looks and share similar brand images perpetuated by all those years of using boy/girl/fun activities type commercials.

All of these endo- and extra-market factors provide 7UP with the opportunity to exploit Coke and Pepsi's traditional sameness in these cola dominated markets.

In late 1973, this problem/opportunity was turned over to our advertising agency. J. Walter Thompson was asked to create something which would communicate 7UP's unique position to people of diverse cultures, intelligence levels and varying degrees of sophistication. A new campaign had to be amusing, yet not contain anything which could be interpreted as denigratory towards our cola competitors.

Because 7UP's market position was very similar to the brand's 1968 position in the United States, thought was first given to exporting the Uncola campaign. This proved not to be practical because the slogan could not be translated into other languages and still retain its special meaning. However, the strategy behind the campaign, that is to position 7UP in consumers' minds as a unique, untraditional, alternative to cola had definite possibilities.

In place of the untranslatable Uncola slogan, J. Walter Thompson created an unusual character who lives in a little green box. The activities of this amusing visual device cuts across many levels of sophistication to develop a style very distinctive from cola. In effect the Uncola campaign strategy is being used on a multinational basis but in a somewhat modified form.

In those three major markets where colas do not dominate or where 7UP is the market leader, a small change in the copy lines of the voice-over film track will enable 7UP to be positioned merely as an untraditional, fun soft drink with no mention of cola.

Now that 7UP is midway through its second year of this campaign, it becomes important to try and measure what effect "Green Box" has had on brand sales. Even under the best of conditions this is a difficult chore with often questionable results. Compounding the problem of comparing sales results for 1974 over 1975 is the sales dampening effect of depression and inflation experienced by most oil importing nations over the past 18 months plus last year's worldwide sugar shortaage. Nevertheless, we selected ten national markets which used our "Green Box" campaign during the months of May, June and July of 1975 and compared them to sales over the same period in ten other markets of comparable size which used different advertising or promotional material. The difference was significant even after we made adjustments for market variations.

The ten "Green Box" markets showed a 16% sales increase for the three month period of 1975 compared to the same period in 1974. Those ten markets which used other material showed an 8% loss in sales over the same time period.

Although these figures are impressive they become somewhat qualified because of the major variables involved. Nonetheless, we are encouraged enough to commission a multinational, qualitative research project to try and determine through focus group sessions in four countries if "Green Box" is being understood by consumers and is reaching its creative objectives. If these results prove positive we will continue the concept into 1976 and beyond.

In summary, there is little doubt that the positioning concept has been used successfully in North America. I contend that this same concept can be used with equal success on a multinational basis as long as the same consistency is exercised in the use of the company's trademark/brand/packaging as is practiced in the United States. An example would be The McDonald's Corporation. They continue to use their famous double arch in international markets which signifies quality hamburgers plus fast, friendly service. McDonald's can position itself against the slow, old-fashioned, take-your-chances-on-quality foreign competitors. Another example would be L'eggs panty hose which will enter the international field in 1976. I

see no reason why they cannot use essentially the same dynamic packaging and name trademark overseas to position itself as a quality product against existing (locally made) competitors.

These strategies were used by both companies to gain a strong market position in the United States . . . and they can be used with equal success overseas. The world is growing "smaller" all the time. Television satellite broadcasting, inexpensive group travel plans, etc. have all contributed to this shrinking phenomenon. In the process we have found that there is really very little difference between worldwide consumers. They all want quality products which will enhance their personal prestige at an affordable price. This is the universality of the average consumer with disposable income. An advertising strategy which has proven to be successful in one country has a fairly good chance of being successful in another. That's what multinational positioning is all about.

12 DOWN-TO-EARTH MARKETING INFORMATION SYSTEMS

Neil Doppelt
Manager, Administrative Services Division
Arthur Andersen & Co.

This article suggests in detail how to set up a basic marketing information system which focuses on the decisions each manager must make. Efficiency results when the attention is concentrated on those accounts that contribute most.

As the cost-price squeeze continues to handicap many companies, increasing attention is being paid, not only to every effort to cut costs, but also to every possible way to increase sales and profits. This has focused attention on marketing efforts—and marketing management—as it has never been directed before.

The accountant, whether he is internal or external, has a vital role to play in this increasing attention to marketing activities.

This concentration, while it is rather belated in some companies, is only an acceleration of trends that have been visible for some time.

Actions to improve the management of marketing activities and to increase senior management's understanding of marketing functions have been prompted by three key factors:

1. More companies are adopting a definition of marketing operations that goes beyond the

From Neil Doppelt, "Down-to-Earth Marketing Informa-tion Systems," Management Adviser, *September-October, 1971, pp. 96-103. Copyright 1971 by the American Institute of Certified Public Accountants, Inc. Reprinted by permission of the publisher.*

simple mechanics of selling products to consumers. This "marketing concept" begins when the company interprets the consumer's needs and desires, both quantitatively and qualitatively; follows through with all the business activities involved in the flow of goods and services from producer to consumer; and ends with those services necessary to aid the consumer in getting the expected utility from the products he has purchased. In order to adopt the marketing concept in deed as well as word, companies must approach the marketplace with respect and flexibility, rather than trying to succeed with brute force.

2. Investments in advertising, sales promotion, market research, salesmen, and new product development are increasing. Possible profit improvements by making more effective use of marketing resources are often much larger than the prospects of achieving significant product cost reductions.

3. The outputs of the marketing department are critical to orderly and efficient operations throughout the organization. Marketing forecasts and budgets become the basis for production schedules, cash flow projections, and profit plans. Conversely, lack of detail, accuracy, or timeliness in marketing planning can impair the profit potential for products or services that are otherwise strong and competitive.

PAST NEGLECT—WHY?

If marketing is so important, why do many companies find themselves with fragmented or nonexistent planning and control systems in this area? Several reasons can be pinpointed:

1. Partially by design and partially by accident, marketing often becomes isolated from other operating departments. Senior executives accustomed to dealing with straightforward information about machine hours, inventory turns, and sales volume are reluctant to dig into the supposedly less precise areas of marketing decisions. In some cases marketing managers themselves have contributed to this situation by overemphasizing subjective judgment as the basis for their strategies—even though most mar-

keting executives are at least as fact-oriented as their counterparts in other functions.

2. Marketing information needs have usually been satisfied on a piecemeal basis by using data sources and reports really designed for other management purposes, such as financial reporting, production control, and accounting. This "hand-me-down" method sometimes looks like an economical way to solve continuing marketing information problems. Basic information needs go unfulfilled, however, since important aspects of customer identification, cost allocations, and external market conditions cannot be captured unless special provisions are made for doing so.

3. EDP techniques have been successfully applied first where dollar savings or operating advantages have been easily recognized; accounting, inventory control, order entry, and production scheduling usually get top priority. The benefits of better information for the marketing function are difficult to quantify in dollars and cents.

4. The concepts behind a marketing information system may be misinterpreted by senior executives. At one extreme, they may expect such systems to deliver the answers to the most difficult kinds of questions—the effectiveness of advertising and promotion, for example. At the other extreme, the systems approach may be dismissed as just another sales reporting scheme. Neither concept is correct. As is detailed in this article, many problems can be solved or their current solutions improved upon with better marketing information. Imperfect answers to tough questions are usually better than no answers at all, and sales reporting is only one element of a basic system.

When the pressures to develop effective systems for marketing become great enough, these historical problems succumb to good management judgment and a "marketing information system" begins to sound like the right answer.

The primary objective of a marketing information system is to improve marketing management's ability to identify profitable sales opportunities, to make the most effective use of sales force personnel, to allocate advertising and sales promotion expenditures efficiently, and to react quickly and correctly to changes in market conditions. The "system" itself can be broadly defined as an organized set of procedures, information-handling systems, and reporting techniques designed to provide the information needed to plan and control marketing activities.

These definitions of objectives and system content are necessarily long because a substantial amount of information is required to manage the marketing function and there are many different kinds of tasks carried out within that function. Regardless of the eventual complexity of a marketing information system, the guiding philosophy is simple: Better information helps capable men do a better job.

A good problem solver usually has the answer sketched out in his mind before he sets to work. The same logic applies to the design of a system to meet the information needs of marketing management—the most important information needs should be anticipated before the first interview is scheduled. The following list is offered as a guide to the kinds of information marketing managers want, whether the products involved are building materials, breadsticks, or bonds:

CUSTOMER INFORMATION

Where is volume concentrated?

Who are specific major customers, both present and potential?

What are their needs for products?

What are their needs for sales coverage and service?

What order activity and volume are expected?

What are the differences in profitability between types and classes of customers?

Where is performance significantly short of expectations?

PRODUCT INFORMATION

What are the relative profitabilities of products at the gross margin level? After direct marketing expenses?

Which elements of variable product cost are influenced by marketing decisions? What is the current cost structure?

Which products tend to respond most favorably to sales promotion at the wholesale, retail, and consumer levels?

What are the major advantages and disadvantages of current products in the eyes of consumers, relative to competitive products?

What factors have the greatest influence on sales volume?

What is the status of volume and profitability relative to objectives?

SALES FORCE INFORMATION

What area and which customers are assigned?

What call activity is required, both for protection of present volume and development of new business?

Do current compensation systems motivate the desired mix of salesmen's activity?

What is current performance relative to objectives?

This list can be expanded, of course, into the detailed questions concerning the "right" strategies for pricing, advertising, sales promotion, and new product development. However, information systems do not make strategic decisions—managers do, by the best use of their experience and the information and analytical tools available to them.

A basic marketing information system should be designed to provide most or all of the customer/product/sales force information listed above. Focusing on the *decisions* each manager must make as part of his normal job responsibility helps to define what his information requirements are and how his outputs of plans and forecasts can best be integrated into the information system.

Like any other systems development project, the design and installation of a marketing information system must be undertaken with care and organized effort. A good first step is to charter a temporary Task Force, including knowledgeable men from marketing, accounting, and data processing. These individuals, assigned full time for the duration of the project, can provide the broad and intensive effort required

to produce a conceptual systems design for all aspects of the system and to participate in the implementation of the design. The Task Force approach helps to avoid the disappointment of sporadic, stop-and-start marketing systems projects.

VARIED SKILLS REQUIRED

Each member of the Task Force can make important contributions to the project. The marketing representatives (there could be more than one) should have overall responsibility for the successful completion of the project. The system will be designed, after all, to meet the needs that they identify and interpret. The accounting representative's skills will be needed because accounting systems in particular are likely to require revision in order to accommodate marketing information needs. The data processing man should participate in the planning of changes in data collection and reporting systems, as well as in their implementation. Given the flexibility and capacity of current electronic data processing techniques (if they are required) and the skills available to design manual systems, the output of the Task Force should be in agreement with user needs.

The users are, of course, marketing managers with a wide variety of responsibilities and outputs, as is illustrated in Exhibit 1. These managers are charged with preparing plans covering sales volume, advertising and promotion programs, customer service, and sales force operations. Each of these plans and associated budgets becomes integrated into a marketing plan (product emphasis) and a sales plan (customer or territory emphasis). Other functional areas, shown on the right of the exhibit, rely on the marketing department's outputs as the basis for their own schedules, projections, and objectives.

The varying tasks of marketing executives might suggest separate data files and reporting systems for each kind of planning and monitoring activity. Such a system would be inefficient, however, and a more economical approach would utilize basic data sources for a variety of purposes.

The interfaces between marketing and other functional areas can present problems if users on

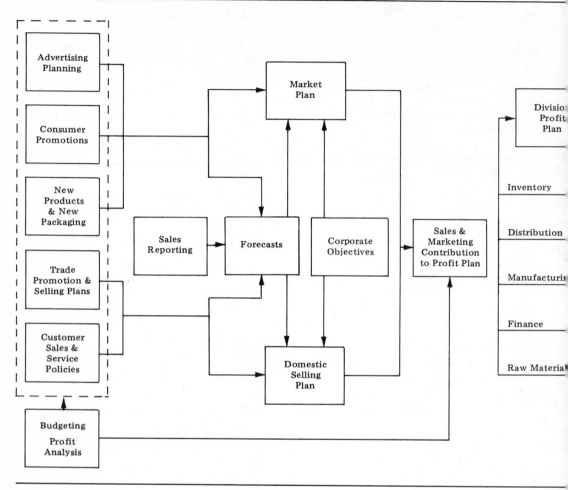

Exhibit 1. Marketing Responsibilities and Key Outputs.

either side are forced to work with data formats and definitions that are cumbersome or unfamiliar, simply to avoid a data processing step. For example, marketing managers may be comfortable with "cases" while production scheduling personnel prefer to work in terms of "pounds." A common unit is not necessarily required for both marketing and production as long as the two different units can be defined in terms of one another and procedures installed to maintain compatibility.

As discussed previously, it is not necessary that each marketing manager have a separate information system. The problems (and oppor-tunities) in marketing information systems design arise from the need to utilize available sources for a wide variety of information requirements. Basic data sources usually consist of the following:

invoices or other documents recording shipments of specific quantities to specific customers;

accounting ledgers recording the disposition of funds for specific purposes;

salesmen's call reports showing the frequency and nature of their activity;

reports of inventory status, product costs, and project status;

planning documents showing expected levels of activity for product volume, price levels, sales force activity, marketing expenditures, and projects, including statistical forecasts based on historical data; and

external data, collected and analyzed for the purpose of establishing priorities among products, customers, and areas.

The list of basic sources has several implications for marketing systems design work. First, most of the documents and records are designed for users in other functional areas such as accounting, production, and distribution. If they are to be utilized as part of a marketing information system, it will be necessary to modify the ways in which other users handle and distribute the basic sources. Second, plans are included as a source of information; they are also important outputs of the marketing management effort. Both aspects of the planning process are critical since information flows *within* as well as *between* functions. Finally, models and simulations are not included in the list; they represent "second generation" information systems projects for most companies. Managers can make better use of these sophisticated tools after they have fully explored the benefits of new procedures and reports.

The following example illustrates how basic data can be rearranged to provide marketing management with valuable information.

Case 1   A manufacturer of cosmetics utilized department stores, chain drug stores, and variety and specialty outlets for his channels of distribution. Each of his many products required substantial support in the form of special promotions, cooperative advertising arrangements with retailers, and partially or completely subsidized in-store sales personnel. As part of a larger effort to exercise more control of these expenditures, procedures were installed to identify expenses directly attributable to the different classes of retail outlets, in addition to product-by-product budget control. These procedures required subsidiary ledgers to accumulate marketing and selling expenses by class of trade. Exhibit 2 shows

COSMETIC COMPANY

	% of Net Sales	
	Drug Stores	Department Stores
Cost of Goods, Freight, Commission, Insurance	56%	53%
Co-op Advertising	3	10
Salesgirl Salary Support	0	21
Commissions in Outlets	12	11
	71%	95%
Contribution to Profit & Overhead	29%	5%

Exhibit 2.   Trade Channel Performance.

one of the resulting trade-class profitability reports.

Customer class profitability data had not been available before, and the new reports enabled management to pinpoint profit improvement opportunities. Exhibit 2 illustrates another key point about marketing information systems: they provide the tools for decision making, but not the decisions themselves. Based on the new cost and profit data, management could conclude that department store business was just not worth having, or it could conclude that the prestige and exposure afforded by department stores was worth the costs and low profit levels involved. Other alternatives involving changes in promotional programs could also be considered. The key to the decision remains the factual information provided by one element of the marketing information system.

In contrast to other functional areas, marketing operations depend heavily on data originating *outside* the organization. External data from government publications, trade associations, business periodicals, and syndicated services provide marketing managers with indicators of market and product potential. In turn, these measures of potential establish the basis for assigning salesmen to particular geographic areas, industries, or customers; for allocating advertising and promotional dollars to specific buying groups or areas; and for forecasting volume performance.

Case 2   A small manufacturer of copper wire relied on his customers' buying expectations, as reported by his salesmen, to establish volume forecasts. Actual performance, however, was usually far short of forecast. By utilizing trade and government publications that reported on activity of his customers' customers, he was able to adjust his projections downward to compensate for the tendency of end-users of copper wire to place multiple orders as protection against stock-outs. It was found that these multiple orders were inflating the purchasing expectations of the manufacturer's direct customers.

The Task Force must identify the most appropriate sources for external data and pinpoint why, how, and by whom such information will be used. The availability of external data can have major effects on the organization and reporting of internal data. For example, geographic definitions used internally (such as districts and regions) may require realignment in order to provide direct comparability with external statistics dealing with countries or accepted industry trade area designations. Product groups also may have to be reorganized in order to match the categories found in trade literature or government publications. The tasks of rearranging and reclassifying internal data usually require extensive recoding and wholesale changes in key master files.

Planning is one of the most important elements of sound management—it provides the basis for evaluating performance and exercising control. Unfortunately, planning procedures that should be part of the most basic marketing information

systems tend to get pushed aside in the rush to design and install new reporting systems. Planning systems are usually an afterthought even though the simplest report serves little purpose without some predetermined benchmark against which results can be measured.

Case 3   The sales manager in a textile company supervised the activities of some 80 salesmen and district managers. He found that continued hiring of salesmen did not seem to improve overall performance, even though his field managers insisted that more men were required to cover the market. A more formal and effective way to plan sales force activity was adopted, as shown in Exhibit 3. The new sales planning procedures called for:

identifying key customers;

defining minimum call frequencies by customer class;

assigning salesmen to territories of approximately equal potential; and

developing sales objectives for key customers and territories based on potential and past performance.

The sales plan in this example covers a six-month selling season and specifies call frequen-

SALESMAN *Morgan*   TERRITORY *27*   YEAR *1971*   SEASON *Fall*

ACCOUNT CLASS	CALLS TO BE MADE						TOTAL	CUMULATIVE VOLUME OBJECTIVES $(000)						TOTAL
	Jul.	Aug.	Sep.	Oct.	Nov.	Dec.		Jul.	Aug.	Sep.	Oct.	Nov.	Dec.	
KEY/MAJOR — —	2	1	1	2	1	1	8	12	16	25	29	32	40	40
OTHER ACTIVE — —	1	1	1	1	1	1	6	1	3	4	6	8	9	9
PROSPECTIVE — —	1	2	—	—	—	—	3							
TERR. TOTALS														

Exhibit 3. Sales Plan.

cies for each major and prospective account, as well as cumulative volume objectives. The summation of such territory plans becomes the basis for assigning salesmen and for checking total volume objectives against corporate goals. The sales manager must adjust the total of the individual account objectives downward to reflect probable account losses from season to season.

Controls over sales force activity were facilitated by regular reports like the one shown in Exhibit 4. The primary measures of performance—volume, call activity, price maintenance, and new account acquisition—are all monitored versus objectives using data from two basic sources, call reports and orders. A profit index is used to give the salesman an indicator of profit contribution without requiring the sales manager to distribute detailed profit margin data throughout his organization.

The Task Force responsible for marketing systems design needs to define the responsibilities, formats, and timing necessary to produce plans for product sales, sales force manpower levels and call frequency, promotion and advertising expenditures, and summary budgets and profit contribution plans for the entire marketing and sales function. Exhibit 5 illustrates the timing of plan preparation and the relationship between planning and reporting. In this example planning begins early in the year with the review and updating of long-range and new product plans. Other basic plans and forecasts are developed throughout the year, some sequentially and others concurrently. A "pause" in the forth quarter provides for updating statistical forecasts with the most recent data available, prior to the final coordination and approval sessions necessary to establish objectives for the coming year. On the reporting side, progress is monitored against each plan on a monthly or quarterly basis.

Once a Task Force begins to ask marketing managers what their reporting needs are, requests are likely to come thick and fast. Some managers have useful personal systems that they would like

SALESMAN _Jones_   TERRITORY _14_   PERIOD THROUGH _March 31, 1991_

| | SALES VOLUME | | | PROFIT INDEX | | CALLS | |
	PLAN	ACTUAL	LAST YR.	PLAN	ACTUAL	PLAN	ACTUAL
KEY/MAJOR							
—	7,200	8,100	6,500	100	104	4	4
—							
—							
ALL OTHER							
—							
NEW							
—							
—							
• TOTAL	90,000	100,000	75,000	100	102	210	196
• COMMISSION	XXX			XXX		XXX	XXX
• ACCOUNTS	PLAN	ACTUAL					
RETAINED	40	43					
NEW	8	10					

Exhibit 4. Performance Report.

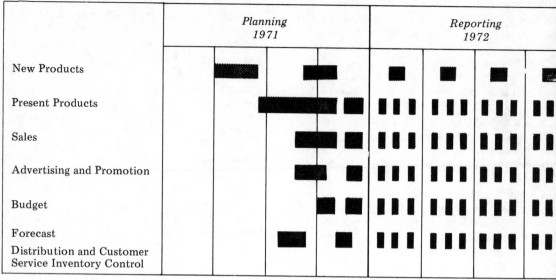

Exhibit 5. Planning Time Frame.

incorporated into any new system. Others will see the project as an opportunity to satisfy their curiosity, but they have no specific uses in mind for the information they request. These requests must be evaluated in light of the overall marketing approach either in use or contemplated by management. Even with experienced assistance on board to help sort out priorities, the eventual list of needs can be very long. The volume of reports can be staggering when levels of detail and reporting frequencies are considered.

Part of this problem comes about from confusion between data and information. Detailed reports of every individual sales transaction and marketing expenditure provide raw data only and are often unusable due to their bulk. Summaries, groupings, and limited report distribution procedures are required to make reports readable and manageable. Exception reporting techniques would also simplify reporting, but few systems utilize exception reports to more than a minor extent. Managers are reluctant to work with less than complete information at the levels of detail most convenient for them.

Exhibit 6 illustrates a technique that parallels the exception report concept. The graph is based on the volume contribution of each

account, arranged largest first. Thus in this example, the top 10 percent of accounts contribute 74 percent of total volume. The importance of these accounts warrants frequent, detailed reporting on their activity, although the reports themselves will be relatively "thin"; key accounts are usually less than 20 percent of the total number of accounts. The small accounts contribute relatively little volume and thus detailed reports of their activity do not add much to a manager's understanding of current market conditions. Some systems are designed to summarize the smallest accounts (perhaps several thousand of them) into a single line for reporting purposes.

The "key account" approach works equally well with product line reporting, especially for those companies that manufacture a large number of product variations that are distinguished by minor differences in size, color, packaging material, or shipping quantity. As the costs of electronic data storage decrease and the time pressures on marketing managers increase, information systems tend to emphasize more storage and less reporting.

Various parts of this article have focused on the reasons for directing effort toward a marketing information system; the basic user needs, data sources, and design techniques for such a system;

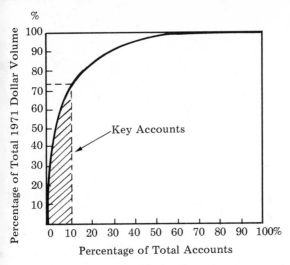

Cumulative %

Accounts	Volume
2 (45)	48
10 (210)	74
20 (430)	86
50 (1100)	97
100 (2200)	100

Exhibit 6. Distribution of Volume by Account.

and some of the potential problems involved. The focus has been on developing a basic system that will reflect the marketing approach and key information needs of marketing management.

The success of any concentrated effort to improve planning and control in the marketing function will depend most heavily, however, on the active support of senior management. "Active support" means defining the scope of the project, assigning qualified personnel on a full-time basis, participating in regular progress report sessions, and recognizing that a broad and detailed examination of needs and alternatives must precede implementation.

Most companies, large and small, have yet to scratch the surface in this critical area. Although designing and installing even a "down-to-earth" marketing information system can involve some hard work, a quick look at the resources allocated to the marketing function should be sufficient incentive to get started.

3 INSIGHTS INTO: THE ANALYTICAL-STRATEGIC APPROACH

How marketing managers plan and execute decisions is the subject of this section of the book.

In marketing there is rarely the *one* "right answer." Why is this so? Principally because marketing managers are dealing with decisions that call for predicting what consumers, suppliers, and others will do in the future—when even *they* don't know.

The key input to decision making, of course, is information. The capturing of relevant information is the constant preoccupation of marketing managers. The models managers use to process this information range from intuitive judgment to the highly quantitative marketing information system.

How to analyze what consumers are doing, and thinking, is discussed in this section. Also: how to probe the industrial sector and the international marketplace.

The seven articles in this section will help managers and students alike in learning what is required to create more useful marketing plans and strategies.

13 ACTIVITIES, INTERESTS, AND OPINIONS

William D. Wells
Professor of Psychology and Marketing
University of Chicago

Douglas J. Tigert
Associate Professor of Marketing
University of Toronto

Lifestyle or psychographic research sounds imposing and difficult. Actually, it is a logical extension
of the demographics approach, which focused on
age, income, and sex. Two marketing professors
describe actual applications of this new tool.

*From William D. Wells and Douglas J. Tigert, "Activi-
ties, Interests, and Opinions," Journal of Advertising Research, 1971, pp. 27-35. Copyright © 1971, by the Advertising Research Foundation. Reprinted by permission of
the publisher.*

In the early 1950s advertising and marketing
were host to an extended and lively fad that came
to be known as Motivation Research. Armed with
"projective techniques" from clinical psychology
and some exciting notions from psychoanalysis,
MR practitioners penetrated deeply into the consumer's psyche, revealing for the first time to
their astounded clients the "real" reasons people
buy products.

The research establishment's reaction was
predictable. Conventional researchers insisted that
MR was unreliable, invalid, unobjective, too expensive, liable to be misleading, and altogether
an instrument of the Devil—and whatever was good
about motivation research had long been standard
practice anyway. The motivation researchers replied that conventional research was sterile, dull,
shallow, rigid, and superficial.

The controversy rolled on through the fifties until everything that could be said had been said too often. As the contestants and the audience wearied, the spotlight moved from MR and the couch to OR and the computer.

But MR left a legacy. Before MR, advertising and marketing research had in fact been a vast wasteland of percentages. The marketing manager who wanted to know why people ate the competitor's cornflakes was told "32 per cent of the respondents said taste, 21 per cent said flavor, 15 per cent said texture, 10 per cent said price, and 22 per cent said don't know or no answer." The copywriter who wanted to know his audience was told: "32.4 years old, 12.62 years of schooling, 90 per cent married with 2.1 children."

To this desert MR brought people. In addition to the exotic (and largely unworkable) projective tests, motivation researchers employed long, free-flowing narrative interviews, and through these interviews marched an array of mothers who worried about getting the kids to school on time, old ladies whose feet hurt, fretful young housewives who didn't know how to make a good pie crust, fathers who felt guilty about watching television when they should be painting the porch and skinny kids who secretly, but sincerely, believed that The Breakfast of Champions had something to do with their batting averages. For the first time, research brought the marketing manager and the copywriter face to face with an audience or a group of customers instead of a bunch of decimals. The marketing manager and the copywriter thought they were—and they probably were in fact—aided in their task of communication.

The rise of OR and the computer did nothing to change this need to have some sensible contact with believable humans. As the mathematical models proliferated, percentages and averages turned into dots, arrows, brackets, boxes, asterisks, and squiggles. The humans who used to show up in motivation research reports disappeared into the computer and emerged as regression coefficients and eigenvalues. The copywriter and the marketing manager, especially the copywriter, still needed some way to appreciate the consumer.

It begins to appear that this need will now be met at least in part by research that focuses on consumers' activities, interests, prejudices, and opinions. Variously called "psychographic" research, "life style" research and even (incorrectly) "attitude" research, it resembles motivation research in that a major aim is to draw recognizably human portraits of consumers. But it also resembles the tougher-minded, more conventional research in that it is amenable to quantification and respectable samples.

This paper is about this new and slightly more sanitary version of motivation research. It starts with a specific example. It mentions various uses. It describes some of the techniques of data gathering and analysis. It ends with a discussion of some criticism and problems, and the usual rosy but cautious predictions about developments in the future.

DESIGN

One thousand questionnaires were mailed to homemaker members of Market Facts' mail panel. In addition to the usual demographics and questions about a variety of products, the questionnaire contained 300 "activity, interest, and opinion" statements to which the respondent indicated degree of agreement on a six-point scale. For instance, the first statement was, "When I set my mind to do something I usually can do it," and the respondent answered on a scale that ran from 1 (definitely disagree) to 6 (definitely agree). The statements covered a wide variety of topics—including day-to-day activities; interests in media, the arts, clothes, cosmetics and homemaking; and opinions on many matters of general interest.

SWINGING EYE MAKEUP USER

One of the products on the questionnaire was eye makeup. Respondents were asked how often they use it on a seven-step scale ranging from "never" to "more than once a day."

The demographic questions showed that eye makeup users tend to be young and well-educated, and tend to live in metropolitan areas. Usage rates were much higher for working wives than for full-time homemakers, and substantially higher in the West than in other parts of the country.

Cross-tabulation with other products showed

the user of eye makeup to be a heavy user of other cosmetics—liquid face makeup base, lipstick, hair spray, perfume, and nail polish, for example. Perhaps less predictably, she also turned out to be an above-average cigarette smoker and an above-average user of gasoline and the long distance telephone.

On television, she liked the movies, the Tonight Show, and Run For Your Life; she didn't like panel programs or Westerns. She read fashion magazines, news magazines and *Life* and *Look*; she didn't read *True Confessions* or *Successful Farming*.

Thus, eye makeup is clearly not an isolated product. Instead, it is part of a behavior pattern, a pattern that suggests an organized set of tastes and values.

Cross-tabulation of eye makeup with the activity, interest, and opinion questions added significant detail to this emerging picture. Compared with the nonuser of eye makeup, the user appeared to be much more interested in fashion. For instance, she was more apt to agree with statements like: "I often try the latest hairdo styles when they change;" "I usually have one or more outfits that are of the very latest style;" "An important part of my life and activities is dressing smartly;" and "I enjoy looking through fashion magazines."

Secondly, she said in a number of ways that being attractive to others, and especially to men, is an important aspect of her self image. (All the respondents in this study were homemakers. The large majority were married.) More than the nonuser of eye makeup, the user said, "I like to feel attractive to all men;" "Looking attractive is important in keeping your husband;" "I want to look a little different from others;" and "I like what I see when I look in the mirror."

She indicated that she is very meticulous about her person: "I comb my hair and put on my lipstick first thing in the morning;" "I take good care of my skin;" "I do not feel clean without a daily bath;" and "Sloppy people feel terrible."

More than the nonuser she said, "I would like to make a trip around the world;" "I would like to spend a year in London or Paris;" "I enjoy going through an art gallery;" and "I like ballet."

She said, "I like parties where there is lots of music and talk;" "I like things that are bright, gay and exciting;" and "I do more things socially than do most of my friends." Not surprisingly, she said "no" to "I am a homebody."

As far as household chores are concerned, she conceded that she is not a compulsive housekeeper. She said "yes" to "I would like to have a maid to do the housework" and "no" to: "I like to go grocery shopping" and "I enjoy most forms of housework."

Her reaction to her home was style-conscious rather than utilitarian: "I like to serve unusual dinners;" "I am interested in spices and seasonings;" "If I had to choose I would rather have a color television set than a new refrigerator." She said "no" to "I furnish my home for comfort, not for style;" "I try to arrange my home for my children's convenience;" and "It is more important to have good appliances in the home than good furniture."

Finally, she ascribed to a number of statements that suggest acceptance of the contemporary and rejection of traditional ideas. More than the nonuser she tended to agree with, "I like to think I am a bit of a swinger;" "I like bright, splashy colors;" and "I really do believe that blondes have more fun." She rejected statements like, "Women should not smoke in public;" "There is too much emphasis on sex today;" "Spiritual values are more important than material things;" and "If it was good enough for my mother, it is good enough for me."

THE HEAVY USER OF SHORTENING

In the same study, another product—shortening—produced a vividly contrasting picture. Compared with the heavy user of eye makeup, the heavy user of shortening was not as young, had a larger family and was much less likely to have a job outside the home. She was also much more apt to be living outside a metropolitan area, and to be living in the South, especially the Southeast.

The clues continued in the product use pattern. Heavy users of shortening tended to be heavy users of flour, sugar, laundry detergent, canned lunch meat, canned vegetables, cooked pudding, mustard, and catsup—all products that go with large families. They were not heavy users of eye makeup or any of the cosmetics that go with it.

In the activity, interest, and opinion questions the contrast deepened. Almost none of the items that correlated with use of eye makeup also correlated with use of shortening. When the same question did correlate with both products, the correlations were usually in opposite directions.

Compared with the light user of shortening, the heavy user expressed a much stronger interest in cooking and baking. With much greater frequency she said "yes" to, "I love to bake and frequently do;" "I save recipes from newspapers and magazines;" "I always bake my cakes from scratch;" and "The kitchen is my favorite room." She also said, "I love to eat" and "I love candy."

Instead of disliking the job of keeping house, she said she likes it: "I enjoy most forms of housework;" "Usually I have regular days for washing, cleaning, etc. around the house;" "I am uncomfortable when my house is not completely clean." She *disagreed* with "I would like to have a maid to do the housework" and "My idea of housekeeping is 'once over lightly.' "

She said she sews: "I often make my own or my children's clothes" and "I like to sew and frequently do."

She indicated heavy involvement with her children and with the positive emotional tone of her family: "I try to arrange my home for my children's convenience," a statement that correlated *negatively* with eye makeup use. She also said, "Our family is a close-knit group;" "There is a lot of love in our family;" and "I spend a lot of time with my children talking about their activities, friends, and problems."

An unexpected and certainly nonobvious finding was that she is unusually health conscious, and this frame of mind extends to a personal interest in fresh air and exercise: "Everyone should take walks, bicycle, garden, or otherwise exercise several times a week;" "Clothes should be dried in the fresh air and sunshine;" "I love the fresh air and out-of-doors;" "It is very important for people to wash their hands before eating each meal;" and "You should have a medical checkup at least once a year."

Finally, she said she is not a party goer, and she is definitely not cosmopolitan: "I would rather spend a quiet evening at home than go to a party" and "I would rather go to a sporting event than a dance." She said "No" to "Classical music is more interesting than popular music;" "I like ballet;" and "I'd like to spend a year in London or Paris."

These two sharply contrasting portraits—the eye makeup user and the shortening user—show how recognizable humans emerge from quantified activity, interest and opinion data.

PORTRAITS OF TARGET GROUPS

Perhaps the most obvious use of this kind of research is the one already mentioned—portraits of target groups in the advertising and marketing of products. If it is granted that all forms of advertising and marketing are in some sense communication, and it is granted that a communicator can usually do a better job when he can visualize his audience than when he cannot, it seems obvious that this level of descriptive detail is a significant improvement over the rather sparse and sterile demographic files that have been traditional in marketing research.

The target group is often, but by no means always, the product's heavy user. The target group may be the light user or the nonuser. It may be some special segment, such as smokers of mentholated cigarettes. It may be some demographic segment, such as young married men with a college education. If the target group can be specified and identified, a useful portrait is at least a possibility.

MEDIA VALUES NOT IN THE NUMBERS

Media representatives insist that an audience quality, as well as its size, should be considered. Activity, interest, and opinion questions provide some insight into audience quality by drawing a portrait of the medium's user. The *Playboy* reader for instance, turns out to be pretty much the male counterpart of the swinging eye makeup user, while the male *Reader's Digest* reader emerges as the soul of conservative middle class values—probusiness, anti-government welfare, anti-union power, interested in politics, interested in community projects and activities. The *Time*-only reader, compared with the *Newsweek*-only reader, emerges as less concerned about job security, less worried about government and union power, less worried about the peril of communism and more favorably disposed toward advertising (Tigert, 1969).

Media analysts know that, compared with magazines, television is a very "blunt" medium. Since magazine audiences select themselves in accordance with the magazine's specialized editorial content, while television program audiences are usually very large and very heterogeneous, it is usually much easier to find distinct demographic differences among the readers of different magazines than among the viewers of different television programs. But work with activity, interest, and opinion variables suggests that television program audiences may be more different than some suspect.

Before Brand Rating Index, Simmons, and other syndicated product-media services became widely available, it was customary to match media with products by demographic "profile": "Our product is used by young, upscale housewives, so we want to be in a book that appeals to young, upscale housewives." It has sometimes been suggested that the psychographic profile be substituted for the demographic profile as a link between product and media: "Our product is used by women with a certain activity, interest, and opinion pattern, so we want to be in books or on TV programs that appeal to people who match that description." But this intuitively appealing idea has the same drawbacks as demographic profile matching. The correlations that link products to media through psychographics are no stronger than the correlations that link products to media through demographics, so a product and a medium can have similar activity, interest, and opinion profiles without being much related to each other. It is always safer to use the direct product-medium link in selecting media than to try to infer this link through some third set of variables.

Where psychographics can be of help in media selection is in improving the analyst's understanding of the product-medium linkages that are found through direct cross-tabulation. For instance, if direct cross-tabulation shows that many heavy users of home permanents are devoted readers of *True Story*, the activities, interests, and opinions of the women who *both use the product and read the magazine* will help explain the reasons behind this relationship by showing what, exactly, home permanent users and *True Story* readers have in

common. That sort of understanding is often of great help in making sensible decisions.

OTHER VARIABLES

Questions about activities, interests, and opinions can shed light on topics other than products and media. They can give additional meaning to the standard demographic classifications by showing how the executive's wife differs from the homemaker in a blue-collar household. They can further define the generation gap. They can add to what is known about sex differences. They can further describe the opinion leader, the new product tryer, the television addict, the trading stamp saver, the discount shopper, the political activist, the lady who thinks there is too much advertising to children on television. For almost any identifiable type of behavior there is at least the possibility of new insight when the behavior is viewed in the context of opinions, interests, and activities. Topics studied in this way include age and social class (Tigert, 1970), opinion leadership and information seeking (Reynolds and Darden, 1971), fashion interest and leadership (Summers, 1970), reactions to new product concepts (Nelson, 1971), furniture store choice and preferences for furniture styles (Good and Suchland, 1970) and Stone's concept of "shopping orientations" (Darden and Reynolds, 1971).

GETTING THE DATA

Since activity, interest, and opinion items are self-administering to literate respondents, data can be obtained through either personal contact or established mail panels. Personal contact permits probability samples. It can also, with enough effort, reach hard-to-find respondents like young single males, transients, hippies, and prisoners. For many purposes, however, established mail panels yield a satisfactory return at a good cost. Because activity, interest, and opinion questions are in general so very interesting to respondents, mail questionnaires as long as 25 pages have yielded usable returns from 75 to 80 per cent of mail panel samples.

Good items come from intuition, hunches, conversations with friends, other research, reading, head scratching, day dreaming, and group or individual narrative interviews. Appendix 1 is a list of items that came from these sources and from Wilson (1966), Pessemier and Tigert (1966), and a set of unpublished studies by Social Research, Inc. for MacFadden-Bartell Corporation. The items are grouped into "scales" through factor analysis.

INDIVIDUAL ITEMS VS. SCALES

The user of activity, interest, and opinion material has the option of employing a large, highly diversified collection of statements that cover as many different topics as possible, or of using a more limited number of multi-item scales. The multi-item scale approach is favored by psychometric tradition because properly constructed scales are invariably more reliable than individual items.

Unhappily, however, scales have four important disadvantages: (1) They limit coverage because they reduce the number of topics covered by any given number of items, and the longer the scales, the greater the reduction. (2) The shorthand of the scale name (e.g., "Credit User," "Fashion Conscious") encourages the analyst to think only in terms of the name rather than the richness of detail in the individual items. (3) Since scale items are never exact duplicates of each other, there are times when the scale as a whole correlates with some other variable but individual items do not, and there are times when individual items correlated with some other variable but the scale as a whole does not. Thus, the scale approach sometimes misses some potentially useful relationships. (4) Use of preestablished scales limits the findings to dimensions the analyst thought would be important, thereby precluding discovery of the unexpected.

The alternative is to throw a wide net and hope to catch something interesting, a practice sometimes disparagingly referred to as a fishing expedition. While this criticism should not be taken lightly, it should also be borne in mind that going on a fishing expedition is one of the best ways to catch fish. The items listed in Appendix 1, and the items cited in the examples, typify items that have worked well in past studies. An item

library too large for reproduction here is available from the authors.

FORCED CHOICE VS. SCALAR RESPONSES

As an alternative to having the respondent mark a scale position to indicate his answer, some analysts prefer to present two AIO statements and ask the respondent to indicate which he agrees with more. Others prefer to ask the respondent to rank a set of statements from most to least agreement. When carefully applied, these alternatives can help suppress the undesirable effects of "yeasaying," social desirability, and other troublesome response styles, and they force discrimination among items that might otherwise be marked at the same scale position. On the other hand, forced-choice and ranking questions are often difficult to administer and difficult for the respondent to handle, and analysis of the data presents certain sticky problems. Studies that used the forced choice approach successfully are described by Nelson (1969, 1971). The analysis problems are described by Hicks (1970).

CLINICAL VS. AIO VARIABLES

Some of the earliest attempts to use this sort of material in advertising and marketing research employed standardized inventories designed to measure general personality traits, with results that were usually somewhat disappointing (Evans, 1959; Westfall, 1962). Much of the later work has tended to move away from general personality traits toward variables that are more closely related to the behavior under consideration—homemaking activities and interests for household products, sociability items for cosmetics, and so on. As a result, it has often been found that significant relationships emerged where none had been found before, and it has often been easier to visualize uses for the relationships that were uncovered.

Nevertheless, the use of general personality traits has not been abandoned. Their value, especially when combined with activity, interest, and opinion items, is clearly demonstrated in studies by Nelson (1969) and Ziff (1971).

ANALYSES

When the sample is large and responses are well scattered, the simplest way to look at AIO material is ordinary cross-tabulation. For instance if the AIO scale has six steps, and the product use scale has seven, the relationship between each AIO and the product would appear in an ordinary 6x7 table.

But when the sample is small, or when either AIO or product responses are highly skewed, a 6 x 7 table will have many empty or nearly empty cells. In these common situations, it is best to condense the data beforehand by grouping scale steps to embrace reasonable numbers of respondents. When using a six-step scale, a strategy that usually works satisfactorily is to group steps 1-2, 3-4, 5-6.

If many relationships must be considered, for instance 100 products × 300 AIO items, the analyst who orders a complete cross-tabulation will find 30,000 tables on his desk before he can shut off the computer. One alternative is to order a product's × AIO's correlation matrix, and to have only those product-AIO correlations that are statistically significant cross-tabulated. This strategy may throw away some significant and potentially interesting curvilinear relationships, but it avoids the stupefying effect of 30,000 tables. A more detailed description of this approach can be found in an article by Plummer (1971).

Once the significant relationships have been found, the problem is to organize and understand them. Here the analyst's skill, experience, and ingenuity come to work, just as they did in the analysis of motivation research interview data. Factor analysis is a great help. R factor analysis can help condense AIO data by putting related statements together into categories. Q factor analysis can further simplify the problem by grouping respondents into types with similar response patterns. Neither of these procedures is automatic or foolproof, however, and there is little danger that the computer will replace the experienced and insightful analyst in the bridge between data gathering and application.

APPLICATIONS

Here are three examples of the way relationships between products and AIO items have been turned into action. They are derived from real situations, but, for obvious reasons, they are heavily disguised.

A new car wax is a significant improvement over products now on the market. The plan is to present this new wax in the context of fantastic and futuristic space gadgetry, a product so much better than anything now available that it belongs in the twenty-first century. An examination of the AIO profile of the target group shows no special interest in the future, in fantasy, in science, or in space. Instead the potential customer appears to be preoccupied with the here and now, and to be most impressed by facts, by proof, by the testimony of others he trusts and by demonstration. The campaign is reoriented to take account of this disposition.

A product traditionally advertised in folksy, homey, small town settings is found to be most heavily used by young housewives with an AIO profile almost as swinging as that of the eye makeup user. This finding fosters consideration of new advertising, and produces recommendations for changes in promotion and packaging.

The advertising for a heavy duty floor cleaner has been emphasizing its ability to remove visible dirt such as mud, dog tracks, and spilled food. The AIO profile of the target group shows great concern about germs and odors, and unusual preoccupation with the appearance of surfaces. The recommendation is to place special emphasis on the product's germicidal qualities and to feature the shiny surface the product leaves when the job is finished.

Further examples of actual and potential uses of AIO material can be found in Husted and Pessemier (1971), Nelson (1971), Plummer (1971) and Tigert (1969, 1971).

CRITICISMS AND PROBLEMS

It has been said that the relationships between AIOs and products or media are merely surface manifestations of the more familiar, more "basic" demographics. The psychographic profile of the *Playboy* reader, for instance, might be thought of as merely a sign that *Playboy's* readers are young, relatively well-educated males. While this assertion is in part correct, two considerations suggest that it would be wrong to depend on demographics only.

First, two products with very similar demographic profiles sometimes turn out to have usefully different psychographic profiles. Fresh oranges and fresh lemons are one example, as noted later in this paper.

Second, a demographic bracket in itself means little unless one has a clear picture of its life style implications. Everyone has some idea of what it means to be a young mother with a college education, or a middle-aged male with a blue-collar job, but such designations can be richly supplemented by information about the activities, interests, and opinions that go with them. Plummer's (1971) study of bank charge card users shows explicitly how AIO data can produce results that did not emerge when only demographic data were available.

LOW CORRELATIONS

When expressed as product-moment correlations, the relationships between AIO items and products or media are low—often around .2, and seldom higher than .3 or .4. Thus, they do not "explain the variance" very well, even when put together in a prediction equation.

It should be remembered, however, that the variance "explained" is the variance in the behavior of individuals, not the variance in the average behavior of groups, so a product-moment correlation of .2 is deceptively small. Consider the following cross-tabulation table. The product-moment correlation is .2—4 per cent of the variance "explained"—yet the relationship is obviously meaningful.

This point has been discussed in detail by Bass, Tigert, and Lonsdale (1968), so it will not be belabored here. Perhaps it is sufficient to say that anyone who refuses to look at the relationships between AIOs and products, or AIOs and media, must also—to be consistent—refuse to look at the relationships between products or media and demographics, because the correlations are the same size, or smaller. Further, anyone who rejects the relationships between AIOs and products, or AIOs and media, must also reject the use of media selection models that depend upon relationships between media use and product use. These relationships, too, when expressed as product-moment correlations, are rarely higher than .3.

Table 1. Cross-Tabulation of Shortening Use and Degree of Agreement with "I Save Recipes from Newspapers and Magazines."*

	Once a Week or Less (286)	Few Times a Week (296)	Once a Day or More (204)
Definitely Agree	42%	52%	63%
Generally Agree	24%	25%	19%
Moderately Agree	20%	12%	14%
Moderately, Generally or Definitely Disagree	14%	11%	4%

To avoid small cell frequencies both variables are condensed by combining adjacent categories.

OVERLAPPING PORTRAITS

AIO portraits do not always differ as much as the portraits of the eye makeup user and the shortening user. Many cosmetics are much alike. The heavy user of sugar looks like the heavy user of shortening and heavy user of flour. These overlaps occur because products themselves overlap, forming families that denote life styles (Wells, 1968).

But even similar portraits sometimes show useful differences, like the differences between heavy users of fresh oranges and heavy users of fresh lemons. Both groups of respondents show a strong interest in cooking and baking, especially with unusual recipes. Both also show unusual interest in community activities. However, the heavy user of fresh oranges, but *not* the heavy user of fresh lemons is distinguished by a strong need for cleanliness: "A house should be dusted and polished at least three times a week." "It is very important for people to brush their teeth at least five times a day." "Odors in the house embarrass me." The heavy user of fresh lemons but *not* the heavy user of fresh oranges, is distinguished by an unusual interest in fresh air and exercise: "I love the fresh air and out-of-doors." "I bowl, play tennis, golf or other active sports quite often." And the heavy user of fresh oranges, but *not* the heavy user of fresh lemons, indicates she is a bargain hunter: "I usually watch the advertisements for announcements of sales," and "I'm not a penny-pincher but I love to shop for bargains."

Thus, the two groups are much alike, but they also differ along interesting and actionable dimensions.

ARE HEAVY USERS ALL ALIKE?

Certain products may be heavily used for two or more quite different purposes. For instance, mouthwash may be used as a precaution against colds, or as a cosmetic. Since the cold user and the cosmetic user have very different life styles (Nelson, 1969), the picture presented by "the heavy user" will be a jumble of the two. It is important to be aware of this possibility and to separate users into subgroups whenever there is reason to suspect that the product plays a variety of roles.

THIN PRODUCTS

Not all products correlate significantly with a large number of activity, interest, and opinion items. In one typical study, of 127 products, 32 correlated significantly with fewer than ten of the 300 AIO items, 67 correlated significantly with more than 10 but fewer than 30, and 35 correlated significantly with more than 30. Since portraits provided by fewer than 10 correlations are usually not very helpful, a general rule of thumb would be that the chances of drawing a blank are about one in four.

It is hard to know why some products are so "thin." It is not because "rich" products are used by small, way-out segments of the population, while "thin" products are used by people in general. Instant coffee, cat food, laxatives, and cold cereal have all show few AIO associations; laundry detergent, stomach remedies, gasoline, and floor wax have shown many. The potential user should be aware that "rich" results are not automatic.

THE FUTURE

In a recent issue of the *Journal of Marketing Research*, James Benson, chairman of Ogilvy and Mather, was quoted: "There is more similarity between the consumer in New England and the consumer in Old England than there is between the consumer in New England and the consumer in New Orleans. Increasingly, markets will need to be segmented more on psychological, social and attitudinal criteria than on the traditional bases of geography and demography."

Partly as a result of such urging, the use of psychographics and related techniques is gaining considerable momentum. A substantial number of large scale proprietary studies have been conducted, with enough success that at least some of the sponsors have come back to ask for more. The approach has sparked interest among academic researchers, and papers on it or using it are beginning to appear.

The danger, of course, is that this somewhat novel way of sizing up consumers will be oversold, and that users will be disappointed when it does not turn out magic answers to all conceivable questions. Readers who respond "definitely agree" to the statement, "Most people have a lot of common sense," will hope that that won't happen.

References

Bass, Frank M., Douglas J. Tigert, and Richard T. Lonsdale. Market Segmentation: Group Versus Individual Behavior. *Journal of Marketing Research*, Vol. 5, No. 3, August 1968, pp. 264-70.

Darden, William R. and Fred D. Reynolds. Mutually Adaptive Effects of the Interpersonal Communication. *Journal of Marketing Research*. November 1971, pp. 449-54.

Evans, Franklin B. Psychological and Objective Factors in the Prediction of Brand Choice: Ford vs. Chevrolet. *Journal of Business*, Vol. 32, October 1959, pp. 340-369.

Good, Walter S. and Otto Suchsland. Consumer Life Styles and Their Relationship to Market Behavior Regarding Household Furniture. Research Bulletin, No. 26, Michigan State University, 1970.

Hicks, Lou E. Some Properties of Ipsative, Normative, and Forced Choice Measures. *Psychological Bulletin*, Vol. 74, No. 3, pp. 167-184.

Husted, Thomas P. and Edgar A. Pessemier. Segmenting Consumer Markets with Activity and Attitude Measures. Paper No. 298, Institute for Research in the Behavioral, Economic and Management Sciences, Krannert Graduate School of Industrial Administration, Purdue University, March, 1971.

Nelson, Allan R. A National Study of Psychographics. Paper presented at the 52nd International Marketing Congress, American Marketing Association, Atlanta, Georgia, June, 1969.

Nelson, Alan R. New Psychographics: Action-Creating Ideas, Not Lifeless Statistics. *Advertising Age*, June 28, 1971, pp. 1, 34.

Pessemier, Edgar A. and Douglas J. Tigert. In J. S. Wright and J. L. Goldstucker (Eds.) *New Ideas for Successful Marketing*, Chicago, Ill.: American Marketing Association, 1966.

Plummer, Joseph T. Life Style and Advertising: Case Studies. Paper given at 54th Annual International Marketing Congress, American Marketing Association, San Francisco, California, April, 1971.

Plummer, Joseph T. Life Style Patterns and Commercial Bank Credit Card Usage. *Journal of Marketing*, Vol. 35, No. 2, pp. 35-41.

Reynolds, Fred D. and William R. Darden. Mutually Adaptive Effects of Interpersonal Communication. *Journal of Marketing Research.* Forthcoming, 1971.

Summers, John O. The Identity of Women's Clothing Fashion Opinion Leaders. *Journal of Marketing Research*, Vol. 7, 1970, pp. 178-185.

Tigert, Douglas J. Life Style Correlates of Age and Social Class. Paper presented at the first annual meeting of the Association for Consumer Research, Amherst, Mass., August, 1970.

Tigert, Douglas J. A Psychographic Profile of Magazine Audiences: An Investigation of a Media's Climate. Paper presented at the American Marketing Association Consumer Behavior Workshop, Ohio State University, Columbus, Ohio, 1969.

Wells, William D. In J. Arndt (Ed.) *Insights into Consumer Behavior.* New York: Allyn and Bacon, 1968.

Westfall, Ralph. Psychological Factors in Predicting Product Choice. *Journal of Marketing*, Vol. 26, April 1962, pp. 34-50.

Wilson, Clark C. In J. S. Wright and J. L. Goldstucker (Eds.) *New Ideas for Successful Marketing*, Chicago, Ill.: American Marketing Association, 1966.

Ziff, Ruth. Psychographics for Market Segmentation. *Journal of Advertising Research*, Vol. 11, No. 2, pp. 3-9.

APPENDIX 1

Price Conscious

I shop a lot for "specials."

I find myself checking the prices in the grocery store even for small items.

I usually watch the advertisements for announcements of sales.

A person can save a lot of money by shopping around for bargains.

Fashion Conscious

I usually have one or more outfits that are of the very latest style.

When I must choose between the two I usually dress for fashion, not for comfort.

An important part of my life and activities is dressing smartly.

I often try the latest hairdo styles when they change.

Child Oriented

When my children are ill in bed I drop most everything else in order to see to their comfort.

My children are the most important thing in my life.

I try to arrange my home for my children's convenience.

I take a lot of time and effort to teach my children good habits.

Compulsive Housekeeper

I don't like to see children's toys lying about.

I usually keep my house very neat and clean.

I am uncomfortable when my house is not completely clean.

Our days seem to follow a definite routine such as eating meals at a regular time, etc.

Dislikes Housekeeping

I must admit I really don't like household chores

I find cleaning my house an unpleasant task.

I enjoy most forms of housework. (Reverse score

My idea of housekeeping is "once over lightly."

Sewer

I like to sew and frequently do.

I often make my own or my children's clothes.

You can save a lot of money by making your own clothes.

I would like to know how to sew like an expert.

Homebody

I would rather spend a quiet evening at home than go out to a party.

I like parties where there is lots of music and talk. (Reverse scored)

I would rather go to a sporting event than a dance.

I am a homebody.

Community Minded

I am an active member of more than one service organization.

I do volunteer work for a hospital or service organization on a fairly regular basis.

I like to work on community projects.

I have personally worked in a political campaign or for a candidate or an issue.

Credit User

I buy many things with a credit card or a charge card.

I like to pay cash for everything I buy. (Reverse scored)

It is good to have charge accounts.

To buy anything, other than a house or a car, on credit is unwise. (Reverse scored)

Sports Spectator

I like to watch or listen to baseball or football games.

I usually read the sports page in the daily paper.

I thoroughly enjoy conversations about sports.

I would rather go to a sporting event than a dance.

Cook

I love to cook.

I am a good cook.

I love to bake and frequently do.

I am interested in spices and seasonings.

Self-Confident

I think I have more self-confidence than most people.

I am more independent than most people.

I think I have a lot of personal ability.

I like to be considered a leader.

Self-Designated Opinion Leader

My friends or neighbors often come to me for advice.

I sometimes influence what my friends buy.

People come to me more often than I go to them for information about brands.

Information Seeker

I often seek out the advice of my friends regarding which brand to buy.

I spend a lot of time talking with my friends about products and brands.

My neighbors or friends usually give me good advice on what brands to buy in the grocery store.

New Brand Tryer

When I see a new brand on the shelf I often buy it just to see what it's like.

I often try new brands before my friends and neighbors do.

I like to try new and different things.

Satisfied with Finances

Our family income is high enough to satisfy nearly all our important desires.

No matter how fast our income goes up we never seem to get ahead. (Reverse scored)

I wish we had a lot more money. (Reverse scored)

Canned Food User

I depend on canned food for at least one meal a day.

I couldn't get along without canned foods.

Things just don't taste right if they come out of a can. (Reverse scored)

Dieter

During the warm weather I drink low calorie soft drinks several times a week.

I buy more low calorie foods than the average housewife.

I have used Metrecal or other diet foods at least one meal a day.

Financial Optimist

I will probably have more money to spend next year than I have now.

Five years from now the family income will probably be a lot higher than it is now.

Wrapper

Food should never be left in the refrigerator uncovered.

Leftovers should be wrapped before being put into the refrigerator.

Wide Horizons

I'd like to spend a year in London or Paris.

I would like to take a trip around the world.

Arts Enthusiast

I enjoy going through an art gallery.

I enjoy going to concerts.

I like ballet.

14
A MODEL OF INDUSTRIAL BUYER BEHAVIOR

Jagdish N. Sheth
Professor of Business
University of Illinois

Although industrial market research has generated large data banks on organizational buyers, not enough of the data seems helpful to management. What is needed, a noted professor maintains, is better understanding of the *process* of industrial buying decisions.

The purpose of this article is to describe a model of industrial (organizational) buyer behavior. Considerable knowledge on organizational buyer behavior already exists[1] and can be classified into three categories. The first category includes a considerable amount of systematic empirical research on the buying policies and practices of purchasing agents and other organizational buyers.[2] The second includes industry reports and observations of industrial buyers.[3] Finally, the third category consists of books, monographs, and articles which analyze, theorize, model, and sometimes report on industrial buying activities.[4] What is now needed is a reconciliation and integration of existing knowledge into a realistic and comprehensive model of organizational buyer behavior.

It is hoped that the model described in this article will be useful in the following ways: first, to broaden the vision of research on organizational buyer behavior so that it includes the most salient

From Jagdish N. Sheth, "A Model of Industrial Buyer Behavior," Journal of Marketing, October 1973, pp. 50-56. Published by the American Marketing Association Reprinted by permission of the publisher.

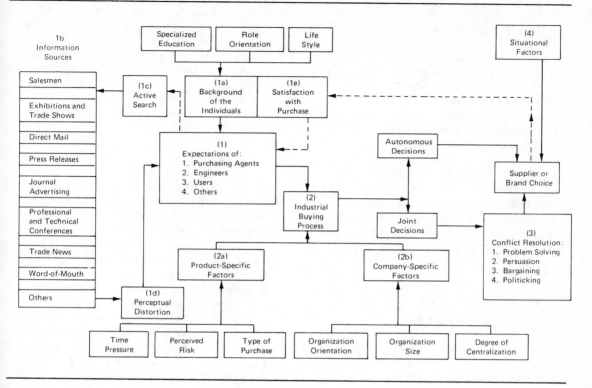

Figure 1. An Integrative Model of Industrial Buyer Behavior.

elements and their interactions; second, to act as a catalyst for building marketing information systems from the viewpoint of the industrial buyer; and, third, to generate new hypotheses for future research on fundamental processes underlying organizational buyer behavior.

A DESCRIPTION OF INDUSTRIAL BUYER BEHAVIOR

The model of industrial buyer behavior is summarized in Figure 1. Although this illustrative presentation looks complex due to the large number of variables and complicated relationships among them, this is because it is a generic model which attempts to describe and explain all types of industrial buying decisions. One can, however, simplify the actual application of the model in a specific study in at least two ways. First, several

variables are included as conditions to hold constant differences among types of products to be purchased (product-specific factors) and differences among types of purchasing organizations. These exogenous factors will not be necessary if the objective of a study is to describe the process of buying behavior for a specific product or service. Second, some of the decision-process variables can also be ignored if the interest is strictly to conduct a survey of static measurement of the psychology of the organizational buyers. For example, perceptual bias and active search variables may be eliminated if the interest is not in the process of communication to the organizational buyers.

This model is similar to the Howard-Sheth model of buyer behavior in format and classification of variables.[5] However, there are several significant differences. First, while the Howard-Sheth model is more general and probably more useful in consumer behavior, the model described in this article is limited to organizational buying alone. Second, the Howard-Sheth model is limited to the individual decision-making process, whereas this model explicitly describes the joint decision-making process. Finally, there are fewer variables in this model than in the Howard-Sheth model of buyer behavior.

Organizational buyer behavior consists of three distinct aspects. The first aspect is the psychological world of the individuals involved in organizational buying decisions. The second aspect relates to the conditions which precipitate joint decisions among these individuals. The final aspect is the process of joint decision making with the inevitable conflict among the decision makers and its resolution by resorting to a variety of tactics.

PSYCHOLOGICAL WORLD OF THE DECISION MAKERS

Contrary to popular belief, many industrial buying decisions are not solely in the hands of purchasing agents.[6] Typically in an industrial setting, one finds that there are at least three departments whose members are continuously involved in different phases of the buying process. The most common are the personnel from the purchasing, quality control, and manufacturing departments. These individuals are identified in the model as purchasing agents, engineers, and users, respectively. Several other individuals in the organization may be, but are typically not, involved in the buying process (for example, the president of the firm or the comptroller). There is considerable interaction among the individuals in the three departments continuously involved in the buying process and often they are asked to decide jointly. It is, therefore, critical to examine the similarities and differences in the psychological worlds of these individuals.

Based on research in consumer and social psychology, several different aspects of the psychology of the decision makers are included in the model. Primary among these are the *expectations* of the decision makers about suppliers and brands ((1) in Figure 1). The present model specifies five different processes which create

differential expectations among the individuals involved in the purchasing process: (1a) *the background of the individuals,* (1b) *information sources,* (1c) *active search,* (1d) *perceptual distortion,* and (1e) *satisfaction with past purchases.* These variables must be explained and operationally defined if they are to fully represent the psychological world of the organizational buyers.

Expectations

Expectations refer to the *perceived* potential of alternative suppliers and brands to satisfy a number of explicit and implicit objectives in any particular buying decision. The most common explicit objectives include, in order of relative importance, product quality, delivery time, quantity of supply, after-sale service where appropriate, and price.[7] However, a number of studies have pointed out the critical role of several implicit criteria such as reputation, size, location, and reciprocity relationship with the supplier; and personality, technical expertise, salesmanship, and even life style of the sales representative.[8] In fact, with the standardized marketing mix among the suppliers in oligopolistic markets, the implicit criteria are becoming marginally more and more significant in the industrial buyer's decisions.

Expectations can be measured by obtaining a profile of each supplier or brand as to how satisfactory it is perceived to be in enabling the decision maker to achieve his explicit and implicit objectives. Almost all studies from past research indicate that expectations will substantially differ among the purchasing agents, engineers, and product users because each considers different criteria to be salient in judging the supplier or the brand. In general, it is found that product users look for prompt delivery, proper installation, and efficient serviceability; purchasing agents look for maximum price advantage and economy in shipping and forwarding; and engineers look for excellence in quality, standardization of the product, and engineering pretesting of the product. These differences in objectives and, consequently, expectations are often the root causes for constant conflict among these three types of individuals.[9]

Why are there substantial differences in expectations? While there is considerable speculation among researchers and observers of industrial buyer behavior on the number and nature of explanations, there is relatively little consensus. The five most salient processes which determine differential expectations, as specified in the model, are discussed below.

Background of Individuals   The first, and probably most significant, factor is the background and task orientation of each of the individuals involved in the buying process. The different educational backgrounds of the purchasing agents, engineers, and plant managers often generate substantially different professional goals and values. In addition, the task expectations also generate conflicting perceptions of one anothers's role in the organization. Finally, the personal life styles of individual decision makers play an important role in developing differential expectations.[10]

It is relatively easy to gather information on this background factor. The educational and task differences are comparable to demographics in consumer behavior, and life-style differences can be assessed by psychographic scales on the individual's interests, activities, and values as a professional.

Information Sources and Active Search The second and third factors in creating differential expectations are the source and type of information each of the decision makers is exposed to and his participation in the active search. Purchasing agents receive disproportionately greater exposure to commercial sources, and the information is often partial and biased toward the supplier or the brand. In some companies, it is even a common practice to discourage sales representatives from talking directly to the engineering or production personnel. The engineering and production personnel, therefore, typically have less information and what they have is obtained primarily from professional meetings, trade reports, and even word-of-mouth. In addition, the active search for information is often relegated to the purchasing agents because it is presumed to be their job responsibility.

It is not too difficult to assess differences among the three types of individuals in their exposure to various sources and types of information by standard survey research methods.

Perceptual Distortion   A fourth factor is the selective distortion and retention of available information. Each individual strives to make the objective information consistent with his own prior knowledge and expectations by systematically distorting it. For example, since there are substantial differences in the goals and values of purchasing agents, engineers, and production personnel, one should expect different interpretations of the same information among them. Although no specific research has been done on this tendency to perceptually distort information in the area of industrial buyer behavior, a large body of research does exist on cognitive consistency to explain its presence as a natural human tendency.[11]

Perceptual distortion is probably the most difficult variable to quantify by standard survey research methods. One possible approach is experimentation, but this is costly. A more realistic alternative is to utilize perceptual mapping techniques such as multidimensional scaling or factor analysis and compare differences in the judgments of the purchasing agents, engineers, and production personnel to a common list of suppliers or brands.

Satisfaction with Past Purchases   The fifth factor which creates differential expectations among the various individuals involved in the purchasing process is the satisfaction with past buying experiences with a supplier or brand. Often it is not possible for a supplier or brand to provide equal satisfaction to the three parties because each one has different goals or criteria. For example, a supplier may be lower in price but his delivery schedule may not be satisfactory. Similarly, a product's quality may be excellent but its price may be higher than others. The organization typically rewards each individual for excellent performance in his specialized skills, so the purchasing agent is rewarded for economy, the engineer for quality control, and the production personnel for efficient scheduling. This often results in a different level of satisfaction for each of the parties involved even though the chosen supplier or brand may be the best feasible alternative in terms of overall corporate goals.

Past experiences with a supplier or brand, summarized in the satisfaction variable, directly influence the person's expectations toward that supplier or brand. It is relatively easy to measure the satisfaction variable by obtaining information on how the supplier or brand is perceived by each of the three parties.

DETERMINANTS OF JOINT vs. AUTONOMOUS DECISIONS

Not all industrial buying decisions are made jointly by the various individuals involved in the purchasing process. Sometimes the buying decisions are delegated to one party, which is not necessarily the purchasing agent. It is, therefore, important for the supplier to know whether a buying decision is joint or autonomous and, if it is the latter, to which party it is delegated. There are six primary factors which determine whether a specific buying decision will be joint or autonomous. Three of these factors are related to the characteristics of the product or service (2a) and the other three are related to the characteristics of the buyer company (2b).

Product-Specific Factors

The first product-specific variable is what Bauer calls *perceived risk* in buying decisions.[12] Perceived risk refers to the magnitude of adverse consequences felt by the decision maker if he makes a wrong choice, and the uncertainty under which he must decide. The greater the uncertainty in a buying situation, the greater the perceived risk. Although there is very little direct evidence, it is logical to hypothesize that the greater the perceived risk in a specific buying decision, the more likely it is that the purchase will be decided jointly by all parties concerned. The second product-specific factor is *type of purchase*. If it is the first purchase or a once-in-a-lifetime capital expenditure, one would expect greater joint decision making. On the other hand, if the purchase decision is repetitive and routine or is limited to maintenance products or services, the buying decision is likely to be delegated to one party. The third factor is *time pressure*. If the buying decision has to be made under a great deal of time pressure or on an emergency basis, it is likely to be delegated to one party rather than decided jointly.

Company-Specific Factors

The three organization-specific factors are *company orientation, company size,* and *degree of centralization.* If the company is technology oriented, it is likely to be dominated by the engineering people and the buying decisions will, in essence, be made by them. Similarly, if the company is production oriented, the buying decisions will be made by the production personnel.[13] Second, if the company is a large corporation, decision making will tend to be joint. Finally, the greater the degree of centralization, the less likely it is that the decisions will be joint. Thus, a privately-owned small company with technology or production orientation will tend toward autonomous decision making and a large-scale public corporation with considerable decentralization will tend to have greater joint decision making.

Even though there is considerable research evidence in organization behavior in general to support these six factors, empirical evidence in industrial buying decisions in particular is sketchy on them. Perhaps with more research it will be possible to verify the generalizations and deductive logic utilized in this aspect of the model.

PROCESS OF JOINT DECISION MAKING

The major thrust of the present model of industrial buying decisions is to investigate the process of joint decision making. This includes initiation of the decision to buy, gathering of information, evaluating alternative suppliers, and resolving conflict among the parties who must jointly decide.

The decision to buy is usually initiated by a continued need of supply or is the outcome of long-range planning. The formal initiation in the first case is typically from the production personnel by way of a requisition slip. The latter usually is a formal recommendation from the planning unit to an ad hoc committee consisting of the purchasing agent, the engineer, and the plant manager. The information-gathering function is typically relegated to the purchasing agent. If the purchase is a repetitive decision for standard item there is very little information gathering. Usually the purchasing agent contacts the preferred supplier and orders the items on the requisition slip. However, considerable active search effort is manifested for capital expenditure items, especially those which are entirely new purchase experiences for the organization.[14]

The most important aspect of the joint decision-making process, however, is the assimilation of information, deliberations on it, and the consequent conflict which most joint decisions entail. According to March and Simon, conflict is present when there is a need to decide jointly among a group of people who have, at the same time, different goals and perceptions.[15] In view of the fact that the latter is invariably present among the various parties to industrial buying decisions, conflict becomes a common consequence of the joint decision-making process; the buying motives and expectations about brands and suppliers are considerably different for the engineer, the user, and the purchasing agent, partly due to different educational backgrounds and partly due to company policy of reward for specialized skills and viewpoints.

Interdepartmental conflict in itself is not necessarily bad. What matters most from the organization's viewpoint is *how* the conflict is resolved (3). If it is resolved in a rational manner, one very much hopes that the final joint decision will also tend to be rational. If, on the other hand, conflict resolution degenerates to what Strauss calls "tactics of lateral relationship,"[16] the organization will suffer from inefficiency and the joint decisions may be reduced to bargaining and politicking among the parties involved. Not only will the decision be based on irrational criteria, but the choice of a supplier may be to the detriment of the buying organization.

What types of conflict can be expected in industrial buying decisions? How are they likely to be resolved? These are some of the key questions in an understanding of industrial buyer behavior. If the inter-party conflict is largely due to disagreements on expectations about the suppliers or their brands, it is likely that the conflict will be resolved in the *problem-solving* manner. The immediate consequence of this type of conflict is to actively search for more information,

deliberate more on available information, and often to seek out other suppliers not seriously considered before. The additional information is then presented in a problem-solving fashion so that conflict tends to be minimized.

If the conflict among the parties is primarily due to disagreement on some specific criteria with which to evaluate suppliers—although there is an agreement on the buying goals or objectives at a more fundamental level—it is likely to be resolved by *persuasion*. An attempt is made, under this type of resolution, to persuade the dissenting member by pointing out the importance of overall corporate objectives and how his criterion is not likely to attain these objectives. There is no attempt to gather more information. However, there results greater interaction and communication among the parties, and sometimes an outsider is brought in to reconcile the differences.

Both problem solving and persuasion are useful and rational methods of conflict resolution. The resulting joint decisions, therefore, also tend to be more rational. Thus, conflicts produced due to disagreements on expectations about the suppliers or on a specific criterion are healthy from the organization's viewpoint even though they may be time consuming. One is likely to find, however, that a more typical situation in which conflict arises is due to fundamental differences in buying goals or objectives among the various parties. This is especially true with respect to unique or new buying decisions related to capital expenditure items. The conflict is resolved not by changing the differences in relative importance of the buying goals or objectives of the individuals involved, but by the process of *bargaining*. The fundamental differences among the parties are implicitly conceded by all the members and the concept of distributive justice (tit for tat) is invoked as a part of bargaining. The most common outcome is to allow a single party to decide autonomously in this specific situation in return for some favor or promise of reciprocity in future decisions.

Finally, if the disagreement is not simply with respect to buying goals or objectives but also with respect to *style of decision making*, the conflict tends to be grave and borders on the mutual dislike of personalities among the individual decision makers. The resolution of this type of conflict is usually by *politicking* and back-stabbing tactics. Such methods of conflict resolution are common in industrial buying decisions. The reader is referred to the sobering research of Strauss for further discussion.[17]

Both bargaining and politicking are non-rational and inefficient methods of conflict resolution; the buying organization suffers from these conflicts. Furthermore, the decision makers find themselves sinking below their professional, managerial role. The decisions are not only delayed but tend to be governed by factors other than achievement of corporate objectives.

CRITICAL ROLE OF SITUATIONAL FACTORS

The model described so far presumes that the choice of a supplier or brand is the outcome of a systematic decision-making process in the organizational setting. However, there is ample empirical evidence in the literature to suggest that at least some of the industrial buying decisions are determined by ad hoc *situational factors* (4) and not by any systematic decision-making process. In other words, similar to consumer behavior, the industrial buyers often decide on factors other than rational or realistic criteria.

It is difficult to prepare a list of ad hoc conditions which determine industrial buyer behavior without decision making. However, a number of situational factors which often intervene between the actual choice and any prior decision-making process can be isolated. These include: temporary economic conditions such as price controls, recession, or foreign trade; internal strikes, walkouts, machine breakdowns, and other production-related events; organizational changes such as merger or acquisition; and ad hoc changes in the marketplace, such as promotional efforts, new product introduction, price changes, and so on, in the supplier industries.

IMPLICATIONS FOR INDUSTRIAL MARKETING RESEARCH

The model of industrial buyer behavior described above suggests the following implications for marketing research.

First, in order to explain and predict supplier or brand choice in industrial buyer behavior, it is necessary to conduct research on the psychology of other individuals in the organization in addition to the purchasing agents. It is, perhaps, the unique nature of organizational structure and behavior which leads to a distinct separation of the consumer, the buyer, and the procurement agent, as well as others possibly involved in the decision-making process. In fact, it may not be an exaggeration to suggest that the purchasing agent is often a less critical member of the decision-making process in industrial buyer behavior.

Second, it is possible to operationalize and quantify most of the variables included as part of the model. While some are more difficult and indirect, sufficient psychometric skill in marketing research is currently available to quantify the psychology of the individuals.

Third, although considerable research has been done on the demographics of organizations in industrial market research—for example, on the turnover and size of the company, workflows, standard industrial classification, and profit ratios—demographic and life-style information on the individuals involved in industrial buying decisions is also needed.

Fourth, a systematic examination of the power positions of various individuals involved in industrial buying decisions is a necessary condition of the model. The sufficient condition is to examine trade-offs among various objectives, both explicit and implicit, in order to create a satisfied customer.

Fifth, it is essential in building any market research information system for industrial goods and services that the process of conflict resolution among the parties and its impact on supplier or brand choice behavior is carefully included and simulated.

Finally, it is important to realize that not all industrial decisions are the outcomes of a systematic decision-making process. There are some industrial buying decisions which are based strictly on a set of situational factors for which theorizing or model building will not be relevant or useful. What is needed in these cases is a checklist of empirical observations of the ad hoc events which vitiate the neat relationship between the theory or the model and a specific buying decision.

Notes

1. For a comprehensive list of references, see Thomas A. Staudt and W. Lazer, *A Basic Bibliography on Industrial Marketing* (Chicago: American Marketing Assn., 1963); and Donald E. Vinson, "Bibliography of Industrial Marketing" (unpublished listing of references, University of Colorado, 1972).
2. Richard M. Cyert, et al., "Observation of a Business Decision," *Journal of Business*, Vol. 29 (October 1956), pp. 237-248; John A. Howard and C. G. Moore, Jr., "A Descriptive Model of the Purchasing Agent" (unpublished monograph, University of Pittsburgh, 1964); George Strauss, "Work Study of Purchasing Agents," *Human Organization*, Vol. 33 (September 1964), pp. 137-149; Theodore A. Levitt, *Industrial Purchasing Behavior* (Boston: Division of Research, Graduate School of Business, Harvard University, 1965); Ozanne B. Urban and Gilbert A. Churchill, "Adoption Research: Information Sources in the Industrial Purchasing Decision," and Richard N. Cardozo, "Segmenting the Industrial Market," in *Marketing and the New Science of Planning*, R. L. King, ed. (Chicago: American Marketing Assn., 1968), pp. 352-359 and 433-440, respectively. Richard N. Cardozo and J. W. Cagley, "Experimental Study of Industrial Buyer Behavior," *Journal of Marketing Research*, Vol. 8 (August 1971), pp. 329-334; Thomas P. Copley and F. L. Callom, "Industrial Search Behavior and Perceived Risk," in *Proceedings of the Second Annual Conference, the Association for Consumer Research*, D. M. Gardner, ed. (College Park, Md.: Association for Consumer Research, 1971), pp. 208-231; and James R. McMillan, "Industrial Buying Behavior as Group Decision Making," (paper presented at the Nineteenth International Meeting of the Institute of Management Sciences, April 1972).
3. Robert F. Shoaf, ed., *Emotional Factors Underlying Industrial Purchasing* (Cleveland, Ohio: Penton Publishing Co., 1959); G. H. Haas, B. March, and E. M. Krech, *Purchasing Department Organization and Authority*, American Management Assn. Research Study No. 45 (New York: 1960); *Evaluation of Supplier Performance* (New York: National Association of Purchasing Agents, 1963); F. A. Hays and G. A. Renard, *Evaluating Purchasing Performance*, American Management Assn. Research Study No. 66

(New York: 1964); Hugh Buckner, *How British Industry Buys* (London: Hutchison and Company, Ltd., 1967); *How Industry Buys/1970* (New York: Scientific American, 1970). In addition, numerous articles published in trade journals such as *Purchasing and Industrial Marketing* are cited in Vinson, same reference as footnote 1, and Strauss, same reference as footnote 2.
4. Ralph S. Alexander, J. S. Cross, and R. M. Hill, *Industrial Marketing*, 3rd ed. (Homewood, Ill.: Richard D. Irwin, 1967); John H. Westing, I. V. Fine, and G. J. Zenz, *Purchasing Management* (New York: John Wiley & Sons, 1969); Patrick J. Robinson, C. W. Farris, and Y. Wind, *Industrial Buying and Creative Marketing* (Boston: Allyn & Bacon, 1967); Frederick E. Webster, Jr., "Modeling the Industrial Buying Process," *Journal of Marketing Research*, Vol. 2 (November 1965), pp. 370-376; and Frederick E. Webster, Jr., "Industrial Buying Behavior: A State-of-the-Art Appraisal," in *Marketing in a Changing World*, B. A. Morin, ed. (Chicago: American Marketing Assn., 1969), p. 256.
5. John A. Howard and J. N. Sheth, *The Theory of Buyer Behavior* (New York: John Wiley & Sons, 1969).
6. Howard and Moore, same reference as footnote 2; Strauss, same reference as footnote 2; McMillan, same reference as footnote 2; *How Industry Buys/1970*, same reference as footnote 3.
7. Howard and Moore, same reference as footnote 2; *How Industry Buys/1970*, same reference as footnote 3; Hays and Renard, same reference as footnote 3.
8. Howard and Moore, same reference as footnote 2; Levitt, same reference as footnote 2; Westing, Fine, and Zenz, same reference as footnote 4; Shoaf, same reference as footnote 4.
9. Strauss, same reference as footnote 2.
10. For a general reading, see Robert T. Golembiewski, "Small Groups and Large Organizations," in *Handbook of Organizations*, J. G. March, ed. (Chicago: Rand McNally & Company, 1965), chapter 3. For field studies related to this area, see Donald E. Porter, P. B. Applewhite, and M. J. Misshauk, eds., *Studies in Organizational Behavior and Management*, 2nd ed. (Scranton, Pa.: Intext Educational Publishers, 1971).
11. Robert P. Abelson, et. al., *Theories of Cognitive Consistency: A Source Book* (Chicago: Rand McNally & Company, 1968).
12. Raymond A. Bauer, "Consumer Behavior as Risk Taking," in *Dynamic Marketing for a Changing World*, R. L. Hancock, ed. (Chicago: American Marketing Assn., 1960), pp. 389-400. Applications of perceived risk

in industrial buying can be found in Levitt, same reference as footnote 2; Copley and Callom, same reference as footnote 2; McMillan, same reference as footnote 2.

13. For some indirect evidence, see Strauss, same reference as footnote 2. For a more general study, see Victor A. Thompson, "Hierarchy, Specialization and Organizational Conflict," *Administrative Science Quarterly*, Vol. 5 (March 1961), p. 513; and Henry A. Landsberger, "The Horizontal Dimension in Bureaucracy," *Administration Science Quarterly*, Vol. 6 (December 1961), pp. 299-332, for a thorough review of numerous theories.

14. Strauss, same reference as footnote 2.

15. James G. March and H. A. Simon, *Organizations* (New York: John Wiley & Sons, 1958), chapter 5; and Landsberger, same reference as footnote 13.

16. George Strauss, "Tactics of Lateral Relationship: The Purchasing Agent," *Administrative Science Quarterly*, Vol. 7 (September 1962), pp. 161-186.

17. Same reference as footnote 16.

15 EXPANDING THE SCOPE OF SEGMENTATION RESEARCH

Nariman K. Dhalla
Associate Research Director
J. Walter Thompson Company

Winston H. Mahatoo
Professor of Marketing
MacMaster University, Ontario, Canada

Segmenting the market groups can be more meaningful if the total marketing problem is taken into account, say these authors. In this way, segmentation research will be both operational and profitable.

Market segmentation helps the firm gear a specific product to the likes or requirements of a particular target group. For many companies, it is far better to capture bigger pieces of fewer markets than to scramble about for a smaller share of every market in sight.

The segmentation concept would be more meaningful to management if research were to cover the entire scope of the problem. This means the inclusion in the initial survey of product-specific measures on both psychographics and communications behavior in addition to the standard attitudinal and usage data. After the segments have been selected, a second-phase research should be conducted to estimate the response elasticities of different submarkets to the firm's communica-

From Nariman K. Dhalla and Winston H. Mahatoo, "Expanding the Scope of Segmentation Research," Journal of Marketing 40 (April 1976), pp. 33-41. Reprinted by permission of Journal of Marketing.

tion mix. In this way, management will be in a firm position to evaluate the profitability of the segmentation strategy.

Most of the research undertaken at present does not adopt this two-fold approach. Even the initial survey is often unsatisfactory. In some cases, the criteria employed for grouping consumers are so general that they cannot discriminate among users of various brands within a product category. In other cases, these bases are so specific that they ignore the different nuances of consumer behavior and thus are not very helpful for developing marketing strategies.

A brief review of the published literature on the subject brings these problems out clearly and sets the stage for a detailed discussion of the proposed two-phase approach. A case history from the food industry illustrates the usefulness of this procedure.

PITFALLS IN EXISTING METHODS

As a rule, markets have been divided on the basis of two types of descriptor variables:[1]

i.   *General variables*, which classify consumers by broad characteristics, such as demographics, personality traits, or life styles
2.   *Situation-specific variables*, which group consumers on some pattern related to consumption, such as frequency of usage, brand loyalty, product benefits, or "perceptual maps"

Although both types of variables have proved useful to marketers, they also have certain drawbacks, as discussed below.

General Variables

Demographics provided the earliest basis for segmentation. Because of the severe limitations of demographics, however, many marketers turned to psychology and began to apply some well-established clinical tests. The Edwards Personal Preference Schedule, the Gordon Personal Profile, the California Personality Inventory, MMPI, and Cattell's 16-Personality Factor Inventory, among

others, have all been used in a marketing context. The results have been disappointing.[2] These instruments were originally designed to measure major personality traits that underlie such psycho-social phenomena as racial prejudice, marital incompatibility, or proneness to commit suicide. It is a different story to use them to predict whether a shopper would buy a particular brand of toilet paper[3] or prefer a certain type of design on the package. The items that tend to discover psychological stability or imbalance do not have much relevance for mundane activities related to marketing.

Equally ineffective have been most attempts to use market-oriented sociological measures such as inner- and other-directedness,[4] self-actualization concepts,[5] cognitive needs and styles,[6] and activity-interest-opinion (AIO) items dealing with leisure, work, and consumption.[7] No doubt, the vast amount of research in these areas has led to deep insights into the basic processes of consumer behavior. In a majority of cases, however, the groups are far too broad to discriminate among users of different brands within a product category.

Sometimes such segments may even turn out to be misleading. A personality trait or a life-style measure in its generalized form may not be related at all to the product under consideration. A buyer may be price conscious in making routine decisions but will still purchase the most expensive brand of wine or perfume. Similarly, an individual may perceive himself to be aggressive and act as such in the office and at home, but he may never choose to express this aggressiveness in his driving behavior or in the type of car he buys.[8]

Situation-Specific Variables

Realizing the futility of adopting wholesale the concepts developed in the social sciences, marketing researchers recently have turned to certain situation-specific descriptors.

The segment that has the most intuitive appeal is the one that distinguishes between *heavy and light users*. But even here the findings have not been encouraging, because not all heavy consumers seek the same kinds of benefits from a product category. For example, heavy coffee drinkers can be divided into two groups: those who drink private brands because cost is an important factor, and those who drink premium brands because taste has greater significance. Obviously, these two groups, although they are both members of the "heavy half" segment, are not equally good prospects for any one brand; nor can they be expected to react favorably to the same advertising claims.[9] Similarly, some products may be heavily used for different reasons. For example, one segment uses a mouthwash to prevent sore throats, while another uses it to eliminate bad breath. Should the two groups have different life styles, the picture presented by the "heavy users" will be a mixture of the two.

Brand loyalty is another favored basis of segmentation, but its effectiveness is also reduced by confounding factors. Loyalty need not be based solely on high satisfaction with the brand. It may be due to sheer force of habit or to a desire to reduce risk associated with the purchase of unknown items.[10] Furthermore, instead of being confined to a single brand, it may extend to two or more brands in the consumer's "evoked set."[11] Because of this lack of within-segment homogeneity, it is not surprising to find that loyal customers do not, as a rule, differ from switchers either in their demographic and psychographic traits, or in their sensitivity to marketing strategies such as pricing, dealing, and retail advertising.[12]

In view of the lackluster performance of these "a priori" classifications, many researchers have turned to "natural" groupings by letting the figures speak for themselves. Thanks to the ready availability of computer software, multivariate methods can be used to extract segments latent in the data. *Benefit segmentation* is a good example of this approach. It uses statistical techniques to group respondents on the basis of the importance they attach to certain combinations of rational, sensory, and emotional benefits expected from the product.

This method is a great improvement over earlier attempts. On several occasions, it has proved valuable for developing new advertising copy or for suggesting alternative marketing strategy, such as the changes in product formulation.[13] Even here, however, the results are not always fruitful. By relying solely on natural groupings, the researcher runs the risk of arriving at purely spurious clusters, since most of the multivariate techniques are simply data-reducing tools and are not based on theoretical concepts of what the segments should look like. This is particularly true of low-salience, frequently purchased products. The brand-benefit profiles often are not sharp enough to permit successful segmentation analysis. Even when meaningful groups are extracted from the data, the benefits in most research studies are confined primarily to product attributes and do not cover the crucial areas of psychographics and communications behavior. Hence, one cannot be sure that a particular cluster selected will help increase sales.

Wilkie attempted to validate this method of segmentation using the Columbia University Buyer Behavior Panel.[14] He found that the classification based on intentions to buy predicted much better subsequent brand purchases than segments derived from the importance that consumers attached to certain sets of product characteristics.

Closely allied to benefit segmentation is *perception mapping*. Here a "map" is prepared of an individual's perceptions of competitive brands on certain product attributes. Then respondents with similar perceptual maps are grouped together. Finally, within each such group further segments are developed on the basis of preference scores. By combining both perceptual and preference data to analyze consumer behavior, the researcher can sometimes obtain unexpected insights into the psychological processes that consumers use for choosing brands.

Like benefit segmentation, however, this method has certain drawbacks. Frequently, the dimensions of the perceptual space cannot be easily interpreted. Also, the segments are derived from perceptions and prefernces, and they totally ignore psychographics and communications behavior. Consequently, there is no guarantee that a favorable sales response will result from the marketing strategy suggested by the mapping procedure.

AN ATTEMPT AT SYNTHESIS

The poor performance of many segmentation criteria tested so far can be attributed to the fact that too often researchers are anxious to find a magic formula that will profitably segment the market in all cases and under all circumstances. As with the medieval alchemists looking for the philosopher's stone, this search is bound to end in vain. There is no single algorithm that can be employed across all market studies. Each case must be viewed as a unique and potentially different situation.[15]

Broad Classifications

A well-designed segmentation study, therefore, does not depend solely on one criterion for grouping consumers. It is flexible enough that one can examine the results from two or more alternative bases. These bases are very general, and it is within them that the segments are later developed. The selection of such broad classifications is governed by conceptual considerations that have bearing on the product under investigation.

In many cases, the theories of attitude reinforcement and attitude change, as formulated by social psychologists, can be of help. Since an individual's reaction to a brand is primarily a function of his overall predisposition, one possible preliminary step would be to have a broad "a priori" classification based on some attitudinal range. The extensive work of Sherif, Sherif, and Nebergall in this area can be effectively used here.[16] Adapting their approach, it may be hypothesized that a buyer, in order to simplify his choice process, is likely to take any one of the following three positions with respect to the brand:

Latitude of acceptance

Latitude of rejection

Latitude of noncommitment

In the noncommitment category, where ego-involvement is low, the consumer will accept without much difficulty a wide discrepancy between his own views and the communications stimuli (e.g., advertising message, point-of-sale display, salesperson's recommendation, etc.). On the other hand, if the brand falls in the latitude of rejection, such a message will be confronted with the mental roadblock of selective exposure, selective perception, and selective retention. In fact,

the influence of this latitude is so strong that even when the communication per se does not deviate from the recipient's own point of view, it is likely to be perceived as being farther from his position than it is in reality (contrast effect). By the same token, there is a strong probability of an assimilation effect in the latitude of acceptance, and advertising or any other communication will be interpreted in a more favorable light than the contents justify. This behavior is in line with the consonance theory, and it has been confirmed by empirical research in both social psychology[17] and marketing.[18]

These findings suggest that the emphasis in research should be directed toward those consumers who are in the latitude of acceptance (mainly current users) or latitude of noncommitment (primarily other consumers who are not against the brand and may purchase it if properly persuaded). It is generally advisable to ignore those falling within the latitude of rejection. Since these consumers violently dislike the brand, the communications stimuli will be either censored from the mind or twisted out of shape.

This grouping is merely an illustration of how consumers can be clustered on some theoretical grounds. To cover all bases, the same study may also explore other product-specific classifications, such as heavy users versus light users, opinion leaders versus followers, and the like. Much will depend on the area under investigation.

For the formulation of a marketing strategy, however, all such classifications are far too general. Within these broad dimensions, the prospects need to be examined in greater detail—much more than is done in most segmentation studies. It is not sufficient to ask the usual product/brand questions, such as volume of usage, switching patterns, demographic profiles, and brand imagery. Information must also be gathered on psychographics and communications behavior. Since these two sectors tend to be ignored or glossed over in research, they are treated in some detail here.

Psychographics

Psychographics are crucial for discovering both the overt and the latent psycho-social motives

that so often spell the difference between acceptance or rejection of the brand. However, the
measures developed are meaningful only when
they are situation-specific and not of a generalized
nature. For example, instead of searching for the
general trait of self-confidence, it is better to
determine the extent to which consumers are self-
confident in evaluating different brands within
the product category. Similarly, anxiety as measured in personality tests does not have much
meaning for businesspeople, but anxiety as connected with the physical or social risks involved
in the purchase of a brand can have significant
implications for marketing. The three key areas
of psychographics are value orientations, role
perceptions, and buying style.

Value Orientations   The term *value* is used
here in the manner employed by social scientists,
namely, as "an enduring belief that a particular
mode of conduct or that a particular end state of
existence is personally and socially preferable to
alternative modes of conduct or end states of
existence."[19] Thus defined, an individual's value
system canalizes motivations, tells him what attitudes he should hold, and provides standards by
which evaluations are made and goals are chosen.

Role Perceptions   These refer to the manner
in which an individual behaves in order to give
positive expression to the type of person he is or
perceives himself to be. This aspect of pscyho-
graphics is important because brands today are
the most universally acknowledged symbols of
roles, and very often they are purchased not so
much for their physical functions as for the impressions they convey about their owners.[20]

Buying Style   This is the extension of value
orientations and role perceptions to one special
milieu, namely, shopping behavior. The premise
is that there will be differences in buyers' reactions
even when they are confronted with the same
purchasing environment, and to some extent this
is a consequence of the differences in buying
style.[21]

Again it is essential to emphasize specificity.
Since these three attributes tend to vary from one
product category to another, the criteria used to
measure them must focus on the product under
investigation. Examples of these criteria with
reference to a food product are given in Table 1.

**Table 1. Typical Examples of Value Orientations,
Role Perceptions, and Buying Style, with Special
Reference to a Food Product.**

Value Orientations

Weight watcher—pays attention to calorie content
   of food
Fond of cooking—loves to prepare food from
   basic ingredients
Time saver—appreciates convenience foods
Nutrition-prone—emphasizes salutary aspects
   of food
Health-conscious—is concerned about the harmful
   effects of food
Connoisseur—is fond of gourmet or exotic dishes
Pro-ecology—dislikes chemical ingredients

Role Perceptions

Social entertainer—frequently invites friends and
   neighbors for snacks or meals
Home-oriented—spends a lot of time in the kitchen
Home-avoider—wants to be emancipated and to
   escape from the drudgeries of the kitchen
Creative—craves preparing novel dishes and finding
   new and interesting ways of serving food
Achievement seeker—measures success on the
   basis of recognition obtained for skill in culi-
   nary activities

Buying Style (related specifically to product
   type under study)

Repeat buyer—sticks to the same brand through
   force of habit
Loyal—repurchase decision is motivated by satisfaction with the brand
Cautious—is high on "perceived risk," confining
   selection to well-known brands of large
   companies
Cognitive—is sensitive to rational claims, evaluating brand on basis of weight and ingredients
Value-inclined—is willing to pay premium for
   quality
Impulsive—tends to buy on the spur of the momen
Economy-minded—prefers low-priced to high-
   priced lines, or giant-sized to small packages
Independent—notices very little difference between brands and switches a lot
Time-pressured—is anxious to finish shopping as
   soon as possible
Conformist—selects brands that friends and neigh-
   bors buy
Hedonist—is affected by sensory benefits, such as
   attractive packaging
Innovator—is eager to try new brands
Variety seeker—changes brands for the sake of
   variety or novelty
Bargain hunter—is susceptible to deals, coupons,
   and premiums, and shops around a lot to
   compare prices

Communications Behavior

To complete the segmentation study, it is necessary to explore the communications behavior of the prospects. The three main categories studied are: media habits, advertising, and decision-making process. (The types of questions that may be asked are shown in Table 2.)

Information on *media habits* may serve as a guide for the selection of media and of a particular vehicle within each medium. This is especially relevant when no one segment is large enough to be profitable. The advertiser can then aim at two or more segments with different appeals in different media, and avoid the danger of overlapping.

As regards *advertising*, some playback about prospects' reactions can be helpful in the effective execution of copy. The creative department is then able to use situational approaches that gener-

ate empathy and tune in well on the consumer's wavelength.

Equally important is knowledge about the prospects' *decision-making* process. Very often, consumers may be persuaded but may still feel the need to reinforce their judgment through personal interaction with their peers. It is then in the interest of the advertiser to direct the appeal to the opinion leaders.[22]

In certain cases, the "source" or corporate image can also play a major role. Consumers often select one brand over others because of their favorable predisposition toward its producer. If they like what the company stands for, then they choose to do business with it rather than with its competitors.[23]

Development of Strategy

Segmentation study of this nature covers a very broad area. At first glance, the tabulation and analysis of the data would seem to be an almost superhuman task. Fortunately, it is possible to extract a few meaningful segments within the broad "a priori" classification by applying multivariate techniques (e.g., Q-type factor analysis) to most of the attitudinal, psychographic, and communications-behavior measures.[24]

In most cases, because of media and budget constraints, only one segment is chosen for proper brand positioning. However, this does not rule out the selection of two or more segments, as long as they can be profitably exploited by the marketer. For example, through product and distribution differentiation, a firm may promote a low-priced line for one segment and a high-priced line for another. Similarly, one segment, which is price-conscious, may be cultivated by means of selective direct-mail couponing, while the other, which is sensitive to emotional appeals, may be won over by advertising that is in tune with its value orientations and role perceptions.

Second-Phase Research: How Much to Spend on Marketing?

Segmentation research by no means stops with the first survey. The financial aspects now

---

Table 2. Typical Examples of the Area Covered by Communications Behavior.

Media Habits

Readership of representative newspapers and magazines
Preference for certain types of television programs
Favorite time periods for watching television and listening to the radio

Advertising

Amount of attention paid to advertising of the product category in various media
Level of confidence in brand advertising
Reaction to situational elements used in advertising

Decision-Making Process

Importance of advertising versus recommendations received by word of mouth or from salespeople
Role of opinion leaders in influencing brand selection
Perception of the manufacturer on such attributes as competence, trust, power, and likability. (The first two characteristics are important when purchase decisions are influenced by problem-solving needs, while the last two play a major role when psycho-social needs are in the forefront.)[a]

[a]Raymond A. Bauer, "Source Effect and Persuasibility: A New Look," in *Risk Taking and Information Handling in Consumer Behavior*, Donald F. Cox, ed. (Boston: Graduate School of Business Administration, Harvard University, 1967), pp. 559-578.

enter the picture. Some guidelines are required on the amount of money that should be spent on marketing strategies so as to optimize profits.

One of the cardinal axioms of micro-economics is that profits are maximized when a firm allocates its expenditures in such a way that the incremental returns are equal for all subsets of markets. More money is spent on segments with greater potential until diminishing returns bring the incremental response down to the level for the less desirable segments.[25] In actual practice, budget constraint stops the process before equality can be achieved, and the less desirable segments are almost always ignored. However, even for a single submarket, the most advantageous procedure continues to be the same: the allocation of the marketing budget in such a way that marginal costs equal marginal revenues.

Consequently, as Frank and Massy point out, *"one crucial criterion for determining the desirability of segmenting a market along any particular dimension is whether the different sub-markets have different elasticities with respect to the price and promotional policies of a firm."*[26] The same idea was expressed by Wendell Smith two decades ago: "In the language of the economist, segmentation is *disaggregative* in its effects and tends to bring about recognition of several demand schedules where only one was recognized before."[27]

This vital information on elasticity cannot be obtained from the first survey. It is necessary to know for each segment the percentage change in sales as a result of a percentage change in some element of the marketing mix, such as price or advertising. This calls for a *second-phase research program* in which weight tests are conducted for a certain period of time in the marketplace. For example, instead of having the same level of advertising or sales promotion all over the country, a few test markets are selected where controlled experimentation is carried out at different levels of expenditure. Data are collected not only on sales but also on extraneous elements that may affect purchase (e.g., competitive activities, socio-economic differences, etc.) in order to factor out their influence mathematically. After all the results are in, multiple regression equations are fitted to obtain the elasticities of the variables tested, so that one segment may be meaningfully compared against the other.[28]

Generally, three options are open for performing the second-phase research. The most convenient way is to carry out the first segmentation study among members of a nationwide consumer panel, provided the sample size is sufficiently large to avoid gross instabilities by subcells. The segmentation strategy can later be validated by analyzing the purchases of selected segments of panel members at different levels of marketing expenditures.

If no panel is available, a second option is to conduct the first survey with a large, well-dispersed random sample and then to contact the same respondents again after a certain lapse of time, preferably a year. On the second interview, questions are confined to attitudinal data and brand usage, on the assumption that the interviewing period is too short to expect any changes in psychographic or communications-behavior variables.

When it is impossible or undesirable to go back to the same people, then an attitude and usage survey should be conducted with the same type of sample as in the first study. Although the respondents must be grouped anew into original segments, only those questions that were particularly discriminating in the first research (e.g., the ones with high loadings in the Q-type factor analysis) need to be asked.

AN ILLUSTRATION

The above procedure is now illustrated with the case history of a food product that had been promoted strictly on the basis of its strong and distinctive taste. Sales had been stagnant for some time, and the company needed to win over a portion of nonusers. A segmentation study was conducted, and the Q-type analysis of those respondents who fell within the latitude of non-commitment revealed the following five clusters: impulse buyers, social conformists, bargain hunters, time savers, and health promoters.

The decision was made to ignore the first four segments even though they represented about 70% of the "neutral" consumers. The impulse buyers were very volatile and did not provide a firm base for building the brand franchise. The social conformists were worrying too much about group norms, and it was unrealistic to expect that the brand's distinctive taste could win universal appeal. The thrifty were essentially bargain hunters, and it was not in the company's interest to compete on price. The time savers were primarily oriented toward convenience in food preparation, a benefit that the brand was not able to provide.

On the other hand, the health promoters held great promise. The housewives in this segment took very seriously their role as custodians of family health and well-being. Their brand selection was governed almost totally by this value orientation. Now it so happened that the strong taste of the brand was mainly due to certain "natural" ingredients, and the firm had a clear edge over competition in this respect. Furthermore, the media habits of health promoters were different from those of loyal users. The latter were primarily heavy viewers of situation comedy shows on television. The former, on the other hand, were fond of documentaries and also tended to be avid readers of certain magazines whose editorial content was slanted toward family health and well-being. As a result, the danger of overlapping of exposures was not serious.

New advertising was built around nutrition, wholesomeness, and natural ingredients. At the same time, in order to retain loyal users, the old 30-second spots, emphasizing strong taste, were continued as before on situation comedy shows.

The company already had on hand from a previous experiment on loyal users the following information on the diminishing marginal effects of advertising on sales:

Equation 1:

$$Q_1 = 5.751 + 5.36A_1 - 1.2(A_1)^2$$

where

Q_1 = Quantity sold in millions of units

A_1 = Advertising expenditures in millions of dollars

(The subscript '1' refers to the first segment, that is, loyal users. The equation also included other exogenous variables, such as competitive advertising and number of prospects, but to simplify the exposition their estimated values have been incorporated into the intercept.)

An attempt was made to obtain a similar type of relationship for health promoters. A media-weight test was initiated in certain markets, and relevant data were collected from the respondents who fell within this segment. The results were then projected to the total universe to derive the following:

Equation 2:

$$Q_2 = 3.9981 + 3.732A_2 - 1.24(A_2)^2$$

The gross margin per unit for the brand was $0.50: the difference between the factory selling price of $1.50 and the variable cost of $1.00, excluding advertising.

Suppose management had only $2 million available for advertising and wanted to know how much to spend on each segment to obtain the highest profit contribution for the brand, minus fixed costs. The problem could be solved by using the standard maximizing procedures found in differential calculus for constrained optima. The formula is:

Equation 3:

$$P = M(Q_1 + Q_2) - A_1 - A_2 + \lambda(A_1 + A_2 - 2)$$

where

P = Profit contribution, excluding fixed costs, in millions of dollars

M = Gross margin (0.50)

λ = Lagrangian multiplier used for the calculation of constrained optima

The results obtained were as follows:

Variable	Loyal Users ($MM)	Health Promoters ($MM)	Total of the two Segments ($MM)
Advertising	1.35	0.65	2.00
Unit Sales	10.80	5.90	16.70
Profit contribution	4.05	2.30	6.35

If the company had spent the entire $2 million of advertising on the loyal users, the profit contribution of the brand, according to Equation 1, would have been $3.84 million, or $2.51 million less than the amount generated by tapping health promoters. Segmentation research in this case may be deemed a success. Of course, as in all equations based on market experiments, the results are only approximations, subject to a margin of random error. Also, such weight tests are time consuming. Yet this approach helps to provide a fairly good yardstick for the profitability of a segmentation strategy.

SUMMARY AND CONCLUSIONS

A review of the segmentation criteria currently in use reveals the existence of two schools of thought: the behaviorally oriented school, which is interested in obtaining insights into the basic processes of consumer behavior, with only secondary consideration given to marketing needs; and the decision-oriented school, which focuses not so much on why there are differences among consumers as on how these differences can be exploited to increase the productivity of the firm's marketing programs.

Real progress can be achieved by fusing the concepts of these two schools. A viable marketing strategy can be formulated when the segmentation study examines all facets of consumer behavior as related to the product category under investigation. Also, the research must not stop with the first survey. Weight tests should be conducted to estimate the demand schedules of different submarkets.

This second research phase is essential because the theoretical route to profit maximization lies in equating marginal revenue with marginal costs. To obtain data on marginal revenue, it is necessary to have equations that show the response elasticities of different segments to the firm's marketing strategies. Only then is the firm in a position to judge the profitability of cultivating each submarket—and this, after all, is the object of all exercises in segmentation.

Notes

1. Ronald E. Frank, William F. Massy, and Yoram Wind, *Market Segmentation* (Englewood Cliffs, N.J.: Prentice-Hall, 1972), pp. 26-89.
2. Harold H. Kassarjian, "Personality and Consumer Behavior: A Review," *Journal of Marketing Research*, Vol. 8 (November 1971), pp. 409-418.

3. Advertising Research Foundation, *Are There Consumer Types?* (New York, 1964).
4. Harold H. Kassarjian, "Social Character and Differential Preference for Mass Communication," *Journal of Marketing Research*, Vol. 2 (May 1965), pp. 146-153. See also, Arch G. Woodside, "Social Character, Product Use, and Advertising Appeals," *Journal of Advertising Research*, Vol. 8 (December 1968), pp. 31-35.
5. B. Curtis Hamm and Edward W. Cundiff, "Self-Actualization and Product Perception," *Journal of Marketing Research*, Vol. 6 (November 1969), pp. 470-472.
6. Stuart U. Rich and Subhash C. Jain, "Social Class and Life Cycle as Predictors of Shopping Behavior," *Journal of Marketing Research*, Vol. 5 (February 1968), pp. 41-49. See also John Wilding and Raymond A. Bauer, "Consumer Goals and Reactions to a Communications Source," *Journal of Marketing Research*, Vol. 5 (February 1968), pp. 73-77.
7. William D. Wells and Douglas J. Tigert, "Activities, Interests and Opinions," *Journal of Advertising Research*, Vol. 11 (August 1971), pp. 27-35.
8. Joseph Pernica, "The Second Generation of Market Segmentation Studies: An Audit of Buying Motivations," in *Life Style and Psychographics*, William D. Wells, ed. (Chicago: American Marketing Assn., 1974), pp. 279-313.
9. Russell I. Haley, "Benefit Segmentation: A Decision-Oriented Research Tool," *Journal of Marketing*, Vol. 32 (July 1968), pp. 30-35; and Haley, "Beyond Benefit Segmentation," *Journal of Advertising Research*, Vol. 11 (August 1971), pp. 3-8.
10. Scott M. Cunningham, "Perceived Risk and Brand Loyalty," in *Risk Taking and Information Handling in Consumer Behavior*, Donald F. Cox, ed. (Boston: Graduate School of Business Administration, Harvard University, 1967), pp. 507-523.
11. John A. Howard and Jagdish N. Sheth, *The Theory of Buyer Behavior* (New York: John Wiley & Sons, 1969), pp. 211-212.
12. Ronald E. Frank and William F. Massy, "Market Segmentation and the Effectiveness of a Brand's Price and Dealing Policies," *Journal of Business*, Vol. 38 (April 1965), pp. 186-200.
13. Same references as footnote 9.
14. William L. Wilkie, "An Empirical Analysis of Alternative Bases of Market Segmentation" (Ph.D. diss., Stanford University, Graduate School of Business, December 1970).
15. Joel P. Baumwoll, "Segmentation Research: The Baker vs. The Cookie Maker," in *1974 Combined Proceedings*, Ronald C. Curhan,

ed. (Chicago: American Marketing Assn., 1975), pp. 3-20.

16. Carolyn W. Sherif, Muzafer Sherif, and Roger E. Nebergall, *Attitude and Attitude Change: The Social Judgment Involvement Approach* (Philadelphia: Saunders, 1965).

17. Muzafer Sherif and Carl I. Hovland, *Social Judgment: Assimilation and Contrast Effects in Communication and Attitude Change* (New Haven, Conn.: Yale University Press, 1961).

18. J. Shable, "The Effects of Message Discrepancy on Attitude Change" (M.A. thesis, Ohio State University, 1968).

19. Milton Rokeach, "The Role of Values in Public Opinion Research," *Public Opinion Quarterly*, Vol. 32 (Winter 1968-69), pp. 547-559.

20. Sidney J. Levy, "Symbols by Which We Buy," in *Advancing Marketing Efficiency*, Lynn H. Stockman, ed. (Chicago: American Marketing Assn., 1965), pp. 222-243.

21. George S. Day, *Buyer Attitudes and Brand Choice Behavior* (New York: Free Press), pp. 75-79.

22. For actual phrasing of questions, see questionnaire in the appendix of Elihu Katz and Paul F. Lazarsfeld, *Personal Influence* (New York: Free Press, 1955), pp. 340-352.

23. Nariman K. Dhalla, "Look to Your Corporate Image," *Canadian Business*, September 1971, pp. 58-66.

24. Nariman K. Dhalla, "How to Find a Winning Advertising Strategy," *Canadian Business*, November 1970, pp. 24-32, and December 1970, pp. 31-34.

25. Joan Robinson, *The Economics of Imperfect Competition* (London: Macmillan & Co., 1954), pp. 179-188.

26. Same reference as footnote 12.

27. Wendell R. Smith, "Product Differentiation and Market Segmentation as Alternative Marketing Strategies," *Journal of Marketing*, Vol. 21 (July 1956), pp. 3-8.

28. It is not possible in this article to discuss controlled experimentation and the development of marketing models therefrom. This topic is covered in Seymour Banks, *Experimentation in Marketing* (New York: McGraw-Hill Book Co., 1965). More detailed analysis may be found in William G. Cochran and Gertrude M. Cox, *Experimental Designs*, 2nd ed. (New York: John Wiley & Sons, 1957); and Karl A. Fox, *Intermediate Economic Statistics* (New York: John Wiley & Sons, 1968).

16 MANAGEMENT CONTROL OF MARKETING RESEARCH

James H. Myers
DeBell Professor of Business Administration
University of Southern California

A. C. Samli
Professor of Marketing
Virginia Polytechnic Institute

What is marketing research worth to the buyer? The marketing research manager who wishes to better control and evaluate his projects will find several worthwhile ideas in this article.

A great deal has been written about marketing research objectives and techniques, but almost no emphasis has been placed on the evaluation and control of research by top marketing management. As a staff function, research has been subject to much less scrutiny than other marketing functions.

Evaluation and control of marketing research is needed at two levels: (1) the individual project and (2) the total research activity within a business firm. Not only must each research effort be evaluated as it arises, but the total program must be examined periodically to assess its contribution to the needs and objectives of the total marketing system of a business firm.

Though various tools for controlling research have been available for some time, use

From J.H. Myers and A.C. Samli, "Management Control of Marketing Research," Journal of Marketing Research, August 1969, pp. 267-77. Published by the American Marketing Association. Reprinted by permission of the authors and the publisher.

of them is inadequate in most business firms today for maybe several reasons:

1. Neither management nor research is aware of the evaluation and control devices that exist.
2. The complexity of research may distinguish it somewhat from other marketing staff functions in that research methodology tends to defy understanding of the research process by top marketing management.
3. Many research techniques are not standardized and do not readily lend themselves to establish norms for control.
4. Because marketing researchers occupy a high status position in many companies, it is often hard to bring research under close examination.

Because management understands little about research, it is often unable to establish effective control over this important function. Marketing management needs criteria for determining the value of research. Furthermore, it needs to develop more effective approaches to the administration and control of research activities. This holds for both one-shot studies and ongoing information-gathering services by research.

This article reviews some evaluation and control devices that can be used by business firms with a marketing research effort of any size. Three specific topical areas are covered. First, the value of information to the decision maker is estimated to indicate whether marketing research is worthwhile and to provide some idea of the maximum amount of money that can feasibly be spent. Second, methods of controlling individual research projects are considered so that execution proceeds efficiently and costs are kept in line. And third, means of systematically guiding and appraising the total marketing research activity are examined. Although the tools and techniques presented here are discussed in detail elsewhere, they are used only minimally (if at all) in marketing research.

VALUE OF INFORMATION

Most difficult business decisons are made under conditions of uncertainty. Normally, the greater the uncertainty, the more difficult the decision. To reduce uncertainty, management moves to acquire information prior to the decision.

Though the logic of this approach is simple, the *cost* of the information must be considered. For any given decision, if the net advantage of the best alternative does not exceed the cost of acquiring the information for that alternative, this information is not worthwhile. The economics of information-gathering is shown in Figure 1.

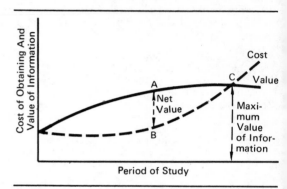

Figure 1. Value of Information.

The solid line in Figure 1 shows the value of information obtained as a function of the time period covered; the dotted line shows the cost of obtaining the information. The net value of information is, of course, the value of information minus the costs of obtaining it. In Figure 1 the dotted line AB represents the maximum net value. After this point diminishing returns set in because the cost of information starts increasing faster than its value. After Point C the value of information is exceeded by the costs involved so that research has no net value and becomes a drain on company resources.

In terms of marketing research information, Ralph Day observed:

> The increasing importance of marketing research, both as an activity and as a use of funds, suggests the need to evaluate more carefully methods of making marketing research decisions. Few management decisions to expend large sums of money are made without careful analysis of the relation-

ship between costs and benefits. Management typically demands careful estimates of the additional revenues or reduced costs resulting from a proposed capital investment and applies stringent criteria in evaluating the economic feasibility. In a very real sense, investments in marketing research should be expected to produce additional revenues or reduce costs in much the same way as a new piece of equipment. Yet there are no widely accepted procedures for evaluating the returns nor is there any standard set of criteria for evaluating the economic feasibility of proposed projects [7, p. 46].

This section of the article presents several methods of establishing the value of marketing research information. Each applies more at the individual project than at the total research effort level. Some methods are applied before undertaking the research, some after. Ideally, the value of information should always be established before undertaking any work, but this is not always feasible for a number of reasons, e.g., projects whose benefits are great may not warrant formal value estimation.

Simple Savings Method

Perhaps the most direct approach to estimating the value of research is the Simple Savings Method [2]. This method assumes that management can make a single reasonably accurate estimate of the cost of making a particular wrong decision. The Simple Savings Method is illustrated as follows for a decision that might cost the company as much as $200,000 if made improperly:

	Chance of correct decision	Estimated cost of mistake
Making decision by flipping coin	50-50	$100,000
Using known facts in decision (no research)	60-40	80,000
Using additional research information	75-25	50,000

Value of research: $80,000 − $50,000 = $30,000

If the cost of a wrong decision is estimated at $200,000, the flip of a coin will result in a 50-per cent chance of making a right decision so that the expected cost of the decision is $100,000. That is, over the long run decisions of this kind will be wrong half the time, and the average cost for all decisions would be $100,000. Information known to management boosts chances to 60-40, and research is expected to increase chances to 75-25. In this situation, the value of research is at most $30,000. Hence, as long as the cost of research does not exceed this amount, research will have a net value to the firm.

The Simple Savings Method is perhaps of more value conceptually than practically, since later methods furnish models for estimating returns and costs in more detailed and useful form. However, this method furnishes a framework for other methods to be discussed, and it may be useful in some decision-making situations whose implications are clearly seen.

Return on Investment

Another approach regards research as an investment and calculates a return on this investment after the research has been completed and acted on. As an illustration, the Oscar Mayer Company reviewed its major marketing research projects during the previous fiscal year. The purpose of the review was to estimate the worth of research findings in terms of the actual application of the information produced, not what it would have been worth had it been used. The evaluations were made by users of the information, not by research personnel.

As Twedt explains [18, p. 62]:

Most marketing research is done to help decide which of one or more alternatives is preferable. Let us assume that in at least 60 per cent of the instances where managerial decisions were required, the correct decision would have been made without the benefit of marketing research information. This correction reduces the 'worth' of the information by 60 per cent, or 40 per cent of the total contribution. A simple formula then estimates the company's return on investment in marketing research:

$$\frac{\textit{Worth of findings} \times .40}{\textit{Annual marketing research budget}} = \textit{return on investment}$$

Thus, if a company has an annual research budget of $500,000 and the contribution of the information provided in a given year is judged to be $2,500,000, the return on investment would be 200 per cent. This estimate would be inflated if only direct costs are included in the research budget, but estimates of indirect costs, e.g., space and fringe benefits, can also be included. Obviously the 60 per cent figure used in this calculation is somewhat arbitrary, and the proper figure may be quite different depending on the circumstances.

In this company at least, it was possible to make an objective estimate of the contribution of most projects to corporate profitability. Some of the contributions were negative in that management decided not to take a course of action that research showed to be unwise.

Twedt concludes:

> Obviously this method of estimating the return on investment is a matter of elementary accounting. It has also turned out to be a matter of good personnel relations within the company, since it provides a reason for a mutually helpful annual review of the dollar value of information supplied by the marketing research department [18, p. 63].

The Present Value Method

The Present Value Method also treats research expenditures as investments and is the proper technique for computing the expected return of an investment. In this method incremental cash benefits expected over the lifetime of an investment are discounted by the marginal cost of capital:

Current	First year	Second year	Final year

$$(R_0 - C_0) + \frac{(R_1 - C_1)}{1 + K} + \frac{(R_2 - C_2)}{(1 + K)^2} + \frac{(R_n - C_n)}{(1 + K)^n}$$

where

R_0 ------ R_n are annual cash receipts attributable to the investment,

C_0 ------ C_n are the incremental cash expenditures, and K is the firm's marginal costs of capital [10].

The Present Value Method can be applied either to individual research projects or to the firm's entire marketing research effort and offers a more effective approach for evaluating marketing research contributions than previous models.

Bayesian Analysis

Perhaps the best way to determine the value of information before doing research is Bayesian Analysis. This technique estimates the value of research by setting an upper limit on the amount of money that profitably can be spent on a particular marketing problem before deciding whether to do research. This amount is based directly on the dollars to be gained or saved by making the correct decision. It can also determine which of several research designs is likely to yield the greatest return relative to cost, as indicated later in this article. Bayesian Analysis is more appropriate for major marketing decisions than for very small research efforts.

Bayesian Analysis differs from the more traditional statistical analysis by allowing the assignment of numerical probabilities to *unique* rather than repetitive events. Furthermore, these probabilities can be subjectively determined, i.e., established by some experienced observer. In this way, Bayesian Analysis allows for the lack of directly comparable experience on which to base the probability of success or to predict the outcome of some decision, but considers that we usually have some meaningful idea as to probable outcome.

To illustrate this in the marketing context, introduction of a new product can be used. Classical statistical models provide no means of estimating the probability of the product's success, unless extensive market testing provides results that can be projected nationwide (and this is often of doubtful accuracy). Nor do they indicate whether research should be done at all and, if done, what upper limit should be set on the dollar amount spent. Bayesian Analysis is helpful for all of these problems.

Bayesians argue that management always has at least some idea of how well the new product will do, based on such factors as experience with the introduction of similar products (either theirs or competitors), their evaluation of the new product in terms of degree of superiority to existing products, amount of promotion expense planned to support the product, and amount and timing of competitive retaliation expected. These feelings can be translated into quantitative terms by asking management to estimate the probabilities of reaching various levels of sales from the new product.

Table 1 shows how this would work for a company trying to decide whether to introduce a new male cosmetic—perhaps eye shadow or wrinkle-remover cream. Column 1 is the number of men who might buy the new product. Column 2 shows management's estimate of the probability that the indicated number of men will buy. Management estimates a 5 per cent probability that 800,000 will buy, a 10 per cent probability that 1,000,000 will buy, and so on up to a 10 per cent probability that 1,800,000 will buy.

Next, total profit or loss is estimated for each sales level, independently of the probability of attainment. The resulting figures are shown in Column 3. The break-even point for this product is 1,400,000 units, with profit ranging up to $450,000 for any reasonable level of sales above this and loss down to $400,000 for minimum expected sales.

Once the first three columns are developed, Bayesian Analysis can be employed. The key concept for this particular type of problem is opportunity loss, which represents either of the following:

1. actual dollars lost from introducing the product and failing to achieve the breakeven level.

2. potential profits lost from failing to introduce the product when sales would have been profitable, i.e., greater than 1.4 million units.

Thus, Column 4 shows that a decision to introduce the product will result in opportunity loss if sales are below breakeven (1.4 million units). Above this sales level there is profit, which means that no opportunity has been lost. Similarly, Column 5 shows that the decision not to introduce the product results in opportunity loss if sales would have exceeded the breakeven point—$200,000 profit loss if sales would have been 1.6 million units and $450,000 profit loss for 1.8 million sales.

Bayesian Analysis provides a means of calculating expected opportunity loss for each action, i.e., introduce versus not introduce, by multiplying the various opportunity losses (Columns 4 and 5) by the probability of these losses (Column 2). Results are shown in Columns 6 and 7 for each level of sales. Summing each of these columns provides the overall expected opportunity loss for each action: $67,500 for introducing the product and $95,000 for not introducing it. In this example, then, the company should choose to introduce the cosmetic, since this action results in the lowest expected opportunity loss.

In addition to suggesting whether to introduce the product, Bayesian Analysis shows how much money might be profitably spent for research in this situation. By its calculation, opportunity loss can never be less than $0. This means that even if perfect information were available, i.e., if the firm knew from a market research

Table 1. Bayesian Analysis for New Product Introduction.

Unit sales	Estimated probability	Profit or loss	Opportunity loss		Expected opportunity loss	
			Introduce	Not introduce	Introduce	Not introduce
(1)	(2)	(3)	(4)	(5)	(6)	(7)
1,800,000	.10	$450,000	0	$450,000	0	$45,000
1,600,000	.25	200,000	0	200,000	0	50,000
1,400,000	.35	0	0	0	0	0
1,200,000	.15	−150,000	$150,000	0	$22,500	0
1,000,000	.10	−250,000	250,000	0	25,000	0
800,000	.05	−400,000	400,000	0	20,000	0
Total	1.00				$67,500	$95,000

study exactly how many men would buy the cosmetic, it could reduce its expected opportunity loss by only $67,500. Therefore, the maximum value of research in this situation is $67,500; it would not be reasonable to spend any more than that amount. This even assumes that research will provide perfect information in telling the correct number of men who would buy the cosmetic. Research is seldom this accurate.

Cost Benefit Approach

Day [7] casts the value of information problem into a cost-benefit framework and proposes three criteria to evaluate the information supplied by marketing research:

1. set a cost figure and maximize the benefits to be obtained from that cost
2. establish the level of benefits to be obtained and minimize the cost of obtaining them
3. maximize the value of benefits.

Day concludes that "benefits minus costs is the logical criterion for evaluating marketing research proposals since it does not imply an arbitrary limit on the benefits to be obtained from research" [7].

Applying the Cost-Benefit Model to the Bayesian Analysis in the previous section, the expected value of perfect information, i.e., lowest expected opportunity loss, places an upper limit on the benefits to be obtained from information provided by marketing research. It also provides a reference point against which the expected value of alternative research designs can be compared.

For example, consider the payoff matrix in Table 2. R_1, R_2, and R_3 are three possible research designs, e.g., standard consumer survey, motivation research, and test market. Entries in the matrix are probabilities that the information provided by the research project will reveal to the decision-maker when each particular sales level will be realized. Thus, there is a 20 per cent chance that the first research design (R_1) will indicate that sales will be 1.8 million units when they will be.

These probabilities are perhaps best estimated by research personnel who are most familiar with

both the sensitivities and limitations of the three research alternatives. For example, research professionals are more likely to know that consumer survey results often tend to overestimate demand for a new product, and they would therefore assign higher probabilities to the larger gross sales for this alternative. Ideally, these estimates should be made independently by two or more researchers and then pooled into a single estimate for review by management.

When these probabilities are weighted by management's estimates of the probabilities of each level of sales (Table 1, Column 2) the result is an expected value for the probabilities that each research design will provide perfect information. As shown below, research design R_1 has the highest conditional probability of predicting the true state of the market place:

$$P(P_1/R_1) = .10(.20) + .25(.30) + .35(.20) + .15(.15) + .10(.05) + .05(.10) = .20$$

$$P(P_1/R_2) = .10(.25) + .25(.10) + .35(.15) + .15(.10) + .10(.05) + .05(.00) = .12$$

$$P(P_1/R_3) = .10(.10) + .25(.15) + .35(.20) + .15(.10) + .10(.20) + .05(.20) = .16.$$

Though R_1 would be chosen as the best research alternative on this basis, it is important to consider its relative cost as well. To consider net return, benefits must first be quantified by multiplying the conditional probabilities above by $67,500, the estimated upper limit for research benefits. This is done in Table 3. Then, deducting the estimated cost for each research alternative from its respective benefit, R_2 is found to be the alternative providing the greatest net return based on cost benefit analysis. In this way, Bayesian Analysis provides a means of choosing from several research alternatives.

Comments

A word of caution is in order in using any of these methods. All methods rely upon estimates for factors such as profits, costs, and probabilities. Estimates of this type may either be accurate or

Table 2. Payoff Matrix for Research Alternatives.

	Research alternative		
Sales of cosmetic	R_1	R_2	R_3
1,800,000	.20	.25	.10
1,600,000	.30	.10	.15
1,400,000	.20	.15	.20
1,200,000	.15	.10	.10
1,000,000	.05	.05	.20
800,000	.10	.00	.20

Table 3. Cost/Benefit Analysis for Three Research Alternatives.

	Benefit	*Estimated Cost*	*Benefit minus cost*
R_1	$67,500(.20) = $13,500	$15,400	−$1,900
R_2	67,500(.12) = 8,100	5,500	2,600
R_3	67,500(.16) = 10,800	9,800	1,000

overly optimistic. When estimating the value of any one service or staff function, other staff functions are often overlooked, which is why some of these estimates turn out to be inflated beyond reason, i.e., the sum of the various contributions is estimated to be far greater than total gross margins or return on investment. Every staff function naturally claims the greatest share of credit. Thus, the estimation of various probabilities may be especially difficult, but by asking several members of management this problem can be ameliorated.

On the other hand, carefully quantified estimates are better than none at all. Usually, it is not too difficult to provide some sort of realistic estimate of sales, of the costs of a mistake, or of the value of research information in a particular decision. Once this is done, the techniques shown can be helpful in preventing management from making decisions that are not consonant with its judgment and experience.

CONTROLLING THE RESEARCH PROJECT

After it has been established that a particular research project is likely to be worth the money

required, the research director usually handles the details of execution. However, there is a growing realization that research in process will be no better than the time and effort devoted to it by top marketing management. Miller warns:

> Today's businessman should also realize that research can be the most wasteful of all his business activities. If the head of a business indulges in research, as many do, just to solace his own fears of the future, he will come to the end of his cycle all the sooner. If research is to be fruitful, it must be a daily concern of top management, and if it is to succeed, those who conduct the research must have a solid understanding of the true needs of their company, of its industry, and of its customers. Unless the top management of a company and its research staff are in the most constant and intimate kind of communication, research will amount to little and can be a great drain on any company [14, p. 59].

This section reviews some of the tools that can help the marketing executive determine exactly what is to be done and keep track of research projects on a daily or weekly basis.

Check Lists

The check list is a venerable tool of management in every part of the business firm. Some executives feel it is one of the most versatile and useful control devices ever developed for business. It is also one of the simplest to use and to construct.

Check lists can be quite useful in the control of marketing research projects [8]. These lists can be long or short and devoted only to more general questions. Figure 2 is an abbreviated short, general list for use by marketing management. It can serve as a starting point for more comprehensive check lists tailored to the needs of a particular business firm or type of research project. This list can be expanded to any level of depth or coverage. It is also possible to construct separate, more specific check lists for typical research studies, such as product testing, advertising effectiveness, or market potentials.

Definition of Objectives

1. What exactly is needed in the way of information?
2. Is marketing research the proper group to execute the assignment?
3. To what extent are other functional areas of the firm involved, both within and outside marketing? What coordination mechanism is necessary?
4. Are the time and budget resources required by the marketing research group reasonable? Will these be justified by the value of the research?
5. Will this research be used as a basis for marketing decisions? Or will it merely collect dust?
6. Are the objectives clearly defined? Are they understood by all involved?
7. Can we obtain agreement in advance as to what constitutes conclusive evidence, e.g., what significance must findings have in order to become a basis for action?

Research Design

1. Are the sources specified by marketing research appropriate—published secondary sources, customer surveys, interviews with key observers?
2. Are the research tools indicated by marketing research reasonable—questionnaires, simple observation, complex experimental designs, projective devices, motivation research?
3. Does marketing research provide a proper balance in its research plan among the various information sources and research techniques?
4. If surveys are proposed, does marketing research require samples large enough to be meaningful? To provide useful breakdowns?
5. Are outside consultation and field work needed? Should there be competitive bids?
6. Do line marketing personnel who will use the results understand the research methodology? Do they know what to expect in the way of results or output?

Figure 2. A Partial Research Check List for Management.

Since check lists tend to become a repository of hints for the solution of errors or serious problems encountered in previous research, they serve as effective reminders for the anticipation and prevention of problems.

Logical Flow Analysis

The next level of control calls for ordering the various elements of a research study usually in terms of time or sequence. Logical flow analysis provides a framework for doing this. It is used by computer technologists as a first step in framing a problem or objective in terms that can be handled by computers. It can be equally effective for the control of marketing research studies of any size.

Logical flow analysis requires a flow model that describes the questions asked or alternative steps taken in sequence over time. These models may deal with either the processing or the administrative sequencing of research activity. In either case both the research practitioner and the marketing administrator can better see the whole picture, thus providing a firmer basis for control activities. The specific strengths of logical flow analysis can be summarized as follows [13]:

1. The ability to reason is enough to construct a flow model; no other specific skills are required.
2. Flow models are useful for the description of simple as well as complicated behavior patterns relating to particular decisions or operations.
3. Not only the models but their analysis as well as their recommendations are easy to comprehend by the user.
4. These models are applicable to a large variety of marketing activities.
5. Flow models can be used jointly with or in the construction of mathematical models.

Since many aspects of research undertakings are known from experience, it is easy to develop a logical flow chart. In such cases the researcher builds the model to establish the constraints of the research process, i.e., formulation of the hypotheses and how they will be tested, or he may spell out only the administrative steps involved in the research undertaking. Though both are valuable, the last is more important for an administrator exogenous to the research project.

Although it is expressed in general terms, Figure 3 displays a portion of a logical flow chart in an image study for a bank. Attempts to determine this image led to a sizable field survey in three income-stratified sections of a small Midwest

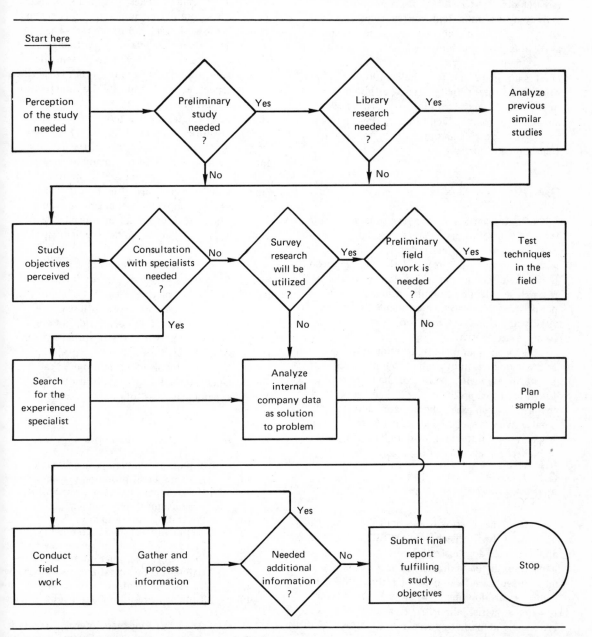

Figure 3. Logical Flow Chart for a Research Project.

town. In the preparation of the flow chart, all aspects of the research process as well as all administrative steps to be taken were considered, although not all are shown in Figure 3. Careful planning using logical flow analysis enabled the research director to control the overall project activity by assigning field workers to jobs. At any given time it was possible to see the next step and, as a whole, how much progress had been made.

One major shortcoming of the logical flow chart is not being able to establish the time dimension for the total activity. Hence, although control of the research activity in terms of effort, talent, and specific action is facilitated by these models, they do not provide an opportunity to control time and total cost.

Gantt Charts

Gantt Charts introduce the time dimension into the control of market research. They force the research planner to think in terms of the logical sequence of the total project and, more importantly, they enable the planner to develop an overall research schedule by assigning a specific time period to each research component. The charts give vitality and a practical means of controlling the total research activity.

Especially in major marketing activities, such as the introduction of a new product, research must be coordinated with the rest of the total marketing function in a carefully sequenced and scheduled manner. In such cases, the horizon date for the total activity is specified and the researcher plans his activities on the basis of date, duration, and sequence in that order of consideration [1, 16].

PERT Networks

Much has been written about Program Evaluation and Review Techniques (PERT) and their application to administrative and production problems. Here the basic discussion of terminology and concepts are treated very lightly. Although some forward-looking firms are using it in their research activities, almost no treatment of PERT is available in marketing research literature. PERT can be used effectively to evaluate progress in a

project where goals as well as monetary and temporal constraints are established [9, 17].

To prepare a PERT network, all the individual tasks needed for the completion of a given project must be visualized clearly. Networks are composed of events and activities. An event is a specialized accomplishment at a given instant in time; it is shown in Figure 4 by a circle. The number in the circle indicates the particular sequence of the event. Activities represent the time needed to progress from one event to another. In this respect, activities indicate the time required for the completion of each event. Typically, three time estimates are utilized in PERT: optimistic, pessimistic, and most likely terms. These estimates reflect the uncertainty of the activity and the probabilistic nature of many of the tasks in nonstandard programs [17, pp. 61, 101-3]. Since research projects are often nonstandard; with the exception of the actual simple events, the total undertakings cannot be routinized. In such cases, PERT appears to be especially applicable.

One research project involving a detailed market potential and behavior study illustrates the use of PERT in marketing research.[1] The project consisted of personal interviews with over 200 businesses, more than 500 households, and 300 on-the-street shoppers to gather information on shopping habits, attitudes, likes, and dislikes.

The events involved in the project that should be considered for the application of PERT were identified as follows:

Event No.	Activity description
10	Submit a complete project design
20	Acceptance of proposed project design
30	Questionnaire construction: business, consumer, and shopper
40	Pre-testing questionnaire
50	Field work—business interviews
60	Field work—consumer interviews
70	Field work—shopper interviews
80	Tabulating results of business interviews
90	Tabulating results of consumer interviews
100	Tabulating results of shopper questionnaires
110	Analysis of business interview results
120	Analysis of consumer interview results

Event no.	Activity description
130	Analysis of shopper interview results
140	Preparation of the report on business section
150	Preparation of report on consumer section
160	Preparation of report on shopper section
170	Preparation of the comprehensive report
180	Submittal of the finalized report

On the basis of these events a network was developed as shown in Figure 4. Optimistic, most likely, and pessimistic times were estimated for each activity on the basis of past experience. The expected time was calcualted for each activity by using the PERT formula of:

$$TE = \frac{a + 4m + b}{6}$$

where

- a is optimistic time,
- m is most likely time,
- b is pessimistic time.

The sum of expected times yielded an earliest expected time (TE) of 50 working days. And the critical path, which indicates the longest of the alternative series of sequences that are needed to fulfill the objectives, was determined to be 10-30-40-60-90-120-150-170-180.

Besides the expected time computations, it was necessary to determine individual latest allowable times (TL). These are computed by adding the expected times for activities on the longest path, when working back from the objective event to the event in question, and subtracting this sum from the total schedule of the objective event. For each event on the critical path TL always equals TE. However, this is not true for the events outside the critical path. There are usually differences between TE and TL which indicate the slack time, TS. This concept represents flexibility on a range of time within which the event can take place without interfering with the project's completion. If a slack time prevails, management resources can be shifted to minimize costs by eliminating idleness implied by this slack time. Figure 4 displays the computations of TE, TL, and TS for each event.

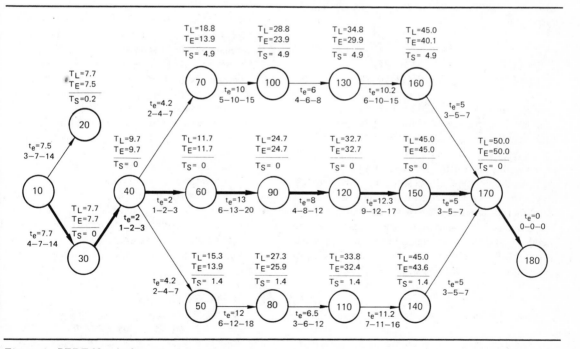

Figure 4. PERT Network.

One significant value in the use of PERT is that it lends itself to probability computations. Uncertainty or probability of success for the total project is computed by using the PERT equation of

$$Z = \frac{Tc - Te}{\sigma \Sigma \sigma^2}$$

where Tc = scheduled completion time, Te = earliest allowable time, $\Sigma \sigma^2$ = the sum of the variances of the activities on the preferred path, $\sigma \Sigma \sigma^2$ = the standard deviation of the sum of variances.[2]

Some Problems

PERT can be used effectively for nonroutine projects that can be broken into simple routine steps. PERT becomes ineffective without a basic knowledge of questionnaire construction or in a field survey where the mechanics of the activity in terms of time, effort, and cost are not known. Furthermore, if the research project is somewhat routinized, the value of PERT tends to disappear. However, PERT can be useful for many of the larger research projects.

CONTROLLING AND GUIDING THE TOTAL RESEARCH PROGRAM

Turning to the total research effort, lack of standardization and uniformity in the output of any staff group makes the control process difficult; therefore, little attempt is normally made to establish meaningful control procedures. In loosely organized companies this results in control passing, in effect, to that function that makes the most demands for the attention of the staff group.

Marketing research, like other staff functions, needs constant orientation and guidance to ensure productive contribution. Various means of accomplishing this are discussed in this section.

Advisory Committees

There is probably no better administrative means for evaluating and controlling the total mar-

keting research effort than the advisory committee. Such a committee is composed of representatives from all functions served by research, both within and outside the marketing operation, normally including representatives from advertising, field sales, product planning, brand management, product development, and similar functions.

The advisory committee does not discuss research techniques, review completed studies, or evaluate proposed research designs for major studies; it is not an executive committee to whom research reports for decisions on problems of a current nature are submitted. Rather, the advisory committee provides the overall direction of the marketing research program toward problem areas of greatest importance to the marketing system and to the total company. This committee identifies the principal information needs over the next three to six months so the research effort will not become diverted or dissipated. Some firms like to have an annual research plan to give even more direction to the research effort.

Auditing Marketing Research

Over 15 years ago, Sessions proposed that the marketing research effort be audited thoroughly in terms of present needs and long-range objectives [15]. Few strides have been made since that time in this important direction. One recent text comments, "If the time was ripe in 1950, how much more ripe it is today!" [12, p. 181].

Sessions suggested that an audit be designed to answer three key questions:

1. Is the research program in keeping with the character of the company as well as its needs?
2. How can the administration of research be made to set the pace for operating efficiency?
3. Is the research staff sufficiently in touch with the realm of ideas which determine sales growth and future market position for the company?

He suggested as a first step that of "qualifying the company, having auditors develop a clear picture of how the company is organized to make and to communicate decisions. Subsequent steps include establishing benchmarks for analysis in terms of the duties and responsibilities of research, auditing the internal research operation against these benchmarks, and finally preparing a complete report of findings and recommendations [15].

The audit could be done by company personnel under the direction of top management. This would appear similar to the advisory committee approach discussed above, although not on such a regular basis. Also Crisp discussed a number of potential sources for an audit of the entire marketing program (self-appraisal, audit from above, task force) and concluded:

> It seems obvious that a marketing audit which is going to make anything approaching a maximum contribution to a small or medium-sized company will have to be spearheaded and directed by someone outside the company . . . working effectively with a team of inside people, the consultant can advise, initiate, and plan—and then get out of the company's hair while the work is being done. Later he can come back to provide analyses, appraisals and recommendations before moving on to the next area [5, p. 44].

An audit directed by an outside consulting firm would provide a perspective based on experience and knowledge gained from working with many business firms. Another promising source is nearby major universities, since faculties of business administration schools normally have a wide variety of backgrounds and experience in various aspects of marketing and marketing research.

Budget Controls

Any discussion of control devices would not be complete without reference to budgets. Although a detailed discussion of budgets is beyond the scope of this article, attention must be given to the monetary dimension of research control. The research budget is an important total constraint on research activities, both single project and total effort.

One budgetary strategy not often used is to establish research funds within the budgets of other functional marketing areas, such as field sales, advertising, product planning, and brand management. Each of these then purchases research services as its own needs arise, thus working backward from identification of operational needs to the fulfillment of these needs. This means that research has no more total budget than the sum of the individual research budgets within the functional areas. And if these areas are either unable or unwilling to obtain funds for this purpose, the research effort shrinks.

Another approach is simply to establish an overall budget for the research function at the beginning of the year, based upon past amounts and tempered by the research activity generally expected for the coming year. Or a company could consult one or more published surveys to find the average amount spent for research by companies of the same size and industry type [6, 19]. Another alternative is to budget a certain amount for each of several research activities, field survey interviewing, continuing panel or audit services, and computer expense, etc. Of course, this would be in addition to such overhead items as personnel salaries, employee benefits, and small equipment needs.

All of the above approaches are subject to the criticism that they leave little room for flexibility in research, by either the research manager or top management. Little scrutiny is given to the need for research, the value of research, and the contribution it can make to the marketing effort, either overall or in part. Specifically, research expenditures should be tied to the objects of these expenditures, using methods discussed earlier in this paper. Management should know in some detail how and when research will be needed during the next six months to a year. In this way, budgets would be established based on the task method, as has been recommended for advertising and other marketing staff functions.

CONCLUSIONS

Control and evaluation is a continual process, as important (and difficult) in marketing research as in other staff functions throughout the firm. It will never be possible to exercise the same degree of control over staff as over line functions, but far more can be done to evaluate and control research in most large manufacturing and service firms than is now being done.

Better control is necessarily related to norms dealing with research inputs and processes. Therefore, it is obvious where the real future progress lies. Being able to evaluate and control these processes in terms of the scarce elements of management (i.e., time, effort, and money) provides the direction for avenues of maturity in marketing research administration.

Notes

1. Most of the discussion and the computations presented in this section were prepared by one of the author's graduate research assistants, Ronald J. Bosgell, instructor, Division of Business, Eastern Illinois University.
2. The variance σ^2 is computed by using the following formula:

$$\sigma^2 = \left(\frac{b-a}{6}\right)^2$$

where a = optimistic time and b = pessimistic time. By determining the corresponding area of the outcome under a normal curve, the probability of the project's completion by the scheduled date can be found.

References

1. Lee Adler, "Phasing Research into the Marketing Plan," *Harvard Business Review*, 38 (May - June 1960), 113-22.
2. Ralph Alexander, "The Marketing Manager's Dilemma," *Journal of Marketing*, 30 (January 1966), 62-3.
3. Seymour Banks, *Experimentation in Marketing*, New York: McGraw-Hill Book Co., Inc., 1965, 15-22.
4. Frank M. Bass, "Marketing Research Expenditures: A Decision Model," *Journal of Business*, 39 (January 1963), 77-90.
5. Richard Crisp, "Auditing the Functional Elements of a Marketing Operation," in *Analyzing and Improving Marketing Performance*, AMA Management Report No. 32, New York: American Management Association, 1959, 37-46.
6. ____, *Marketing Research Organization and Operation*, American Management Association, Research Study No. 35, 1958.
7. Ralph L. Day, "Optimizing Market Research Through Cost-Benefit Analysis," *Business Horizons*, 9 (Fall 1966), 45-54.
8. E. L. Eldridge, "Check List for Eldridge Marketing Plan," in Steuart H. Britt and Harper W. Boyd, eds., *Marketing Management and Administrative Behavior*, New York: McGraw-Hill Book Co., Inc., 1963, 194-202.
9. Harry F. Evarts, *Introduction to PERT*, Boston: Allyn and Bacon, Inc., 1964.
10. Morriss J. Gottlieb and Irving Roshwolb, "The Present Value Concept in Evaluating New Products," in J. S. Wright and J. I. Godstucker eds., *New Ideas for Successful Marketing*, Chicago: American Marketing Association, 1966, 387-400.
11. Paul E. Green and Donald S. Tull, *Research for Marketing Decisions*, Prentice-Hall, Inc., 1966.
12. Hector Lazo and Arnold Corbin, *Management in Marketing*, New York: McGraw-Hill Book Co., Inc., 1964.
13. W. F. Massy and J. D. Sarvas, "Logical Flow Models for Marketing Analysis," *Journal of Marketing*, 28 (January 1964), 32-7.
14. J. I. Miller, "The Real Challenge of Research," *Business Horizons*, 1 (Winter 1958), 58-64.
15. Richard E. Sessions, "A Management Audit of Marketing Research," *Journal of Marketing*, 14 (Summer 1950), 111-9.
16. E. C. Soistman, "Research and Development Can Be Controlled," *Research Management*, 9 (January 1966), 15-27.
17. Gabriel M. Stillion, *et al.*, *PERT, A New Management Planning and Control Technique*, New York: American Management Association, 1962.
18. Dik W. Twedt, "What is the 'Return on Investment' in Marketing Research," *Journal of Marketing*, 30 (January 1966), 62-3.
19. ____, *A Survey of Marketing Research*, Chicago: American Marketing Association, 1963.

17 POSITIONING CUTS THROUGH CHAOS IN THE MARKETPLACE

Jack Trout
Vice President
Ries, Cappiello, Colwell, Inc.

Al Ries
President
Ries, Cappiello, Colwell, Inc.

"Advertising is entering an era where strategy is king," say two agency executives. Positioning, a venerable term in product development, has now been extended to the advertising world.

As far as advertising is concerned, the good old days are gone forever.

As the president of a large consumer products company said recently, "Count on your fingers the number of successful new national brands introduced in the last two years. You won't get to your pinky."

Not that a lot of companies haven't tried. Every supermarket is filled with shelf after shelf of "half successful" brands. The manufacturers of these me-too products cling to the hope that they can develop a brilliant advertising campaign which will lift their offspring into the winner's circle.

Meanwhile, they hang in there with coupons, deals, point of purchase displays. But profits are hard to come by and that "brilliant" advertising campaign, even if it comes, doesn't ever seem to turn the brand around.

From Al Ries and Jack Trout, "Positioning Cuts Through Chaos in the Marketplace," **Advertising Age,** *May 1, 1972, pp. 51-54. Reprinted by permission of the publisher.*

No wonder management people turn skeptical when the subject of advertising comes up. And instead of looking for new ways to put the power of advertising to work, management invents schemes for reducing the cost of what they are currently doing. Witness the rise of the house agency, the media buying service, the barter deal.

Ads Don't Work Like They Used To

The chaos in the marketplace is a reflection of the fact that advertising just doesn't work like it used to. But old traditional ways of doing things die hard. "There's no reason that advertising can't do the job," say the defenders of the status quo, "as long as the product is good, the plan is sound and the commercials are creative."

But they overlook one big, loud reason. The marketplace itself. The noise level today is far too high. Not only the volume of advertising, but also the volume of products and brands.

To cope with this assault on his or her mind, the average consumer has run out of brain power and mental ability. And with a rising standard of living the average consumer is less and less interested in making the "best" choice. For many of today's more affluent customers, a "satisfactory" brand is good enough.

Advertising prepared in the old, traditional ways has no hope of being successful in today's chaotic marketplace.

In the past, advertising was prepared in isolation. That is, you studied the product and its features and then you prepared advertising which communicated to your customers and prospects the benefits of those features.

It didn't make much difference whether the competition offered those features or not. In the traditional approach, you ignored competition and made every claim seem like a preemptive claim. Mentioning a competitive product, for example, was considered not only bad taste, but poor strategy as well.

In the positioning era, however, the rules are reversed. To establish a position, you must often not only name competitive names, but also ignore most of the old advertising rules as well.

In category after category, the prospect already knows the benefits of using the product. To climb on his product ladder, you must relate your brand to the brands already there.

Avis Took 'Against' Position

In today's marketplace, the competitor's image is just as important as your own. Sometimes more important. An early success in the positioning era was the famous Avis campaign.

The Avis campaign will go down in marketing history as a classic example of establishing the "against" position. In the case of Avis, this was a position against the leader.

"Avis is only Number 2 in rent-a-cars, so why go with us? We try harder."

For 13 straight years, Avis lost money. Then they admitted they were No. 2 and have made money every year since. Avis was able to make substantial gains because they recognized the position of Hertz and didn't try to attack them head-on.

VW Made "Ugly" Position Work

A company can sometimes be successful by accepting a position that no one else wants. For example, virtually all automobile manufacturers want the public to think they make cars that are good looking. As a result, Volkswagen was able to establish a unique position for themselves. By default.

The strength of this position, of course, is that it communicates the idea of reliability in a powerful way. "The 1970 VW will stay ugly longer" was a powerful statement because it is psychologically sound. When an advertiser admits a negative, the reader is inclined to give them the positive.

A similar principle is involved in Smucker's jams and jellies. "With a name like Smucker's," says the advertising, "you know it's got to be good."

Battle of the Colas

The advantage of owning a position can be seen most clearly in the soft drink field. Three major cola brands compete in what is really not a contest. For every ten bottles of Coke, only four bottles of Pepsi and one bottle of Royal Crown are consumed.

While there may be room in the market for a No. 2 cola, the position of Royal Crown is weak. In 1970, for example, Coca-Cola's sales increase over the previous year (168,000,000 cases) was more than Royal Crown's entire volume (156,000,000 cases).

Obviously, Coke has a strong grip on the cola position. And there's not much room left for the other brands. But, strange as it might seem, there might be a spot for a reverse kind of product. One of the most interesting positioning ideas is the one currently being used by Seven-Up. It's the "Un-Cola" and it seems silly until you take a closer look.

"Wet and Wild" was a good campaign in the image era. But the "Un-Cola" is a great program in the positioning era. Sales jumped something like 10 per cent the first year the product was positioned against the cola field. And the increases have continued.

The brilliance of this idea can only be appreciated when you comprehend the intense share of mind enjoyed by the cola category. Two out of three soft drinks consumed in the U.S. are cola drinks.

By linking the product to what's already in the mind of the prospect, the Un-Cola position establishes Seven-Up as an alternative to a cola drink.

A somewhat similar positioning program is working in the media field. This is the "third newsweekly" concept being used by *Sports Illustrated* to get into the mind of the media buyer.

It obviously is an immensely successful program. But what may not be so obvious, is why it works. The "third newsweekly" certainly doesn't describe *Sports Illustrated*. (As the Un-Cola doesn't describe Seven-Up.)

What it does do, however, is to relate the magazine to a media category that is uppermost in the prospect's mind (as the Un-Cola relates to the soft drink category that is uppermost in the mind).

Both the Seven-Up and the *Sports Illustrated* programs are dramatic reminders that positioning is not something you do with the product. Positioning is something you do with the mind. That is, you position the product in the mind of the prospect.

You Can Reposition Competitor

In order to position your own brand, it's sometimes necessary to reposition the competitor.

In the case of Beck's beer, the repositioning is done at the expense of Lowenbrau: "You've tasted the German beer that's the most popular in America. Now taste the German beer that's the most popular in Germany."

This strategy works because the prospect had assumed something about Lowenbrau that wasn't true.

The current program for Raphael aperitif wine also illustrates this point. The ads show a bottle of "made in France" Raphael and a bottle of "made in U.S.A." Dubonnet. "For $1.00 a bottle less," says the headline, "you can enjoy the imported one." The shock, of course, is to find that Dubonnet is a product of the U.S.

Plight of Airline X

In the positioning era, the name of a company or product is becoming more and more important. The name is the hook that allows the mind to hang the brand on its product ladder. Given a poor name, even the best brand in the world won't be able to hang on.

Take the airline industry. The big four domestic carriers are United, American, TWA and an airline we'll call Airline X.

Like all airlines, Airline X has had its ups and downs. Unfortunately, there have been more downs than ups. But unlike some of its more complacent competitors, Airline X has tried. A number of years ago, it brought in big league marketing people and pushed in the throttle.

Airline X was among the first to "paint the planes," "improve the food" and "dress up the stewardesses" in an effort to improve its reputation.

And Airline X hasn't been bashful when it comes to spending money. Year after year, it has one of the biggest advertising budgets in the industry. Even though it advertises itself as "the second largest passenger carrier of all the airlines in the free world," you may not have guessed that Airline X is Eastern. Right up there spending with the worldwide names.

For all that money, what do you think of Eastern? Where do you think they fly? Up and down the East Coast, to Boston, Washington, Miami, right? Well, Eastern also goes to St. Louis, New Orleans, Atlanta, San Francisco, Acapulco. But Eastern has a regional name and their competitors have broader names which tell the prospect they fly everywhere.

Look at the problem from just one of Eastern's cities, Indianapolis. From Indianapolis, Eastern flies *north* to Chicago, Milwaukee and Minneapolis. And *south* to Birmingham and Mobile. They just don't happen to fly *east*.

And then there is the lush San Juan run which Eastern has been serving for more than 25 years. Eastern used to get the lion's share of this market. Then early last year American Airlines took over Trans Caribbean. So today, who is number one to the San Juan sun? Why American, of course.

No matter how hard you try, you can't hang "The Wings of Man" on a regional name. When the prospect is given a choice, he or she is going to prefer the national airline, not the regional one.

B. F. Goodrich Has Identity Crisis

What does a company do when its name (Goodrich) is similar to the name of a much larger company in the same field (Goodyear)?

Goodrich has problems. They could reinvent the wheel and Goodyear would get most of the credit.

If you watched the Super Bowl last January, you saw both Goodrich and Goodyear advertise their "American-made radial-ply tires." But which company do you think got their money's worth at $200,000 a pop?

We haven't seen the research, but our bet would be on Goodyear, the company that owns the tire position.

Beware of the No-Name Trap

But even bad names like Eastern and Goodrich are better than no name at all.

In *Fortune's* list of 500 largest industrials, there are now 16 corporate nonentities. That is, 16 major American companies have legally changed their names to meaningless initials.

How many of these companies can you recognize: ACF, AMF, AMP, ATO, CPC, ESB, FMC, GAF, NVF, NL, PPG, RCA, SCM, TRW, USM and VF?

These are not tiny companies either. The smallest of them, AMP, has more than 10,000 employees and sales of over $225,000,000 a year.

What companies like ACF, AMF, AMP and the others fail to realize is that their initials have to stand for something. A prospect must know your name first before he or she can remember your initials.

GE stands for General Electric. IBM stands for International Business Machines. And everyone knows it. But how many people knew that ACF stood for American Car & Foundry?

Furthermore, now that ACF has legally changed its name to initials, there's presumably no way to even expose the prospect to the original name.

An exception seems to be RCA. After all, everyone knows that RCA stands for, or rather used to stand for, Radio Corp. of America.

That may be true today. But what about tomorrow? What will people think 20 years from now when they see those strange initials? Roman Catholic Archdiocese?

And take Corn Products Co. Presumably it changed its name to CPC International because it makes products out of lots of things besides corn, but you can't remember "CPC" without bringing Corn Products Co. to mind. The tragedy is, CPC made the change to "escape" the past. Yet the exact opposite occurred.

Line Extension Can Be Trap, Too

Names are tricky. Consider the Protein 21/29 shampoo, hair spray, conditioner, concentrate mess.

Back in 1970, the Mennen Co. introduced a combination shampoo conditioner called "Protein 21." By moving rapidly with a $6,000,000 introductory campaign (followed by a $9,000,000 program the next year), Mennen rapidly carved out a 13 per cent share of the $300,000,000 shampoo market.

Then Mennen hit the line extension lure. In rapid succession, the company introduced Protein 21 hair spray, Protein 29 hair spray (for men), Protein 21 conditioner (in two formulas), Protein 21 concentrate. To add to the confusion, the original Protein 21 was available in three different formulas (for dry, oily and regular hair).

Can you imagine how confused the prospect must be trying to figure out what to put on his or her head? No wonder Protein 21's share of the shampoo market has fallen from 13 per cent to 11 per cent. And the decline is bound to continue.

Free Ride Can Be Costly

Another similar marketing pitfall recently befell, of all companies, Miles Laboratories.

You can see how it happens. A bunch of the boys are sitting around a conference table trying to name a new cold remedy.

"I have it," says Harry. "Let's call it Alka-Seltzer Plus. That way we can take advantage of the $20,000,000 we're already spending to promote the Alka-Seltzer name."

"Good thinking, Harry," and another money-saving idea is instantly accepted.

But lo and behold, instead of eating into the Dristan and Contac market, the new product turns around and eats into the Alka-Seltzer market.

And you know Miles must be worried. In every TV commercial, the "Alka-Seltzer" gets smaller and smaller and the "Plus" gets bigger and bigger.

Related to the free-ride trap, but not exactly the same, is another common error of judgment called the "well-known name" trap.

Both General Electric and RCA thought they could take their strong positions against IBM in computers. But just because a company is well known in one field doesn't mean it can transfer that recognition to another.

In other words, your brand can be on top

of one ladder and nowhere on another. And the further apart the products are conceptually, the greater the difficulty of making the jump.

In the past when there were fewer companies and fewer products, a well-known name was a much greater asset than it is today. Because of the noise level, a "well-known" company has tremendous difficulty trying to establish a position in a different field than the one in which it built its reputation.

You Can't Appeal to Everyone

A human emotion called "greed" often leads an advertiser into another error. American Motors' introduction of the Hornet is one of the best examples of the "everybody" trap.

You might remember the ads, "The little rich car. American Motors Hornet: $1,994 to $3,589."

A product that tries to appeal to everyone winds up appealing to no one. People who want to spend $3,500 for a car don't buy the Hornet because they don't want their friends to think they're driving a $1,900 car. People who want to spend $1,900 for a car don't buy the Hornet because they don't want a car with $1,600 worth of accessories taken off of it.

Avoid the F.W.M.T.S. Trap

If the current Avis advertising is any indication, the company has "forgotten what made them successful."

The original campaign not only related No. 2 Avis to No. 1 Hertz, but also exploited the love that people have for the underdog. The new campaign (Avis is going to be No. 1) not only is conventional "brag and boast" advertising, but also dares the prospect to make the prediction not come true.

Our prediction: Avis ain't going to be No. 1. Further prediction: Avis will lose ground to Hertz and National.

Another company that seems to have fallen into the forgotten what made them successful trap is Volkswagen.

"Think small" was perhaps the most famous advertisement of the sixties. Yet last year VW ran an ad that said, "Volkswagen introduces a new kind of Volkswagen. Big."

O.K., Volkswagen, should we think small or should we think big?

Confusion is the enemy of successful positioning. Prediction: Rapid erosion of the Beetle's position in the U.S. market.

The world seems to be turning faster.

Years ago, a successful product might live 50 years or more before fading away. Today, a product's life cycle is much shorter. Sometimes it can be measured in months instead of years.

New products, new services, new markets, even new media are constantly being born. They grow up into adulthood and then slide into oblivion. And a new cycle starts again.

Yesterday, beer and hard liquor were campus favorites. Today it's wine.

Yesterday, the well-groomed man had his hair cut every week. Today, it's every month or two.

Yesterday, the way to reach the masses was the mass magazines. Today, it's network TV. Tomorrow, it could be cable.

The only permanent thing in life today is change. And the successful companies of tomorrow will be those companies that have learned to cope with it.

The acceleration of "change" creates enormous pressures on companies to think in terms of tactics rather than strategy. As one respected advertising man commented, "The day seems to be past when long-range strategy can be a winning technique."

But is change the way to keep pace with change? The exact opposite appears to be true.

The landscape is littered with the debris of projects that companies rushed into in attempting to "keep pace." Singer trying to move into the boom in home appliances. RCA moving into the boom in computers. General Foods moving into the boom in fast-food outlets. Not to mention the hundreds of companies that threw away their corporate identities to chase the passing fad to initials.

While the programs of those who kept at what they did best and held their ground have been immensely successful. Maytag selling their reliable appliances. Walt Disney selling his world of fantasy and fun. Avon calling.

And take margarine. Thirty years ago the first successful margarine brands positioned themselves against butter. "Tastes like the high-priced spread," said a typical ad.

And what works today? Why the same strategy. "It isn't nice to fool Mother Nature," says the Chiffon commercial, and sales go up 25 per cent. Chiffon is once again the best selling brand of soft margarine.

Long-Range Thinking Important

Change is a wave on the ocean of time. Short-term, the waves cause agitation and confusion, but long-term the underlying currents are much more significant.

To cope with change, it's important to take a long-range point of view. To determine your basic business. Positioning is a concept that is cumulative. Something that takes advantage of advertising's long-range nature.

In the seventies a company must think even more strategically than it did before. Changing the direction of a large company is like trying to turn an aircraft carrier. It takes a mile before anything happens. And if it was a wrong turn, getting back on course takes even longer.

To play the game successfully, you must make decisions on what your company will be doing not next month or next year, but in five years, ten years. In other words, instead of turning the wheel to meet each fresh wave, a company must point itself in the right direction.

You must have vision. There's no sense building a position based on a technology that's too narrow. Or a product that's becoming obsolete. Remember the famous *Harvard Business Review* article entitled "Marketing Myopia"? It still applies.

If a company has positioned itself in the right direction, it will be able to ride the currents of change, ready to take advantage of those opportunities that are right for it. But when an opportunity arrives, a company must be ready to move quickly.

Because of the enormous advantages that accrue to being the leader, most companies are not interested in learning how to *compete* with

the leader. They want to be the leader. They want to be Hertz rather than Avis. *Time* rather than *Newsweek*. General Electric rather than Westinghouse.

Historically, however, product leadership is usually the result of an accident, rather than a preconceived plan.

The xerography process, for example, was offered to 32 different companies (including IBM and Kodak) before it wound up at the old Haloid Co. Renamed Haloid Xerox and then finally Xerox, the company has since dominated the copier market. Xerox now owns the copier position.

Were IBM and Kodak stupid to turn down xerography? Of course not. These companies reject thousands of ideas every year.

Perhaps a better description of the situation at the time was that Haloid, a small manufacturer of photographic supplies, was desperate, and the others weren't. As a result, it took a chance that more prudent companies couldn't be expected to take.

When you trace the history of how leadership positions were established, from Hershey in chocolate to Hertz in rent-a-cars, the common thread is not marketing skill or even product innovation. The common thread is seizing the initiative before the competitor has a chance to get established. In someone's oldtime military terms, the marketing leader "got there firstest with the mostest." The leader usually poured in the marketing money while the situation was still fluid.

IBM, for example, didn't invent the computer. Sperry Rand did. But IBM owns the computer position because they built their computer fortress before competition arrived.

And the position that Hershey established in chocolate was so strong they didn't need to advertise at all, a luxury that competitors like Nestle couldn't afford.

You can see that establishing a leadership position depends not only on luck and timing, but also upon a willingness to "pour it on" when other stand back and wait.

Yet all too often, the product leader makes the fatal mistake of attributing its success to marketing skill. As a result, it thinks it can transfer that skill to other products and other marketing situations.

Witness, for example, the sorry record of Xerox in computers. In May of 1969, Xerox exchanged nearly 10,000,000 shares of stock (worth nearly a billion dollars) for Scientific Data Systems Inc. Since the acquisition, the company (renamed Xerox Data Systems) has lost millions of dollars, and without Xerox's support would have probably gone bankrupt.

And the mecca of marketing knowledge, International Business Machines Corp., hasn't done much better. So far, the IBM plain-paper copier hasn't made much of a dent in Xerox's business. Touche.

The rules of positioning hold for all types of products. In the packaged goods area, for example, Bristol-Myers tried to take on Crest toothpaste with Fact (killed after $5,000,000 was spent on promotion). Then they tried to go after Alka-Seltzer with Resolve (killed after $11,000,000 was spent). And according to a headline in the February 7 [1972] issue of *Advertising Age*, "Bristol-Meyers will test Dissolve aspirin in an attempt to unseat Bayer."

The suicidal bent of companies that go head-on against established competition is hard to understand. They know the score, yet they forge ahead anyway. In the marketing war, a "charge of the light brigade" happens every day. With the same predictable result.

One Strategy for Leader

Successful marketing strategy usually consists of keeping your eyes open to possibilities and then striking before the product leader is firmly fixed.

As a matter of fact, the marketing leader is usually the one who moves the ladder into the mind with his or her brand nailed to the one and only rung. Once there, what can a company do to keep its top-dog position?

There are two basic strategies that should be used hand in hand. They seem contradictory, but aren't. One is to ignore competition, and the other is to cover all bets.

As long as a company owns the position, there's no point in running ads that scream, "We're

No. 1." Much better is to enhance the product category in the prospect's mind. Notice the current IBM campaign that ignores competition and sells the value of computers. All computers, not just the company's types.

Although the leader's advertising should ignore the competition, the leader shouldn't. The second rule is to cover all bets.

This means a leader should swallow his or her pride and adopt every new product development as soon as it shows signs of promise. Too often, however, the leader pooh-poohs the development, and doesn't wake up until it's too late.

Another Strategy for Non-Leaders

Most companies are in the No. 2, 3, 4 or even worse category. What then?

Hope springs eternal in the human breast. Nine times out of ten, the also-ran sets out to attack the leader, a la RCA's assault on IBM. Result: Disaster.

Simply stated, the first rule of positioning is this: You can't compete head-on against a company that has a strong, established position. You can go around, under or over, but never head-to-head.

The leader owns the high ground. The No. 1 position in the prospect's mind. The top rung of the product ladder.

The classic example of No. 2 strategy is Avis. But many marketing people misread the Avis story. They assume the company was successful because it tried harder.

Not at all. Avis was successful because it related itself to the position of Hertz. Avis preempted the No. 2 position. (If trying harder were the secret of success, Harold Stassen would be president.)

Most marketplaces have room for a strong No. 2 company provided they position themselves clearly as an alternative to the leader. In the computer field, for example, Honeywell has used this strategy successfully.

"The other computer company vs. Mr. Big," says a typical Honeywell ad. Honeywell is doing what none of the other computer companies seems to be willing to do. Admit that IBM is, in fact, the leader in the computer business. Maybe that's why Honeywell and Mr. Big are the only large companies reported to be making money on computers.

Some 'Strong' Positions Aren't

Yet there are positions that can be taken. These are positions that look strong, but in reality are weak.

Take the position of Scott in paper products. Scott has about 40 per cent of the $1.2 billion market for towels, napkins, toilet tissues and other consumer paper products. But Scott, like Mennen with Protein 21, fell into the line-extension trap.

ScotTowels, ScotTissue, Scotties, Scottkins, even BabyScott. All of these names undermined the Scott foundation. The more products hung on the Scott name, the less meaning the name had to the average consumer.

When Procter & Gamble attacked with Mr. Whipple and his tissue-squeezers, it was no contest. Charmin is now the No. 1 brand in the toilet-tissue market.

In Scott's case, a large "share of market" didn't mean they owned the position. More important is a large "share of mind." The housewife could write "Charmin, Kleenex, Bounty and Pampers" on her shopping list and know exactly what products she was going to get. "Scott" on a shopping list has no meaning. The actual brand names aren't much help either. Which brand, for example, is engineered for the nose, Scotties or Scot-Tissue?

In positioning terms, the name "Scott" exists in limbo. It isn't firmly ensconced on any product ladder.

Eliminate Egos from Decision Making

To repeat, the name is the hook that hangs the brand on the product ladder in the prospect's mind. In the positioning era, the brand name to give a product is probably a company's single, most important marketing decision.

To be successful in the positioning era, advertising and marketing people must be brutally frank. They must try to eliminate all ego from the decision making process. It only clouds the issue.

One of the most critical aspects of "positioning" is being able to evaluate objectively products and how they are viewed by customers and prospects.

As a rule, when it comes to building strong programs, trust no one, especially managers who are all wrapped up in their products. The closer people get to products, the more they defend old decisions or old promises.

Successful companies get their information from the marketplace. That's the place where the program has to succeed, not in the product manager's office.

A company that keeps its eye on Tom, Dick and Harry is going to miss Pierre, Hans and Yoshio.

Marketing is rapidly becoming a worldwide ball game. A company that owns a position in one country now finds that it can use that position to wedge its way into another.

IBM has 62 per cent of the German computer market. Is this fact surprising? It shouldn't be. IBM earns more than 50 per cent of its profits outside the U.S.

As companies start to operate on a worldwide basis, they often discover they have a name problem.

A typical example is U.S. Rubber, a worldwide company that marketed many products not made of rubber. Changing the name to Uniroyal created a new corporate identity that could be used worldwide.

Creativity Takes Back Seat

In the seventies, creativity will have to take a back seat to strategy.

Advertising Age itself reflects this fact. Today you find fewer stories about individual campaigns and more stories about what's happening in an entire industry. Creativity alone isn't a worthwhile objective in an era where a company can spend millions of dollars on great advertising and still fail miserably in the marketplace.

Consider what Harry McMahan calls the "Curse of Clio." In the past, the American Festival has made special awards to "Hall of Fame Classics." Of the 41 agencies that won these Clio awards, 31 have lost some or all of these particular accounts.

But the cult of creativity dies hard. One agency president said recently, "Oh, we do positioning all the time. But after we develop the position, we turn it over to the creative department." And too often, of course, the creativity does nothing but obscure the positioning.

In the positioning era, the key to success is to run the naked positioning statement, unadorned by so-called creativity.

Ask Yourself These Questions

If these examples have moved you to want to apply positioning thinking to your own company's situation, here are some questions to ask yourself:

1. What position, if any, do we already own in the prospect's mind?

Get the answer to this question from the marketplace, not the marketing manager. If this requires a few dollars for research, so be it. Spend the money. It's better to know exactly what you're up against now than to discover it later when nothing can be done about it.

2. What position do we want to own?

Here is where you bring out your crystal ball and try to figure out the best position to own from a long-term point of view.

3. What companies must be out-gunned if we are to establish that position?

If your proposed position calls for a head-to-head approach against a marketing leader, forget it. It's better to go around an obstacle rather than over it. Back up. Try to select a position that no one else has a firm grip on.

4. Do we have enough marketing money to occupy and hold the position?

A big obstacle to successful positioning is attempting to achieve the impossible. It takes money to build a share of mind. It takes money to establish a position. It takes money to hold a position once you've established it.

The noise level today is fierce. There are just too many "me-too" products and too many "me-too" companies vying for the mind of the prospect. Getting noticed is getting tougher.

5. Do we have the guts to stick with one consistent positioning concept?

With the noise level out there, a company has to be bold enough and consistent enough to cut through.

The first step in a positioning program normally entails running fewer programs, but stronger ones. This sounds simple, but actually runs counter to what usually happens as corporations get larger. They normally run more programs, but weaker ones. It's this fragmentation that can make many large advertising budgets just about invisible in today's media storm.

6. Does our creative approach match our positioning strategy?

Creative people often resist positioning thinking because they believe it restricts their creativity. And it does. But creativity isn't the objective in the seventies. Even "communications" itself isn't the objective.

The name of the marketing game in the seventies is "positioning." And only the better players will survive.

18
SINGLE FAMILY:

Stop Thinking Basic House, Start Thinking Basic Market

Natalie Gerardi
Associate Editor
House and Home *magazine*

One of the last bastions of "seat-of-the-pants" marketing is the fragmented housing industry. A trade journal for home builders tells its readers how several marketing specialists have analyzed today's buyers.

Ever since single-family emerged as the only relatively crunch-proof market, the so-called basic house has been getting most of the headlines. The idea seems to be that if you reduce the house to a minimum-sized box and strip it of all its amenities, sales will soar and boom times will return to homebuilding.

This has an unpleasantly familiar ring. It sounds like the same kind of oversimplification that during the past six years led to deep trouble in both the rental housing and condo markets.

So in preparing this issue, *House & Home's* editors turned to four experts whose business depend on accurate judgment of the housing market: Kenneth Agid, residential marketing director of the giant Irvine Co.; George Fulton, marketing vice president of Walker & Lee, the largest new-home realty firm in the country; William Mitchell, president of Market Profiles, a comprehensive marketing company; and Alfred Gobar, president

From Natalie Gerardi, "Single Family: Stop Thinking Basic House, Start Thinking Basic Market," House & Home *(February 1976), pp. 59-63. Reprinted by permission of* House & Home.

of Alfred Gobar Associates, one of the most respected market research firms in the country.

The experts agreed on a fundamental point: Single-family isn't a market—it's three markets. Specifically:

> *The price-sensitive market,* which is just what its name says it is. This is potentially the biggest single-family market, but also the one most vulnerable to rising construction costs.

> *The discretionary market,* made up chiefly of trade-up buyers. This is a tricky market, but right now it's the strongest of the three.

> *The luxury market.* Price is not much of a factor here, but the size of the market is limited and the buyers are discriminating and demanding.

These markets are not delineated so much by price—for example, the same house that costs $25,000 in Alabama will cost nearly $40,000 in Orange County, California—as by the characteristics of the buyers. Moreover, within the three basic markets there are subcategories that also have their own special characteristics.

The Price-Sensitive Market

The price-sensitive market includes two groups of buyers. First, there are the young professionals. They're strapped for cash because they're just beginning their careers. But they know they'll be making much more money in a few years.

Then there are the static-income buyers—blue-collar workers and municipal employees who can look forward to cost-of-living raises, but no great jump in income.

Rising property taxes and construction costs have made it hard for both of these groups to afford a home. "We know a builder who has to sell just about every house five times before the lender qualifies a buyer," says Al Gobar. "This situation is beginning to show up in a number of markets around the country."

And George Fulton points to a recent Walker & Lee survey that showed that, typically, price-sensitive buyers have to double their current monthly shelter payments—from 15% of gross income to as much as 32%—to buy a new home today.

The Discretionary Market

The discretionary market consists of families who already own homes. They are under no great pressure to move, and luring them out of their present homes is a real challenge for it often means doubling their monthly payments. In the subdivision surveyed by Walker & Lee, for example, the discretionary buyers had upped their monthly payments from 12% of gross income to 27%.

"High-income households are allocating more of their income to housing than ever before," says Gobar. He points out that as recently as 1970, a family making $50,000 a year would typically spend only 1.7 times its income for a house, while a family making $25,000 would spend 2.3 times income. Now they're both spending 2.3 times income.

Gobar's national statistics are borne out by Walker & Lee's buyer profiles. Discretionary buyers bought homes priced at 2.6 times the husband's income or 2.5 times family income; price-sensitive buyers bought homes costing 2.6 times the husband's income or 2.1 times family income.

So today's discretionary buyers must often make the same sacrifices—fewer luxuries, cars, vacations, etc.—that price-sensitive buyers have traditionally made to buy a new home. And often a family can afford to move up only if the wife goes to work.

The Luxury Market

The luxury market doesn't have to make any sacrifices. These buyers can afford to wait around until they find just what they want, and then buy it. Bill Mitchell likes to compare the luxury buyer to a 1,000-lb. gorilla—he sits where he wants to.

It's important to remember that there's no inherent market here, he says. The demand has to be created, and it's dependent on a unique, even flamboyant product plus effective promotion.

Also there's a danger that too many builders will jump into this market at the same time. It's not very large, and can easily be overbuilt.

YOU HAVE TO KNOW WHAT TURNS THESE THREE MARKETS ON

The Luxury Buyer

The luxury buyer is turned on by more and more. So you keep adding features—and they'll differ in different parts of the country—until you create the right feeling of exclusivity. Within reason, the higher the price the better; image is what the luxury buyer is after.

The Price-Sensitive Buyer

The price-sensitive buyer is just the opposite. Price is the determining factor. So you keep subtracting things from the house until you reach the point of market resistance.

Both groups of price-sensitive buyers—the young professionals and the static-incomes—are willing to make sacrifices in such things as lot size, extra bathrooms and appliances.

But what may be a basic house for a static-income family may not be a basic house for a young professional. Static-income buyers fear they will soon be priced out of the market altogether, and thus are willing to make great sacrifices to buy a home now. The young professionals, on the other hand, would prefer to stay in an apartment until they can afford what they want, rather than settle for housing that's not up to their standards.

It's particularly important to the young professionals that they live among people like themselves. Nor will they compromise on community amenities, such as schools and recreation. That's why in Orange County, for example, which has a high concentration of young professionals because of the types of job opportunities available, the lowest-priced homes are the slowest sellers.

Potentially, the price-sensitive market is the largest. A substantial part of the demand, however, cannot be satisfied under today's conditions.

"It will take major changes in such areas as consumer expectations, financing methods and dependence on the automobile," says Ken Agid, "before much of the low-end demand can be satisfied."

Agid does not see the stripped-down house as a viable long-range solution to housing the price-sensitive market. "In some parts of the country even the stripped-down house is edging towards $50,000," he says. "And there's only so much you can cut out before you're down to the point where you no longer have a salable commodity."

Agid also cautions against trying to compete with existing housing stock.

"You can't build a new $30,000 house with all the features a buyer can get in a used $30,000 house," he says. "But if you pull someone out of a $30,000 home and put him into a $45,000 home, you have sold a new home to a discretionary buyer and you've put a low-priced home on the market."

The Discretionary Buyer

And what about the discretionary buyer? The discretionary buyer is looking for something better. He may want a new home because he's gotten a higher-status job, is making more money or has had more children.

But unless he's a transferee, he isn't pressed to buy. And, if you can't convince him that what you're offering is not only better as well as newer than his present home, he's a prime candidate for a remodeling job.

Before the advent of planned communities it was easier to lure the discretionary buyer into a new home. Then, most people lived in tract housing and there was a degree of social and functional obsolescence built into the typical 1950's tract house.

"Also, people were always worrying that an apartment house or industrial complex or supermarket could open across the street. So they were anxious to get into a more stable residential environment," says Mitchell.

But as more planned communities sprang up and single-family design became more sophisticated, this all changed. So it's harder to get people to move, especially in the face of today's high interest rates.

Still, the existing homeowner with inflated equity in his present house is today's best prospect for a new home. That's why you've got to make the discretionary buyer disenchanted with what he's got. "Make the weakest area in his present home the strongest area in yours," says Agid. As a start, he suggests going on some of the house tours offered by the local Real Estate Board to see how the trade-up prospect currently lives. Are there vanities in the bathrooms? Hard-surfaced entries What kind of light fixtures are there? Wall surfaces? Wall treatments?

"Decide which features within the house you want to attack—and I do mean attack," says Agid. "As with any good military strategy, you've got to study the opportunity and place your greatest strength at the points of greatest weakness."

You should design with the working wife in mind. She's getting to be the rule rather than the exception these days (in one of the subdivisions surveyed by Walker & Lee, 56% of the wives worked). And she offers a great opportunity to make existing houses seem obsolete.

What does she want? First of all, easy maintenance. That goes for floors and other surfaces. And appliances: A trash compactor starts to make sense, for it turns a daily chore into a weekly chore And to speed food preparation a working wife might want a microwave oven. (But don't substitute it for one of the two regular ovens: most women aren't ready to give up their second oven.)

And then there's the master bath: Both husband and wife will be getting ready for work at the same time in the morning, so they'll appreciate a double lavatory setup. And extra closet space becomes more of a selling point than ever for a working wife with her two different wardrobes.

Then, too, a working couple often has divergent commitments in the evening. One member may be away on business and the other is forced to eat alone. He (or she) probably doesn't want to eat in a large formal dining room; there should be a dining nook of some kind. And there should also be a defined space in the living room or a separate space adjacent to it or the master bedroom where one person can relax without rattling around in a big room.

And you should capitalize on the energy crisis. You can design a house that's far more energy-efficient than an old house can ever become. Mitchell offers a caveat, however: Be sure you don't spend so much that the tradeoff doesn't make sense.

"My old Cadillac gets 11 miles to the gallon and my friend's Seville gets 16 miles to the gallon," says Mitchell. "But he just paid $15,000 for this, while mine is paid off."

And you've got to understand the changing psychology of today's discretionary buyer. We seem to be moving from an age of affluence to an age of guarded optimism, says Agid. "Bigger is no longer better to us. And I think that's the key to the marketplace."

We're also in a period when job promotions don't come as rapidly as they once did, and people are becoming resigned to spending more time in the middle ranks of management. So they're expressing themselves a little differently, with social concerns and community involvement. No longer do they feel they have to become president of the company and have the biggest house and car on the street.

"People today aren't judged as much for what they have as they once were," says Agid. "And so they're more concerned with quality than quantity," adds Mitchell.

It's now smart to be energy-conscious, for example: "I don't remember the last time I heard a discussion about a car's horsepower," says Mitchell. "But I sure hear a lot of talk about miles per gallon. And it's the same with housing: People are recognizing the waste of past years, and the house of the future is going to be a little more sleek, more compact."

An Irvine Co. survey confirms this. When 2,000 shoppers were asked how many bedrooms they wanted in their next home, some 15% wanted two, and less than 5% wanted five or more. When this same question was asked in 1970-71, less than 1% wanted two bedrooms and more than 20% wanted five or more. Similarly, people want three rather than four bedrooms and small rather than large yards.

A smaller, sleeker house is not a basic house, however. "It's just that the dollars have been put into design and efficiency rather than square footage," says Mitchell.

And Agid agrees: "People feel that the smaller, prudently utilized, highly decorated house that's an expression of themselves is far better than the large barn that they can't afford to decorate."

19 INTERNATIONAL RESEARCH IS DIFFERENT

Paul Howard Berent
Managing Director
ERMB Limited

A British researcher points out the very real difficulties involved in conducting multi-country research. For example, on the Continent, the proportion of adults who speak English ranges from 5% in Spain to 41% in the Netherlands.

Although international research could refer to market research in one country only—as long as this country is not the country of the originator of the research—this paper is mainly concerned with market research on a multi-country basis. Market research on a multi-country basis or, in short, multi-country research is defined as market research whose purpose it is to help in the solution of a multi-country marketing problem, as opposed to a purely national marketing problem. It is irrelevant to this definition whether the actual research is carried out simultaneously in all the countries involved, or whether it is carried out consecutively in one country after another. After all, an international product introduction or promotion strategy may be phased over a period of months or even years, and the appropriate market research might well be timed accordingly.

Moreover, multi-country research in this sense does not necessarily involve the exact replication of research techniques in all the countries under investigation. It serves little purpose to define multi-country research in a narrow technical

Reprinted from Paul Howard Berent," International Research Is Different," Proceedings, 1975, Edward M. Mazze, ed. Published by the American Marketing Association.

sense, namely as the simultaneous application of the same sampling and the same questionnaire techniques across a number of countries. It is only too often taken to mean that somebody in New York, or London, or Paris, or wherever, produces a questionnaire and sample specifications, and some weeks or months later there emerges a neat set of tables with the names of the countries at the top, and a standard list of attributes at the side. The exact replication of research methods in all countries under investigation is wrongly dignified by the term of "comparability," and far too much of the effort in this field has been devoted to attempts to iron out the nasty little differences between countries, such as differences in language or social class divisions, so as to achieve a perfect uniformity of data collection. If one could only get all respondents to speak English, or even Esperanto, if only all countries would have the same social and economic structures, if only the sun would shine for exactly the same number of hours everywhere, all our problems would disappear.

The trouble is that multi-country research does involve dealing with countries that differ not only in language, but also have very different economic and social structures, behavior and attitude patterns. These differences must be taken into account in the formulation of the design of a multi-country survey, and they may well necessitate variations in the research methods to be applied in individual countries. To ignore these differences in the interests of a spurious comparability is to commit the cardinal sin of so many researchers—both national and international—namely to take a technique rather than a problem-oriented view of their function. In fact it is the differences between the countries covered, and the necessity to allow for them, that renders international research a very different type of operation from national research.

NATIONAL DIFFERENCES AND RESEARCH DESIGN

International research involves dealing with countries that differ not only in language but also differ considerably in their economic, legal and social structures, their behavior and attitude pat-

terns. These differences would, of course, be reflected in the results of multi-country research, just as differences between areas, sex, age or social class groups would be reflected in the results of single-country research. However, if national differences were relevant only to the outcome of multi-country research, then the procedures involved would be very similar to those pertaining to single-country research. In fact, national differences can have a very considerable effect on the formulation of the initial design of a multi-country survey. Unless these differences are understood and appreciated at the planning stage, and allowed for in the design of the survey, the survey may completely fail to achieve its objectives.

An example of the sort of thing that can happen if national differences are not taken into account at the planning stage occurred in the Reader's Digest Survey of 1963,[1] which, amongst a wealth of other information gave the impression that the consumption of spaghetti and macaroni was significantly higher in France and Western Germany than in Italy. The results for spaghetti and macaroni in the home were:

France	90%
Western Germany	71%
Italy	63%
Luxembourg	61%
Belgium	45%
Netherlands	45%

Taken at their face value, these results suggest that popular notions about Italian eating habits are quite mistaken, and that spaghetti is really the national dish of France or Germany rather than of Italy. In fact, the public press seized on this particular result as one of the surprising items of information to come out of the survey. The trouble was that the relevant question in all countries was concerned with packaged and branded spaghetti, and many Italians buy their spaghetti loose. In a footnote the Reader's Digest report quite properly estimates that if the question had been asked in a different way the result for Italy would have been 98-100%. The trouble was that the question as asked did not provide—as it was intended to—a valid comparison between the food habits of the six nations.

In contrast, here is an example of a multi-country survey in the design of which national differences were taken into account. This example concerns a questionnaire we were administering to women in each of seven countries. The information we were trying to obtain at the beginning of the questionnaire was of a very simple type: we were trying to establish whether the respondent was married or engaged, whether she had received an engagement ring, and the type of engagement ring received. The first three questions on the questionnaire used in England were:

1. Are you married?   IF YES: in what year were you married?
   IF NO: are you engaged to be married (again)?

   IF MARRIED OR ENGAGED ASK:

2. Do you own an engagement ring or did you obtain one or more rings at the time of engagement?

   IF YES:

3. What type of ring is it/was it?
   No stones/Single diamond only/Several diamonds but no other stones/Diamond(s) and other stones; Other stones only.

This looks like a very simple list of questions, involving no difficulty of direct translation, and yet, if they had been applied as they stood in all seven countries the results would have been meaningless. The first trouble was with the word "engaged": although the word "engaged" can be directly translated into Spanish or Italian, it does not by any means have the same significance to a young woman in Italy or Spain as it has to a young woman in England, or, for that matter, Germany or Sweden. While in England to be engaged involves a formal or semi-formal agreement to marry, an Italian, or Spanish woman will refer to almost any man who has taken her to the cinema more than once as her fiance, whether she intends to marry him or not. In other words, to be engaged in Spain or Italy means no more than to have a boyfriend, and if we had used the questionnaire as it stood we would have obtained wildly inflated results for the number of women who were engaged, and—what is even more serious —significant understatements with regard to the ownership of engagement rings in the target group.

In these countries, instead of asking the respondent whether she was engaged, we had to use the following questions:

1. Are you thinking of getting married in the near future?

   IF YES:

2. Has your hand been asked in marriage?

This is a very simple example of the use of different questions to obtain comparable information, while the use of the same questions would have resulted in information that was not comparable.

Our difficulties, however, did not end there: the question "Do you own an engagement ring?" would not have worked in Germany, since many German women receive a plain gold band at the time of engagement which they later transfer to the other hand and use as a wedding ring. Frequently there is an exchange of rings between the couple at the time of engagement and we had to use a whole battery of questions to obtain information from Germany that was equivalent to that for the other six countries.

Another modification we had to make was in the list of pre-coded ring types in Question 3. Although pearl rings were relatively unimportant in most countries covered, they accounted for a high proportion of engagement rings in Japan, and a significant proportion in France. To include pearl rings as a separate category in most of the countries might have unnecessarily complicated the list: however, to exclude them in Japan or France would not only have resulted in a loss of information but also in confusion arising from the list of ring types being incomplete.

Differences in behaviour and attitude patterns may necessitate considerable differences in survey design. In England, Germany and Scandinavia, for instance, beer is generally regarded as an alcoholic beverage, and the factors underlying its consumption are similar to those underlying the consumption of other alcoholic beverages: in Greece, Spain or Italy beer is regarded as much more like a soft drink such as Coca-Cola or orangeade. A survey designed to aid a beer manufacturer in the determination of his marketing strategy in Europe would have to obtain information on behavior and attitudes in relation to soft drinks in some countries and in relation to alcoholic beverages in others. However, quite apart from the expense involved, there would be little point in obtaining information about both soft drinks and alcoholic beverages in all countries covered by the survey.

Another example in the beverage field is that in England many people consume hot milk drinks such as Horlicks, Ovaltine or Bournvita before going to bed, and the advertising claims for these products are generally concerned with their abilities to induce sound sleep. In Thailand, where charcoal is the normal cooking fuel, and since it takes a long time to heat, very few people have any hot nourishment before they leave home for work. They will, therefore, try to get some quick energy before work by taking a hot nourishing drink at a street cafe, and the drinks they choose are precisely the same brands chosen by the English before they go to bed. In other words, what wakes up the Thais sends the English to sleep. The slogan used in England "Sleep sweeter, Bournvita" would hardly be suitable for the Thai situation. Certainly one would have to ask very different questions if one were researching hot milk drinks in Thailand than if one were researching them in England.

In a survey we carried out for an international hotel chain we established that while a third of all German and Dutch businessmen took their wives with them on business trips, 85% of the English and French tended to leave them at home. For this reason alone, German and Dutch businessmen would judge hotels on rather different criteria from their English or French equivalents, and this factor would have to be taken into consideration during the planning stage of a survey.

Legal circumstances surrounding the products or services surveyed might also affect research design. We were recently engaged in an eight country survey amongst doctors on an ethical pharmaceutical product. In Holland general practitioners are very restricted in the drugs they are allowed to prescribe, and there was no possibility of the product under examination being included in the Dutch national insurance list. We therefore limited our interviews to hospitals and specialists. In Belgium general practitioners have considerable freedom in the drugs they prescribe, and most of

our interviews were, therefore, carried out with this group. The problem was the same in both countries, namely to establish the acceptability of the product amongst the medical profession. There would have been no point, however, in interviewing general practitioners in Holland, or concentrating on specialists in Belgium. Comparability at the interpretation stage was achieved, in so far as the relative acceptability of the product in the two countries was established, but the methods of data collection were very different.

Facilities for market research differ considerably between countries. Below, for instance, are the 1972/73 figures for telephone ownership in a number of European countries:

Households with Telephones

Sweden	90%
Switzerland	88%
Denmark	54%
Netherlands	43%
U.K.	34%
W. Germany	31%
Italy	27%
France	19%

While it would be perfectly feasible to obtain a reasonable representative cross-section of the population by the use of telephone research in Switzerland or Sweden, this would be out of the question in Britain, Germany or France. In Britain or Germany, however, postal research can be used to solve a variety of problems. High illiteracy rates in Italy and Spain, however, would render the use of postal research inadvisable in those countries. Let us assume that one wanted to obtain some very simple and fairly approximate information in Sweden, Switzerland, England, Germany, Spain and Italy. To collect the data in the same way throughout the survey area, it would be necessary to carry out personal interviews in all six countries. However, some problems might well be solved with sufficient accuracy—and at much lower cost—by the use of telephone interviews in Sweden and Switzerland, postal interviews in Germany and the U.K. and personal interviews in Italy and Spain.

Other circumstances may also affect research techniques. It is relatively easy to get eight or ten German working class women to come into an office or hall for a group discussion: if one asked eight or ten working class women in southern Spain or Sicily to come to a strange place for this purpose, they would be terrified and one would probably first have to contact the local priest or the representative of the Mafia.

The differences that may be encountered by the multi-country researcher include:

1. Language differences.
2. Differences in consumption patterns.
3. Differences in actual and potential target groups.
4. Differences in the way that products or services are used.
5. Differences in the criteria for assessing products or services.
6. Differences in economic and social conditions.
7. Differences in marketing conditions.
8. Differences in market research facilities.
9. Differences in market research capabilities.

All these differences must be taken into account at the planning stage of a multi-country survey, and they may have a considerable effect on the research design.

NATIONAL DIFFERENCES AND COMPARABILITY

Many multi-country marketing problems can be solved by research that uses exactly the same sample design and asks exactly the same questions in all the countries under investigation. The examples quoted show, however, that there are many instances where the research design has to be modified—sometimes drastically—from one country to another to allow for national differences. In such cases the attempt to impose a rigid research structure on a number of very different countries may defeat the very objectives that the research is trying to achieve.

Where such an attempt is made, it is generally made in the name of comparability. It confuses comparability with the replication of research methods, assuming that comparability in the sense of comparability of results involves

or depends on comparability of techniques. There is a very clear distinction between:

1. Comparability at the data-collection stage.
2. Comparability at the interpretation stage.

While the achievement of comparability at the data-collection stage may be no more than an academic research exercise, comparability at the interpretation stage is absolutely essential for any research which has been set up to provide a basis for an international market decision. Whether the marketing decision is concerned with priorities between countries for a new product introduction, or the advisability of a product modification in a number of existing markets, or the viability of an international advertising campaign, the research must be structured in such a way that the results can be used to make valid comparisons between the countries covered. In other words, a multi-country survey must be able to provide a basis for the solution of marketing problems such as "how should marketing expenditure be distributed between various countries?" or "to what extent should the product, or the pack, or the advertising be varied between one country and another?" Multi-country research can only help in the solution of these or similar international marketing problems if the results enable one to measure one country against another, in other words if comparability is achieved at the interpretation stage.

Moreover, the achievement of comparability at the interpretation stage does not necessarily involve:

1. That the same type of information is collected in each country.
2. That the information is collected in the same way in each country.

One very useful paper on this subject[2] says "Research methods might differ considerably but still allow comparability on the indirect or interpretative level" and quotes a case history where "we were able, even though utilising varying methods, to provide information comparable in the sense of answering the same marketing questions for all three markets." Another paper[3] on this subject asks, "Should not our main concern be the comparability of the responses which are obtained with *similar* instruments of measurement, instead of *equality* of these instruments of measurement themselves?"

While comparability of results is regarded as all-important, practitioners in the multi-country research field are increasingly coming to realise that techniques may have to be varied between countries to achieve their objectives. Comparability is concerned with the end, not the means.

COMPARABILITY AND COORDINATION

The achievement of comparability of results involves a high degree of coordination and central control, it involves:

1. Central planning.
2. Central control.
3. Central interpretation.

To achieve these objectives, the method we have found best is to subcontract local fieldwork and basic editing only, while all the planning, questionnaire development, analysis and interpretation is carried out centrally. Moreover, the work of local subcontractors is closely supervised on the spot by the executives of our company, to the extent that we almost invariably brief the local interviewers ourselves (the executives concerned are, of course, multi-lingual). In the case of some surveys, the executive responsible has visited each country as many as three times, to discuss the results of the pilot survey, to provide coding and editing instructions, to check the progress of the fieldwork and the processing, as well as to brief the local interviewers and agencies.

It is essential that an organisation carrying out multi-country research is staffed by executives who not only have considerable experience of the countries covered, but also speak the languages involved. Only a minority of continental Europeans, for instance, speak English. The proportions of adults in various countries who claim to speak English are:[4]

Adults Who Claim to Speak English

Netherlands	41%
Scandinavia	33%
W. Germany	21%

Switzerland	21%
Belgium	14%
France	10%
Italy	5%
Spain	5%

Central ownership or membership of a chain of local research agencies is not in itself the equivalent of central control and coordination. Central control and coordination involves that one researcher or research group is responsible for a multi-country project in all the countries covered much as an international brand manager is responsible for his brands in all his markets. It involves horizontal rather than vertical lines of responsibility. While this may happen in chains of research agencies, in a centrally controlled and coordinated multi-country research study, it is irrelevant whether the local agencies used for fieldwork belong to the same chain or not.

The case against chains was very powerfully put by a recent paper:[5] "We think this structure lacks fundamental business sense. A chain even if originally entered into by reasonably well-established companies, soon suffers from the breakup of its weakest members and the impossibility of finding equivalent institutes to replace them. There is a problem (of) . . . a lack of credibility vis à vis research buyers in that work is being subcontracted, not to the best possible institute in that country, but to a chain member, however unsuitable that member concerned might be for the job on hand.

Finally, in the past and in the likely future, a successful chain member is going to receive such a small proportion of his turnover from the chain itself that he is unlikely to structure his services or procedures on an internationally coordinated basis, whilst a member who is failing will be sustained by the amount of business he receives through the chain."

NATIONAL DIFFERENCES AND COORDINATION

In the first part of this paper I have emphasised the necessity of taking national differences into account in the planning and execution of multi-country research: in the second part of my paper I have emphasised the necessity for central control and coordination. These two principles may appear to be in contradiction, since it may be felt that if national differences have so much effect on the research design, the best way of carrying out multi-country research may be to leave the determination of techniques and the interpretation of results in the hands of a separate locally-based company in each of the countries covered. Excessive anxiety over the problem of dealing with a number of different and alien countries simultaneously can result in using six different research organisations for a six country study and letting them get on with it in their own way, on the comforting principle that "the local man knows best." Frequently the main criterion for selecting a local research company is that somebody there speaks English, or whatever the language of the originators of the research.

One of the snags of this procedure is that the local man frequently does not know best and may tend to have a very subjective view of conditions in his own country. The acquisition of knowledge of local conditions should not depend exclusively on the views of one company, which may have a vested interest in doing things in a particular way, but on a combination of the study of published statistics and previous research findings, and an objective examination of the experience of a number of people involved in marketing and other relevant fields in the country concerned.

Another danger of over-fragmentation is that research companies in different countries may differ not only in the quality of their work but also in the techniques they employ. Many research companies have their own favourite techniques which are not necessarily determined by the particular conditions of the country in which they operate. In fact, the differences—both in approach and quality—between one research company and another in the same country frequently are greater than the differences between research companies in different countries. While it may well be necessary to vary the research approach from country to country, these variations should certainly not depend on the quirks of individual research companies. Nothing is more dangerous in multi-country research than to have to brief six or more different research companies, each of them with its own background of experience and its own way of working. It is quite possible that each of

these organisations may interpret and execute the brief in a different way. Moreover, it is unlikely that a research organisation operating in one country only—and especially a small country—will have the knowledge and experience of all the research techniques applicable to any particular research problem.

A project director responsible for the survey in all the countries covered is not only more likely to have a deeper overall understanding of the marketing problem to be solved than a research agency in any one of the countries to be covered; he is also much more likely to be experienced in a wide variety of research approaches and techniques. Moreover, he is in a position to assess objectively the value, or otherwise, of the research methods practiced by local research agencies, and frequently he is able to suggest alternative methods to the benefit of both parties involved.

CONCLUSIONS

The design of a research project normally involves four steps: problem definition, decision on survey techniques, sample design and questionnaire formulation—or, in other words, what to find out, how to go about it, whom to ask and what to ask. A single-country survey usually involves the use of one set of survey techniques, a sample design applying to the whole area of the survey and a uniform questionnaire. A multi-country survey may necessitate the use of more than one survey technique, a number of different questionnaires, and sample designs varying from one country to another. It also involves the coordination and supervision of work in countries with different languages and differing conditions.

These considerations make it clear that multi-country research is a very different type of operation from single country research. They also have an important bearing on the type of people or organisations that are able to carry out multi-country research. A researcher or research organisation that thinks in terms of one country only is unlikely to have the adaptability, knowledge and experience for the conduct of multi-country research. Researchers or research organisations operating on an international scale not only have to think internationally (and speak a number of languages), but also have to have a considerable

amount of experience of and an extensive fund
of knowledge about individual countries and
international conditions. They must be constantly
prepared to draw on this fund of knowledge or
obtain new information when faced with a specific
research problem. Moreover, they must be capable
of using this knowledge—as well as their knowledge
of research techniques—when designing a multi-
country survey. In other words, they must be
international marketing men as well as market
researchers.

References

1. Readers Digest European Survey, 1963.
2. R. Day: "The Meaning of Comparability in
      Multi-Country Research and how to achieve
      it," ESOMAR Congress, 1966.
3. P. de Jong, F. Myers: "Some Reflections on
      the Measurement of Basic Attitudes in a
      Multi-Country Context," ESOMAR Seminar
      on Multi-Country Research, 1971.
4. *Reader's Digest:* "A Survey of Europe
      Today," 1970.
5. R. W. Goldsmith, I. C. Jarvis: "Multi-National
      Marketing and its Research Requirements,"
      ESOMAR Congress, 1974.

4 INSIGHTS INTO MANAGING THE MARKETING ACTIVITY

How does a manager develop and manage a marketing program?

With great care, since he must balance four sets of decision areas simultaneously. The decisions revolve around:

the product,
its pricing,
its promotion, and
the distribution system.

Providing a point of reference in all these decisions is the notion that, to a consumer, the product represents an array of values for providing satisfaction. In other words, the producer will be more right than wrong if he matches his product(s) to the consumer's view of his own wants.

Twelve articles in this section offer new ideas in the care and development of this "marketing mix."

20
HOW DECISIONS ARE MADE TO STOP DEVELOPING OR TESTING NEW PRODUCTS

Cornelius S. Muije
Director of Marketing Research Services
Brown and Williamson Tobacco Corporation

How marketing research is involved in the managerial decision-making process at a major tobacco company is described by the department manager. Specifically, he focuses on two new product test results.

This is a presentation about a managerial process rather than a presentation of research techniques. I am not going to discuss new research approaches or new research techniques—no new breakthroughs—in fact, not even old breakthroughs. This is a presentation on how, at Brown

Reprinted from Cornelius S. Muije, "How Decisions Are Made to Stop Developing or Testing New Products," pp. 160-62, Proceedings, 1973, published by the American Marketing Association.

& Williamson, marketing research is integrated into the decision process.

U.S. CIGARETTE MARKET

Here is some information on the characteristics of the cigarette business that would be helpful in understanding the marketing research role at B & W.

1. In 1972, close to 525 billion cigarettes were sold in the United States. This translates to about 26 billion packs, or in retail dollars, close to $11,000,000,000.

2. The manufacturers, wholesalers, and retailers receive about half of this. The Federal Government gets about 2.1 billion dollars in cigarette taxes, and the states, with a variety of different taxes, receive about 3.2 billion dollars. As you can see, we have some real partners.

3.   You can also see that a one-share point cigarette generates annual retail sales of $110 million dollars. The manufacturer of such a one-share brand will probably have an after-tax profit of about 5 million dollars per year, but this does vary significantly between companies.

4.   Contrary to most product classes, price competition is minimal.

5.   Cigarette smoker loyalties are, compared to other product categories, extremely high, and a typical life cycle of a brand is in excess of 20 years, which makes the present worth of a one-share cigarette probably close to 50 million dollars.

6.   Ours is one of the most segmented markets— with 120 brands or brand styles. Talking about the total category is relatively meaningless. There are plain cigarettes, filter cigarettes, menthol cigarettes, extra-long cigarettes, female cigarettes, high-filtration cigarettes, and several more subclassifications. This obviously has all kinds of testing implications.

In the past ten years there have been 97 visible, but unsuccessful, attempts to launch a new brand or brand style. By visible, I mean those that were launched in test market or nationally. The invisible attempts—those that were abandoned at some stage prior to test market—must number in the hundreds.

BROWN & WILLIAMSON ORGANIZATION AND CHARACTERISTICS

Within the cigarette industries, Brown & Williamson, with about 18 share points of total cigarette sales, ranks No. 3 among the major six. Brown & Williamson sales at wholesale prices exceeded one billion in 1972.

Marketing Research reports to the vice-president of Marketing. The Marketing vice-president, in addition to Marketing Research, has a Sales Department and an Advertising/Brand Group Department reporting to him.

There is also a four-member Marketing Committee consisting of the vice-president of

Marketing, the directors of Sales and Advertising, and myself.

Furthermore, I am a member of the Product Development Committee. This committee consists of members from Marketing, Law, Finance, Manufacturing, Leaf, Research & Development, and Marketing Research.

There are many companies where committees are an effective way to impede progress. Let me point out that this committee is chaired by the Senior Executive Vice-President and has one more Executive Vice-President and two Vice-Presidents as members. Of the hundreds of recommendations made by this committee over the years, no more than a dozen have been rejected by our president.

In our organization, one other committee should be mentioned and that is the Executive Committee consisting of the president and four other senior executives.

The Marketing Research Department generally presents the research results to either the Marketing Committee, the Product Development Committee, or the Executive Committee. Sometimes results are presented to two or all three of these committees.

This depends on the type of test and on the importance of the test. It is a basic expectation of my management—and happily coincides with my viewpoint—that recommendations are always made.

I will not claim that our executives are experts in decision theory, but I will state that we are familiar with the concepts. We recognize the implications of decision trees with their associated probabilities and payouts. Basically, our process of testing stages takes alternatives, investments, and probabilities of success into account.

In a process of this type, the costs are usually, but not always, relatively easy to estimate. Estimating the likelihood of successful development in R & D or successfully passing the various testing stages is a lot more difficult.

This is why I consider it exceedingly important that the Marketing Research Department give presentations—with recommendations—to the decision makers. After each presentation, lively discussions usually take place; penetrating questions are raised; additional knowledge and research information not specific to the project is brought out, and a decision or decisions are usually made during this same meeting.

Sometimes the Marketing Research Department is embarrassed—it is not comfortable—but educational for future meetings. In two of the three committees, I am placed in the peculiar position of being the director of the department making the recommendation and then become a committee member voting on the recommendation.

TYPE OF TESTING CONDUCTED AT BROWN & WILLIAMSON

Now, we turn to our various types of testing. We generally conduct the following on potential new products:

1. Product Test(s)
2. Name Test(s)
3. Package Test(s)
4. Advertising Test(s)
5. Ad-Product-Name-Package/Concept Test(s)
6. Controlled Store Mini-Market Test(s)
7. Trial and Switching Surveys

The sequencing of these stages is not always the same; for instance, name tests may precede or follow product tests. Frequently, we parallel-test, even though, from a research standpoint, this is inefficient. When parallel testing of stages is performed, it is done with the clear recognition that time is gained in exchange for money.

Touching on each of these stages, I shall first point out that we have never called off a project at either the name or package testing stage. If research indicates that names or packages are inadequate, we will always develop or test new names or packages.

In our company there are examples of calling off a new product development project at each of the other tests I have listed.

For the product testing stage, we have tested as many as 112 different products, and we have recycled through this stage as many as four times.

For the advertising stage, we have had as many as three agencies writing different copy approaches and competing for the brand. Some-

times we have simultaneously tested several approaches from the same agency.

At Brown & Williamson we do not believe in what I call pure concept tests, that is, in some way, directly asking the consumer whether they think a certain type of product is a good idea. Ideally, concept tests should include all elements: advertising, product, name, and package. In practice, we have often tested with only two of the four elements. We have also used descriptive brochures in lieu of finished advertising.

The controlled store mini-market tests have been recycled, and we have also simultaneously conducted two different mini-market tests on the same product. The trial and switching surveys are always associated with test-market activity.

SOME "NEW PRODUCT" TEST RESULTS

Next, I would like to discuss two new products—one that demonstrates a failure in the system—and one that can be considered a part-failure.

First, the failure—our product called "Hallmark." This one is relatively easy to handle.

Our Hallmark brand is a concept with great inherent appeal. The usual cigarette delivers about 1 mg. of tar during the first machine puff and close to 3 mgs. at the last puff. Hallmark has a rapid burn chemical imprinted as a checkered pattern on the paper which quickly burns back as the fire cone reaches the checks. This opens up air ventilation holes right below the fire cone. As a result, the tar delivery from the first to the last puff is close to the same. Conceptually, this is so appealing that I might say that we—our management—fought this all the way to the final test-market failure.

In our first product test, the Marketing Research Department stated that we had a burn rate perception problem. Even though lab measurements proved that Hallmark smoked no faster than other cigarettes, since the smoker could visually see the burn run back across the checkmark, he generally stated that the cigarette burned too fast.

The Marketing Research Department in the presentation pointed out, *possibly not emphati-*

cally enough, that the cigarette had a burn rate perception problem that needed correction. A number of product/concept tests were conducted with a brochure in lieu of advertising. Every time the "fast burn" was a problem. This happened in spite of attempts to resolve this with reassurances on the pack, in the brochure, and even trying an extra-long cigarette rather than a king-size cigarette.

Let me emphasize the "burn rate" problem. It did not appear in advertising testing—it only appeared when smokers used the product. It is troublesome to recognize that our "science" still has some methodological problems.

In spite of all the warning flags, we went all the way to test market. The product failed in test market, and the major negative feedback was a "fast burn" perception. Trial was adequate, but conversion was miserable.

What does all of this prove?—that the best laid programs and plans sometimes fail. We were either too optimistic or failed to recognize the seriousness of the red flags.

In our defense I should say that, after the test-market failure with the king-size version, we conducted a product-advertising/concept test on an extra-long version. In this test we even put burn rate reassurance on the back of the package. When we got the same "burn rate" negatives, we did not proceed to test market.

Our product "Laredo" was a success. A success in the sense that investments were paid back and a profit made on the product. I call it a part-failure because certain research recommendations were not accepted. Acceptance of these recommendations would have led to greater profits.

Laredo is a filter roll-your-own product. Roll-your-own products are not subject to the normal taxes and can therefore be sold for 20 cents less than what an equivalent pack of cigarettes would cost.

Laredo would not have been a viable proposition without a machine that makes good filter cigarettes. None of the available machines were adequate, and we spent years trying to have a good machine developed.

Our efforts were successful, and we ended up with a patented making machine that could be retailed for $1.00, but at this price generated

no profit for us. Like the razor blade industry, we decided to make our profit on the tobacco and not on the making machine.

The concept then was: tobacco identical in quality to factory-made cigarettes; fresher cigarettes than were purchased in the store; machines to be sold at a self-liquidating price; and cigarettes to the consumer at 20 cents per pack.

In this project we had a testing stage that is not normally encountered. We tested the clarity of the "use" instructions, the strength and stability of the machine, and also the price the consumer would be willing to pay for the machine.

Selling the machine at $3.00 rather than $1.00 depressed interest moderately. Initial small-scale testing had indicated that the maker might have novelty appeal. For this reason the Marketing Research Department recommended that the maker should be sold for more than $1.00—in fact, for $3.00. Not only would this price generate a profit on the maker, but it was further argued that in the face of the possible novelty appeal, depressing immediate demand would be desirable. We were faced with severe initial capacity restrictions and equipment investment costs.

Also, Marketing Research believed that a smoker was more likely to continue using a machine that cost him $3.00 rather than $1.00. Throwing a $1.00 machine away would be a relatively easy decision. Management decided to stay with the $1.00 price.

Early mini-test market results showed good initial sales followed by a disturbing decline.

Again, the Marketing Research Department recommended that a new mini-market test with a higher priced machine be conducted. Just at this point, Pennsylvania added 5 cents a pack to the cigarette tax and Laredo sales boomed. Although we saw a subsequent decline parallel to the initial decline, the decision point for expansion beyond Erie had been reached. Again management decided to proceed with the initial pricing.

During our national launch, 5,300,000 Laredo machines were sold. Current Laredo tobacco sales are equivalent to the full-time smoking needs of about 150,000 smokers. Either 5,000,000 plus machines are stuck away in drawers or have ended up in the trash can.

CONCLUSIONS

I have emphasized a failure and a semi-failure of our testing approach. You might ask why. Our Marketing Research effort is fully integrated into the decision-making process. We have direct access to all levels of management, including the very top. I can further characterize our efforts as being integrated into the planning and very responsive to needs. This, both in terms of the type of research conducted and in the speed with which we bring back information.

If these things were not true, I could probably discuss a dozen research failures rather than the one-and-a-half that I just presented.

The major points I want to make with this presentation are that a good Marketing Research operation must:

Be involved in all planning stages.

Be integrated into the decision process.

Provide research results, together with firm recommendations, and be willing to be wrong once in awhile.

And, last but not least, have direct access to top management, who realize they will be wrong once in awhile.

In my view, the presence of the above environment is far more important than research methods that might work but are not accepted for use, or when used, not acted upon.

21
THE DEATH AND BURIAL OF SICK PRODUCTS

R. S. Alexander
Professor Emeritus of Marketing
Columbia University

Products, like men, are mortal. They flourish for a time, then decline and die. This fact of life is almost as vital to the marketing manager as the introduction of new products, in the view of this author.

Euthanasia applied to human beings is criminal; but aging products enjoy or suffer no such legal protection. This is a sad fact of business life.

The word "product" is used here not in its broad economic sense of anything produced—such as wheat, coal, a car, or a chair—but in its narrower meaning of an article made to distinct specifications and intended for sale under a separate brand or catalogue number. In the broader sense of the word, certain products may last as long as industrial civilization endures; in the narrow sense, most of them are playthings of change.

Much has been written about managing the development and marketing of new products, but business literature is largely devoid of material on product deletion.

This is not surprising. New products have glamor. Their management is fraught with great risks. Their successful introduction promises growth in sales and profits that may be fantastic.

But putting products to death—or letting them die—is a drab business, and often engenders much of the sadness of a final parting with old and tried friends. "The portable six-sided, pretzel

From R. S. Alexander, "The Death and Burial of Sick Products," Journal of Marketing, April 1964, pp. 1-7. Published by the American Marketing Association. Reprinted by permission of the author and publisher.

polisher was the first product The Company ever made. Our line will no longer be our line without it."

But while deletion is an uninspiring and depressing process, in a changing market it is almost as vital as the addition of new products. The old product that is a "football" of competition or has lost much of its market appeal is likely to generate more than its share of small unprofitable orders; to make necessary short, costly production runs; to demand an exorbitant amount of executive attention; and to tie up capital that could be used more profitably in other ventures.

Just as a crust of barnacles on the hold of a ship retards the vessel's movement, so do a number of worn-out items in a company's product mix affect the company's progress.

Most of the costs that result from the lack of an effective deletion system are hidden and become apparent only after careful analysis. As a result, management often overlooks them. The need for examining the product line to discover outworn members, and for analysis to arrive at intelligent decisions to discard or to keep them, very rarely assumes the urgency of a crisis. Too often, management thinks of this as something that should be done but that can wait until tomorrow.

This is why a definite procedure for deletion of products should be set up, and why the authority and responsibility for the various activities involved should be clearly and definitely assigned. This is especially important because this work usually requires the cooperation of several functional groups within the business firm, including at least marketing, production, finance, and sometimes personnel.

Definite responsibility should be assigned for at least the following activities involved in the process:

1. selecting products which are candidates for elimination;
2. gathering information about them and analyzing the information;
3. making decisions about elimination; and
4. if necessary, removing the doomed products from the line.

SELECTION OF PRODUCTS FOR POSSIBLE ELIMINATION

As a first step, we are not seeking the factors on which the final decision to delete or to retain turns, but merely those which indicate that the product's continuation in the product mix should be considered carefully with elimination as a possibility. Although removal from the product line may seem to be the prime aim, the result is not inevitably deletion from the line; instead, careful analysis may lead to changes in the product itself or in the methods of making or marketing it.

Sales Trend If the trend of a product's sales is downward over a time period that is significant in relation to the normal life of others like it, its continuation in the mix deserves careful examination. There may be many reasons for such a decline that in no way point toward deletion; but when decline continues over a period of time the situation needs to be studied.

Price Trend A downward trend in the price of a new product may be expected if the firm introducing it pursues a skimming-price policy, or if all firms making it realize substantial cost savings as a result of volume production and increased processing know-how. But when the price of an established product whose competitive pattern has been relatively stabilized shows a downward trend over a significant period of time, the future of that product should receive attention.

Profit Trend A declining profit either in dollars or as a per cent of sales or investment should raise questions about a product's continued place in the product line. Such a trend usually is the result of a price-factory cost squeeze, although it may be the outcome of a loss in market appeal or a change in the method of customer purchase which forces higher marketing expenditures.

Substitute Products When a substitute article appears on the market, especially if it represents an improvement over an old product, management must face the question of whether to retain or discard the old product. This is true regardless of who introduces the substitute. The problem is especially difficult when the new product serves the same general purpose as the old one but is not an exact substitute for it.

Product Effectiveness Certain products may lose some of their effectiveness for the purposes they serve. For example, disease germs may develop strains that are resistant to a certain antibiotic. When this happens, the question of whether to keep or delete the drug involves issues not only of the interests of the firm but of the public welfare.

Executive Time A possible tipoff as to the location of "illness" in a product mix lies in a study of the amount of executive time and attention devoted to each of the items in the product line. Sick products, like sick people, demand a lot of care; but one must be careful to distinguish the "growing pains" of a new product from the more serious disorders of one that has matured and is now declining.

The six indicators mentioned do not of themselves provide evidence justifying deletion. But they can help management to single out from a line of products those upon which it can profitably spend time and money in analyzing them, with elimination from the line as a *possibility*.

ANALYSIS AND DECISION MAKING ABOUT "SICK" PRODUCTS

Although the work of analyzing a sick or decrepit product is usually done by people other than the management executives who decide what to do about it, the two processes are interdependent. Unless the right factors are chosen for analysis and unless the work is properly done, the decision is not likely to be an intelligent one. Accordingly, these two factors will be discussed together.

What information does a decision maker need about a product, and what sort of analysis of it should he have in order to render a sound verdict as to its future? The deletion decision should not turn on the sole issue of profitability. Profit is the most important objective of a business; but individual firms often seek to achieve both long-run and short-run objectives other than profit.

So, in any individual case the critical factors and the weights assigned them in making a decision must be chosen in the light of the situation of the firm and the management objectives.

Profits

Profit management in a firm with a multiproduct line (the usual situation in our economy)

is not the simple operation generally contemplated in economic theory. Such a firm usually has in its product mix

1. items in various stages of introduction and development, some of which may be fantastically profitable and others deep "in the red";
2. items which are mature but not "superannuated," whose profit rate is likely to be satisfactory; and
3. declining items which may yield a net profit somewhat less than adequate or may show heavy losses.

The task is to manage the whole line or mix so that it will show a satisfactory profit for the company. In this process, two questions are vital; What is a profit? How much profit is satisfactory?

Operating-statement accounting makes it possible to determine with reasonable accuracy the total amount of net profit a company earns on an overall basis. But when the management of a multiproduct firm seeks to determine how much of this total is generated by its activities in making and marketing each product in its mix, the process is almost incredibly complex; and the results are almost certain to be conditioned on a tissue of assumptions which are so debatable that no management can feel entirely comfortable in basing decisions on them.

This is because such a large portion of the costs of the average multiproduct firm are or behave like overhead or joint expenses. Almost inevitably several of the items in the product mix are made of common materials, with the same equipment, and by manpower which is interchangeable. Most of the company's marketing efforts and expenses are devoted to selling and distributing the mix or a line within the mix, rather than individual items.

In general, the more varied the product mix of a firm, the greater is the portion of its total expense that must be classified as joint or overhead. In such a company, many types of cost which ordinarily can be considered direct tend to behave like overhead or joint expenses. This is particularly true of marketing costs such as advertising that does not feature specific items; personal selling; order handling; and delivery.

This means that a large part of a company's costs must be assigned to products on some arbitrary basis and that however logical this basis may be, it is subject to considerable reasonable doubt in specific cases. It also means that if one product is removed from the mix, many of these costs remain to be reassigned to the items that stay in the line. As a result, any attempt to "prune" the product mix entirely on the basis of the profit contribution, or lack of it, of specific items is almost certain to be disappointing and in some cases disastrous.

But if a multiproduct firm could allocate costs to individual items in the mix on some basis recognized as sound and thus compute product-profit accurately, what standards of profit should be set up, the failure to meet which would justify deletion?

Probably most managements either formally or unconsciously set overall company profit targets. Such targets may be expressed in terms of dollars, although to be most useful in product management they usually must be translated into percentages on investment, or money used. As an example, a company may have as its profit target 15 per cent on investment before taxes.

Certainly *every* product in the mix should not be required to achieve the target, which really amounts to an average. To do so would be to deny the inevitable variations in profit potential among products.

Probably a practical minimum standard can be worked out, below which a product should be eliminated unless other considerations demand its retention. Such a standard can be derived from a balancing out of the profit rates among products in the mix, so as to arrive at the overall company target as an average. The minimum standard then represents a figure that would tip the balance enough to endanger the overall target.

1. Management probably will be wise to recognize an overall company target profit in dollars or rate on investment, and to set in relation to it a minimum below which the profit on an individual product should not fall without marking that item for deletion (unless other special considerations demand its retention).

2. Management should cast a "bilious eye" on all arguments that a questionable product be kept in the mix because it helps to defray overhead and joint costs. Down that road, at the end of a series of decisions to retain such products, lies a mix entirely or largely composed of items each busily "sopping up" overhead, but few or none contributing anything to net profit.

3. This does not mean that management should ignore the effect of a product deletion on overhead or joint costs. Decision makers must be keenly aware of the fact that the total of such costs borne by a sick product must, after it is deleted, be reallocated to other products, and with the result that they may become of doubtful profitability. A detailed examination of the joint or overhead costs charged against an ailing product may indicate that some of them can be eliminated in whole or in part if it is eliminated. Such costs are notoriously "sticky" and difficult to get rid of; but every pretext should be used to try to find ways to reduce them.

4. If a deletion decision involves a product or a group of products responsible for a significant portion of a firm's total sales volume, decision makers can assess the effects of overhead and joint costs on the problem, by compiling an estimated company operating statement after the deletion and comparing it with the current one. Such a forecasted statement should include expected net income from the use of the capital and facilities released by deletion if an opportunity for their use is ready to hand. Surviving joint and overhead expenses can even be reallocated to the remaining products, in order to arrive at an estimate of the effect that deletion might have, not only on the total company net income but on the profitability of each of the remaining products as well. Obviously such a cost analysis is likely to be expensive, and so is not justified unless the sales volume stakes are high.

Financial Considerations

Deletion is likely not only to affect the profit performance of a firm but to modify its financial structure as well.

To make and sell a product, a company must invest some of its capital. In considering its deletion, the decision makers must estimate what will happen to the capital funds presently used in making and marketing it.

When a product is dropped from the mix, most or all of the circulating capital invested in it—such as inventories of materials, goods in process, and finished goods and accounts receivable—should drain back into the cash account; and if carried out in an orderly fashion, deletion will not disturb this part of the capital structure except to increase the ratio of cash to other assets.

This will be true, unless the deletion decision is deferred until product deterioration has gone so far that the decision assumes the aspect of a crisis and its execution that of a catastrophe.

The funds invested in the equipment and other facilities needed to make and market the "sick" product are a different matter. If the equipment is versatile and standard, it may be diverted to other uses. If the firm has no need of it and if the equipment has been properly depreciated, management may find a market for it at a price approaching or even exceeding its book value.

In either case, the capital structure of the company is not disturbed except by a shift from equipment to cash in the case of sale. In such a case management would be wise, before making a deletion decision, to determine how much cash this action promises to release as well as the chances for its reinvestment.

If the equipment is suited for only one purpose, it is highly unlikely that management can either find another use for it or sell it on favorable terms. If it is old and almost completely depreciated, it can probably be scrapped and its remaining value "written off" without serious impairment of the firm's capital structure.

But if it is only partly depreciated, the decision makers must weigh the relative desirability of two possible courses of action:

1. to delete immediately, hoping that the ensuing improvement in the firm's operating results will more than offset the impairment in capital structure that deletion will cause; or
2. to seek to recapture as much as possible of its value, by continuing to make and market the product as long as its price is enough to cover out-of-pocket costs and leave something over to apply to depreciation.

This choice depends largely on two things: the relation between the amount of fixed and circulating capital that is involved; and the opportunities available to use the funds, executive abilities, manpower, and transferable facilities released by deletion for making profits in other ventures.

This matter of opportunity costs is a factor in every deletion decision. The dropping of a product is almost certain to release some capital, facilities, manpower skills, and executive abilities. If opportunities can be found in which these assets can be invested without undue risk and with promise of attractive profits, it may be good management to absorb considerable immediate loss in deleting a sick product.

If no such opportunities can be found it is probably wise to retain the product so long as the cash inflow from its sales covers out-of-pocket costs and contributes something to depreciation and other overhead expenses. In such a case, however, it is the part of good management to seek actively for new ventures which promise satisfactory profits, and to be ready to delete promptly when such an opportunity is found.

Employee Relations

The effect which product elimination may have on the employees of a firm is often an important factor in decisions either to drop or to retain products.

This is not likely to be a deciding factor if new product projects are under development to which the people employed in making and marketing the doubtful product can be transferred, unless such transfer would deprive them of the earning power of special skills. But when deletion of a product means discharging or transferring unionized employees, the decision makers must give careful thought to the effect their action is likely to have on company-union relations.

Even in the absence of union pressure, management usually feels a strong sense of responsibility for the people in its employ. Just how far management can go in conserving specific jobs at the expense of deferring or foregoing necessary deletions before it endangers the livelihood of all the employees of the firm is a nice question of balance.

Marketing Factors

Many multiproduct firms retain in their marketing mixes one or more items which, on the basis of profits and the company financial structure, should be deleted. To continue to make and market a losing product is no managerial crime. It is reprehensible only when management does not know the product is a losing one or, knowing the facts, does not have sound reasons for retaining it. Such reasons are very likely to lie in the marketing area.

Deletions of products are often deferred or neglected because of management's desire to carry a "full line," whatever that means. This desire may be grounded on sound reasons of consumer patronage or on a dubious yearning for the "prestige" that a full line is supposed to engender. But there is no magic about a full line or the prestige that is supposed to flow from it. Both should be evaluated on the basis of their effects on the firm's sales volume, profits, and capacity to survive and grow.

Products are often associated in the marketing process. The sale of one is helped by the presence of another in the product mix.

When elimination of a product forces a customer who buys all or a large part of his requirements of a group of profitable items from the firm to turn to another supplier for his needs of the dropped product, he might shift some or all of his other patronage as well. Accordingly, it is sometimes wise for management to retain in its mix a no-profit item, in order to hold sales volume of highly profitable products. But this should not be done blindly without analysis.

Rarely can management tell ahead of time exactly how much other business will be lost by deleting a product, or in what proportions the losses will fall among the remaining items. But in many cases the amount of sales volume can be computed that will be *hazarded* by such action; what other products will be subject to that hazard; and what portion of their volume will be involved. When this marketing interdependence exists in a deletion problem, the decision makers should seek to discover the customers who buy the sick product; what other items in the mix they buy; in what quantities; and how much profit they contribute.

The firm using direct marketing channels can do this with precision and at relatively little cost. The firm marketing through indirect channels will find it more difficult, and the information will be less exact; but it still may be worthwhile. If the stakes are high enough, marketing research may be conducted to discover the extent to which the customer purchases of profitable items actually are associated with that of the sick product. Although the results may not be precise, they may supply an order-of-magnitude idea of the interlocking patronage situation.

Product interrelationships in marketing constitute a significant factor in making deletion decisions, but should never be accepted as the deciding factor without careful study to disclose at least the extent of the hazards they involve.

Other Possibilities

The fact that a product's market is declining or that its profit performance is substandard does not mean that deletion is the *only* remedy.

Profits can be made in a shrinking market. There are things other than elimination of a product that can be done about deteriorating profit performance. They tend to fall into four categories.

1. *Costs.* A careful study may uncover ways of reducing factory costs. This may result from improved processes that either eliminate manpower or equipment time or else increase yield; or from the elimination of forms or features that once were necessary or worthwhile but are no longer needed. The natural first recourse of allocating joint and overhead costs on a basis that is "kinder" to the doubtful product is not to be viewed with enthusiasm. After reallocation, these costs still remain in the business; and the general profit picture has not been improved in the least.

2. *Marketing.* Before deleting a product, management will be wise to examine the methods of marketing it, to see if they can be changed to improve its profit picture.

Can advertising and sales effort be reduced without serious loss of volume? A holding operation requires much less effort and money than a promotional one.

Are services being given that the product no longer needs?

Can savings be made in order handling and delivery, even at some loss of customer satisfaction?

For example, customers may be buying the product in small orders that are expensive to handle.

On the other hand, by spending more marketing effort, can volume be increased so as to bring about a reduction in factory cost greater than the added marketing expense? In this attempt, an unexpected "assist" may come from competitors who delete the product and leave more of the field to the firm.

By remodeling the product, "dressing it up," and using a new marketing approach, can it be brought back to a state of health and profit? Here the decision makers must be careful not to use funds and facilities that could be more profitably invested in developing and marketing new products.

3. *Price.* It is natural to assume that the price of a failing product cannot be raised. At least in part, its plight is probably due to the fact that it is "kicked around" by competition, and thus that competition will not allow any increases.

But competitors may be tired of the game, too. One company that tried increasing prices found that wholesalers and retailers did not resent a larger cost-of-goods-sold base on which to apply their customary gross profit rates, and that consumers continued to buy and competitors soon followed suit.

Although a price rise will not usually add to the sum total of user happiness, it may not subtract materially from total purchases. The decision makers should not ignore the possibility of using a price reduction to gain enough physical volume to bring about a more-than-offsetting decline in unit costs, although at this stage the success of such a gambit is not likely.

4. *Cross Production.* In the materials field, when small production runs make costs prohibitive, arrangements may sometimes be made for Firm A to make the *entire* supply of Product X for itself and Competitor B. Then B reciprocates with another similar product. Such "trades," for instance, are to be found in the chemical business.

Summation for Decision

In solving deletion problems, the decision makers must draw together into a single pattern the results of the analysis of all the factors bearing on the matter. Although this is probably most often done on an intangible, subjective basis, some firms have experimented with the formula method.

For example, a manufacturer of electric motors included in its formula the following factors:

> Profitability
> Position on growth curve
> Product leadership
> Market position
> Marketing dependence of other products

Each factor was assigned a weight in terms of possible "counts" against the product. For instance, if the doubtful item promised no profits for the next three years, it had a count of 50 points against it, while more promising prospects were assigned lesser counts. A critical total for all factors was set in advance which would automatically doom a product. Such a system can include other factors—such as recapturability of invested capital, alternate available uses of facilities, effects on labor force, or other variables peculiar to the individual case.

The use of a formula lends an aura of precision to the act of decision making and assures a degree of uniformity in it. But obviously the weights assigned to different factors cannot be the same in all cases. For example, if the deletion of a doubtful product endangers a large volume of sales of other highly profitable items, that alone should probably decide the matter.

The same thing is true if deletion will force so heavy a writeoff of invested funds as to impair the firm's capital structure. Certainly this will be true if all or most of the investment can be recaptured by the depreciation route if the product stays in the mix.

This kind of decision requires that the factors be weighted differently in each case. But when managers are given a formula, they may tend to quit thinking and do too much "weighing."

THE DELETION OF A PRODUCT

Once the decision to eliminate a product is made, plans must be drawn for its death and burial with the least disturbance of customer relations and of the other operations of the firm.

Such plans must deal with a variety of detailed problems. Probably the most important fall into four categories: timing; parts and replacements; stocks; and holdover demand.

Timing It is desirable that deletion be timed so as to dovetail with the financial, manpower, and facilities needs for new products. As manpower and facilities are released from the dying product and as the capital devoted to it flows back into the cash account, it is ideal if these can be immediately used in a new venture. Although this can never be completely achieved, it may be approximated.

The death of a product should be timed so as to cause the least disturbance to customers. They should be informed about the elimination of the product far enough in advance so they can make arrangements for replacement, if any are available, but not so far in advance that they will switch to new suppliers before the deleting firm's inventories of the product are sold. Deletion at the beginning of a selling season or in the middle of it probably will create maximum customer inconvenience, whereas at the end of the season it will be the least disturbing.

Parts and Replacements If the product to be killed off is a durable one, probably the deleting firm will find it necessary to maintain stocks of repair parts for about the expected life of the units most recently sold. The firm that leaves a trail of uncared-for "orphan" products cannot expect to engender much good will from dealers or users. Provision for the care and maintenance of the orphan is a necessary cost of deletion.

This problem is much more widespread than is commonly understood. The woman who buys a set of china or silverware and finds that she cannot replace broken or lost pieces does not entertain an affectionate regard for the maker. The same sort of thing is true if she installs draperies and later, when one of them is damaged, finds that the pattern is no longer available.

Stocks The deletion plan should provide for clearing out the stocks of the dying product and materials used in its production, so as to recover the maximum amount of the working capital invested in it. This is very largely a matter of timing—the tapering off of purchase, production, and selling activities. However, this objective may conflict with those of minimizing inconvenience

to customers and servicing the orphan units in use after deletion.

Holdover Demand However much the demand for a product may decline, it probably will retain some following of devoted users. They are bound to be disturbed by its deletion and are likely to be vocal about it; and usually there is little that management can do to mitigate this situation.

Sometimes a firm can avoid all these difficulties by finding another firm to purchase the product. This should usually be tried before any other deletion steps are taken. A product with a volume too small for a big firm to handle profitably may be a moneymaker for a smaller one with less overhead and more flexibility.

NEGLECT OR ACTION?

The process of product deletion is important. The more dynamic the business, the more important it is.

But it is something that most company executives prefer not to do; and therefore it will not get done unless management establishes definite, clearcut policies to guide it, sets up carefully articulated procedures for doing it, and makes a positive and unmistakable assignment of authority and responsibility for it.

Exactly what these policies should be, what form these procedures should take, and to whom the job should be assigned are matters that must vary with the structure and operating methods of the firm and with its position in the industry and the market.

In any case, though, the need for managerial attention, planning, and supervision of the deletion function cannot be overemphasized. Many business firms are paying dearly for their neglect of this problem, but unfortunately do not realize how much this is costing them.

22 COMMUNICATIONS AND INDUSTRIAL SELLING

Theodore Levitt
Professor of Business Administration
Harvard University

The "sleeper effect" and other important considerations for industrial marketers are outlined in a study from Harvard. The research points to differences in strategies for established as well as unknown companies in various industrial fields.

Does corporate or institutional advertising by industrial-product companies pay?

Do the salesmen of well-known industrial products companies have an automatic edge over the salesmen of little-known or unknown companies?

Is it better for an industrial product company to spend its limited funds on aggressive advertising of its general competence or on more careful selection and training of its salesmen?

Are the decisions of prospective buyers of new industrial products affected by the amount of personal risk these decisions expose them to?

Are the buying decisions of practicing purchasing agents affected more by the reputation of a vendor-company than are the decisions of practicing engineers and scientists?

Does the effect of a company's reputation on a customer's buying decision hold up over time, or does it erode as time passes?

From Theodore Levitt, "Communications and Industrial Selling," Journal of Marketing, April 1967, pp. 15-21. Published by the American Marketing Association, Reprinted by permission of the author and publisher.

These are some of the questions that have been investigated in a study recently completed at the Harvard Graduate School of Business Administration. Specifically, the questions focused on the extent to which an industrial-product company's generalized reputation affects its ability to launch new products. The accelerating flood of new and often complex industrial products, coupled with the continuing shortage of capable salesmen and the rising costs of advertising make the above questions particularly timely.

'Source Effect'

This timeliness is further enhanced by studies by Harvard Business School Professor Raymond A. Bauer, which have suggested that business communicators have been inadequately aware of the extent to which their audiences influence the communicators, rather than the usual one-way preoccupation with how the communicators (or advertisers) influence their audiences.[1] To illustrate:

Research shows that a newspaper editorial identified to one group of Americans as emanating, say, from *The New York Times* and to a similar group of Americans as emanating, say, from *Pravda* would lead one to expect that a change in audience opinion in the direction advocated by the editorial would be greater for those who believed it was a *New York Times* editorial than those who believed it to be a *Pravda* editorial. In other words, the audience's feelings about the credibility of the message source help determine the persuasive effectiveness of the message itself. The greater the prestige or the more believable the message source, the more likely that it will influence the audience in the direction advocated by the message. The less prestigeful or believable the source, the less likely that it will influence the audience in the direction advocated by the message.

This phenomenon is now generally referred to as "source effect." Obviously what source effect amounts to is some sort of independent judgment by the audience such that it is either more or less affected by the message. The audience takes a form of initiative, independent of the message, which affects its susceptibility to the message.[2]

If in their private lives people such as busi-

nessmen and scientists exhibit source effect and
audience initiative in response to political communications and propaganda, there is the question of
whether they do this same thing in their business
lives in response to advertising and direct sales
presentations. McGraw-Hill expresses its belief
that source effect works powerfully in industrial
selling in its famous advertisement of a stern-
looking purchasing agent facing the reader (salesman) from behind his desk and saying:

> I don't know who you are.
> I don't know your company.
> I don't know your company's product.
> I don't know what your company stands for.
> I don't know your company's customers.
> I don't know your company's record.
> I don't know your company's reputation.
>
> Now—what was it you wanted to sell me?
>
> MORAL: Sales start before your salesman
> —with business publication advertising.

To test this and a variety of related hypotheses, an elaborate communications simulation was
devised and administered. Participants included
113 practicing purchasing agents from a wide
variety of companies, 130 engineers and scientists,
and 131 business school graduate students. (For
simplifying purposes, the engineers and scientists
are in this article referred to as "chemist.") This
article is a report on the results of this simulation.
But while it is a "report," it is not a simple document. As will be seen, it is full of moderating
qualifications and carefully-phrased conclusions.
It cannot be read with easy speed or casual comfort. The more complex a subject, the more
involuted its rhetoric. In the present case, the
reader must be prepared to go slow along an agon-
izing path.

Methodology

Basically what was done in the research was
to divide each audience group (purchasing agents,
chemists, and students) into six separate subgroups
and then to expose each subgroup to a ten-minute
filmed sales presentation for a new, but fictitious,
technical product for use as an ingredient in making
paint. Each audience member was put into the

position of assuming he was listening to the presentation as it would be given by a salesman sitting
across his desk. Some groups were asked to assume
they were purchasing agents for a paint firm and
some were asked to assume they were chemists.
The film presentation technique and audience
setup were created to make conditions as realistic
as possible, with great care taken to prevent communications between subgroups and to create
realistic and thoughtful responses by the subjects.
All saw what was basically the same ten-minute
film with the same actors. However, some subgroups saw a relatively good presentation and some
a relatively poor one; for some the selling company was identified in the film as a relatively high-
credibility company (the Monsanto Company), for
other subgroups it was identified as a relatively
lower credibility and less well known company
(the Denver Chemical Company), and for still
others the company identity was kept anonymous.
Immediately after the film was run, and then again
in five weeks, each respondent filled out a detailed
questionnaire.[3]

RESULTS

Let us now take up each of the question
areas posed at the outset of this article, and see
how our findings respond to them.

Does Corporate or Institutional Advertising by Industrial-Product Companies Pay?

For complex industrial products or materials, a company's generalized reputation does
indeed have an important bearing on how its sales
prospects make buying decisions. While the research did not specifically investigate the influence
of corporate or institutional advertising, the results
show that to the extent that such advertising helps
in building a company's reputation it clearly helps
in making sales. Whether such advertising specifically helps build a reputation is, however, a separate question. But the presumption is that mere
visibility of a company is in some way helpful and
reassuring, provided that the impressions that are
created are not negative.

Generally speaking, the better a company's reputation, the better are its chances (1) of getting a favorable *first hearing* for a new product among customer prospects, and (2) of getting early *adoption* of that product. Vendor reputation influences buyers, decision makers, and the decision-making process. But since industrial products, and particularly new products, generally require direct calls by salesmen, does the value of company reputation automatically give an edge to the salesman from a well-known company over the salesman from a less well known or anonymous one?

Do Well-Known Company Salesmen Have an Edge Over the Salesmen of Other Companies?

The answer is "yes," but it is a more complex answer than one might offhand suspect. Just because his company is favorably well known and to this extent puts the customer in a more favorable frame of mind toward that company, does not give the saleman a simple and automatic leg up over the salesman of a less-known company. The fact seems to be that customers *expect* more, or at least a better sales presentation job, from well-known company salesmen. Hence they judge their performance somewhat differently from the way they judge the performance of other salesmen. Indeed there is some indication that some types of customers (or "audiences" of sales presentations) almost unconsciously "help" the salesmen of lesser-known companies by lowering their expectations in order to encourage competition between vendors. Thus, when they eventually make buying decisions, while these customers tend clearly to favor the better-known companies, they seem to give disproportionate encouragement to the salesmen of the less well known companies.

Still, everyone knows from experience that a good sales presentation is always better than a poor one, regardless of company reputation. A vital question that therefore arises is whether it is generally better for an industrial products company to spend its limited funds on more aggressive or effective advertising of its general competence, or on more careful selection and training of its salesmen?

Is It Better to Advertise More or to Select and Train Salesmen Better?

As would be expected, the research found that the quality of a salesman's presentation in support of a technically complex new product is an important variable in obtaining a favorable customer reaction. In other words, there is a "presentation effect" in favor of the product supported by a well-done sales presentation.

When the influences of source effect and presentation effect are combined, the research suggests that when a relatively unknown or anonymous company makes a good direct sales presentation, it may be just as effective in getting a favorable first hearing for a complex new industrial material as a well-known company making a poor presentation. Thus a well-known company loses the advantage of its reputation if its direct sales presentation is clearly inferior to that of an unknown or little-known company. Against a good sales presentation by a little-known company, a well-known one must also have a good presentation if the customer-getting value of its reputation is to be realized. Conversely, a little-known company, by concentrating strongly on training its salesmen to make good presentations, may be able to make considerable progress toward overcoming the liability of its relative anonymity.

Combining this with the finding that certain buyers apparently want to favor less well known companies and expect more of better-known companies, even though they are strongly attracted to the latter, the conclusion seems to be that the lesser-known company—particularly when its resources are limited—can do an unexpectedly effective job for itself through more careful salesman selection and training.

On the other hand, everyone knows that every buying decision for a new product, and some for an established product, involves a certain amount of risk for the buyer. Moreover, the buyer's personal risk (as opposed to the risk for his company) varies as between whether he has sole personal responsibility for the buying (or, indeed, the "rejection") decision or whether it is a shared or committee decision. To what extent does the degree of the decision maker's personal risk affect the importance of vendor reputation and quality of a sales presentation in the buyer's decision process?

The Role of Personal Risk in Buying Decisions

The amount of personal risk to which the individual decision maker is exposed in a buying or rejection decision proves to be a vital factor in his decisions. And it is vital in the extent to which source effect is influential. Company reputation clearly results in a higher proportion of high-risk decisions in favor of the well-known company. Presentation quality tends substantially to strengthen the position of the less well known company in high-risk buying situations, but not as much in low-risk buying situations. While careful attention to salesman selection and training can be said to help equalize greatly the competitive position of lesser-known firms, these help it more to get a foot in the door than help it get an immediate adoption for its product. When it comes to the most important and most risky of customer actions—actually deciding to buy or reject a new product—assuming the various suppliers' products to be equal in all respects, source credibility exerts a dominant influence over other considerations.

But this still leaves unanswered the question of whether and to what extent all of these influences are equal among customers with varying degrees of technical competencies. Do they apply equally, for example, to purchasing agents and technically-trained personnel such as chemists?

The Influence of Customer 'Competence'

The research found that the power of source effect (company reputation for credibility) varies by the character and "competence" of the recipient of a sales message. Thus, there is some indication that, in the case of complex industrial materials, purchasing agents, who are usually highly competent as professional buyers, may be less influenced by a company's generalized reputation than are technical personnel, who are presumably less competent as buyers but more competent as judges of a complex product's merits. In first appraising complex new materials on the basis of sales presentations made directly to them, technically-sophisticated personnel seem to be influenced by the seller's reputation to a point that is unexpectedly higher than the influence of that reputation on such technically less sophisticated personnel as

purchasing agents. In short, technical personnel are probably influenced far more by company reputation than has been widely assumed, and certainly more than such technically less sophisticated people as purchasing agents.

While all audiences seem to be influenced by the quality of the sales presentation, important differences apparently exist between purchasing agents and technical personnel. In the lower-risk decision situation of whether to give a newly presented complex new product a further hearing, technical personnel are more powerfully influenced by the quality of a direct sales presentation than are purchasing agents. Put differently, on low-risk purchasing decisions, the technically less sophisticated purchasing agents seem to rely less heavily on the quality of the sales presentation than do the technically more sophisticated personnel in making their decisions. But on high-risk decisions (whether actually to buy the product) the reverse is true: that is, the greater the risk, the more favorably purchasing agents are influenced by good sales presentations, and the less favorably technical personnel are influenced by such presentations. The greater the risk, the more likely technical personnel are to rely on their technical judgments about a new product's virtues rather than on the quality of the sales presentation in favor of that product. But purchasing agents, being technically less sophisticated, seem forced, in high-risk situations, to rely more heavily on the seller's presentation.

The Durability of Vendor Reputation on Buying Decisions

Philip Wrigley, of the chewing gum empire, is alleged to have answered a query about why his company continues to spend so much on advertising now that it is successful with this observation: "Once you get a plane up in the air you don't turn off the engines." For industrial-product companies, a related question concerns the durability of buying inclinations (and even of buying decisions) that sales prospects exhibit immediately after hearing a sales presentation. Since few new industrial products are immediately purchased on the making of a sales presentation to a customer—since, for many reasons, there is generally a time lag before a decision is made, the question is: Does source effect hold up over time? For example, with the passage of time does the prospect forget the source of a new product presentation, remembering only the facts and the claimed product performance, such that when the actual buying decision is made at some later time the vendor's reputation plays little or no role? Similarly, does the importance of quality of the sales presentation hold up over time?

The present research indicates that there is in industrial purchasing a phenomenon which communications researchers call the "sleeper effect." The favorable influence of a company's generalized good reputation (source effect) does indeed erode with the passage of time. But the conditions under which this happens appear to be quite special. Based on what the present research was able to test, what can be said is that this erosion occurs specifically when there is no intervening reinforcement or reinstatement of the identity of the source. Put differently, in the absence of repeated sales callbacks or advertisements to reinstate the identity of the source, the seller tends, over time, to lose the favorable impact of his good reputation on the attitudes and actions of his sales prospects.

But the declining power of source effect over time on audience decision making works *in opposite directions* for the well-known company than for the lesser-known company. Sleeper effect, in a manner of speaking, hurts the well-known company but helps the lesser-known company. In the case of the former, as the sales prospect forgets the well-known source, his originally favorable attitude toward the product declines; and in the case of the latter, as he forgets the lesser-known source his originally less favorable attitude toward the product also declines. That is, the likelihood of his buying from the high-credibility company declines while the likelihood of his buying from the low-credibility company rises—even though the high-credibility company is still likely to get more customers in absolute terms.

IMPLICATIONS AND RESERVATIONS

The implications of the present research for industrial products companies are numerous, but so also are the reservations and qualifications which must be attached to the research findings. While the research sought to simulate reality as carefully as possible, it still remains only a simulation. Moreover, individual competitive situations, product characteristics, and a vast variety of other conditions can greatly affect the value of these findings in specific cases. But in the absence of better information and research, the present findings may be viewed as at least a beginning toward unravelling some age-old mysteries.

Reputation and Presentation

From the point of view of a producer of industrial materials or components, it seems safe to conclude that the cultivation of a good reputation among potential customers will have some payoff in the sense that it will help his salesmen to get "a foot in the door" of a prospect. But the value of cultivating a good reputation seems to be considerably less when it comes to its effect on the likelihood of the prospect's *actually buying* a new product on being first exposed to it. A good reputation always helps, but it helps less as the riskiness of the customer's decision rises and as he has something else to rely or draw on.

Hence it seems safe also to suggest that a producer of technically advanced products which are used as components or as ingredients by other manufacturers would be wise systematically to cultivate for himself a strongly favorable generalized reputation among technical personnel of prospective manufacturing customers. In other words, in trying to sell such products to technically trained personnel it may not be wise to rely so extensively, as many such companies do, on the product's inherent virtues and on making strong technical product presentations. Technical personnel are not human computers whose purchasing and product-specification decisions are based on cold calculations and devoid of less rigorously rational influences. They do indeed seem to be influenced by the seller's general reputation.

However, as might have been expected, the quality of a salesman's presentation in support of a product is an important variable in obtaining favorable buyer reactions, regardless of the technical or purchasing competence of the audience. A good direct sales presentation is generally more effective than a poor one. There is a "presentation effect" in favor of the product supported by a well-done sales presentation. But, as in the case of source effect, the research indicates that a good sales presentation is generally more useful in getting a favorable first hearing for a new product (that is, in what is, for the prospect, a low-risk decision) than it is in getting a favorable buying decision (that is, a high-risk decision). A good sales presentation is definitely better than a poor one in getting product adoption, but it has even more leverage than a poor one in getting a favorable first hearing for a product.

All this indicates that both the reputation of a vendor company and the quality of its direct sales presentations are important elements in sales success, but that the way the importance of these elements varies as between audiences and between types of audience decision situations greatly affects how a vendor might wish to shape his marketing tactics.

'Sleeper Effect'

The findings on "sleeper effect" are particularly interesting in that, contrary to the other findings, they suggest that some policies appropriate for the well-known company may not be appropriate for the lesser-known company. Thus, repeat advertising and sales callbacks reinstate the well-known company's identity and therefore influence the prospect in its favor. But since the sales prospect tends to forget the source over time and therefore makes a more "objective" decision, reinstating the identity of the lesser-known company could actually tend to hurt that company. All other things being equal, the lesser-known company may find it better to leave well enough alone. But whether "all other things" are equal is highly doubtful, and in any case varies by the situation. The most that can be said here is that there can conceivably be circumstances in which sleeper effect can work to the advantage of the lesser-known company.

However, the research also found that the passage of time has different consequences for source effect than for presentation effect. A good sales presentation is more effective over time than a good reputation. Moreover, the better the original sales presentation, the greater the durability of its influence over the audience with the passage of time. That is, regardless of the presence of sleeper effect (the declining influences of source credibility with the passage of time), if the original sales presentation was relatively good, the prospects tend more strongly to favor the product in question at a later date than if that presentation had been poor. The originally favorable influence of the highly credible source declined less, and the originally unfavorable influence of the less credible source hurt less, as the original sales presentation was better. A good sales presentation has greater durability than a good company reputation. Company reputation, in order to work for that company, has to be more regularly reinforced (possibly through advertising repetition) than does the effect of a good sales presentation.

A related finding on the dynamics of sleeper effect involves the strength of a sales prospect's reaction to a sales presentation. Thus, there is some evidence that the more self-confidently a prospect refuses at the outset to permit a new product to be viewed and reviewed by others in his firm, the greater the likelihood later that he will change his mind and give such permission. That is, a strong outright refusal for a further hearing at the time of the first sales call may suggest greater probability of getting permission later than does a weak and vacillating original refusal. Hence the very vigor with which a new product is at first rejected by a prospect may, instead of signaling that it is a lost cause, actually signal that a later repeat call is likely to get a good hearing.

High Risk Situations

But this refers only to relatively low-risk decisions—decisions in which the prospect is asked merely to give the product serious consideration, not actually to buy it at that time. In high-risk decision situations the findings were different. The research confirms the common-sense expectation that the greater the personal risk to the responding sales prospect, the more persuasion it takes to get him to switch from a product he is currently using. Moreover, once a prospect has made a decision in a high-risk situation, the seller will generally have considerable difficulty both in getting the negative respondent subsequently to change his mind and in keeping the affirmative respondent from changing his mind. This means that, especially in high-risk situations, it pays to try to get a favorable customer decision at the outset. Once he has rejected a product, it appears to be extremely difficult to get the prospect to be willing to reopen the discussions. Similarly, once he has accepted a new product under high-risk conditions, the customer appears to suffer from considerable self-doubt about whether he has made the right decision. He is probably very susceptible to being "unsold" by a competitor. This suggests the need for continuous followup by the original seller to reassure the customer and thus keep him sold.

Salesman or Company?

It has already been pointed out that, generally speaking, the more credible the source the more likely it is that its message will get a favorable reception. But the question arises as to who "the" source is: Is it the salesman who makes the sales call, or is it the company he represents? Do customers perceive this "source" as being one and the same or different? The present research indicates that they think of them as being two different sources. The salesman is not automatically thought of as being the company. When asked to rank the trustworthiness of the salesman on the one hand and then the trustworthiness of the company he represented, respondents consistently scored the salesman lower than his company.

While this might reflect the relatively low esteem with which salesmen are generally held, paradoxically, in our highly sales-dependent society, a closer look at the results suggests a great deal more. It was found, for example, that respondents are more likely to favor the products of salesmen whom they rank low in trustworthiness when these salesmen represent well-known companies than they are to favor the products of salesmen whom they rank relatively high in trustworthiness but who represent unknown companies. A similar result occurred in connection with respondents' feelings about how well informed and competent the salesmen from high-vs.-low credibility companies are. Thus, offhand it would seem that favorably well known companies operate at the distinct advantage of being able to afford to

to have less "trustworthy" and less "competent" salesmen, at least in the short run, than little-known or anonymous companies. But close examination suggests something else. It suggests that source effect is such a uniquely powerful force that for respondents to favor well-known companies, their need to trust the salesmen of these companies and to think highly of their competence is much less urgent than it is in order for them to favor less well known and anonymous companies. In other words, the favorably well known company does indeed have an advantage over its less well known competitor in that its salesmen need to *seem* less trustworthy and competent in order to be effective. Well-known companies need not be as scrupulous in their hiring and training of salesmen. Source effect seems almost to conquer everything.

But not entirely everything. As noted above, presentation quality and quality of the message can overcome some of the disadvantages of being relatively anonymous. So can, of course, trust in the salesman. What is it then that makes for an appearance of salesman trustworthiness? First of all, the results of the present research suggest that trustworthiness of the communicator (such as, for example, a salesman, television announcer, etc.) is not as clearly related to the audience's feeling about his knowledge or understanding of the product he is selling as might be expected. While there is some relationship, trust is much more closely related to the overall quality or character of the salesman's sales presentation. Poor presentations in particular reduce trust in the message transmitter (salesman). They also reduce trust in the message source (the salesman's company). The better the presentation the more trustworthy both the company and the salesman are perceived to be. To say this, and what has been said before, is equivalent to saying that there is obvious merit in making sure that salesmen have quality sales presentations, and this holds true particularly for less well known companies.

It is interesting to note from the research that there was only a very modest, certainly not a clear, connection between audience ratings of a salesman's trustworthiness and their judgments regarding the extent of his product competence. An audience's willingness either to recommend or adopt a product was not clearly related to its judgment about a salesman's product knowledge. Nor was it related, in the short run, to how much of the information which the salesman gave out was actually retained by the audience.

All this suggests that in making his adoption decisions the customer is influenced by more than what the salesman specifically says about the product or even how effectively he communicates product facts. It seems very probable that the communicator's personality and what he says about things other than the product in question play a vital role in influencing his audience. The effective transmission of product facts seems to be more important in the long run than in the short run. With the passage of time since the date of the original sales presentation, persons who retained more product information right after that presentation were more likely to make and hold decisions favorable to the source. Hence the importance of the effective transmission of product facts during the original presentation seems to increase as the product-adoption decision is delayed. But it is not clear that detailed recall of product facts ever becomes a paramount ingredient in obtaining favorable buying decisions.

SUMMARY

It seems clear that company reputation is a powerful factor in the industrial purchasing process, but its importance varies with the technical competence and sophistication of the customer. The quality of a sales message and the way it is presented are capable of moderating the influence of this source effect, but again it varies by audience. Generally speaking, it pays for a company to be favorably well known, and perhaps especially among customers having some degree of technical sophistication, such as engineers and scientists. But superior sales messages and well-trained salesmen can help less well known companies to overcome some of the disadvantages of their relative anonymity. A well-planned and well-executed direct sales presentation can be an especially strong competitive weapon for the less well-known company. Moreover, the greater the riskiness of the purchasing decision the customer is asked to make, the more likely it is that a good sales presentation will produce a customer decision in favor of the direction advocated by the source.

Notes

1. Bauer, "The Obstinate Audience," *American Psychologist*, Vol. 19 (May 1964), pp. 319-328, and "Communication as a Transaction," *Public Opinion Quarterly*, Vol. 27 (Spring 1963), pp. 83-86.
2. For the seminal research in this area, see Carl I. Hovland and Walter Weiss, "The Influence of Source Credibility on Communication Effectiveness," *Public Opinion Quarterly*, Vol. 15 (Winter 1951-1952), pp. 635-650, and Carl I. Hovland, A. A. Lumsdaine, and Fred D. Sheffield, *Experiments in Mass Communication* (Princeton: Princeton University Press, 1949).
3. The details of the research mechanism are spelled out in Theodore Levitt, *Industrial Purchasing Behavior: A Study in Communications Effects* (Boston, Massachusetts: Division of Research, Harvard Business School, 1965).

23 THE NEW SUPERSALESMAN: WIRED FOR SUCCESS

By the Editors of
Business Week

What is a supersalesman and why is he or she here
to stay? This article discusses the increasingly
important role of the salesperson in today's corporate stucture.

If you want to rile Herbert D. Eagle, just
slide a copy of *Webster's New Collegiate Diction-
ary* in front of him. "Have you ever read the
definition of 'sell'?" fumes Eagle, vice-president
of marketing for Transamerica Corp. "Things like
'betray' and 'cheat' are capitalized, and there are
phrases such as 'to deliver up or give up in violation of duty, trust, or loyalty.' I've been carrying
on a running battle with G. & C. Merriam Co. to
change that definition."

If anyone can sell Merriam on a new definition, it is 54-year-old Herb Eagle. As marketing
vice-president for giant, fast-growing Transamerica
Corp. ($1.6-billion in sales last year), Eagle
coordinates the marketing and sales strategies for
42 companies that field more than 6,000 internal
salesmen and handle everything from insurance
and financial services to car rentals. Eagle also
doubles as president of Sales & Marketing Executives International, a professional society of
25,000 members scattered through 49 countries.
As the official pick of his peers and thus the
closest thing to industry's top salesman, Eagle is a

From "The New Supersalesman: Wired for Success,"
Business Week *(January 6, 1973), pp. 238-242. Copyright
© 1973 McGraw-Hill Inc. Reprinted by permission of
McGraw-Hill Inc.*

drumbeater in the cause of supersalesmanship and
the enormous change that is coming over that
fine, old American institution: personal selling.

"A few years back," says Eagle, "it was
usually the salesman out there alone, pitting his
wits against the resistance of a single corporate
purchasing agent. Now, more and more companies
are selling on many different levels, interlocking
their research, engineering, marketing, and upper
management with those of their customers. This
way, today's salesman becomes a kind of committee chairman within his company. Some manufacturers call them 'account managers.' Either way,
his job is to exploit the resources of his company
in serving the customer."

As industries consolidate and larger corporations continue to swallow up the small fry, a
growing number of companies are also "preselling"
their products through massive promotion,
advertising, and improved communications between buyer and seller. The result is that the
average salesman's prime responsibility is no
longer selling, so much as clinching a sale that has
already been set in motion even before he makes
his first spiel.

MORE SALES PRODUCTIVITY

At the consumer level, this shows up in the
cutback of retail sales help and the huge expansion
of self-service merchandising. At the industry
level, it shows up in a whole new function for the
industrial salesman. No longer is he simply a pitch-
man or prescriber of his company's products. Now
he must go beyond that and become a diagnosti-
cian.

"If a supplier's job is to service the customer,
then the role of the salesman becomes one of
problem-identifier first, problem-solver second,
and prescriber third," says Charles S. Goodman,
professor of marketing at the University of
Pennsylvania's Wharton School. "I don't say this
is common today. But as the economy becomes
more consumer-oriented"—and thus open to
greater challenge on product performance—"it has
to go that way."

An even greater goad is today's spiraling
cost of selling, which demands that industry get
far more out of its sales dollar. Rex Chainbelt,

Inc., for instance, spends $5,000 to $20,000 to train a salesman and $30,000 to $35,000 a year to keep him on the road. That averages out to $52.80 per sales call, double the figure of 10 years ago. What is more, as product lines proliferate and product technology gets more complex, manufacturers and wholesalers have gradually boosted their number of internal salesmen to more than 1 million. And some experts claim that the demand for salesmen will grow by another 250,000 jobs a year over the next few years, not including replacements. "Obviously," as Transamerica's Eagle notes, "something has to give."

To cut costs and raise sales efficiency, more and more companies are reexamining the ways that they recruit, train, pay, equip, and manage their salesmen. Many companies are reorganizing their selling structures. Some are experimenting with new compensation and incentive programs. Nearly all are moving away from the old straight commission system to salary-plus-bonus.

"This is primarily the product of looking upon salesmen as account managers," says William E. Cox, professor of marketing at Case Western Reserve University. "You begin asking him to take on a lot of additional duties other than just simply writing an order. He becomes the company's broader marketing representative."

Industry is also drawing on a whole new battery of selling tools, ranging from audio/visual cassettes and special slide projectors to remote portable terminals that can plug the salesman straight into his home-office computer. The computer itself, of course, has become one of selling's biggest tools of all. It can lay out sales territories, budget the salesman's time by customer and product, and keep track of sales costs, time use, itineraries, payables and receivables, expenses, orders, inquiries, and over-all performance.

"Fifteen years ago when I first started selling," says Frederick H. Stephens, Jr., sales vice-president for Gillette Co.'s Safety Razor Div., "we couldn't tell at any point how much volume we did on promotional items, for instance, compared with open stock. Now we have monthly IBM printouts that tell our salesmen how much business he's doing with promotions compared to open stock and total business, how much business is being done in his territory, and how much each customer bought of each item. We used to tell a salesman, 'You're up 4.6% this year, that's pretty good.' Now we can say, 'You're up 4.6% but down 1.6% in discount stores and up only 2.1% over your territory.' And we have the information to get him back in the ballgame."

IDENTIFYING CUSTOMER NEEDS

Unfortunately, most salesmen are still somewhere between the locker room and the playing field. "Selling is very, very inefficient compared to what it could be," says Edward J. Feeney, vice-president of the Systems Performance Div. of Emery Air Freight Corp. "Most salesmen," Feeney claims, "are sitting in lobbies. They're calling on wrong accounts. They're calling on accounts that give them all the business that they can. They're calling on people they think can make the buying decision when, in fact, they do not or cannot make much of it at all. They are efficient in talking about what they do—what their company provides—but not in how it fills the customer's need, because they haven't probed to find out what those needs are."

Those needs usually go far beyond the purchase of any one supplier's equipment or services. Hugh Hoffman, chairman of Opinion Research Corp., cites the experience of one of his company's clients, a major chemical producer. "Its salesmen told us," he says, "that if they're trying to sell plastic film to a packager who has several million dollars' worth of packaging equipment designed to use some other material, they must now know how to unload the present equipment, purchase new equipment, and work out the intricacies of amortization. Without that background, they cannot persuade the customer to accept delivery of a single carload of plastic film."

This is because today's major competitor is no longer one broom salesman against another. It is alternate uses of money. "And the modern salesman," says John R. Robertson, sales manager for the Business Systems Markets Div. of Eastman Kodak Co., "must be able to convince his customer that spending money on the salesman's product is a better investment than spending it elsewhere."

Above all, the supersalesman tries to build

more than the old-style buyer-seller relationship. A top marketing executive at International Business Machines Corp., which is one of the companies that has spearheaded the development of superselling, claims that today's salesman must develop a "long-range partnership" with his clients. "The installation of a data-processing system," he emphasizes, "is only the beginning, not the end, of IBM's marketing effort."

To serve their customers better, IBM salesmen not only specialize by product and market, they also specialize by function: installation, equipment protection or maintenance, and upgrading of systems. To sharpen the focus of its salesmen even more, IBM—like most consumer-goods companies—is "segmenting" or targeting its markets. "The costs of developing new accounts by the cold-call approach," says the IBM marketer, "have risen so drastically that we are moving toward far more selective prospecting" —including a special computer experiment for picking only "high-potential prospects."

Among the other special qualities that set off the supersalesman:

Universality "Ten years ago when I hired a salesman," says James Schlinkert, Pittsburgh-area branch manager for Olivetti Corp. of America, "I was looking for someone who would make a lot of calls and, through sheer effort and exposure, be reasonably successful. Now I want someone more versed in things unrelated to our business. Today's salesman must be able to talk on any and all current subjects—from the economy to world affairs—because these often affect his business." Not too many years ago, adds the marketing vice-president for a major information-systems company, "you'd hire somebody with personality that you thought would wear well, and you'd point him out the door." Now it takes more. "A top manager's time is very precious," he says, "and we have to give him a meaningful message when we meet with him."

Patience Because product technology has become more complex and salesmen are interrelating more products and moving deeper into systems selling, the time that it takes to close a sale has stretched out. "There are no quick sales today," says Anthony E. Schiavone, an assistant development manager for Rohm & Haas Co. "It may take a year just to get to know a new cus-

tomer and his problems." Philip Rosell, western regional sales manager for Singer's Business Machines Group, claims that he was on the verge of quitting Singer two years ago after he had gone his first full year without writing an order. "You have to gear yourself psychologically for a long haul," he says.

Persistence With growing cost-consciousness, upper management is increasingly involved in major buying decisions. So the supersalesman often tries to go beyond the first level of decision-making. "This is not usually the best-paid or most creative guy around anyway," says one Boston salesman. "It's when you go beyond this level that you can sell the extras. And it's not true that the top guy never sees salesmen. You can often enlist the aid of your own top people and set up a meeting."

More Work, Less Pay Lavish wining and dining of buyers is out. In fact, Don H. Hartmann, president of Crutcher Resources Corp., calls this "probably the biggest thrust of all—the trend away from the massive entertainment of a few years ago." One top eastern salesman adds, of his relations with his customers: "We're no longer a bunch of drinking buddies. I never have lunch with a man I haven't met before, and I never hesitate to talk business at lunch. After all, our relationship is business and not personal."

RESTRUCTURING THE TERRITORIES

Whether he is selling insurance, computers, catalytic crackers, or wholesale cosmetics, today's supersalesman has two big things going for him: improved transportation and communications. This allows him to cover more territory faster and to draw closer to his markets. As the president of a Houston industrial-goods company describes his ideal salesman: "He starts his day flying out nonstop from North Carolina to Chicago, then gets a midafternoon plane to Los Angeles to make two or three calls, and catches a night plane to Dallas. It's a fast-moving situation today. Five years ago, because of aircraft and flight scheduling, we couldn't do this."

Yet how much territory is too much? As far back as 10 years ago, adman and marketing seer E. B. Weiss, a senior vice-president at Doyle Dane Bernbach, was calling for a whole new approach to the organization of sales territories and to the basic corporate selling structure. Then, as now, the problem was to minimize unproductive calls and contacts and to get close to the prospects who had both the need and purchasing authority to buy a given product or service. "The sales organization," Weiss wrote, "must be reorganized so as to be able to open up its channels of communication to those who make buying decisions, rather than to limit itself primarily to buyers who make merely buying motions. This calls for new sales organizational blueprints."

Those changes are finally beginning to come. Today's three basic levels of selling—manufacturing, wholesaling, and consumer and industrial services—are spawning dozens of highly-specialized sub-categories aimed at shortening the lines of communication between buyer and seller. IBM is even experimenting with administrative specialists who help its sales specialists handle order preparation, scheduling, collections, and other paperwork. Along the way, more and more companies are organizing against markets, rather than products. For maximum productivity, a few are even organizing against profits.

"Historically," says Gennaro A. Filice, Jr., vice-president of U.S. marketing for Del Monte Corp., "most food companies have been case-volume oriented. As long as we could push out a lot of volume, we let the profits take care of themselves. That's no longer true. As products multiply and the competition for shelf space increases, salesmen have to be far more sophisticated in their approach to product management, and the company has to learn to identify those with the most profit potential."

To help pinpoint that potential, Del Monte recently restructured its entire field sales force, expanding from nine regional divisions to 21. "As our emphasis shifted away from case sales," says Filice, "and as the chains got bigger and more dominant, it became more difficult for a salesman to write an order. This restructuring was also designed to get us as close to the customer as possible."

Under Del Monte's new system, the actual selling is handled by an "account representative." He makes the direct calls on retailers and writes up the orders. Then one level below him is the sales representative. He is the junior type who works with store managers on shelf management, restocking, display, and other merchandising chores. Sales representatives are also information-gatherers. Using a new computerized system called "Key Facts," which the company plans to expand nationwide next spring, Del Monte's California salesmen fill out a form during each store visit, listing shelf position, pricing, advertising support, and other basic marketing data. This is fed into the computer and later compared against actual product performance to arrive at maximum profitability.

WOMEN IN THE SALES FORCE

Hunt-Wesson Foods, Gillette, Allied Chemical, and several other companies have found another productivity booster for their field organizations: part-time female-workers. Gillette maintains an auxiliary force of 150 middle-aged housewives who operate one rung below the individual store salesmen. The women work 24 hours a week for $3 an hour, plus expenses, and handle retail displays, distribution, and stock replenishment.

"In 1958, when I started selling," says one sales executive at Gillette, "I spent 30% of my time calling on direct customers and 70% calling on local stores to work on display and distribution, and writing up turnover orders"—orders passed on to wholesalers to replenish out-of-stock items. "Today, our salesmen spend 85% of their time on direct accounts and only about 15% of their time at local stores on display and distribution."

Along with tightening the focus of their field forces, more and more companies are also creating broader "account executives," whose job is to crack that tricky, old marketing problem: how to deal with the big chains or a large, diversified company with a variety of product needs. Some suppliers, of course, simply send a battalion of salesmen swarming into such companies at all levels. Now a growing number are creating account executives who oversee all product needs of a single customer, often at the headquarters level.

This way, the big customer has one sales contact that can satisfy and interrelate all its needs.

Over the last few years, Dow Chemical Co. has created 14 corporate account managers who operate one notch above the salesman and handle all 1,200 Dow products for a given customer. "There are no firm rules about how big an account must be before a corporate account manager takes over," says M. C. Carpenter, Dow's director of marketing communications. "But they are basically potential multimillion-dollar customers."

At the same time, Dow is trying to crack

Supersalesman Eagle Talks Selling

On the changing role: "As today's salesman becomes part of a larger marketing team, some people claim that his individual role begins to diminish. This is not true. In 1950, for instance, there were 3,000 items in the average supermarket. Today, there are 8,000. The salesman thus helps position and differentiate that product for the chain."

On corporate backup: "The salesman needs plenty of management and marketing support. He does not always get it. Take insurance. One of the problems of that business is that the industry spends 30 times as much for advertising to tell people what and when to buy as it spends on market research. This is not an indictment of advertising but an indictment of how much we have been telling and how little we've been listening."

On upward mobility: "Today's salesman is moving higher faster. One out of every three publicly-owned U. S. corporations is now headed by a man whose background is primarily marketing or sales. And this ratio is bound to grow as companies become more sensitive to consumerism."

On resilience: "The salesman gets paid for the number of times he hears 'no.' The well-adjusted salesman knows in advance that he may close one sale out of 25 calls. He is mentally prepared to suffer those 24 turndowns. Still, it takes its toll. So he gets paid for hearing 'no.'"

On picking a sales career: "Nothing really happens until somebody sells something. Or, as Robert Louis Stevenson once put it, 'Everyone lives by selling something.'"

another problem that comes with the bigness of a customer: the difficulty of getting a territorial fix on where a sale actually occurs. In the past, Dow credited a sale to the office in the territory where the customer was located. Thus, any sale in the Houston area was chalked up to the Houston office, even though the key initiative may have come in New York. Now each sale is credited to the office where the sale originates. "That makes the accounting more complicated and subjective," Carpenter concedes. "But it gives sales managers a better idea of what's really going on in the field. We find out where the key marketing man is."

As sales organizations grow bigger and more complex, the challenge, of course, is to avoid costly duplication of sales effort. Hewlett-Packard Co. ran into this problem. It started out with a highly centralized organization that did most of its selling through outside manufacturers' representatives. By 1963, the company's product line had become so broad and complicated that Hewlett-Packard decided to acquire most of its reps and turn them into a corporate sales staff. "We stayed with reps longer than most companies," says Robert L. Boniface, marketing vice-president. "We felt that it was important to have the sales force represent the customer's viewpoint as much as Hewlett-Packard's. By acquiring them rather than cutting them off, we kept all their experience and momentum."

As Hewlett-Packard moved into medical instruments, calculators, electronic components, and other diverse new markets, the company split its sales staff into eight organizations. "Right away, we developed overlaps," says Alfred P. Oliverio, marketing manager for the Electronic Products Group. "We didn't want two salesmen calling on one customer if the product was not really all that different."

In Hewlett-Packard's most recent shift, the old product-oriented structure gave way to a combined product/market-oriented system. In electronic products, for instance, separate sales groups now concentrate on electrical manufacturing, aerospace, communications, and transportation equipment. Within each group, Hewlett-Packard tries to build a cadre of salesmen, application engineers, and software specialists. "We probably have better than one support person for every salesman," says Oliverio.

SELLING THE 'DREAM LIST'

Hans G. Moser, field director for Northwestern Mutual Life Insurance Co. and a chartered life underwriter, sold $4.5-million worth of life insurance last year. That makes him 29th out of the company's 2,900 agents. Moser's distinctive selling approach is typical of how today's supersalesman tackles his customer.

Like a consumer-goods maker who targets his market, Moser ignores "run-of-the-mill types" and zeroes in on prospects who can either afford heavy insurance now or who are obviously on the way up and will be able to in the future. Moser adopted this tactic when he broke into the insurance business in 1960. "Many of my earlier customers," he says, "are now in a position to set up trust accounts, dabble with stocks, and deal with other sophisticated methods of estate planning. And, of course, I am right in there, making a pitch for life insurance and other securities."

Moser keeps two lists of prospects: one made up of day-to-day business that he expects to close within a month, and the other composed of "dream cases"—each ranging anywhere from $100,000 to $500,000 or more of coverage—that may take three months to a year to close. His goal is to add a new dream case every month and maintain a working inventory of at least 10 or 12 such cases. This way, he closes one every four to six weeks. As part of the same goal, Moser keeps a chart of his best January, February, and so on, and uses it as a composite yearly goal.

In pitching the customer, Singer Business Machines' Philip Rosell has come up with such a winning technique for selling electronic point-of-sale systems to retailers that Singer even asked him to write it up in PERT chart fashion. Salesman Rosell's opening strategy is a letter to the prospect's top operating officer, requesting a meeting. Rosell starts at the top because of the big investment involved in buying his equipment. "We seldom get turned down," Rosell says of his request for that first big meeting. Then Rosell teams up with a local salesman and system engineer, and the three go in together and discuss what the system can do for the prospect. "We don't try to sell him any hardware," Rosell says. "That's what he has a purchasing agent for."

THE LESSONS TAUGHT BY FAILURE

If the first meeting is encouraging, Rosell follows it up with store surveys and endless conferences and demonstrations for the store's credit, merchandising, data processing, and financial executives. "We infiltrate the whole company," says Rosell. "In every case where we've made a major sale, the company has felt we were part of its team." Rosell recalls only two occasions when he did not follow his usual selling approach. This was at the insistence of the customer, who wanted a consultant to act as go-between. Both times the sale was lost.

What happens when you do blow the big sale? H. Glen Haney, a marketing director for the Univac Div. of Sperry Rand Corp., makes it a point to go back and find out why. "We lost a $4.5-million sale to a large state agency about a year ago," Haney says. "In a four-hour debriefing with the agency head, the state budget bureau people, and all other principals that were involved in the purchase, we found out that the loss of the sale really had nothing to do with the quality of our marketing effort. We lost because we had not clearly enough defined the conversion effort that the customer faced. Though our cost-performance was better than the competition, the agency decided to stay with its current vendor for that reason." Yet the lost sale was not a total loss. "As a result of that session," says Haney, "we have developed a series of conversion tools for our salesmen, aimed at solving that problem."

Owens-Corning Fiberglas Corp. took the same approach when a big customer, a thermoplastic compounder in Detroit, considered switching to an Owens-Corning competitor, which had cut its prices 1½¢ per lb. The competitor had a plant near the compounder, and the compounder decided to pick up its materials there, saving on freight. "It was a legitimate saving," says James MacLean, national sales manager for Owens-Corning's Textile & Industrial Group. "So we put our heads together." The local salesman, along with the group's marketing and packaging experts, finally developed a special package for shipping the material that the compounder could then use to ship his finished product. Savings: 2¢ per lb.

for the customer and one industrial account for Owens-Corning.

Sam Jackson, an assistant sales manager for U.S. Steel Corp. in Philadelphia, calls it the difference between moving a product for its own sake and fitting the same product to a customer's system. One of Jackson's customers was bemoaning a 10% hike in the cost of castings. "I suggested that the part could be converted from a casting to welded steel," says Jackson, "and got together with our metallurgical and research people to test the conversion." The customer finally accepted it, saving the 10% boost in cost that he would have paid had he continued to cast the part.

"What makes Jackson stand out is that he knows the different types of metals, the industry that he is selling to, and how to cut costs," says Irwin Rashkover, director of procurement for Gindy Mfg. Corp., a Budd Co. subsidiary. "Jackson knows how to help us save money by working out different tolerances for the steel we buy—for instance, by going to the high side of sheet tolerances. The supersalesman knows this. The ordinary steel salesman doesn't."

DON'T TAKE 'NO' FOR AN ANSWER

Robert Hawkins, who sells radio communications systems for Motorola, Inc., has the simplest—and oldest—selling technique of all: he refuses to take "no" for an answer. When Hawkins was pitching the field service organization of a national equipment supply house, he insisted that Motorola's one-way paging system could improve service and cut manpower needs. When a purchasing agent shrugged him off, Hawkins went above him to a vice-president and received grudging permission for a one-year study of the company's service coverage and performance in 20 cities. Yet when he completed the study, which showed the need for a paging system, Hawkins still did not receive an order. So he offered to follow that up with an intensive three-month test of the paging system in a single city.

"For the entire three months," says Hawkins, "a day never went by when I didn't spend some time with the prospect." Hawkins even helped the dispatcher to design more efficient routes, while soothing the ruffled nerves of its servicemen. "They were afraid of the dispatcher becoming a Big Brother and controlling their every move," he says. Finally convinced, the company has decided to go nationwide with the paging system.

Sometimes, such indecision can go too far. That is when Olivetti's James Schlinkert calls a halt. "To close a tough sale," he says, "you must establish yourself—not the buyer—as the authoritative person." Schlinkert describes just such a sale that he ran up against a few months ago. A small corporation of five people had a definite need for an accounting system. "We had them all at our office one evening and presented our solution to their problem," says Schlinkert. "They were a hard-nosed lot that had evaluated every other accounting system available. After a couple of hours of haggling over a $15,000 sale, I finally shut off the machine, put the key in my pocket, and virtually threatened to throw them out of my office. Immediately, they became very docile and signed a contract. I shocked my salesman when I did that. But I had to take a calculated risk. The need and solution had been established."

TRAINING TODAY'S SALESMAN

Developing such instincts takes years. Some salesmen never develop them, and that puts a heavier burden than ever on today's sales recruiting and training. "In years past," says Transamerica's Herb Eagle, "you figured you could take a new salesman and help him develop the qualities that he needed. With today's higher costs and greater complexity of selling, you have to look for those qualities first off. And if they aren't there, you don't hire."

Five or 10 years ago, for instance, most large technical or engineering companies automatically recruited from engineering schools. Now, many of these same companies are seeking salesmen with a broader outlook and thus are looking for liberal arts, marketing, and other nonengineering backgrounds. "We have even successfully used English, history, and physical education majors," marvels Baxter T. Fullerton, sales vice-president

of Warner & Swasey Co.'s Cleveland Turning
Machine Div. The trick, of course, is to gain a
universal man with broad interests, yet avoid what
one Houston educator calls "the round man who
is so round that he just rolls and develops no depth
or substance."

Other companies are looking less for college
graduates and more for seasoned professionals.
"We used to steer clear of the retreads," says
Peter Warshaw, a division national products manager for Powers Regulator Co. "Today when
there's a vacancy, we don't contact colleges at
all. We contact employment agencies, professional
societies, and use referrals within the industry. We
just can't afford to take the guy, make the major
investment in him for two or three years, and then
have him sell the training that we gave him to
someone else." The new man, Warshaw stresses,
must also be productive immediately. "The sales
quotas are now so large and selling costs so high
that we can't afford to have the backup man or
batboy anymore."

At the same time, sales training has broadened out. A growing number of companies offer
continuing instruction for all their salesmen—and
for good reason. Armour-Dial, Inc., a consumer-
goods division of Greyhound Corp., ran a study
on salesmen who had attended a recent session
at its Aurora (Ill.) sales training center. The result:
a boost of 12% in the number of calls per day,
25% in new-product retail placements, 100% in
case sales, 62% in displays sold, and 250% in sales
to direct-buying or chain accounts.

The big changes coming in sales recruiting
and training—and in the salesman's whole approach
to his markets—promise to usher in a broad new
relationship between him and his company.
Robert W. DeMott, Jr., vice-president and general
manager of Rex Chainbelt's Industrial Sales Div.,
notes that about 10 years ago, industry's overall
marketing effort seemed to eclipse selling in
importance. "Now, and more so in the future,"
he claims, "the trend will be to place selling on a
par with marketing."

Wharton's Goodman goes one step further,
claiming that the supersalesman of the future will
even be ahead of company management when it
comes to understanding his markets. "This is
going to sound heretical," he admits, "but I see
emerging a situation in which the salesman's

function within a company is recognized as most
important, with management performing a
largely supportive role."

While he might get an argument on that, no
one can dispute his larger point: the supersalesman
is here to stay.

24 REPETITIVE ADVERTISING AND THE CONSUMER

Andrew S. C. Ehrenberg
Professor of Marketing
London Graduate School of Business Studies

What consumer advertising can and cannot do is told in a very straightforward manner by a marketing professor who is also a research consultant. His conclusion: advertising's main role is to reinforce feelings of satisfaction.

Advertising is in an odd position. Its extreme protagonists claim it has extraordinary powers and its severest critics believe them. Advertising is often effective. But it is not as powerful as is sometimes thought, nor is there any evidence that it actually works by any strong form of persuasion or manipulation.

Instead, the sequence, awareness/trial/reinforcement, seems to account for the known facts. Under this theory, consumers first gain awareness or interest in a product. Next, they may make a trial purchase. Finally, a repeat buying habit may be developed and reinforced if there is satisfaction after previous usage.

Advertising has a role to play in all three stages. But for frequently bought products, repeat buying is the main determinant of sales volume and here advertising must be reinforcing rather than persuasive.

These conclusions are based largely on studies of consumer behavior and attitudinal

From Andrew S. C. Ehrenberg, "Repetitive Advertising and the Consumer," Journal of Advertising Research *14:2 (April 1974), pp. 25-34. Reprinted by permission of the publisher.*

response. They are important both to our understanding of advertising's social role and to the execution and evaluation of advertising as a tool of marketing management.

In this paper I first examine advertising and the consumption of goods in general. I then discuss competition among brands and the factors affecting consumers' brand choice, particularly for established brands of frequently bought goods.

THE DEMAND FOR GOODS

Advertising is widely credited with creating consumer demand. Sol Golden was quoted in 1972 in the *Journal of Advertising Research* as saying:

> "Advertising is the lynch-pin by which everything in the system hangs together—the consumer benefits, the economic growth, the corporate profits, the technological advancement."

Some years earlier John T. Connor (1966), then Secretary of Commerce, said:

> "Without advertising, we most certainly could not have had the unprecedented prosperity of the last 67 months, because advertising is an absolutely indispensable element in the economic mix of the free enterprise system that produced that prosperity.
> "We would not have had, without advertising, a drop in unemployment from over 7 percent to less that 4 percent."

And we would not have had, without advertising, a rise in unemployment since. Many of advertising's critics from Professor Galbraith downwards also believe it has such powers—to create demand, to manipulate the consumer, to build our acquisitive society. But let us look at these supposed powers.

Product class advertising as a whole—"Buy more cars," "Drink more tea," etc.—certainly cannot be held responsible for consumer demand. For one thing, there is relatively little of this form of advertising. For another it generally has only minor effects, increasing a market by a few percentage points or slightly slowing a rate of decline. These effects are worthwhile to the producer, but neither can be credited with creating demand or manipulating the consumer on any substantial scale.

The primary target of criticism is repetitive advertising for individual brands—"Buy Fords," "Drink Lipton's Tea," etc. This is where the bulk of mass advertising is concentrated. Such competitive advertising for different brands can lead to a higher level of consumption of the product class as a whole than would exist without it, but there is no evidence that such secondary or even unintended effects are either big or particularly common. There are not even any dramatic claims in the literature (if I have missed one, that is the exception). In many product classes with heavy competitive advertising, total consumption is rising little if at all; in some it is falling. On the other hand, there are many product classes with little if any mass media advertising—like sailboats or marijuana—where consumption is increasing quickly.

Advertising for new products cannot bear the blame for consumer demand either. Undoubtedly advertising can help to speed up the initial adoption of a new product by creating awareness and, indirectly, by gaining retail distribution and display. But advertising works as a lubricant in such cases—to ease and speed things—and not as the prime mover. Getting an initial purchase for a new product is not the point at issue in understanding society's continuing demand for goods.

The key question is whether people continue to buy something *after* they or their friends and neighbors have used it. This applies equally to frequently bought goods like frozen foods and cigarettes and to once only or once in a while purchases like atomic power stations or lawn mowers, where the satisfied user's influence makes itself felt through word of mouth recommendation over the garden fence (or the industrial equivalent), through retailer and press comments, and so on.

By and large, one cannot go on selling something which people do not like after they have had it. Sometimes people are sold a new kind of product, by advertising or other means, which they find afterwards they did not really want. Some initial sales volume may be created in this way, but generally that is all.

The usual reason why people buy things is that they want them. Anyone who has washed dishes knows that the demand for nonstick frying pans or dishwashers did not have to be created. Rather, suitable products had to be developed, and then advertising undoubtedly helped to speed their adoption.

There is no need to suppose that the role of advertising here is fundamental. It is a peculiar form of snobbism to suppose that if *other* people want to smoke cigarettes, to smell nice, to have bathrooms, or to drive in motor cars, it is only because they have been manipulated by advertising. Sometimes this view can go as far as John Hobson's statement at his Cantor Lectures (1964):

> "Almost certainly the increase in motoring has been the result of competitive petrol [gasoline] advertising."

The alternative is to suppose that people want to go from A to B, or like driving, or want to get away for weekends, and that rightly or wrongly they often find cars more convenient or pleasing than walking or other forms of transport.

An often-quoted example of the alleged effects of advertising in "creating" demand is the growth of men's toiletries. But this has been part of the great nonadvertised change in men's fashions: clothing, hair styles, etc. Advertising by itself could not have created such a toiletries market 20 or 40 years ago. Instead of leading it, advertising generally follows fashion or product innovation. Anything else would be bad marketing—spending millions to convince people to buy something just because someone can produce it.

The effects of paid advertising on consumer demand must not be confused with the effects of the mass media as such or with people's developing education and greater mobility. People increasingly see how other people live and this has led to vastly increased expectations.

People "want" many things once they have become aware of their existence—food, warmth, good looks, money, power, to drive a car, to be a concert pianist, to avoid washing dishes, etc. Some of these things are very difficult to achieve, others are easier. To acquire goods, one only needs some money, someone to produce them, and a precedent of other people owning them in order to overcome cultural habits or inhibitions.

People go on wanting things because they like them. Increased if highly uneven affluence, increased availability of products, and vastly increased awareness through mass communication and education are three factors which account for the growing acquisitive nature of Western society. The glossy images of affluence shown in advertisements and in the media generally reflect a real demand. Eliminating advertising would not eliminate the demanding consumer.

The products he demands are mostly genuinely wanted or even needed by him. Manufacturers seldom create the needs, but they do attempt to fill them. As a result we have competition and competitive advertising among different brands or makes of the same product. This we now examine in more detail.

COMPETITION AND PERSUASIVE ADVERTISING

Most advertising aims to promote a particular brand or make of product in a competitive situation. Because it often takes an emotional instead of an informative tone, such advertising is generally thought to work by persuasion. A typical critic like Boulding (1955), as quoted for instance by Achenbaum (1972) in the *Journal of Advertising Research*, wrote in his economics text:

> "Most advertising, unfortunately, is devoted to an attempt to build up in the mind of the consumer *irrational preferences for certain brands or goods*. All the arts of psychology—particularly the art of association—are used to persuade consumers that they should buy Bingo rather than Bango."

It is generally recognized that advertising's effects on sales are not necessarily immediate or direct. Instead, it is thought to work through people's attitudes as an intermediary stage to changing their behavior.

Advertising therefore is often thought of as aiming to attach an image or some special consumer benefits to a brand, in an effort to distinguish it from its competitors in the mind of the consumer. This is attempted especially in situations where there are no physical or quality characteristics to differentiate it. Gasoline advertising that stresses "extra mileage," or "smoothness," or "enjoyment," or "power," is

a case in point, and Rosser Reeves' Unique Selling Proposition (USP) was an extreme version of the view that advertising can only work by offering buyers of Brand X something which no other similar brand has.

In the last 50 years, various theories have been put forward to try to explain how advertising works, taking attitudes into account (e.g., Joyce, 1967). One simple version is the well-known AIDA model, which stands for the chain:

$$\text{Awareness} \rightarrow \text{Interest} \rightarrow \text{Desire} \rightarrow \text{Action.}$$

This sequential pattern—or something like it put in different words—is treated as common sense: it only says that people need to be aware of a brand before they can be interested in it, and that they need to desire it before they can take action and buy it. This imputes two roles to advertising: (1) an informational role—making them aware of the product—and (2) a persuasive role—making people desire it before they have bought it.

In its informational role, it might seem that when there are no deeper benefits to guide a consumer's brand choice, he will be influenced by the last advertisement seen or by the general weight of past advertising. This assumption has led to the use of awareness and recall measures in pretesting and monitoring advertisements. But there is little direct evidence that advertising for established brands works like this. The evidence that does exist is either negative (e.g., Achenbaum, 1972) or at best shows effects which are not dramatically large and which still require confirmation (e.g., McDonald, 1970; Barnes, 1971).

In its persuasive role, advertising is thought to create a desire or conviction to buy, or at least to "add value to the brand as far as the consumer is concerned" (e.g., Treasure, 1973). For this reason advertisements take on persuasive methods like creating a brand image, selling a USP, or informing consumers that they need a special product to meet a special need (e.g., a special shampoo for oily hair). But again, there is no empirical evidence that advertising generally succeeds in this aim, when there are no real differences to sell.

In fact, these models of hierarchical or sequential effects have been generally criticized on the grounds of lack of evidence (e.g., Palda,

1966). They also fail to explain many of the known facts.

For example, they do not explain stable markets where shares of advertising and shares of sales are roughly in line for each brand. The small and medium-sized brands survive year-in and year-out, even though their consumers are exposed to vast amounts of advertising for the brand leaders.

Nor do the models account for the situation where, following a drop in sales revenue, advertising expenditure is cut and yet no catastrophe results. If consumers must be continually persuaded to buy a brand, then surely a cut in advertising should turn a minor setback into a major disaster. But it generally is not so.

Again, the models fail to account for the fact that four out of five new brands fail. There is no suggestion that failure occurs less often for highly advertised new brands.

More generally, the models do not explain why advertising generally has only a marginal effect on total demand for a product group; nor why it is only rarely capable of shifting people's attitudes and behavior on social issues like smoking, racial discrimination, voting, etc.

It is not enough to claim that persuasive advertising depends on the quality of the campaign or that advertising in general is inefficient. What is needed is a new explanation of the ways in which advertising actually works.

In recent years a good deal of attention has been paid to alternative explanations of the advertising process, based on mechanisms like satisfaction after previous usage, reinforcement, reduction of dissonance and selective perception. The argument later in this paper is grounded on these processes. But the most direct advances have been in our understanding of consumers' buying behavior and attitudinal responses in a competitive brand situation.

BUYER BEHAVIOR

Brand choice and repeat buying are regular and predictable aspects of buyer behavior.

The economic viability of any frequently bought product depends on repeat buying. It follows simple patterns. If 10 percent of consumers buy Brand X an average of 1.5 times each in a given time period, then in the next time period 45 percent of that group can be expected to buy the brand again on an average of 1.8 times each (as modeled for example by the "NBD" theory [e.g., Ehrenberg 1972, Table B4]). This is what is normally found under a wide range of conditions, both for food and nonfood products, in the U.S. and the U.K., for leading brands and smaller ones, and so on.

The 55 percent who do *not* buy the brand in the second period are, however, not lost for good. Instead, they are merely relatively infrequent buyers of the brand who buy it regularly but not often. No special efforts have therefore to be made either to bring them back or to replace them (the "leaky bucket" theory). Few things about the consumer in competitive markets can be more important than knowing this, and a successful theory of repeat buying was needed to establish it.

The existence of regular and predictable patterns of repeat buying for a brand, however, does not mean that people mostly buy one brand only. Instead, the majority of buyers of a brand regularly purchase other brands as well. In general there are relatively few 100 percent loyal or sole buyers of a brand, especially over any extended period of time. A typical and predictable finding for frequently bought grocery products is that in a week, 80 or 90 percent of buyers of a brand buy only that brand, that in half a year the proportion is down to 30 percent, and that in a year, only 10 percent of buyers are 100 percent loyal (Ehrenberg, 1972). To expect any substantial group or segment of consumers to be uniquely attracted to one particular selling proposition or advertising platform would therefore generally seem entirely beside the point.

Although many consumers tend to buy more than one brand, this does not signify any dynamic brand switching. Instead, the evidence shows that individual people have a repertoire of brands, each of which they buy fairly regularly. Consistent clustering or segmentation of the brands over the whole population is, however, relatively rare. When it occurs, it is usually an *above normal* tendency for buyers of Brand A also to purchase Brand B, compared with the patterns for all the other brands, rather than any special tendency for buyers of one brand not to buy the other (e.g., Collins, 1972). But consumers generally buy brands which are similar as if they were directly substitutable.

In general then, repeat buying and brand switching patterns do not vary materially from one brand or product to another. A particularly simple result is that in a relatively short time period the frequency with which consumers buy a brand varies only marginally within the same product group. The main difference between a leading and a small brand is that the leader has more buyers. With ready-to-eat breakfast cereals, for example, consumers make on average three purchases of a brand over a three-month period. This varies between only 2½ and 3½ for different brands (Charlton, et al., 1972), and this small variation is itself highly predictable from buyer behavior theory, with the larger selling brands being generally bought slightly more frequently by their buyers.

This is what occurs in relatively short time periods. In periods which are very long compared with the product's average purchase cycle (e.g., a year or more), the opposite sort of effect appears to operate because most consumers will have had *some* experience of most brands (even if only a single purchase). This leads to the view that a brand's sales can only increase if people buy it more often (e.g., Treasure, 1973). But in a shorter period, like three months for cereals, higher sales show themselves in terms of having to have more people buy in that period.

These various results are no longer isolated empirical regularities but are becoming increasingly well explained and integrated into coherent theory (e.g., Ehrenberg, 1972; Goodhardt and Chatfield, 1973). The theory applies primarily when a brand's sales are more or less steady. This holds true most of the time—it is a basic characteristic of the market structure of branded frequently bought products that sales levels are *not* in a constant state of flux.

Occasional trends and fluctuations caused by promotions, etc., may be important from a marketing management point of view, perhaps adding up to five percent more sales in a year or 20 percent more in a particular month. But they do not amount to big, dynamic changes in consumer behavior as such. The individual's buying behavior remains broadly characterized as being steady and habitual rather than as dynamic and erratic.

ATTITUDES AND ATTITUDE CHANGE

Since on the whole there are no large behavioral differences among brands except that more people buy one than another, there are not many things that need to be explained by differing motivations and attitudes. In fact, attitudinal responses to branded products tend to be fairly simple.

The evidence shows that most attitudinal variables are largely of an "evaluative" kind, plus some highly specific "descriptive" differences for certain brands (Bird, et al., 1969; 1970; Collins, 1973; Chakrapani and Ehrenberg, 1974).

An "evaluative" response to a brand is equivalent to saying "I like it" or perhaps even only "I have heard of it." Evaluative attitudes therefore differ between users and nonusers of a brand, but they do not differ between brands. For example, 67 percent of users of Brand A say it has the "right taste" with only six percent of nonusers of A saying so about it, and 69 percent of users of Brand B that B has the "right taste" with only five percent of nonusers of B saying so, and so on, as illustrated in Table 1. Brand A may therefore have more people in all saying it has the "right taste" than Brand B, but only because more people use Brand A, not because its users look at it differently: to give an evaluative response about a brand largely depends on whether or not one is using it.

Certain large exceptions to this pattern occur. These usually reflect some physical "descriptive" characteristics of one particular brand. For example, if a brand is fairly new, consumers tend to be aware of this and dub that brand exceptionally "modern," compared with older brands. If one brand of indigestion remedies can be taken without water and the others not, people notice this and far more regard it as "convenient," as is illustrated for Brand C in Table 1. Promotional policies can also make a brand appear "descriptively" different: a slim cigarette advertised in women's magazines as being smoked by feminine women may be rated

Table 1. Typical "Evaluative" and "Descriptive" Attitudinal Responses to Different Brands.

| | Evaluative: E.g., "Right Taste" | | Descriptive (for Brand C): E.g., "Convenient" | |
	Users of the stated brand %	Nonusers of the brand %	Users of the stated brand %	Nonusers of the brand %
Brand A	67	6	19	3
Brand B	69	5	17	2
Brand C	62	4	55	48
Brand D	60	3	17	2
etc.				

more "female" than a standard full-flavored cigarette packaged predominantly in red, with advertisements placed in sporting magazines and featuring cowboys.

A "descriptive" characteristic is usually perceived also by people who do not use the brand. A "female" cigarette will be seen so by people who smoke it and by those who do not. Nonusers of an indigestion remedy which does not require water will *also* regard it as exceptionally "convenient," as for Brand C in Table 1, but they nonetheless do not use it. "Descriptive" differences between one brand and another therefore seldom relate to whether anyone actually *uses* the brand. "Evaluative" responses on the other hand, while distinguishing between users and nonusers, generally do not differentiate one brand from another. Such results are therefore simple but not very helpful in explaining brand choice.

Attitude Change   The conventional results of research into consumers' attitudes show how they feel about products, but not how they *change* their feelings. Very little work has been reported about changes in attitude. What work there is is difficult to interpret (Fothergill, 1968).

It seems to be generally assumed that improving the attitudes of a nonuser towards a brand should make him use the brand, or at least become more predisposed to doing so. But this amounts to assuming that people's attitudes or image of a brand can in fact be readily changed, and that such attitude changes must precede the desired change in behavior. There is little or no evidence to support these assumptions.

The example of a successful change in image that is commonly quoted is for Marlboro cigarettes —few people volunteer another. Marlboro as a brand dates back to the turn of the century. It was considered a "ladies" brand, at one stage holding a major share of the "older society women's market." But in the 1950s, Phillip Morris, the maker, started advertising it very differently, in a male, outdoor manner—Marlboro Country, the Marlboro Man, and the famous tatoo. Sales rose dramatically and Marlboro became a market leader. There is little doubt that Marlboro's advertising had much to do with its success. But there is no evidence that the advertising created a change in "image" or that a change in consumers' attitudes caused the vast increase in sales. The explanation is much simpler.

The change in Marlboro was a change in *product*. The new Marlboro of the 1950s was a standard tipped cigarette, full-flavored, packed in the new flip-top package, with a strong design, and introduced at the start of the growth of the tipped market (the tipped sector of the U.S. market grew from one percent in 1950 to more than 60 percent by the mid-sixties). For the first half of the century, Marlboro had been expensive, high quality, and with a pink paper wrapper (so as not to show up lipstick). No wonder people thought of it as different.

Subsequent attitude surveys in fact showed that smokers thought of Marlboro not as a ladies cigarette but as male, outdoor, for young people, for people with average jobs, etc. But it did not have a special image—it differed little in these respects from other brands of similar product formulation. It scored extra on points where its advertising was played back (male, outdoor), but these differences—some 11 or 12 percentage points in a recent survey—were "not as great as might have been anticipated," to quote Stephen Fountaine, Phillip Morris' director of marketing research. The change in Marlboro was real—it became a standard tipped cigarette—and not one merely in the mind of the consumer.

Other Factors   Conventional thinking about how advertising works rests on the sequence,

Awareness → Attitudes → Behavior

Although this appears like common sense, various studies in social psychology have cast doubt on it. There are well-established psychological mechanisms which can act in the opposite direction—with behavior actually affecting attitudes.

For instance, behavior (the act of buying or using a brand) can lead to greater awareness of information to which one is normally exposed (selective perception). Behavior can even lead to the deliberate seeking out of information, and to changes in attitude (notions of congruence and reduction of dissonance). The well-known illustration is the study where buyers of Ford cars were found to look at Ford advertisements *after* their purchases. This is common.

Usually a consumer is not convinced that a brand he has not bought before has all the advantages over the alternatives. To reduce the "dissonance" between what he has done and what he knows or feels, he changes his attitudes after the purchase to make his chosen brand appear adequate. He needs to do this even more if the chosen brand in fact differs little from the others, because there is then no tangible reason or "reward" to justify his choice—e.g., "maybe it is not very good but at least it cost less."

These processes are consistent with the known facts of consumer attitudes, such as those illustrated in Table 1. We will now see how they also fit into the broader picture.

BRAND CHOICE AND THE CONSUMER

The consumer's choice among different brands or products is widely thought of as irra-tional and based on ignorance. This is how advertising is supposed to get its effect:

> "The scope of advertising depends on the ignorance of the people to whom it is addressed. The more ignorant the buyer, the more he relies on advertising."
> (Scitovsky, 1951)

No one doubts or criticizes advertising's role when it is a question of supplying basic information or creating awareness—e.g., a house for sale, a job vacancy, a play at the theatre, or even for a new consumer product. But where advertising is regarded as persuasive rather than informational, there *is* criticism because of the view that the ignorant consumer's choice is influenced by the last advertisement seen or by the brand image he is being told to believe.

But this is all wrong. Buyers of frequently bought goods are not ignorant of them. They have extensive usage experience of the products—after all, they buy them frequently. As we have seen earlier, they usually have direct experience of more than one brand, plus indirect word of mouth knowledge of others. The average housewife is far more experienced in buying her normal products than the industrial purchaser buying an atomic power station. She is also far less likely to make a mistake.

In regarding the private consumer's brand choice as irrational, the view seems to be that if there is little real difference among the brands, then it is not possible to choose rationally among them. This ignores the fact that the consumer *knows* there is little difference and that he *wants* to buy the product. In choosing between similar brands, it is equally rational to choose the same brand as last time, or to deliberately vary it, or even to toss a coin. Any brand would do because the differences do not matter.

Just because Brand X is advertised as having some specific "consumer benefit," it does not follow that anyone buying that brand must have believed or been influenced by that aspect of the advertising.

In practice, people seem to find it simplest to develop repeat buying habits covering a limited repertoire of brands. Our task is to discover and understand the consumer's reasons for choosing brands, instead of imposing our own preconceptions of how he ought to think and behave and dubbing anything else as irrational. The questions are: How do these habits develop, and what is advertising's role in this?

ATR: AWARENESS, TRIAL AND REINFORCEMENT

Three main steps can account for the known facts of brand choice behavior: (1) gaining awareness of a brand, (2) making a first or trial purchase, and (3) being reinforced into developing and keeping a repeat buying habit.

Some initial awareness of a brand usually has to come first, although occasionally one may find out a brand's name only after buying it. Awareness operates at different levels of attention and interest and can be created in many different ways, of which advertising is clearly one. Awareness may build up into the idea of looking for more information about the brand, asking someone about it, and so on.

A trial purchase, if it comes, will be the next step. This does not require any major degree of conviction that the brand is particularly good or special. Buyers of Brand A do not usually feel very differently about A from how buyers of Brand B feel about B, as was illustrated in Table 1. If that is how one feels afterwards, there is therefore no reason why a consumer should feel strongly about a different brand *before* he has tried it. All that is needed is the idea that one might try it. A trial purchase can arise for a variety of reasons: a cut price offer, an out of stock situation of the usual brand, seeing an advertisement or display, boredom, etc.

After trying a different brand, people usually return to their habitual brands as if nothing had happened. This is so even when new purchasers have been attracted on a large scale, with free samples or an attractive short term promotion (e.g., Goodhardt and Ehrenberg, 1969; Ehrenberg, 1972).

But sometimes a repeat buying habit develops. This is the crucial determinant of long term sales. The way this habit develops for a particular brand is primarily a matter of reinforcement after use. Any feeling of satisfaction—that the brand is liked at least no less than the previously bought

ones—has to be nurtured. Evaluative attitudes have to be brought into line with the product class norms. But no exceptional "liking" need arise, because similar brands are known to be similar and the consumer does not inherently care whether he buys Bingo or Bango (which only matters to the manufacturer).

According to this viewpoint, development of a repeat buying habit remains a fragile process, probably influenced by a variety of almost haphazard factors. The consumer knows there is little to choose between, but he must choose. The critical factor is experience of the brand and no other influences seem to be needed. Thus it has been found that something close to the normal repeat buying habits can develop without any explicit external stimuli such as product differentiation or advertising (Ehrenberg and Charlton, 1973), and preferences for particular price levels can also develop without any external support or manipulation, just by trial and the development of habits (McConnell, 1966; Charlton and Ehrenberg, 1973).

But this process does not in itself determine how *many* people become aware, make a trial purchase, and are reinforced into a repeat buying habit. This—and hence the sales level of a brand—can therefore be influenced by other marketing factors, including advertising.

THE PLACE OF REPETITIVE ADVERTISING

Advertising can act in the various stages of the ATR process.

Firstly, it can create, reawaken, or strengthen awareness. Secondly, it is one of the factors which can facilitate a trial purchase. For an established brand, the consumer may already have been aware of it and even have tried it, but this would have been in the past. The problem is that now he is ignoring the brand and may even be imperceptive of the general run of its advertising. Typically, a special effort like a new product feature, a new package, a new price or special offer, or a new campaign—anything "new"—is needed to give the advertising an edge for this purpose and be noticed. Obtaining awareness and trial for a brand is nonetheless relatively easy.

The difficulty is at the third stage, of turning new triers into satisfied and lasting customers. This generally has to be achieved in the context of consumers already having a repertoire of one or more other brands which they are buying more or less regularly.

What happens in detail is not yet known—do heavy buyers of X switch to being heavy buyers of Y, or is this a gradual process, or is it the *light* buyers who are most easily affected? What is it in fact that advertising has to try and support or accelerate? The knowledge of buyer behavior outlined earlier puts some constraints on the possibilities, but this is one of the purely descriptive features of consumer behavior which is not yet understood.

The process can, however, seldom amount to manipulating the consumer. Real conversion from virgin ignorance to full-blooded, long term commitment does not happen often. A substantial leap forward in sales occurs only once in a while and sales levels of most brands tend to be fairly steady. Trends and even short term fluctuations tend to be smaller and more exceptional than is often thought.

The role of repetitive advertising of well-established brands is therefore predominantly defensive—to reinforce already developed repeat buying habits. The consumer tends to preceive advertising for the brands he is already buying, and repetitive advertising enables the habit to continue to operate in the face of competition. The consumer does not have to be persuaded to think of his habitual brands as better than others, but has to be reinforced in thinking of them as at least no worse.

This view of repetitive advertising—mainly a defensive role of reinforcing existing customers and only occasionally helping to create new customers or extra sales—seems in accord with many of the known facts. It deals also with some of economists' fears about the social costs of advertising and its possibly oligopolistic tendencies (see Doyle, 1968, for a review).

It is consistent with the fact that advertising by itself generally is not very effective in creating sales or in changing attitudes. It also explains why most people feel they are not personally affected by advertising. They are right. Advertising for Brand X does not usually work by persuading people to rush out and buy it.

The primarily reinforcement function of repetitive advertising is in line with the fairly steady sales levels of most brands in most markets. Advertising is not produced by evil men trying to manipulate the consumer. (If it is, these men must be very ineffective.) No one is more eager to cut advertising expenditure than the advertiser himself, who actually has to *pay* for it. For an established brand he sees advertising mainly as a price that has to be paid for staying in business, but he dare not cut it, and he is right (unless *all* manufacturers act together—e.g., aided by government edict, as in the case of TV advertising for cigarettes). For the consumer, large fluctuations in a firm's market share would also not be helpful, in terms of availability, quality control, or lower prices.

According to the ATR model, increasing the amount of advertising would not by itself have much effect on sales, but cutting it is likely to lose sales. This is because some reinforcing action would be withdrawn, allowing competitive brands to gain customers more easily. For an established brand the loss of sales would by definition be quite slow, and no special theory of lagged effects of advertising is needed. Furthermore, reducing an advertising budget *after* a drop in sales to bring the two in line would not necessarily lead to any further substantial drop in sales. The ATR model is consistent with a more or less constant advertising to sales ratio.

The model also explains the survival of a small brand with a small advertising budget. For its users, the large amount of advertising for a larger brand which they do not use performs no function and generally is not even noticed. When a consumer buys two or more brands, some more heavily advertised than the others, each brand's advertising primarily reinforces that brand and the status quo can continue.

High levels of advertising mostly occur in product fields where consumer demand is strong and the product is easy to supply (because of low capital costs, or excess capacity). This leads to active competition and hence the need to defend one's share of the market, either by price cutting or by heavy advertising.

Economists are frequently concerned that high advertising levels act as a barrier to entry for new brands and hence deter competition. This is wrong on two accounts. Firstly, it is the high risk of *failure* with a new brand that acts as the barrier—"four out of five new products fail." The barrier is spending a million and probably having nothing to show for it. Secondly, heavily advertised product fields are in fact characterized by heavy competition and a high incidence of new brands—but generally launched by firms already in the market. Simply having a million to spend on advertising is not enough; general marketing skills and experience of the other factors in the marketing mix (e.g., a suitable sales force) are also needed.

REMAINING PROBLEMS

The ATR approach outlined here is no more than a broad verbal statement of how advertising works that seems consistent with the known facts. Detailed quantitative flesh needs to be put on the model, but its differences with the theory of *persuasive* advertising already raise many questions—e.g., about the content of advertising, about the setting of advertising appropriations and the evaluation of advertising, and about product policy.

As regards content for example, use of attitudinal research results to try to improve one's image or to produce persuasive messages of how Brand X is "best" seem mostly to mislead the advertiser and critic rather than the consumer. Advertising research has failed to show that consumers think of their chosen brands as necessarily better than do buyers of *other* brands think of *theirs*. The consumer needs merely to be told that the brand has all the good properties he expects of the product, and there can be a renewed emphasis on creative advertising telling a good advertising story well.

More generally, since consumers rightly see competitive brands in most product fields as very similar, it seems unnecessary to strive compulsively to differentiate brands artificially from each other. The clutter of marginally different brands, types, and sizes and the corresponding costs of product development and distribution may be unnecessary. This is not a plea for uniformity but for real research into consumers' attitudes and motives to gain a better understanding of their, rather than the advertiser's, needs for product differentiation.

CONCLUSION

Most mass media advertising is for competitive brands. It is a defensive tool and a price the producer pays to stay in business.

Consumers' attitudes to similar brands are very similar. Purchasers of frequently bought goods usually have experience of more than one brand and they mostly ignore advertising for brands they are not already using.

It follows that there can be little scope for persuasive advertising. Instead, advertising's main role is to reinforce feelings of satisfaction for brands already being used. At times it can also create new sales by reawakening consumers' awareness and interest in another brand, stimulating them to a trial purchase and then sometimes, through subsequent reinforcement, helping to facilitate the development of a repeat buying habit. This is the main determinant of sales volume.

The Awareness-Trial-Reinforcement model of advertising seems to account for the known facts, but many quantitative details still need elucidation. Such developments could markedly influence the planning, execution, and evaluation of advertising.

With persuasive advertising, the task might be seen as persuading the pliable customer that Brand X is better than other brands. Under the ATR model, advertising's task is to inform the rather experienced consumer that Brand X is as good as others. The language of the advertising copy might sometimes look similar (still "better" or "best"), but the advertiser's aims and expectations would differ.

[This paper is based on a report prepared for the J. Walter Thompson Company in New York.]

References

Achenbaum, A. A. Advertising Doesn't Manipulate Consumers. *Journal of Advertising Research*, Vol. 12, No. 2, pp. 3-13.

Barnes, M. *The Relationship Between Purchasing Patterns and Advertising Exposure*. London: J. Walter Thompson Co., 1971.

Bird, M., C. Channon, and A. S. C. Ehrenberg. Brand Image and Brand Usage. *Journal of Marketing Research*, Vol. 7, 1969, pp. 307-314.

Bird, M. and A. S. C. Ehrenberg. Consumer Attitudes and Brand Usage. *Journal of the*

Market Research Society, Vol. 12, 1970, pp. 233-247; Vol. 13, pp. 100-101, 242-243; Vol. 13, pp. 57-58.

Boulding, K. *Economic Analysis*. New York: Harper and Row, 1955.

Chakrapani, T. K. and A. S. C. Ehrenberg. "The Pattern of Consumer Attitudes," AAPOR Conference, Lake George, May 1974.

Charlton, P., A. S. C. Ehrenberg, and B. Pymont. Buyer Behaviour Under Mini-Test Conditions. *Journal of the Market Research Society*, Vol. 14, 1972, pp. 171-183.

Charlton, P. and A. S. C. Ehrenberg. McConnell's Experimental Brand-Choice Data. *Journal of Marketing Research*, Vol. 11, 1973, pp. 302-307.

Collins, M. A. Market Segmentation—The Realities of Buyer Behaviour. *Journal of the Market Research Society*, Vol. 13, 1971, pp. 146-157.

Collins, M. A. The Analysis and Interpretation of Attitude Data. Market Research Society, Course on Consumer Attitudes, Cambridge, March 1973.

Connor, J. T. "Advertising: Absolutely Indispensable." Address before the Cleveland Advertising Club, Cleveland, Ohio. New York: American Association of Advertising Agencies, 1966.

Doyle, P. Economic Aspects of Advertising: A Survey. *The Economic Journal*, Vol. 78, 1966, pp. 570-602.

Ehrenberg, A. S. C. *Repeat-Buying: Theory and Applications*. Amsterdam: North Holland; New York: American Elsevier, 1972.

Ehrenberg, A. S. C. *Data Reduction*. London and New York: John Wiley, 1974.

The Analysis of Simulated Brand-Choice. *Journal of Advertising Research*, Vol. 13, No. 1, 1973, pp. 21-33.

Ehrenberg, A. S. C. and F. G. Pyatt (Eds.). *Consumer Behavior*. London and Baltimore: Penguin Books, 1971.

Fothergill, J. G. Do Attitudes Change Before Behaviour? *Proceedings of ESOMAR Congress, Opitija*. Amsterdam: ESOMAR, 1968.

Goodhardt, G. J. and C. Chatfield. The Gamma-Distribution in Consumer Purchasing. *Nature*, Vol. 244, No. 5414, p. 316.

Goodhardt, G. J. and A. S. C. Ehrenberg. Evaluating a Consumer Deal. *Admap*, Vol. 5, 1969, pp. 388-393.

Hobson, J. The Influence and Techniques of Modern Advertising. *Journal of the Royal Society of Arts*, Vol. 112, 1964, pp. 565-604.

Joyce, T. *What Do We Know About How Advertising Works?* London: J. Walter Thompson Co., 1967.

McConnell, J. D. The Development of Brand Loyalty: An Experimental Study, and The Price-Quality Relationship in an Experimental Setting. *Journal of Marketing Research*, Vol. 5, 1968, pp. 13-19 and pp. 300-303.

McDonald, C. D. P. What Is the Short-Term Effect of Advertising? *Proceedings of the ESOMAR Congress, Barcelona*. Amsterdam: ESOMAR, 1970.

Palda, K. S. The Hypothesis of a Hierarchy of Effects: A Partial Evaluation. *Journal of Marketing Research*, Vol. 3, 1966, pp. 13-24.

Scitovsky, T. *Welfare and Competition*. Chicago: Richard Irwin, 1951.

Treasure, J. A. P. The Volatile Consumer. *Admap*, Vol. 9, 1973, pp. 172-182.

25 CONFLICT AND COOPERATION IN MARKETING CHANNELS

Bruce Mallen
Professor, Faculty of Commerce & Administration
Sir George Williams University, Montreal

The act of exchange takes place between any kind of buyer and seller in each level of the distribution channel. This exchange quite often leads to conflict as retailer, wholesaler and manufacturer struggle for domination of the channel.

The purpose of this paper is to advance the hypotheses that between member firms of a marketing channel there exists a dynamic field of conflicting and cooperating objectives; that if the conflicting objectives outweigh the cooperating ones, the effectiveness of the channel will be reduced and efficient distribution impeded; and that implementation of certain methods of cooperation will lead to increased channel efficiency.

DEFINITION OF CHANNEL

The concept of a marketing channel is slightly more involved than expected on initial study. One author in a recent paper[1] has identified "trading" channels, "nontrading" channels, "type" channels, "enterprise" channels, and "business-unit" channels. Another source[2] refers to channels as all the flows extending from the producer to the user. These include the flows of physical possession, ownership, promotion, negotiation, financing, risking, ordering, and payment.

From Bruce Mallen, "Conflict and Cooperation in Marketing Channels," Progress in Marketing, *American Marketing Association Proceedings, 1964, pp. 65-85, L. George Smith, editor. Reprinted by permission of the author and publisher.*

The concept of channels to be used here involves only two of the above-mentioned flows: ownership and negotiation. The first draws merchants, both wholesalers and retailers, into the channel definition, and the second draws in agent middlemen. Both, of course, include producers and consumers. This definition roughly corresponds to Professor Breyer's "trading channel," though the latter does not restrict (nor will this paper) the definition to actual flows, but to "flow-capacity." "A trading channel is formed when trading relations, making possible the passage of title and/or possession (usually both) of goods from the producer to the ultimate consumer, is consummated by the component trading concerns of the system."[3] In addition, this paper will deal with trading channels in the broadest manner and so will be concentrating on "type-trading" channels rather than "enterprise" or "business-unit" channels. This means that there will be little discussion of problems peculiar to specific channels and firms.

CONFLICT

Palamountain isolated three forms of distributive conflict.[4]

1. Horizontal competition—this is competition between middlemen of the same type; for example, discount store *versus* discount store.
2. Intertype competition—this is competition between middlemen of different types in the same channel sector; for example, discount store *versus* department store.
3. Vertical conflict—this is conflict between channel members of different levels; for example, discount store *versus manufacturer.*

The first form, horizontal competition, is well covered in traditional economic analysis and is usually referred to simply as "competition." However, both intertype competition and vertical conflict, particularly the latter, are neglected in the usual microeconomic discussions.

The concepts of "intertype competition" and "distributive innovation" are closely related and require some discussion. Intertype competition will be divided into two categories, (a) "traditional intertype competition" and (b) "innovative intertype competition." The first category includes the usual price and promotional competition between two or more different types of channel members at the same channel level. The second category involves the action on the part of traditional channel members to prevent channel innovators from establishing themselves. For example, in Canada there is a strong campaign, on the part of traditional department stores, to prevent the discount operation from taking a firm hold on the Canadian market.[5]

Distributive innovation will also be divided into two categories; (a) "intrafirm innovative conflict" and (b) "innovative intertype competition." The first category involves the action of channel member firms to prevent sweeping changes within their own companies. The second category, "innovative intertype competition," is identical to the second category of intertype competition.

Thus the concepts of intertype competition and distributive innovation give rise to three forms of conflict, the second of which is a combination of both:

1. traditional intertype competition,
2. innovative intertype competition, and
3. intrafirm innovative conflict.

It is to this second form that this paper now turns before going on to vertical conflict.

Innovative Intertype Competition

Professor McCammon has identified several sources, both intrafirm and intertype, of innovative conflict in distribution, i.e., where there are barriers to change within the marketing structure.[6]

Traditional members of a channel have several motives for maintaining the channel status quo against outside innovators. The traditional members are particularly strong in this conflict when they can band together in some formal or informal manner—when there is strong reseller solidarity.

Both entrepreneurs and professional managers may resist outside innovators, not only for economic reasons, but because change "violates group norms, creates uncertainty, and results in a

loss of status." The traditional channel members (the insiders) and their affiliated members (the strivers and complementors) are emotionally and financially committed to the dominant channel and are interested in perpetuating it against the minor irritations of the "transient" channel members and the major attacks of the "outside innovators."

Thus, against a background of horizontal and intertype channel conflict, this paper now moves to its area of major concern; vertical conflict and cooperation.

Vertical Conflict—Price

The Exchange Act The act of exchange is composed of two elements: a sale and a purchase. It is to the advantage of the seller to obtain the highest return possible from such an exchange and the exact opposite is the desire of the buyer. This exchange act takes place between any kind of buyer and seller. If the consumer is the buyer, then that side of the act is termed shopping; if the manufacturer, purchasing; if the government, procurement; and if a retailer, buying. Thus, between each level in the channel an exchange will take place (except if a channel member is an agent rather than a merchant).

One must look to the process of the exchange act for the basic source of conflict between channel members. This is not to say the exchange act itself is a conflict. Indeed, the act or transaction is a sign that the element of price conflict has been resolved to the mutual satisfaction of both principals. Only along the road to this mutual satisfaction point or exchange price do the principals have opposing interests. This is no less true even if they work out the exchange price together, as in mass retailers' specification-buying programs.

It is quite natural for the selling member in an exchange to want a higher price than the buying member. The conflict is subdued through persuasion or force by one member over the other, or it is subdued by the fact that the exchange act or transaction does not take place, or finally, as mentioned above, it is eliminated if the act does take place.

Suppliers may emphasize the customer aspect of a reseller rather than the channel member aspect. As a customer the reseller is somebody to persuade, manipulate, or even fool. Conversely, under the marketing concept, the view of the reseller as a customer or channel member is identical. Under this philosophy he is somebody to aid, help, and serve. However, it is by no means certain that even a large minority of suppliers have accepted the marketing concept.

To view the reseller as simply the opposing principal in the act of exchange may be channel myopia, but this view exists. On the other hand, failure to recognize this basic opposing interest is also a conceptual fault.

When the opposite principals in an exchange act are of unequal strength, the stronger is very likely to force or persuade the weaker to adhere to the former's desires. However, when they are of equal strength, the basic conflict cannot so easily be resolved. Hence, the growth of big retailers who can match the power of big producers has possibly led to greater open conflict between channel members, not only with regard to exchange, but also to other conflict sources.

There are other sources of conflict within the pricing area outside of the basic one discussed above.

A supplier may force a product onto its resellers, who dare not oppose, but who retaliate in other ways, such as using it as a loss leader. Large manufacturers may try to dictate the resale price of their merchandise; this may be less or more than the price at which resellers wish to sell it. Occasionally, a local market may be more competitive for a reseller than is true nationally. The manufacturer may not recognize the difference in competition and refuse to help this channel member.

Resellers complain of manufacturers' special price concessions to competitors and rebel at the attempt of manufacturers to control resale prices. Manufacturers complain of resellers' deceptive and misleading price advertising, nonadherence to resale price suggestions, bootlegging to unauthorized outlets, seeking special price concessions by unfair methods, and misrepresenting offers by competitive suppliers.

Other points of price conflict are the paperwork aspects of pricing. Resellers complain of delays in price change notices and complicated price sheets.

Price Theory   If one looks upon a channel as a series of markets or as the vertical exchange mechanism between buyers and sellers, one can adapt several theories and concepts to the channel situation which can aid marketing theory in this important area of channel conflict.[7]

Vertical Conflict—Nonprice

Channel conflict not only finds its source in the exchange act and pricing, but it permeates all areas of marketing. Thus, a manufacturer may wish to promote a product in one manner or to a certain degree while his resellers oppose this. Another manufacturer may wish to get information from his resellers on a certain aspect relating to his product, but his resellers may refuse to provide this information. A producer may want to distribute his product extensively, but his resellers may demand exclusives.

There is also conflict because of the tendency for both manufacturers and retailers to want the elimination of the wholesaler.

One very basic source of channel conflict is the possible difference in the primary business philosophy of channel members. Writing in the *Harvard Business Review*, Wittreich says:

> In essence, then, the key to understanding management's problem of crossed purpose is the recognition that the fundamental (philosophy) in life of the high-level corporate manager and the typical (small) retailer dealer in the distribution system are quite different. The former's (philosophy) can be characterized as being essentially dynamic in nature, continuously evolving and emerging; the latter, which are in sharp contrast, can be characterized as being essentially static in nature, reaching a point and leveling off into a continuously satisfying plateau.[8]

While the big members of the channel may want growth, the small retail members may be satisfied with stability and a "good living."

ANARCHY[9]

The channel can adjust to its conflicting-cooperating environment in three distinct ways.

First, it can have a leader (one of the channel members) who "forces" members to cooperate; this is an autocratic relationship. *Second*, it can have a leader who "helps" members to cooperate, creating a democratic relationship. *Finally*, it can do nothing, and so have an anarchistic relationship. Lewis B. Sappington and C. G. Browne, writing on the problems of internal company organizations, state:

> The first classification may be called "autocracy." In this approach to the group the leader determines the policy and dictates or assigns the work tasks. There are no group deliberations, no group decisions. . . .
>
> The second classification may be called "democracy." In this approach the leader allows all policies to be decided by the group with his participation. The group members work with each other as they wish. The group determines the division and assignment of tasks. . . .
>
> The third classification may be called "anarchy." In anarchy there is complete freedom of the group or the individual regarding policies or task assignments, without leader participation.[10]

Advanced in this paper is the hypothesis that if anarchy exists, there is a great chance of the conflicting dynamics destroying the channel. If autocracy exists, there is less chance of this happening. However, the latter method creates a state of cooperation based on power and control. This controlled cooperation is really subdued conflict and makes for a more unstable equilibrium than does voluntary democratic cooperation.

CONTROLLED COOPERATION

The usual pattern in the establishment of channel relationships is that there is a leader, an initiator who puts structure into this relationship and who holds it together. This leader controls, whether through command or cooperation, i.e., through an autocratic or a democratic system.

Too often it is automatically assumed that the manufacturer or producer will be the channel leader, and that the middlemen will be the channel followers. This has not always been so, nor will

it necessarily be so in the future. The growth of mass retailers is increasingly challenging the manufacturer for channel leadership, as the manufacturer challenged the wholesaler in the early part of this century.

The following historical discussion will concentrate on the three-ring struggle between manufacturer, wholesaler, and retailer rather than on the changing patterns of distribution within a channel sector, i.e., between service wholesaler and agent middleman or discount and department store. This will lay the necessary background for a discussion of the present-day manufacturer-dominated *versus* retailer-dominated struggle.

Early History

The simple distribution system of Colonial days gave way to a more complex one. Among the forces of change were the growth of population, the long distances involved, the increasing complexity of new products, the increase of wealth, and the increase of consumption.

The United States was ready for specialists to provide a growing and widely dispersed populace with the many new goods and services required. The more primitive methods of public markets and barter could not sufficiently handle the situation. This type of system required short distances, few products, and a small population, to operate properly.

Nineteenth Century History

In the same period that this older system was dissolving, the retailer was still a very small merchant who, especially in the West, lived in relative isolation from his supply sources. Aside from being small, he further diminished his power position by spreading himself thin over many merchandise lines. The retailer certainly was no specialist but was as general as a general store can be. His opposite channel member, the manufacturer, was also a small businessman, too concerned with production and financial problems to fuss with marketing.

Obviously, both these channel members were in no position to assume leadership. However, somebody had to perform all the various marketing functions between production and retailing if the economy was to function. The wholesaler filled this vacuum and became the channel leader of the nineteenth century.

The wholesaler became the selling force of the manufacturer and the latter's link to the widely scattered retailers over the nation. He became the retailer's life line to these distant domestic and even more important foreign sources of supply.

These wholesalers carried any type of product from any manufacturer and sold any type of product to the general retailers. They can be described as general merchandise wholesalers. They were concentrated at those transportation points in the country which gave them access to both the interior and its retailers, and the exterior and its foreign suppliers.

Early Twentieth Century

The end of the century saw the wholesaler's power on the decline. The manufacturer had grown larger and more financially secure with the shift from a foreign-oriented economy to a domestic-oriented one. He could now finance his marketing in a manner impossible to him in early times. His thoughts shifted to some extent from production problems to marketing problems.

Prodding the manufacturer on was the increased rivalry of his other domestic competitors. The increased investment in capital and inventory made it necessary that he maintain volume. He tended to locate himself in the larger market areas, and thus, did not have great distances to travel to see his retail customers. In addition, he started to produce various products; and because of his new multiproduct production, he could reach— even more efficiently—these already more accessible markets.

The advent of the automobile and highways almost clinched the manufacturer's bid for power. For now he could reach a much vaster market (and they could reach him) and reap the benefits of economics of scale.

The branding of his products projected him to the channel leadership. No longer did he have as great a need for a specialist in reaching widely dispersed customers, nor did he need them to the same extent for their contacts. The market knew where the product came from. The age of wholesaler dominance declined. That of manufacturer dominance emerged.

Is it still here? What is its future? How strong is the challenge by retailers? Is one "better" than the others? These are the questions of the next section.

Disagreement Among Scholars

No topic seems to generate so much heat and bias in marketing as the question of who should be the channel leader, and more strangely, who is the channel leader. Depending on where the author sits, he can give numerous reasons why his particular choice should take the channel initiative.

Authors of sales management and general marketing books say the manufacturer is and should be the chief institution in the channel. Retailing authors feel the same way about retailers, and wholesaling authors (as few as there are), though not blinded to the fact that wholesaling is not "captain," still imply that they should be, and talk about the coming resurrection of wholesalers. Yet a final and compromising view is put forth by those who believe that a balance of power, rather than a general and prolonged dominance of any channel member, is best.

The truth is that an immediate reaction would set in against any temporary dominance by a channel member. In that sense, there is a constant tendency toward the equilibrium of market forces. The present view is that public interest is served by a balance of power rather than by a general and prolonged predominance of any one level in marketing channels.[11]

John Kenneth Galbraith's concept of countervailing power also holds to this last view.

For the retailer:

In the opinion of the writer, "retailer-dominated marketing" has yielded, and will continue to yield in the future greater net benefits to consumers than "manufacturer-dominated marketing," as the central-buying mass distributor continues to play a role of ever-increasing importance in the marketing of goods in our economy. . . .

. . . In the years to come, as more and more large-scale multiple-unit retailers follow the central buying patterns set by Sears and Penney's, as leaders in their respective fields (hard lines and soft goods), ever-greater benefits should flow to consumers in the way of more goods better adjusted to their demands, at lower prices.[12]

. . . In a long-run buyer's market, such as we probably face in this country, the retailers have the inherent advantage of economy in distribution and will, therefore, become increasingly important.[13]

The retailer cannot be the selling agent of the manufacturer because he holds a higher commission; he is the purchasing agent for the public.[14]

For the wholesaler:

The wholesaling sector is, first of all, the most significant part of the entire marketing organization.[15]

. . . The orthodox wholesaler and affiliated types have had a resurgence to previous 1929 levels of sales importance.[16]

. . . Wholesalers have since made a comeback.[17] This revival of wholesaling has resulted from infusion of new management blood and the adoption of new techniques.[18]

For the manufacturer:

. . . the final decision in channel selection rests with the seller manufacturer and will continue to rest with him as long as he has the legal right to choose to sell to some potential customers and refuse to sell to others.[19]

These channel decisions are primarily problems for the manufacturer. They rarely arise for general wholesalers. . . .[20]

Of all the historical tendencies in the field of marketing, no other so distinctly apparent as the tendency for the manufacturer to assume greater control over the distribution of his product. . . .[21]

. . . Marketing policies at other levels can be viewed as extensions of policies established by marketing managers in manufacturing firms; and, furthermore, . . . the nature and function can adequately be surveyed by looking at the relationship to manufacturers.[22]

Pro-Manufacturer

The argument for manufacturer leadership is production-oriented. It claims that they must assure themselves of increasing volume. This is needed to derive the benefits of production scale economies, to spread their overhead over many units, to meet increasingly stiff competition, and to justify the investment risk they, not the retailers, are taking. Since retailers will not do this job for them properly, the manufacturer must control the channel.

Another major argumentative point for manufacturer dominance is that neither the public nor retailers can create new products even under a market-oriented system. The most the public can do is to select and choose among those that manufacturers have developed. They cannot select products that they cannot conceive. This argument would say that it is of no use to ask consumers and retailers what they want because they cannot articulate abstract needs into tangible goods; indeed, the need can be created by the goods rather than vice-versa.

This argument may hold well when applied to consumers, but a study of the specification-buying programs of the mass retailers will show that the latter can indeed create new products, and need not be relegated to simply selecting among alternatives.

Pro-Retailer

This writer sees the mass retailer as the natural leader of the channel for consumer goods under the marketing concept. The retailer stands closest to the consumer; he feels the pulse of consumer wants and needs day in and day out. The retailer can easily undertake consumer research right on his own premises and can best interpret what is wanted, how much is wanted, and when it is wanted.

An equilibrium in the channel conflict may

come about when small retailers join forces with big manufacturers in a manufacturer leadership channel to compete with a small-manufacturer-big-retailer leadership channel.

Pro-Wholesaler

It would seem that the wholesaler has a choice in this domination problem as well. Unlike the manufacturer and retailer though, his method is not mainly through a power struggle. This problem is almost settled for him once he chooses the type of wholesaling business he wishes to enter. A manufacturers' agent and purchasing agent are manufacturer-dominated, a sales agent dominates the manufacturer. A resident buyer and voluntary group wholesaler are retail-dominated.

Methods of Manufacturer Domination

How does a channel leader dominate his fellow members? What are his tools in this channel power struggle? A manufacturer has many domination weapons at his disposal. His arsenal can be divided into promotional, legal, negative, suggestive, and, ironically, voluntary cooperative compartments.

Promotional   Probably the major method that the manufacturer has used is the building of a consumer franchise through advertising, sales promotion, and packaging of his branded products. When he has developed some degree of consumer loyalty, the other channel members must bow to his leadership. The more successful this identification through the promotion process, the more assured is the manufacturer of his leadership.

Legal   The legal weapon has also been a poignant force for the manufacturer. It can take many forms, such as, where permissible, resale price maintenance. Other contractual methods are franchises, where the channel members may become mere shells of legal entities. Through this weapon the automobile manufacturers have achieved an almost absolute dominance over their dealers.

Even more absolute is resort to legal ownership of channel members, called forward vertical integration. Vertical integration is the ultimate in

manufacturer dominance of the channel. Another legal weapon is the use of consignment sales. Under this method the channel members must by law sell the goods as designated by the owner (manufacturer). Consignment selling is in a sense vertical integration; it is keeping legal ownership of the goods until they reach the consumer, rather than keeping legal ownership of the institutions which are involved in the process.

Negative Methods   Among the "negative" methods of dominance are refusal to sell to possibly uncooperative retailers or refusal to concentrate a large percentage of one's volume with any one customer.

A spreading of sales makes for a concentrating of manufacturer power, while a concentrating of sales may make for a thinning of manufacturer power. Of course, if a manufacturer is one of the few resources available and if there are many available retailers, then a concentrating of sales will also make for a concentrating of power.

The avoidance and refusal tactics, of course, eliminate the possibility of opposing dominating institutions.

Suggestives   A rather weak group of dominating weapons are the "suggestives." Thus, a manufacturer can issue price sheets and discounts, preticket and premark resale prices on goods, recommend, suggest, and advertise resale prices.

These methods are not powerful unless supplemented by promotional, legal, and/or negative weapons. It is common for these methods to boomerang. Thus a manufacturer pretickets or advertises resale prices, and a retailer cuts this price, pointing with pride to the manufacturer's suggested retail price.

Voluntary Cooperative Devices   There is one more group of dominating weapons, and these are really all the voluntary cooperating weapons to be mentioned later. The promise to provide these, or to withdraw, can have a "whip and carrot" effect on the channel members.

Retailer's Dominating Weapons

Retailers also have numerous dominating weapons at their disposal. As with manufacturers, their strongest weapon is the building of a consumer franchise through advertising, sales promotion, and branding. The growth of private brands is the growth of retail dominance.

Attempts at concentrating a retailer's purchasing power are a further group of weapons and are analogous to a manufacturer's attempts to disperse his volume. The more a retailer can concentrate his purchasing, the more dominating he can become; the more he spreads his purchasing, the more dominated he becomes. Again, if the resource is one of only a few, this generalization reverses itself.

Such legal contracts as specification buying, vertical integration (or the threat), and entry into manufacturing can also be effective. Even semi-production, such as the packaging of goods received in bulk by the supermarket can be a weapon of dominance.

Retailers can dilute the dominance of manufacturers by patronizing those with excess capacity and those who are "hungry" for the extra volume. There is also the subtlety, which retailers may recognize, that a strong manufacturer may concede to their wishes just to avoid an open conflict with a customer.

VOLUNTARY COOPERATION

But despite some of the conflict dynamics and forced cooperation, channel members usually have more harmonious and common interests than conflicting ones. A team effort to market a producer's product will probably help all involved. All members have a common interest in selling the product; only in the division of total channel profits are they in conflict. They have a singular goal to reach, and here they are allies. If any one of them fails in the team effort, this weak link in the chain can destroy them all. As such, all members are concerned with one another's welfare (unless a member can be easily replaced).

Organizational Extension Concept

This emphasis on the cooperating, rather than the conflicting objectives of channel members, has led to the concept of the channel as simply an extension of one's own internal organization. Conflict in such a system is to be expected even as it is

to be expected within an organization. However, it is the common or "macroobjective" that is the center of concentration. Members are to sacrifice their selfish "microobjectives" to this cause. By increasing the profit pie they will all be better off than squabbling over pieces of a smaller one. The goal is to minimize conflict and maximize cooperation. This view has been expounded in various articles by Peter Drucker, Ralph Alexander, and Valentine Ridgeway.

> Together, the manufacturer with his suppliers and/or dealers comprise a system in which the manufacturer may be designated the primary organization and the dealers and suppliers designated as secondary organizations. This system is in competition with similar systems in the economy; and in order for the system to operate effectively as an integrated whole, there must be some administration of the system as a whole, not merely administration of the separate organizations within that system.[23]

Peter Drucker[24] has pleaded against the conceptual blindness that the idea of the legal entity generates. A legal entity is not a marketing entity. Since often half of the cost to the consumer is added on after the product leaves the producer, the latter should think of his channel members as part of his firm. General Motors is an example of an organization which does this.

> Both businessmen and students of marketing often define too narrowly the problem of marketing channels. Many of them tend to define the term channels of distribution as a complex of relationships between the firm on the one hand, and marketing establishments exterior to the firm by which the products of the firm are moved to market, on the other. . . . A much broader, more constructive concept embraces the relationships with external agents or units as part of the marketing organization of the company. From this viewpoint, the complex of external relationships may be regarded as merely an extension of the marketing organization of the firm. When we look at the problem in this way, we are much less likely to lose sight of the interdependence of the two structures and more likely to be constantly aware that they are closely

related parts of the marketing machine. The fact that the internal organization structure is linked together by a system of employment contracts, while the external one is set up and maintained by a series of transactions, contracts of purchase and sale, tends to obscure their common purpose and close relationship.[25]

Cooperation Methods

But how does a supplier project its organization into the channel? How does it make organization and channel into one? It accomplishes this by doing many things for its resellers that it does for its own organization. It sells, advertises, trains, plans, and promotes for these firms. A brief elaboration of these methods follows.

Missionary salesmen aid the sales of channel members, as well as bolster the whole system's level of activity and selling effort. Training of resellers' salesmen and executives is an effective weapon of cooperation. The channels operate more efficiently when all are educated in the promotional techniques and uses of the products involved.

Involvement in the planning functions of its channel members could be another poignant weapon of the supplier. Helping resellers to set quotas for their customers, studying the market potential for them, forecasting a member's sales volume, inventory planning and protection, etc., are all aspects of this latter method.

Aid in promotion through the provision of advertising materials (mats, displays, commercials, literature, direct-mail pieces), ideas, funds (cooperative advertising), sales contest, store layout designs, push money (PMs or spiffs), is another form of cooperation.

The big supplier can act as management consultant to the members, dispensing advice in all areas of their business, including accounting, personnel, planning, control, finance, buying, paper systems or office procedure, and site selection. Aid in financing may include extended credit terms, consignment selling, and loans.

By no means do these methods of coordination take a one-way route. All members of the channel, including supplier and reseller, see their own organizations meshing with the others, and so

provide coordinating weapons in accordance with their ability. Thus, the manufacturer would undertake a marketing research project for his channel, and also expect his resellers to keep records and vital information for the manufacturer's use. A supplier may also expect his channel members to service the product after the sale.

A useful device for fostering cooperation is a channel advisory council composed of the supplier and his resellers.

Finally, a manufacturer or reseller can avoid associations with potentially uncooperative channel members. Thus, a price-conservative manufacturer may avoid linking to a price-cutting retailer.

E. B. Weiss has developed an impressive, though admittedly incomplete list of cooperation methods (Table 1). Paradoxically, many of these instruments of cooperation are also weapons of control (forced cooperation) to be used by both middlemen and manufacturers. However, this is not so strange if one keeps in mind that control is subdued conflict and a form of cooperation—even though perhaps involuntary cooperation.

Extension Concept is the Marketing Concept

The philosophy of cooperation is described in the following quote:

> The essence of the marketing concept is of course customer orientation at all levels of distribution. It is particularly important that customer orientation motivate all relations between a manufacturer and his customer— both immediate and ultimate. It must permeate his entire channels-of-distribution policy.[27]

This quote synthesizes the extension-of-the organization system concept of channels with the marketing concept. Indeed, it shows that the former is, in essence, "the" marketing concept applied to the channel area in marketing. To continue:

> The characteristics of the highly competitive markets of today naturally put a distinct premium on harmonious manufacturer-distributor relationships. Their very mutuality of interest demands that the manufacturer

Table 1. Methods of Cooperation as Listed.[26]

1. Cooperative advertising allowances	19. Delivery costs to individual stores of large retailers
2. Payments for interior displays including shelf-extenders, dump displays, "A" locations, aisle displays, etc.	20. Studies of innumerable types, such as studies of merchandise management accounting
3. PMs for salespeople	21. Payments for mailings to store lists
4. Contests for buyers, salespeople, etc.	22. Liberal return privileges
5. Allowances for a variety of warehousing functions	23. Contributions to favorite charities of store personnel
6. Payments for window display space, plus installation costs	24. Contributions to special store anniversaries
7. Detail men who check inventory, put up stock, set up complete promotions, etc.	25. Prizes, etc., to store buyers when visiting showrooms—plus entertainment, of course
8. Demonstrators	26. Training retail salespeople
9. On certain canned food, a "swell" allowance	27. Payments for store fixtures
10. Label allowance	28. Payments for new store costs, for more improvements, including painting
11. Coupon handling allowance	29. An infinite variety of promotion allowances
12. Free goods	30. Payments of part of salary of retail salespeople
13. Guaranteed sales	31. Deals of innumerable types
14. In-store and window display material	32. Time spent in actual selling floor by manufacturer, salesmen
15. Local research work	33. Inventory price adjustments
16. Mail-in premium offers to consumer	34. Store name mention in manufacturer's advertising
17. Preticketing	
18. Automatic reorder systems	

base his distribution program not only on what he would like from distributors, but perhaps more importantly, on what they would like from him. In order to get the cooperation of the best distributors, and thus maximum exposure for his line among the various market segments, he must adjust his policies to serve their best interest and, thereby, his own. In other words, he must put the principles of the marketing concept to work for him. By so doing, he will inspire in his customers a feeling of mutual interest and trust and will help convince them that they are essential members of his marketing team.[28]

SUMMARY

Figure 1 summarizes this whole paper. Each person within each department will cooperate, control, and conflict with each other (notice arrows). Together they form a department (notice department box contains person boxes) which will

be best off when cooperating (or cooperation through control) forces weigh heavier than conflicting forces. Now each department cooperates, controls, and conflicts with each other. Departments together also form a higher level organization—the firm (manufacturer, wholesaler, and retailer). Again, the firm will be better off if department cooperation is maximized and conflict minimized. Finally, firms standing vertically to each other cooperate, control, and conflict. Together they form a distribution channel that will be best off under conditions of optimum cooperation leading to consumer and profit satisfaction.

CONCLUSIONS AND HYPOTHESES

1. Channel relationships are set against a background of cooperation and conflict; horizontal, intertype, and vertical.

2. An autocratic relationship exists when one channel member controls conflict and forces the others to cooperate. A democratic

Organizational

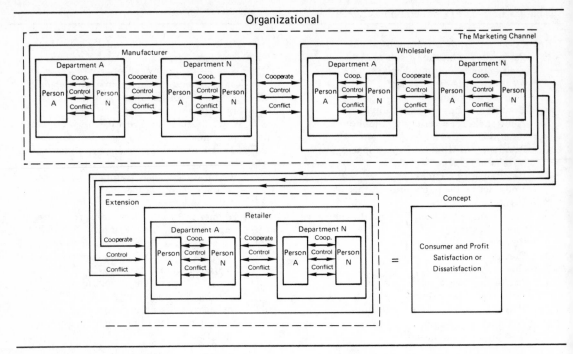

Figure 1. Organizational.

relationship exists when all members agree to cooperate without a power play. An anarchistic relationship exists when there is open conflict, with no member able to impose his will on the others. This last form could destroy or seriously reduce the effectiveness of the channel.

3. The process of the exchange act where one member is a seller and the other is a buyer is the basic source of channel conflict. Economic theory can aid in comprehending this phenomenon. There are, however, many other areas of conflict, such as differences in business philosophy or primary objectives.

4. Reasons for cooperation, however, usually outweigh reasons for conflict. This has led to the concept of the channel as an extension of a firm's organization.

5. This concept drops the facade of "legal entity" and treats channel members as one great organization with the leader providing each with various forms of assistance. These are called cooperating weapons.

6. It is argued that this concept is actually the marketing concept adapted to a channel situation.

7. In an autocratic or democratic channel relationship, there must be a leader. This leadership has shifted and is shifting between the various channel levels.

8. The wholesaler was the leader in the last century, the manufacturer now, and it appears that the mass retailer is next in line.

9. There is much disagreement on the above point, however, especially on who should be the leader. Various authors have differing arguments to advance for their choice.

10. In the opinion of this writer, the mass retailer appears to be best adapted for leadership under the marketing concept.

11. As there are weapons of cooperation, so are there weapons of domination. Indeed the former paradoxically are one group of the latter. The other groups are promotional, legal, negative, and suggestive methods. Both manufacturers and retailers have at their disposal these dominating weapons.

12. *For maximization of channel profits and consumer satisfaction, the channel must act as a unit.*

Notes

1. Ralph F. Breyer, "Some Observations on Structural Formation and the Growth of Marketing Channels," in *Theory in Marketing*, Reavis Cox, Wroe Alderson, Stanley J. Shapiro, editors, (Homewood, Ill.: Richard D. Irwin, 1964), pp. 163-175.
2. Ronald S. Vaile, E. T. Grether, and Reavis Cox, *Marketing in the American Economy* (New York: Ronald Press, 1952), pp. 121 and 124.
3. Breyer, *op. cit.*, p. 165.
4. Joseph C. Palamountain, *The Politics of Distribution* (Cambridge: Harvard University Press, 1955).
5. Isaiah A. Litvak and Bruce E. Mallen, *Marketing: Canada* (Toronto: McGraw-Hill of Canada, Limited, 1964), pp. 196-197.
6. This section is based on Bert C. McCammon, Jr., "Alternative Explanations of Insitutional Change and Channel Evolution," in *Toward Scientific Marketing*, Stephen A. Greyser, editor (Chicago: American Marketing Association, 1963), pp. 477-490. [See p. 289.]
7. Bruce Mallen, "Introducing The Marketing Channel To Price Theory," *Journal of Marketing*, July, 1964, pp. 29-33.
8. Warren J. Wittreich, "Misunderstanding The Retailer," *Harvard Business Review*, May— June, 1962, p. 149.
9. The term "anarchy" as used in this paper connotes "no leadership" and nothing more.
10. Lewis B. Sappington and C. G. Browne, "The Skills of Creative Leadership," in *Managerial Marketing*, rev. ed., William Lazer and Eugene J. Kelley, editors (Homewood, Ill.: Richard D. Irwin, 1962), p. 350.
11. Wroe Alderson, "Factors Governing The Development of Marketing Channels," in *Marketing Channels For Manufactured Products*, Richard M. Clewett, editor (Homewood, Ill.: Richard D. Irwin, 1954), p. 30.
12. Arnold Corbin, *Central Buying in Relation To The Merchandising of Multiple Retail Units* (New York, Unpublished Doctoral Dissertation at New York University, 1954), pp. 708-709.
13. David Craig and Werner Gabler, "The Competitive Struggle for Market Control," in *Readings in Marketing*, Howard J. Westing, editor (New York: Prentice-Hall, 1953), p. 46.
14. Lew Hahn, *Stores, Merchants and Customers* (New York: Fairchild Publications, 1952), p. 12.
15. David A. Revzan, *Wholesaling in Marketing Organization* (New York: John Wiley & Sons, 1961), p. 606.
16. *Ibid.*, p. 202.
17. E. Jerome McCarthy, *Basic Marketing* (Homewood, Ill.: Richard D. Irwin, 1960), p. 419.
18. *Ibid.*, p. 420.
19. Eli P. Cox, *Federal Quantity Discount Limitations and Its Possible Effects on Distribution Channel Dynamics* (Unpublished Doctoral Dissertation, University of Texas, 1956), p. 12.
20. Milton Brown, Wilbur B. England, John B. Matthews, Jr., *Problems in Marketing*, 3rd ed. (New York: McGraw-Hill, 1961), p. 239.
21. Maynard D. Phelps and Howard J. Westing, *Marketing Management*, Revised Edition (Homewood, Ill.: Richard D. Irwin, 1960), p. 11.
22. Kenneth Davis, *Marketing Management* (New York: Ronald Press, 1961), p. 131.
23. Valentine F. Ridgeway, "Administration of Manufacturer-Dealer Systems," in *Managerial Marketing*, rev. ed., William Lazer and Eugene J. Kelley, editors (Homewood, Ill.: Richard D. Irwin, 1962), p. 480.
24. Peter Drucker, "The Economy's Dark Continent," *Fortune*, April 1962, pp. 103ff.
25. Ralph S. Alexander, James S. Cross, Ross M. Cunningham, *Industrial Marketing*, rev. ed. (Homewood, Ill.: Richard D. Irwin, 1961), p. 266.
26. Edward B. Weiss, "How Much of a Retailer Is the Manufacturer," in *Advertising Age*, July 21, 1958, p. 68.
27. Hector Lazo and Arnold Corbin, *Management in Marketing* (New York: McGraw-Hill, 1961), p. 379.
28. Lazo and Corbin, *loc. cit.*

26 TOWARD MORE RESPONSIVE MARKETING CHANNELS

M. S. Moyer
Professor of Administrative Studies
York University, Ontario, Canada

One of the costs of a maturing retail industry, maintains the author, is a lack of responsiveness to the consumer. In a recent cartoon, the salesperson told a matron, "Madam, in this store, you are a voice crying in the wilderness."

THE PROBLEM OF RESPONSIVENESS

One of the most significant changes in the shape of North America's distributive network is the advance of vertical marketing alliances. In fact, it has been argued that "Conventional marketing systems are being rapidly replaced by vertically organized marketing systems as the dominant distribution mechanism in the American economy."[1]

Typically, these systems are captained by a major channel participant. Some have concluded that "the emergence of a leader within such a system is not likely, but inevitable."[2]

One candidate for this role is the leading retailer in the channel. Indeed, it would appear that the rise of retailing organizations sufficiently strong to challenge the earlier dominance of wholesalers and manufacturers is one of the marks of an advanced marketing system.

These two developments—the emergence

From M. S. Moyer, "Toward More Responsive Marketing Channels," Journal of Retailing 51:1 (Spring 1975), pp. 7-19, 112. Reprinted by permission of Journal of Retailing.

of vertical marketing systems and the rise of retailers as channel captains—raise important policy questions. One central issue is whether these new channel forms, with their highly systematized operations, can be sufficiently responsive to changing market requirements.

The question of adaptability is important for scholars, marketers, and consumers alike. Especially in recent years, it has been emphasized that "The market system is so central to the functioning of American society that the students of that system . . . cannot afford to pass over questions concerning the performance of that system"[3] and that one aspect of performance must be "the adjustment of the system to the consumer needs."[4]

The purpose of this article is to highlight a problem of responsiveness in retailer-led marketing channels and to suggest how scholars and marketers might begin to deal with it.

THE CAUSES OF UNRESPONSIVENESS

From Cottage Industry to Mature Industry

Briefly, the problem is that channels led by retailers, and therefore sizable parts of our marketing system, are suffering a loss of responsiveness.

To redeem this loss, one must examine its causes. In general, they lie in the advancing maturity of the retailing industry. In considerable part, retailing continues to be a cottage industry: run from the home, using unpaid family workers, operating on a small scale, dependent on the capital of its suppliers, and led by untrained and unprofessional managers. Its prototype is the marginal mom and pop store. In recent decades, however, growing sectors of the retailing industry have adopted the attitudes, aims, forms, and methods of "big business." Their prototype is the "free-form corporation . . . with a newfound willingness to go anywhere and do anything in distribution."[5]

In many respects, this trend must be welcomed. It has produced increases in real output per retail worker, gains in real income for the marketing labor force, and, in many ways, more efficient operations at the point where marketing channels touch their customers.

But these gains have not been costless. In the retailing industry, the cost of maturity has been the loss of some sensitivity to the consumer. As a consequence, the price of progress in marketing has been the loss of some adaptability in retailer-led vertical marketing systems. The following sections analyse that process in greater detail.

Capital Intensiveness

First, a maturing industry tends to become less labor-intensive and more capital-intensive. In this, the marketing process has lagged the production process. However, with the passage of time, retailing's production function is almost surely giving less weight to labor and more weight to capital. Off the sales floor the modern retail organization is equipped with increasingly expensive capital equipment, notably for materials handling and data processing. On the sales floor, it is becoming a self-service operation staffed by fewer manual workers. Moreover, the industry is converting to "automated front ends"—systems made up of electronic cash registers, optical scanners, and in-store mini-computers—which save labor costs but raise equipment costs. In a very real way, then, the modern store is becoming a factory of distribution.

This development has its price. How high a price was illustrated by a recent cartoon set in a supermarket. It appeared at about the same time that some food chains were advertising that one should "Get to know the friendly man behind the meat counter." It pictured that friendly man seated at his meat counter, holding a snuffling matron on his knee, his face shining with compassion as he murmured, "Now Mrs. Swartz, tell me about last Thursday's pot roast."

The cartoonist was picturing the other side of capital intensiveness: the widespread disappearance of the salesperson for whom retailing is a chosen career and a serious calling. His departure tends to remove from the point of purchase one agent that retail managers once had in their efforts to know their clientele and to understand their markets. Thus industrial maturity in the form of capital intensiveness has probably reduced the openness of retailing enterprises.

Mass Production

Second, as Knauth[6] and Galbraith[7] have emphasized, a maturing industry moves from sporadic activities to continuous operations. "Businessmen, in meeting the exigencies of the modern world, have fashioned a new . . . system of production and distribution . . . whose main idea is to administer the business . . . in the interest of continuity."[8] In other industries, the quest for continuity takes the form of mass production methods and round-the-clock operations.

Here, too, retailing seems to be adopting the animus of other, more mature sectors of the economy. Being increasingly capital intensive, merchandising facilities, like manufacturing plants, must avoid down time. In retailing, this imperative is manifested in the extension of evening hours and the advance of open Sundays. Significantly, it has generally been the independent merchant, whose operations are not large-scale and capital-intensive, who has not supported the stretching of store hours.

Again, industry leaders have incurred some concomitant costs. To mass produce retail transactions the merchant must follow another formula of the factory, which is shift work. To staff tnose extra shifts, he must use more part-time people. Now these workers have in common that for them retailing is an occasional and incidental activity. Large retailing organizations rely on such personnel for a large portion of their total revenues. This means that as dominant retailing organizations move toward continuous high-level operations, a growing proportion of their personnel are amateurs.

Such people can have some difficulty in knowing the merchandise and substantial difficulty in knowing the market. One evidence of this is that the "want book"—a device whereby knowledgable salespeople signalled unmet needs to their superiors—has all but disappeared from the point of purchase. To that extent, management loses another link with its constituency.

Alderson showed how the routinization of transactions can lead directly to efficiency in a marketing system.[9] It must be added that mass production methods at the point of purchase can lead indirectly to insensitivity in a distributive system.

The Selling of Systems

Third, a maturing industry seems to shift to the selling of systems rather than isolated products. That trend is evident elsewhere in marketing.[10] Again, so it is with retailing. There was a day when the merchant sold merchandise and little else. Now it is recognized that just as the package can sell, so can the outlet. Consequently, as one retail president has put it, "Retailing is . . . changing from the selling of products to the marketing of stores."[11] Moreover, merchants and scholars are recognizing that, in a market with more discretionary time and money, a widening range of human needs can be met in the shopping experience.[12] Hence the retailer, like other marketers, is becoming a seller of systems: systems of satisfactions.

As a result, along with other marketers, the merchant is finding that his conventional sensing devices are insufficient for understanding the environment. When pennies counted, comparison shoppers checking competing prices could report fairly accurately the relative appeal of rival stores. When merchandise had primarily to be serviceable to be salable, a department manager with little more than an innate feel of the cloth could reckon reasonably well his relative drawing power. When shopper's needs were unsubtle, a merchandising manager by merely patrolling the sales floor could come close to divining consumer needs. "We've got the greatest market testing place in the world right here in our store. You can stand on the floor of our store and get more ideas. It's fantastic." At an earlier stage of market maturity, then, retail decision-makers could sensibly rely on information systems that were personal, informal, and unsophisticated.

But the selling of systems is a more demanding undertaking. As proponents of the marketing concept have so clearly established, the vending of "bundles of value satisfactions" requires not only an imaginative definition of corporate mission, but an insightful reading of market needs. Large retailing organizations share this problem. Systems of satisfaction cannot be accurately priced by comparison shoppers, cannot be readily felt by central buyers, and cannot be easily calibrated by department managers standing on the sales floor waiting for insight to strike.

In short, as leading merchants move more explicitly to defining and designing systems of satisfactions, their existing contact with the consumer becomes relatively crude and increasingly inadequate. In this way, too, as large retailing organizations progress as marketers they may well be losing some of their empathy with their markets.

Larger Enterprises

Fourth, a maturing industry seems to cluster into larger units. In retailing, this trend takes the form of larger outlets, larger companies, and more economic concentration.

The enlargement of the typical store is well-documented. During the last three decades, the average output per retail establishment, in real terms, has increased more than three times.[13] Measures of company growth are more fragmentary, but a similar trend is indicated. "Those data available indicate that the retailing sector has participated fully in the merger movements that swept all of American industry."[14] The most comprehensive study on the subject concludes that "Through the most recent period we have seen a continuing consolidation of the retail sector in the hands of fewer and fewer large-scale firms."[15]

In developing these aggregations, retailers have paid another penalty: executive isolation. As one critic has said, ". . . many . . . mass retailers have retreated to . . . penthouse offices . . . over-looking artificial gardens—far from the madding shopper. . . ."[16] One of the dangers of executive isolation is a poverty of intelligence on the environment. This problem is inherent in evolving organizations; it threatens the leadership ability of large enterprises in industry, in government, in religion, and elsewhere.[17] It is therefore an inescapable issue for "leading" retailing firms.

Central Staff Specialists

Fifth, a maturing industry appears to use more central staff specialists. While measures are unavailable, retailing is almost surely doing so. "Centrally coordinated systems are gradually displacing conventional marketing channels as the dominant distribution mechanism. . . ."[18] As part of this situation, key decisions are moving from the sales floor to the upstairs office, from the hustings to head office, and from the jack-of-all-trades to the master of one.

In this case it could be argued that one encounters an exception to the rule; that the effect of maturity is not to reduce contact with consumers, but to increase it. For one of these specialists is the central buyer, whose mandate is to keep the company in tune with the market.

On the face of it, that seems a reasonable conclusion. The central buyer does seem well connected to the environment of the enterprise. His reports are voluminous, his travels are wide, and his knowledge is impressive. But one must observe his activities. In a large distributive organization, he visits retail stores, but briefly and infrequently, and then it is usually to meet retailers, not to consult customers. He skims trade journals, but they tend to tell him how other merchants are merchandising, not how his own markets are moving. He scans sales and inventory reports, but because the computer can convey no more than it can capture, his reports deal with the past rather than the future; they tell him about his merchandise rather than his customers, and they tell him how he is doing rather than why. In short, they tell him about the market needs that he is meeting rather than about the market needs that he is neglecting.

Also, he spends much time with his suppliers. Here the information he gets is enormous; it should not be underestimated. But neither should it be overestimated. Most of the intelligence available from suppliers concerns their own offerings. Needless to say, it is detailed and direct. Intelligence about end users is much scarcer. And when it is offered it is of much lower quality, for it comes from company executives, many of whom have conducted no direct investigations among consumers, none of whom share the full results of such studies as have been made, and all of whom have an ax to grind. Therefore, suppliers' insights on the market must be deduced from recent sales, inferred from other retailers' takings, and spun together from the talk of the trade. Altogether, a second look reveals a somewhat different picture. When it is said that the central buyer knows the market, what is meant is that he knows what his sales figures (a reflection

rather than a picture of the market) *imply* about the market, and what his suppliers (themselves twice removed from the market) *say* about the market.

These differences have not been widely remarked. Indeed, it is a measure of the unconsciously inverted orientation of a maturing retailing industry that when a central buyer states that he is going "into the market" he means that he is going to visit, not his customers, but his suppliers.

Thus, on closer inspection, central buying emerges as a mixed blessing. About the supply of merchandise it makes information more direct, detailed, and authoritative; about the wants of consumers, it makes information more indirect, crude, and speculative. About products, then, the organization knows much; about markets, it knows much less. The difference is profound. Again, maturity has imposed its penalty.

The Full Price

In many ways, therefore, as retailing progresses it pays a price. In particular, as the industry matures, the firms in it undergo five key changes which increase internal efficiency but decrease external empathy.

This unspoken exchange can alter the strengths and weaknesses of leading retailing organizations. It can make them more powerful, but less permeable. It can make them more informed about operations, but less insightful about shoppers. It can make them more dominant in the marketplace, but less directed by market demand. It is a tradeoff which deserves to be weighed.

EMERGING EVIDENCE

These conclusions find some support in empirical studies. In recent years several researchers have tested a retailer's understanding of his market and found it often misinformed. For example, a probe of a sizable group of major electrical appliance dealers concluded that "Many . . . demonstrated little knowledge about their customers' characteristics. . . . Such results were quite unexpected, since it has generally been hypothesized that the retailer is particularly knowledgeable about his customers and the manufacturer often depends on the dealer as a primary source of consumer information."[19] In the same way, in an examination of seventeen retail businesses, again in a variety of product fields, other researchers found that none of the firms had at hand a summary profile of its credit customers by income, occupation, sex, or age.[20] On examining the market information available in eight leading retailing organizations in fields as diverse as food, auto accessories, apparel, hardware, and variety merchandise, the author also frequently found that key decision-makers lacked basic, actionable facts about their markets.

The process does not end with the absence of information. When a decision-maker continually lacks facts, he can be moved to invent them. When merchants lack data on their markets, they fall back on plausible hypotheses. This leads to unsupported generalizations about shoppers, their characteristics, motivations, and behavior. The result can be misguided marketing effort.

Again, scholarly investigations attest to this phenomenon. One was a study of both the customers and executives of department stores and specialty stores. In their beliefs that delivery was a less wanted service on small packages than on large items, that lower-income women bought more often by phone than others, and that telephone sales tended to replace floor sales, management was largely contradicted by examination of shoppers themselves. The study concluded that "those findings . . . which revealed a situation somewhat different from what many store executives had assumed, suggest that these two services might play a large role in building sales"[21] for the stores involved.

Another was a study of householders and retailers of refrigerators, stoves, and automatic washers. It found that the retailers concerned often overestimated the price differences that consumers perceived between competing brands, and consistently underestimated the weight that consumers gave to service and warranty, ease of use, and style in the purchase decision. It concluded that many of the stores examined could be pursuing ill-considered marketing strategies.[22]

Another was a study of the buyers and retailers of bathing suits. It found that on the importance of brand names, on the relative frequency of visits to rival stores, and on the best and least liked features of each store, the merchants' beliefs were badly mistaken when tested against the actual behavior and attitudes of the customers themselves. It closed with the conclusion that "Most retailers do not even know the key strengths and weaknesses of their own stores," with the result that each type of outlet tudied was missing major opportunities to develop a uniquely effective marketing strategy.[23]

Another was a study of the patrons, reputed and real, of a particular department store. It found that in visualizing a separate "basement store customer" and "upstairs customer," store executives had invented largely fictional characters and that the biggest customer for either a basement or upstairs department was, unexpectedly, the customer who bought from both. It concluded that, having developed a marketing mix to insulate the basement customer from the upstairs customer, management was discouraging its best patrons.[24]

This evidence cannot show how often retailers hobble themselves for lack of facts or bemuse themselves with believable misinformation. However, it does demonstrate that it is not difficult for modern mass retailers to make basic marketing decisions, on behalf of consumers and suppliers, using facts about the market which are implicit, plausible, and wrong. To the extent that such mistakes occur, they reduce the responsiveness of marketing channels and invite a search for corrective action.

POSSIBLE RESPONSES

Actions by Academics

For scholars, the major consequence should be a re-examination of accepted views on channel leadership.

The emergence of vertical marketing systems has raised the question, "Who should lead this extracorporate organization?"[25] Most academics have leaned toward the retailer as leader. On this there has not been unanimity, of course; the wholesaler and the manufacturer have had their champions. Nevertheless, it seems fair to say that most would concur with the conclusion that "the mass retailer appears to be best adapted for leadership under the marketing concept."[26]

The endorsement of retailer-captained channels has had various origins. Those who have sought a more rationalized marketing process have reasoned that the retailer-led channel is the most streamlined one attainable.[27] Those who have sought to preserve traditional price competition have valued the retailer's private label as a beneficent threat to entrenched national brands and ossified channel margins.

But there is one line of reasoning that has had broad appeal. It has seemed unarguable that, relative to other marketing institutions, the retailing firm is close to the consumer. "The retailer . . . feels the pulse of consumer wants and needs day in and day out."[28] From there it has been easy to reason that, of all marketers, it is the retailer who is best able to consult the consumer, to comprehend his wishes, and to reflect his wants. Moreover, retailers are seen to be relatively uncommitted to any particular, partisan brand. In keeping with this preferred position, retailers cast themselves in a heroic role; as one has said, "The retailer cannot be the selling agent of the manufacturer because he holds a higher commission; he is the purchasing agent for the public."[29] It has therefore seemed a reasonable conclusion that, relative to other possible channel leaders, the retailing organization is the most likely to capture a vertical marketing system which is truly responsive to consumer needs. Thus one close student of retailing concludes that "As the . . . mass distributor continues to play a role of ever-increasing importance in the marketing of goods in our economy . . . ever-greater benefits should flow to consumers in the way of more goods better adjusted to their demands, at lower prices."[30]

That chain of logic now seems to underestimate the price of progress. In particular, it tends to disregard the several ways in which, in becoming large enought to lead marketing channels, mass retailers have lost their ready communion with the consumer. This unacknowledged cost could revise the case for retailers as channel leaders. It could be that as major merchandising firms become more able to control marketing channels, they become less qualified to guide them. For proximity does not equal empathy. The prior

analysis underlines that "Just as an organism may literally starve to death in the presence of available food, so can a management gradually succumb to factual malnutrition while . . . necessary information abounds on all sides."[31] Scholars should consider the possibility that as retailers captain channels, it could lead to vertical marketing systems which are more effective in terms of transaction efficiency but less effective in terms of responsiveness.

Actions by Practitioners

Among retailers, several actions would be opportune. To compensate for their loss of automatic communion with the consumer, merchants should aggressively adopt the new point-of-sale devices which are now becoming available. These include electronic cash registers, in-store mini-computers, and optical scanners. Together, they make it possible for the retailer to capture, in machine language and at the moment of purchase, every detail of every transaction, including the identity of the item and of the buyer. Thus "electronic checkouts" or "automated front ends" allow a breakthrough in the marketer's quest for full and timely information on the sources of his sales.[32] This opportunity should be grasped.

Even "automated front ends" have their limitations, however. Thus, to further enrich their understanding of their marketers, major retailers should adopt another practice uncommon in retailing today: formal market research. Contrary to many merchant's fears, this research need not be elaborate, expensive, inconclusive, or slow. Properly managed, it can produce large payoffs.[33]

Armed with the kind of commercial intelligence that is available from emerging informational technology and established market research techniques, large retailing organizations would then be better able to respond to marketing opportunities. Two examples will illustrate the new capabilities that could follow.

Retailers as Product Innovators

Captained channels have "high vertical programming potential."[34] In retailer-led marketing channels, an attractive use of that potential is to absorb some of the manufacturer's product planning function through specification buying. But here the merchant's paucity of market information becomes an increasing penalty. In unambitious forms of private branding, retailers can get by on simple "knockoffs" of supplier's makes. Most do. To date then, private branding has required the ability to imitate rather than innovate. But if retailers are to grasp their full potential as channel captains, they will need to develop forms of specification buying that can generate something more than "me too" products. Then there will be a new need to discover unique, wanted, product features. As has been shown, the price of progress is that they lack that capability. However, if through market research and automated front ends, retailers could steep themselves more deeply in consumer's unmet wants and needs, then retailer-managed marketing systems could more fully exploit their vertical programming potential.

Retailers as Consumer Advocates

Similarly, there might be another role the leading retailer could play: that of consumer advocate. The complexity and impersonality of the modern marketplace have created, in the public mind, a need for new allies who will champion the consumer's cause.

Filling that need has activated several institutions outside of conventional marketing channels. Newspaper actionlines, radio hotlines, and government complaint bureaus attract a considerable chorus of consumer questions, complaints, and suggestions, many of them concerning retailers and their channel partners. By contrast, large retailers have often been so insulated from consumers as to be largely untouched by this traffic in feelings and ideas. As a salesclerk reminded a matron in a recent cartoon, "Madam, in this store you are a voice crying in the wilderness." Again one sees the enervating effects of inadequate consumer contact.

Aggressive consumer advocacy is not a role suited to all large retailers. On the other hand, it has been employed by some leading merchants, especially grocery chains.[35] It is a strategic opportunity that should be accepted or rejected on its merits, not lost by default. In this way, too, by

moving to improved instruments for understanding their markets, retail management would open up for themselves new marketing options.

CONCLUSION

In an era of advancing vertical marketing systems, it is increasingly realistic to see the channel of distribution as a unit of competition. If these units are to be truly responsive to public needs and expectations, they must be led by channel captains who are well tuned to their constituencies.

In the marketplace, mass retailers are important channel captains, and in academia they are usually favored ones. Yet they are often less understanding of their environments than has been commonly thought. Their unresponsiveness stems less from lack of will than from fundamental changes in the retailing industry. However, the retailer's capacity and credentials for channel captaincy are correspondingly diminished.

This situation has consequences for scholar and marketer alike. For academics, it should mean less reliance on deductive derivations of plausible abstractions about how distribution works, more empiricism in addressing the question of where channel leadership should lie, and a scrapping of the maxim that large retailers are automatically well endowed for channel captaincy. For retailers it should mean abandonment of the comfortable untruth that they are by definition "close" to the market, and early conversion to automated front ends, a discriminating use of formal market research, an imaginative exploitation of the information generated by "automated front ends," and an opportunistic exploration of those roles—such as product innovator and consumer advocate—which capitalize on a combination of market knowledge and marketing power.

Out of these actions should come more responsive marketing channels.

Notes

1. William R. Davidson, "Changes in Distributive Institutions," *Journal of Marketing*, 34, No. 1 (January 1970), p. 7.
2. Louis W. Stern, "Channel Control and Interorganization Management," in Peter D.

Bennett (ed.), *Marketing and Economic Development* (Chicago: American Marketing Association, 1965), p. 665.

3. Frederick D. Sturdivant, "Distribution in American Society: Some Questions of Efficiency and Relevance," in Louis P. Bucklin (ed.), *Vertical Marketing Systems* (Glenview, Ill.: Scott, Foresman and Company, 1970), p. 99.

4. Louis P. Bucklin and Stanley F. Stasch, "Problems in the Study of Vertical Marketing Systems," in Louis P. Bucklin (ed.), *Vertical Marketing Systems* (Glenview, Ill.: Scott, Foresman and Company, 1970), p. 5-6.

5. Davidson, "Changes in Distributive Institutions," p. 9.

6. Oswald Knauth, *Managerial Enterprise: Its Growth and Methods of Operation* (New York: W. W. Norton & Company, Inc., 1948).

7. John Kenneth Galbraith, *The New Industrial State*, 2d ed., rev. (Boston: Houghton Mifflin, 1971).

8. Knauth, *Managerial Enterprise*, p. 11.

9. Wroe Alderson, *Marketing Behavior and Executive Action* (Homewood, Ill.: Richard D. Irwin, Inc., 1957), pp. 296-304.

10. Elmer P. Lotshaw, "Industrial Marketing: Trends and Challenges," *Journal of Marketing*, 34, No. 1 (January 1970), pp. 23-24.

11. Dean Muncaster, "The Marketing Function in Retail Merchandising," (address to the 14th Annual Management Seminar of the Toronto Chapter of the American Marketing Association. Toronto, January 11, 1964).

12. Philip Kotler, "Atmospherics as a Marketing Tool," *Journal of Retailing*, 49, No. 4 (Winter 1973-1974).

13. Louis P. Bucklin, *Competition and Evolution in the Distributive Trades* (Englewood Cliffs, N.J.: Prentice-Hall, Inc., 1972), p. 74.

14. *Ibid.*, p. 134.

15. *Ibid.*, p. 167.

16. Steven Masters, in an address to a seminar of the National Retail Merchants Association, in New York, 1962.

17. Harold L. Wilensky, *Organizational Intelligence: Knowledge and Policy in Government and Industry* (New York: Basic Books, Inc., 1967).

18. Bert C. McCammon, Jr., and Albert D. Bates, "The Emergence and Growth of Contractually Integrated Channels in the American Economy," in P. D. Bennett (ed.), *Economic Growth, Competition, and World Markets* (Chicago: American Marketing Association, 1965), p. 496.

19. John K. Ryans, Jr., "An Analysis of Appliance Retailer Perceptions of Retail Strategy and Decision Processes," in Peter D. Bennett (ed.), *Marketing and Economic Development* (Chicago: American Marketing Association, 1965), p. 669.

20. Thomas V. Greer and Charles G. Walters, "Credit Records: Information Tool for Planning," *Journal of Retailing*, 42, No. 1 (Spring 1966), 11-18 ff.

21. Stuart U. Rich, *Shopping Behavior of Department Store Customers* (Boston: Division of Research, Graduate School of Business Administration, Harvard University, 1963), p. 227.

22. Peter J. McClure and John K. Ryans, Jr., "Differences Between Retailers' and Consumers' Perceptions," *Journal of Marketing Research*, 5, No. 1 (February 1968), pp. 35-40.

23. H. Lawrence Isaacson, *Store Choice: A Case Study of Consumer Decision Making* (New York: Retail Research Institute, National Retail Merchants Association, 1966), p. 78.

24. Donald F. Blankertz, "The Basement-Store Customer," *Journal of Marketing*, 15, No. 1 (January 1951), pp. 336-340.

25. Robert W. Little, "The Marketing Channel: Who Should Lead This Extracorporate Organization," *Journal of Marketing*, 34, No. 1 (January 1970), pp. 31-38; David R. Craig and Werner K. Gabler, "The Competitive Struggle for Market Control," *The Annals of the American Academy of Political and Social Science*, 209 (May 1940), pp. 84-107; and Valentine F. Ridgeway, "Administration of Manufacturer-Dealer Systems," *Administrative Science Quarterly* (March 1957), pp. 464-467.

26. Bruce Mallen, "A Theory of Retailer-Supplier Conflict, Control and Cooperation," *Journal of Retailing*, 39, No. 2 (Summer 1963), p. 32.

27. Craig and Gabler, "The Competitive Struggle."

28. Mallen, "A Theory of Retailer-Supplier Conflict," p. 31.

29. Lew Hahn, *Stores, Merchants and Customers* (New York: Fairchild Publications, 1952), p. 12.

30. Arnold Corbin, "Central Buying in Relation to the Merchandising of Multiple Retail Units (New York: Unpublished doctoral dissertation, New York University, 1954), pp. 708-9.

31. Charles K. Ramond, "How to Starve in the Midst of Plenty," *Journal of Advertising Research*, 3, No. 4 (December 1963), p. 59.

32. M. S. Moyer, "The Marketing Implications of Point-of-Sale Systems," *The Business Quarterly*, Spring 1975.

33. M. S. Moyer, "Market Intelligence for Modern Merchants," *California Management Review*, 14, No. 4 (Summer 1972), pp. 63-69.

34. Davidson, "Changes in Distributive Institutions," p. 8.

35. Esther Peterson, "Consumerism as a Retailer's Asset," *Harvard Business Review*, 52, No. 3 (May-June 1974), pp. 91-101.

27
THE
CONTRIBUTION OF
THE PROFESSIONAL
BUYER TO
A STORE'S SUCCESS
OR FAILURE

Claude R. Martin, Jr.
Associate Professor of Marketing
University of Michigan

What a retail store has on its shelves available to sell is its product. This article presents the results of research about the person who determines the store's product mix, the professional buyer.

Two department stores operate in the same state, do not compete directly with each other, and have shared the details of their operations over the past ten years. One is a success and the other is not. Why?

The complexity of reasons for such a difference is obvious to any manager: there are differences in management ability and performance, in the physical plant, and in the economic condition of the individual markets. Certainly the marketing expert could attribute these reasons to differences in the marketing mix for each store. But one executive for the successful store said: "The bulk of the answer lies with who does the buying for the store and what they buy. If you don't have the goods the customer wants, you cannot be successful!" While the importance of different

From Claude R. Martin, Jr., "The Contribution of the
Professional Buyer to a Store's Success or Failure,"
Journal of Retailing *49:2 (Summer 1973), pp. 69-80.*
Reprinted by permission of Journal of Retailing.

factors is debatable, it seems reasonable to assume that what a store has to sell—its product—makes a major contribution to the sales success of that store.

PURPOSE

The purpose of this article is to present the results of a study into the differences between the people who do the purchasing for the two stores— the professional buyers. These are the people who determine the retailer's product mix. Our contention is that differences between the two stores' buyers help explain the differences in sales performance of the two firms. The hypothesis that we tested is that there are both demographic and behavioral differences between the buyers for the two stores and that these differences are the result of management policies and procedures.

The goal is to provide a profile of the professional buyers for each of the two stores so that possible guidelines for success might be drawn.

SUCCESS VERSUS FAILURE

The criterion used for characterizing success is simply sales performance. The trend of total sales during the past five years was studied for each store. The percentage of change in the sale of total merchandise for Store X and Store Y from 1965 to 1969 (Figure 1) clearly indicates sales growth for Store X and sales decline for Store Y.

While the trend of total sales is indicative of success, a better indicator is the performance of each store in certain key merchandise areas or departments. Interviews with department store owners, general merchandise managers, and the professional buyers in seven midwestern states and an analysis of data collected over thirty years by the Bureau of Business Research at the University of Michigan reveal an increasing reliance on the so-called "fashion goods" for department store sales. The definition of a fashion good is arguable, but there is general agreement that certain lines of clothing are more susceptible to constant and rapid changes in taste and can be labelled as fashion merchandise. For this study

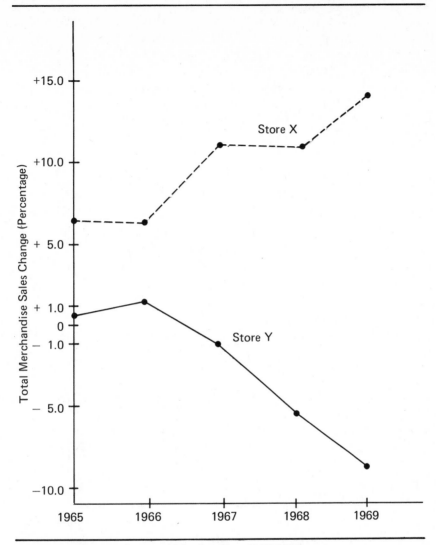

Figure 1. Sales Trends—Total Merchandise, 1965-1969.

we arbitrarily designated five categories of fashion goods:

Women's coats
Women's dresses (both junior and misses sizes)
Women's sportswear (both junior and misses sizes)
Men's clothing
Men's furnishings

The department store members of Research Group B of the University of Michigan report that their sales growth in these five areas is approximately double the sales growth in other merchandise lines and that these five areas constitute more than a 40 percent share of their department sales.

Analysis of the median growth of sales in these fashion categories for X and Y from 1965 to 1969 (Figure 2) indicates that X had a marked

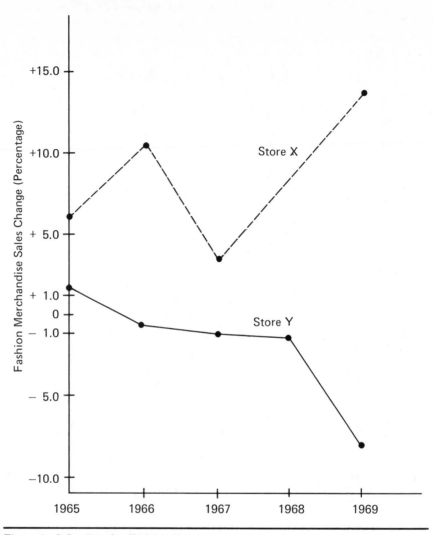

Figure 2. Sales Trends—Fashion Merchandise, 1965-1969.

growth in sales while Y showed an increasing decline. In summary, Store X shows a growth in sales over the past five years in both its total merchandise classifications and in selected fashion goods, while Store Y showed declining sales in both. Added to this is the fact that X had a sales increase in each of the five fashion categories during 1969, while Y showed a decrease in four of the five with only a small sales increase in men's clothing. All this indicates that we should label Store X a success and Store Y a failure.

The Study

Store X and Y are members of Research Group B, a group of department stores in seven midwestern states who share details of their operations in an effort to improve their proficiency. Both X and Y have been members since at least 1965 and have been subject to the joint exchanges of ideas and information. In fact, Store Y (the failure) had access to all internal operating data of Store X (the success).

The professional buyers of both X and Y were interviewed during the summer of 1970, and information was obtained about their socioeconomic status, their self-evaluation of performance and capabilities, and their actual departmental performance. The management of each store was responsible for identifying their buyers. Each buyer was then given a questionnaire to complete and return directly to the University of Michigan. The respondents were assured that the study was confidential and that it was controlled solely by the Bureau of Business Research. A 100 percent response was obtained from both stores.

All the differences cited were statistically tested and were found to be significant at the .05 level.[1]

RESULTS

Demographic Differences

There are striking demographic differences between the buyers for X and Y. Store X buyers are better paid and rely more heavily on their income from Store X as the sole source of financial support for their family unit (Table 1). Store X has a greater number of young and novice

Table 1. Demographic Differences Between Buyers' Income Characteristics (In Percentage of Buyers).

Differences	X	Y
Percentage of buyers who rely on income from store as sole family income*	43	22
Salary scale[†]		
Under $5,000	3	28
$5,000 to $8,999	26	39
$9,000 to $12,999	31	33
Over $13,000	40	—

*The difference between these percentages was tested and is significant at the .05 level.

[†]The two distributions are significantly different at the .05 level.

Source: Samuel Richmond, *Statistical Analysis* (New York: Ronald Press, 1964), pp. 205-07, 290-303.

buyers (Table 2), but the significance in these data appears to be that the distribution of X buyers is closer to normal than the skewed distribution of Y buyers toward age and experience.

An axiom for success held by athletic teams is balance—the successful blending of the experience and wisdom of older players with the energy and enthusiasm of younger players. Clearly, Store X (the success) shows more of this balance in its team of buyers than does Store Y (the failure).

Table 2. Demographic Differences: The Age and Experience of Buyers (In Percentage of Buyers).

Differences	X	Y
*Age**		
18 to 25 years	11	—
26 to 30 years	8	—
31 to 39 years	17	11
40 to 49 years	33	17
50 to 59 years	17	22
Over 59 years	14	50
Experience (years as a buyer)		
1 to 5 years[†]	44	23
6 to 15 years[†]	36	29
Over 15 years[†]	20	48

*The two distributions are significantly different at the .05 level.

[†]The difference between these percentages was tested and is significant at the .05 level.

Source: Same as for Table 1.

Perception of Self-Confidence

Each buyer was asked to evaluate his confidence in his general abilities and in his specific functions as a buyer. The objective was to compare the self-confidence of buyers of the two stores, not to measure the level of self-confidence and relate that to other factors as Cox and Bauer[2] have done. However, the questions eliciting data on self-confidence were similar to those used by Cox and Bauer, and we have categorized the responses similarly as general and specific self-confidence.

Buyers for Store X perceive that they have a higher degree of both general and specific self-confidence in their judgment of both new trends and new resources (Table 3). Reinforcement for this result came from the answers to questions concerning the buyers' self-evaluation of the certainty with which their decisions satisfied both their customers and themselves. This self-evaluation

Table 3. Buyers' Perceived Self-Confidence* (In Percentage of Buyers).

Kind of Self-Confidence	X	Y
General self-confidence		
Q. How do you feel about your abilities in general?		
Very confident	31	22
Usually confident	69	67
Sometimes confident	—	11
Almost never confident	—	—
Special self-confidence		
Q. How confident are you, as a professional buyer, in selecting a new buying resource?		
Very confident	43	12
Usually confident	54	71
Sometimes confident	3	12
Almost never confident	—	6
Q. How confident are you, as a professional buyer, in your ability to select new trends?		
Very confident	22	—
Usually confident	72	67
Sometimes confident	6	33
Almost never confident	—	—

*Chi-Square tests show significant differences in these distributions at .05 level.
Source: Same as for Table 1.

covered decisions regarding both style and resources. The buyers for Store X exhibit a higher degree of certainty and confidence that their decisions are both customer-satisfying and self-satisfying (Table 4).

A possible cause for this self-confidence differential is the difference in the buyers' perceptions of the amount of their own decision-making discretion, both in evaluating new merchandise trends and in adding or dropping re-

Table 4. Certainty Concerning Merchandise and Resource Decisions* (In Percentage of Buyers).

Degree of Certainty	X	Y
Q. How certain are you that a style you have not tried will satisfy your customers as well as a style you now have in inventory?		
Very certain	14	—
Usually certain	69	61
Sometimes certain	14	39
Almost never certain	03	—
Q. How certain are you that a style you have not tried will satisfy you as well as a style you now have in inventory?		
Very certain	28	22
Usually certain	58	39
Sometimes certain	14	33
Almost never certain	—	06
Q. How certain are you that a resource you have not bought from before will satisfy as well as a resource from which you now buy?		
Very certain	22	06
Usually certain	61	65
Sometimes certain	08	24
Almost never certain	08	06

*Chi-Square tests show significant differences in these distributions at .05 level.
Source: Same as for Table 1.

sources. While cause and effect may be arguable, the buyers for X perceived that management gave them more leeway for discretion in their decision-making (Table 5) and that they had a higher degree of self-confidence in their performance than did the buyers for Y.

Leaders versus Followers

Another difference between the X and Y buyers was in their tendency toward leadership in new trends. The following is the description of "new trend" merchandise which was given to them:

Each buying season there are new trends available on the market. During recent seasons these have included the midi and

Table 5. Perceived Discretion in Merchandise and Resource Selection* (In Percentage of Buyers).

Amount of Discretion	X	Y
In merchandise selection		
Very much	80	35
Some	20	59
Not much	—	06
None	—	—
In resource selection		
Very much	80	50
Some	14	39
Not much	03	11
None	03	—

*Chi-Square tests show significant differences in these distributions at .05 level.
Source: Same as for Table 1.

maxi in ready-to-wear; colored shirts and coordinated neckwear in men's furnishings; and the softening of the "squared-look" in shoes. These new trends have existed in all categories . . . for example, in such diverse areas as children's wear, furniture, and cosmetics.

The buyers were asked to choose among the following five alternate courses which they felt their store should take in following the trends:

1. They should be first in town.
2. They should be first in the area.
3. They should follow after the high-fashion stores in the major metropolitan areas.
4. They should not follow until the offices recommend it.
5. They should not follow until shown by regular resources.

Those buyers who chose 1 and 2 show initiative—a leadership—in new trends, while those who chose 3, 4, and 5 rely on others—they are followers. Of the X buyers 70 percent were classified as leaders, and, by sharp contrast, 76 percent of the Y buyers were classified as followers.

Aggressiveness

The final factor that distinguished X from Y buyers was their aggressiveness in seeking and obtaining additional factors from their buying resources. Each buyer was asked whether he normally asked for dating, advertising money, markdown money, or return privileges from buying resources. This was verified by the actual performance records of the individual buyer in obtaining these "extras." A higher percentage of X than Y buyers replied affirmatively that they did ask for each of these factors and did obtain the "extras" (Table 6).

Table 6. Buyers' Aggressiveness with Resources* (In Percentage of Buyers).

Buyers' Actions	X	Y
Asked for and obtained dating	47	17
Asked for and obtained advertising money	78	61
Asked for and obtained markdown money	23	17
Asked for and obtained return privileges	67	50

*Chi-Square tests show significant differences in these distributions at .05 level.
Source: Same as for Table 1.

An index of aggressiveness for the buyers was constructed by assigning a value of 1 to every yes answer and 0 to every no answer for the four questions on the "extras." Those with the total score of 4 or 3 were labelled very aggressive, those with a score of 1 or 2 were labelled somewhat aggressive, and those with a score of 0 were labelled nonaggressive. The buyers in each of these groups were then asked whether they had sole responsibility for adding or dropping buying resources. Those who exhibited more aggressiveness showed a more significant amount of perceived discretion in these decision-making activities than did those with little or no aggressiveness (Table 7).

Implications

The buyers for the successful store are more aggressive, more self-confident, and show a greater tendency for leadership in new merchandise trends than the buyers for the failing store. The contention is that these traits have contrib-

Table 7. Perceived Discretion of Aggressive versus Nonaggressive Buyers.*

	Percentage of Type of Buyer		
	Very Aggressive	*Somewhat Aggressive*	*Not Aggressive*
Need management approval to add resources?			
Yes	13	47	61
No	88	53	39
Need management approval to drop resources?			
Yes	25	51	52
No	75	49	48

*Chi-Square tests show significant differences in these distributions at .05 level.
Source: Same as for Table 1.

uted to the successful pattern of sales growth for Store X, while the "follower" behavior, the lack of aggressiveness, and the lower self-confidence of Y buyers have made a significant contribution to the store's sales decline.

The higher salary scale for X buyers may indeed be the result of, rather than the cause of, the sales growth. However, there are two factors under management control that distinguish the successful store from the failing store. First, the organization recognizes the importance of balance in the buyer cadre so that the older, more experienced buyer is integrated with the younger, more novice buyer. This implies that the firm's personnel administration must continually review the makeup of the buyer corps. Personnel administrators should recognize the direct contribution they may make to the sales growth of the store. Second, the organization should recognize that discretion, both actual and perceived, is important. This discretion is in the decision-making powers given to buyers to determine both merchandise and resources. The implication for management is that what is important is not just the dispensing of actual discretion, but also the perception that the buyers have of their discretionary range.

The objective of this article has been to pinpoint differences between the people making the product decision for two department stores, one a success at sales growth and the other a failure. In summary the results of the interviews with professional buyers for the two firms

indicate that balance in the buyer team and the discretion given to buyers may be two of the keys to success.

Notes

1. Samuel Richmond, *Statistical Analysis* (New York: Ronald Press, 1964), pp. 184-214, 290-303.
2. Donald F. Cox and Raymond A. Bauer, "Self-Confidence and Persuasibility in Women," *Public Opinion Quarterly*, Fall 1964.

28 SWEEPING CHANGES IN DISTRIBUTION

James L. Heskett
Professor of Business Logistics
Harvard Business School

Improving productivity in logistics will come about through institutional rather than technological change, according to the author. This means the reordering of functions and facilities within the organization.

Near the conclusion of World War II, the wartime T-2 tanker, with a rating of 15,600 tons, was thought by many to be too large for expected peacetime petroleum needs and also too large to be handled safely in most ports. Yet just 20 years later, marine architects were designing ships 20 times larger than the T-2, ships exceeding 300,000 deadweight tons which have since been built and now sail the world's oceans.

Only 25 years ago, a respectably advanced rate at which to handle bulk materials was about 500 tons per hour. Recently, a number of installations have been built capable of handling bulk materials at 40 times that rate.

Just a generation ago, there were three basic alternatives for transporting most commodities: rail, water, and truck. Since then, we have witnessed a vast increase in opportunities for transporting commodities other than petroleum by pipeline. Airfreight has become a viable alternative for many shippers. And the development of unitized freight handling and coordinated methods of transporting freight has produced a number of new modal combinations, including piggyback and trailers and containers on ships which, for all practical purposes, did not exist 20 years ago.

Since the inauguration of modern-day containerized service just 8 years ago, ocean transportation to and from the United States has seen an enormous growth of containerized freight in the general cargo sector. In the North Atlantic trade, it is estimated that 60% of all containerizable freight now moves in containers.

As late as 1950, the Interstate Highway System, although conceived, had yet to be financed for construction.

The computer, whose rapid development was another by-product of World War II, has made possible only within the past 15 years the application of techniques and managerial models so vital to the successful management of logistics activities.

Clearly, the generation just ended has produced remarkable technological advances in transportation, materials handling, and information processing.

Partly in response to technological change, industrial, commercial, and governmental organizations have reorganized to improve the management of logistics activities and to make intelligent use of the newly available technology. Increased breadth, in terms of both the backgrounds of individuals attracted to the field and the scope of responsibilities which they have been given, has facilitated a trend toward the purchase of carrier services, physical facilities, and logistics equipment as elements in a broader system of related activities.

In this sense, the past decade can fairly be termed an era of organizational as well as technological change in logistics.

TOWARD INSTITUTIONAL CHANGE

If we have witnessed significant technological and organizational change in the recent past, what does the foreseeable future hold? What are the implications of the fact that the U.S. population, and to some degree the size of the market that it represents, appears to be leveling out as emphasis on birth control increases? What will be the effect if pressures for new products and product individuality continue?

Similarly, what types of responses will be required by the growing congestion in city centers and the continuing dispersion and rapid growth of suburban markets? Will new technology continue to provide the primary means with which to deal with logistics problems arising from all these and other trends?

There are signs which suggest that the answer to my last question is *no*. While technological and organizational change will, of course, continue, major challenges will be met primarily by institutional change involving the spatial reordering of functions and facilities within an organization and among cooperating organizations.

This represents a logical progression in logistics from emphasis on decision making based on *internal cost analyses* to emphasis on *internal profit analyses* and on *interorganizational cost and profit analyses* of the sort suggested in Exhibit 1.

Factors in Shift of Emphasis

We will turn our interest during the foreseeable future to institutional (as opposed to technological) change, for a variety of reasons. Included among these are the seven possibilities that:

1.   There are physical constraints on certain methods of transportation and materials handling, as well as restrictive public attitudes toward the further technological development of others.

2.   Certain technological developments appear to be "topping out," at least for the time being.

3.   Existing technologies, to an increasing extent, require for their success a rationalization of activity which can be brought about largely through institutional cooperation and new types of institutions.

4.   Technological advances have made institutional cooperation not only possible, but in some cases necessary.

5.   There are changing attitudes toward inter-organizational coordination among individuals in business as well as government.

6.   Continued emphasis on logistics management will yield information necessary to justify institutional change.

7.   Perhaps of greatest importance, the economic benefits from institutional coordination and change will far exceed any that foreseeable technological developments can offer.

I shall consider each of these factors in the shift of emphasis to institutional change in the course of this article.

1. Constraints on Technology   Certain transportation modes, such as rail and highway, have natural constraints imposed on them by the existing physical facilities. The height of a rail car can be increased to the point where any further increase would require massive expenditures for greater clearances at bridges, tunnels, and underpass or overpass intersections that have replaced grade-level railroad crossings.

Truckers now speak in terms of a 6-inch increase in the width of a vehicle instead of a 10-foot increase in length, which was more feasible when highway carriers were operating with 27- and 30-foot trailers. And they will have difficulty getting even that small increase in width.

Public attitude now comprises a growing constraint on the further development of other transportation technologies. The refusal to support the development of the supersonic transport, however temporary a victory for such forces it may represent, was an important indicator. It may be

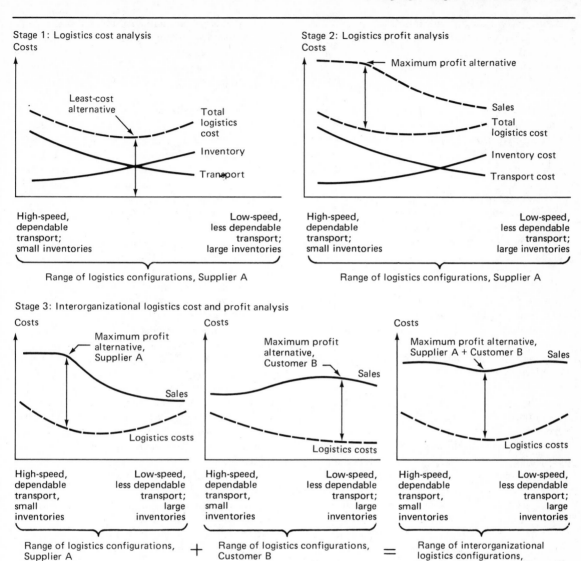

Exhibit 1. Stages in the Scope of Analyses for Logistics Decision Making.

significantly more difficult in the future to obtain funds for the development of an ecologically and economically uncertain device such as the SST than for, say, an expanded system of bicycle paths for urban commuters.

When we throw in the growing opposition to supertankers and the fear of the potential disasters they could create, and the issues and arguments over possible ecological impacts of pipelines in the tundra of the Far North, we have a clear indication that technology in the late 1970s and 1980s may be in for close scrutiny.

2. **Temporary 'Topping Out'** Several years ago, it was popular to look ahead to the "era of the 747," the great hope of airfreight advocates. These "boxcars of the sky" were to eliminate the economic barriers to the use of airfreight. Closer analysis at the time could have shown that the most significant development, the introduction of the DC-8-63F airplane, already had occurred. Furthermore, few anticipated the problems of assembling a sufficient volume of freight in one place at one time to meet the 747's vastly greater requirements for efficient operation. Finally, with their attention diverted to developments in the sky, most airfreight advocates paid too little heed to the significant improvements needed in the problem area of handling airfreight on the ground.

The same marine architects who produced the 300,000-ton ship designs now tell us that, although designs of 1,000,000 tons are possible, the economics of building and operating such ships quite likely precludes their construction in the foreseeable future, public attitude aside. Certain diseconomies of scale begin to assert themselves.

While ingenious devices for introducing automation in the warehouse have been developed in recent years, the promise of automated warehousing is yet to be realized. In fact, the requirements which it imposes on freight flow for effective utilization may in many cases be achieved only through the type of institutional cooperation I shall discuss later.

We now have the computers and the concepts to achieve significant savings through effective control of inventories. More important, economical computer and communication capacity will make possible the use of models offering more individual attention to product-line items,

inventory locations, and customers. But the gains which improved technology in this area could make possible are small compared with the improvements in operations that could be achieved through proper application of currently available machines and methods.

3. **Rationalization of Activity** Typified by improved allocation of effort and responsibility among cooperating and even competing institutions, rationalization of activity has been required by the introduction of certain technologies. Conversely, technological advances have so badly outstripped institutional changes that the absence of the latter now imposes significant constraints on the former.

Perhaps the best example of this is the introduction of containerization on a wholesale basis in North Atlantic shipping several years ago.

Prospective container-ship operators planned for massive capital investment in fast, expensive ships, and the containers they would carry. Even the most forward-looking ship operators, however, did not provide for the numbers of containers which would ultimately be required for the service. They did not properly anticipate the problems of controlling container usage in the hinterlands surrounding the ports which they would serve. And they paid dearly for their traditional lack of interests in, and institutional separation from, freight before it arrived and after it left the docks.

In response to this problem, operators are making extensive efforts to: (a) acquire freight-forwarding, trucking, and other organizations which control freight in the hinterlands; (b) seek out arrangements under which containers can be jointly owned; (c) collect and transmit information in such a way that more effective control can be maintained over container usage.

4. **Necessity for Institutional Cooperation** We have already noted that effective utilization of the 747 jetliner requires the assembly of large quantities of freight at a given place and time for shipment to a common destination. It is quite possible that, until airfreight volume increases significantly on a general front, self-organized groups of shippers with common origins and destinations may offer the best potential for providing this kind of volume.

In view of current computer capabilities

and concepts, perhaps the most acute need in inventory control activities has been for more accurate data on which to base forecasts of future demand. As we have seen, the data have always existed. They needed to be collected and transmitted in a timely way. This has led to the establishment of direct lines of communications between customers and suppliers.

Production technologies have made possible smaller, lighter products that perform jobs better than their larger, heavier predecessors. At the same time, improvements in our intercity transportation systems have made it easier and less expensive to transport larger quantities of these smaller products, at least to the outskirts of large metropolitan areas.

Yet, in a growing number of cities, we have congestion and chaos.

This is clearly a case in which technology has contributed to a problem that will be solved either by more technological development, perhaps in the form of subterranean freight-access routes, or by institutional cooperation to create more efficient freight flows.

5. **Changing Attitudes** Many forms of organizational coordination not only are legal, but are becoming more and more attractive as problem-solving means to businessmen and government officials alike. The growing interest in coordinating inbound freight movements to congested city centers is just one example of a response by government and industry leaders to a difficult problem. Recently, this has led to the organization of the first symposium in this country to explore approaches to the problem of urban freight movements.[1]

Efforts in other countries are more advanced. For example, a recent study of freight movements into Utrecht, Holland, disclosed that the consolidation and systematic delivery of certain types of freight moving typically in small shipments could reduce the number of delivery vehicles in the city center from over 600 to 6.[2]

The Supermarket Institute has supported investigation into the feasibility of consolidated distribution facilities which might be operated as a joint venture by competing grocery product manufacturers and chain food-store organizations utilizing the same regional distribution centers. Essentially, such facilities would enable manufac-turers and retailers to eliminate duplicated warehouse space.

In commenting on the concept of consolidated distribution facilities, the president of a large retail food chain recently remarked that "the idea may not be so farfetched, and it might have advantages to both segments of the industry." Of course, the concept will have arrived when a manufacturer or a store organization closes all or a part of its own warehouse facility to take advantage of a consolidated distribution service.

6. **Continued Organizational Development** In the past 15 years, there has been a rebirth in the concern for coordinated management of transportation, warehousing, materials handling, inventory-control, order-processing, and procurement activities. Evidence for this can be found in the rapidly increasing number of job titles like Physical Distribution Manager, Materials Manager, and Manager of Logistics, particularly in larger corporations. Further, the growth in membership in organizations such as the 10-year-old National Council of Physical Distribution Management (NCPD) and the even younger Society of Logistics Engineers (SOLE) has mushroomed.

Explanations for this concern and interest range from the competitive advantage that the effective management of logistics activities provides to organizational "me-too" faddism in certain industries. But an analysis of the roster of the NCPD suggests that the base of membership has spread from a few large companies in different industries to many more organizations in those same industries and then to other industries as well. Included among these are grocery and chemical product manufacturers, and manufacturers and distributors of products requiring extensive parts distribution activities. Other industries in which substantial costs of logistics, compared with sales, must be balanced against rigorous demands for customer service will see organizational change and emphasis on logistics.

As a further development in this area, managements will devote more attention to, and change the nature of, responsibility for coordinated product flow. For example, expansions in product lines without commensurate increases in sales produce higher inventory carrying costs as a percentage of sales.

As a result, in order to maintain a given level of customer service, retailers and wholesalers are limiting their speculative risk by reducing stocks of any one item (or by investing a commensurate amount of money in inventory for a broader product line) while at the same time expecting, and in fact depending on, manufacturers making speedy responses to their orders. This customer expectation, stated in the form of a willingness to substitute one manufacturer's product for another's in the event of the latter's inability to meet the customer's demands, in effect raises the incentive for speculation by manufacturers.

Thus caught in a squeeze between broader product lines and increasing demands for faster service from channel institutions, a number of manufacturers have responded by holding larger quantities of stock in semifinished form closer to markets, typically in distribution centers. There they can be cut, assembled, or packaged to order, thus postponing the company's commitment to specific stock-keeping unit locations until the last possible moment while reducing speculation (measured in terms of the elapsed time between customer order and delivery) for the customer.

To an increasing degree, logistics management will involve the operation of light manufacturing as well as distribution facilities. Perhaps the automobile assembly plant offers the most extreme example of this phenomenon. It is the closest thing to a distribution center in the channel of distribution for automobiles produced in the United States; it also houses light manufacturing activities. Because of the complexity of the latter, however, these plants typically fall under the responsibility of production management.

However, in other industries with less complex field requirements—such as the cutting to order of plate glass, paper products, lumber, and so on, and the packaging to order of common commodities—light manufacturing in the field will to an increasing extent fall within the purview of those concerned with logistics.

7. *Increased Economic Benefits*   Technological change can enable a company in a channel of distribution to perform its functions more efficiently. Typically, institutional change can eliminate the cost of performing a function by shifting the function to another point in the channel, where it can be integrated into other activities. Only occasionally, as with momentous developments such as containerization, can technology accomplish as much. And even then, it can do this only with the institutional change necessary to implement its introduction and growth.

INSTITUTIONAL RESPONSES

Basic functions performed in a channel of distribution, such as selling, buying, storing, transporting, financing, providing information, and others, can only be shifted, not eliminated. They must be performed by some institution at some point in a channel. Distribution opportunities can be pinpointed by identifying the basic functions which can be performed most effectively by each institution in the channel, and the types of institutional change needed to accommodate efficient product flow.

The types of institutional change called for include at least four, arrayed in terms of their organizational impact on companies in a channel of distribution:

1. The coordination of policies and practices to enable cooperating channel members to perform their existing functions more effectively.
2. The shift of functions and responsibilities from one institution to another in a channel.
3. The creation of joint-venture or third-party institutions to eliminate duplication of the performance of functions in such channels.
4. The vertical integration of channel functions which are currently performed by different organizations.

It may be useful to take a closer look at each of these four types of institutional change prompted by the forces I have discussed.

1. Coordination of Practices

The unitized handling of products by means of such devices as pallets is one example of a

technological development that has had a profound effect on interorganizational coordination.
In order to reap the maximum benefits of palleti-
zation, buyers and sellers have to coordinate their
materials handling systems to make use of the
same size pallet, or at least pallet sizes with
modular compatibility.

Thus industry standards for pallet sizes have
been established for the shipment of such things
as tin cans and paper products. Where standards
have not been established, certain wholesalers
have adapted their materials handling systems to
conform with those of a dominant supplier.
Companies electing not to abide by such standards
do so at a price which is reflected in increased
costs for handling goods.

2. Shifting of Responsibilities

A large distributor of personal care and
houseware products that employed a network of
direct sales personnel desired recently to gain
greater control over product delivery to its distributors without actually going into the trucking
business. It offered truckers an interesting proposition: a guaranteed, high profit on their investment in return for the full authority to schedule
and control their trucks, reductions of up to 40%
in existing charges, and access to the truckers'
books to verify profit levels.

This case suggests the tremendous potential
benefits made possible by a shift of functions
between organizations.

A shift of stock-keeping responsibility
from inventory-conscious retailers to wholesalers
and manufacturers has taken place in recent years.
This has resulted in part from the desire of retailers to reduce speculation and unsalable stocks
in an age of expanding product lines as well as a
realization that warehousing and materials handling costs may be significantly lower per unit
for manufacturers and wholesalers than for their
retailer customers.

In this case, the shift of responsibility for
the performance of these functions in the channel
of distribution is a logical result of interorganizational analysis and management.

3. Third-Party Arrangements

Cooperative interorganizational approaches
in the form of joint ventures or third parties[3] can
provide the objectivity and "arm's length" management often needed when large, proud organizations wish to create a product or service requiring inputs from several participating companies.
They are particularly attractive in a field that has
been typified by fragmented, duplicated services—
logistics.

. . . in distribution utilities: We are now seeing
joint ventures and third-party arrangements used
in the creation of so-called distribution utilities—
companies that are capable of providing a complete range of warehousing, transportation, order-
processing, and inventory-control services to
shipper customers. A distribution utility contracts
with a small to medium-sized manufacturer or a
division of a larger company to remove finished
stock from the end of the latter's production line
and make it available for sale—when, where, and in
the quantities desired—with some pre-agreed-on
level of customer service. This allows the manufacturer's marketing organization to concentrate
on selling.

The distribution utility, to the extent that
it takes possession of a product without taking
title to it, is the converse of what, in common
marketing parlance, is termed a broker—one
who buys and sells goods without ever taking
possession of them.

However, substantial resources are required
to (a) construct or acquire a network of distribution centers (warehouses), (b) support the design
and installation of extensive communication and
information-processing facilities, and (c) create
an organization in which naturally skeptical
manufacturer-customers can have confidence. The
joint venture provides a convenient means of
assembling such resources.

. . . in consolidated regional centers: The movement of carload quantities of stocks directly from
the production lines of competing manufacturers
into common regional distribution centers for
consolidated delivery direct to retail stores has
been under discussion for some time, particularly
in the grocery products industry. Until now,

objections regarding loss of control over the product, possible disclosure of competitive information, and the elimination of an area of potential competitive advantage have overruled the economic benefits of eliminating the manufacturer-operated and the retailer-operated distribution center as shown in Exhibit 2. But consolidated distribution of this type is now a reality.

A. Without consolidated distribution

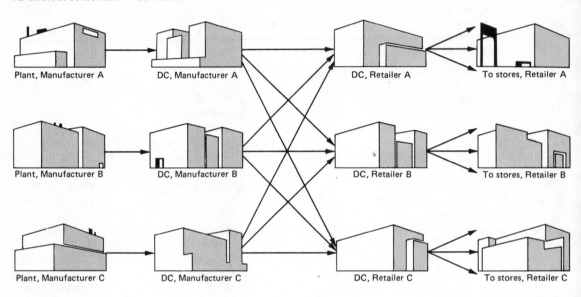

B. With consolidated distribution

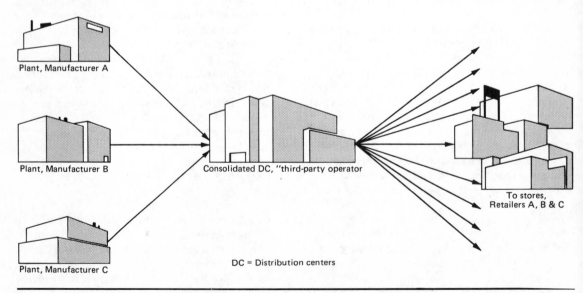

Exhibit 2. Impact of Consolidated Distribution on Product Flow to Regional Markets.

The concept has been recently implemented in Canada with the creation of a distribution center in Vancouver, shared jointly by leading manufacturers and their chain-store customers. The success of this experiment, conducted by a task force of the Canadian Grocery Manufacturers Association, which reports that it has reduced the cost of dry grocery distribution by at least 10%, has led to its rapid expansion to two other provinces of Canada.

. . . in central cooperative facilities: The benefits of consolidating outbound freight can usually be enjoyed by a well-managed, medium-sized or large manufacturer. However, companies typically receiving small shipments from many sources have found that they must establish cooperative arrangements to enjoy similar benefits.

Thus far, such arrangements have been confined to the formation of shippers' cooperatives for the consolidation of merchandise purchased by several companies for delivery to the same destination (a metropolitan area). Transportation cost savings, in the form of pro rata rebates, from the replacement of small package shipments by carload and truckload shipments have been remarkable.

Now, at the urging of city officials, these same companies are beginning to explore the creation of consolidated storage and merchandise-processing facilities, located in low-cost suburban areas, as well as the coordination of delivery to retail store sites.

An unpublished feasibility study in which I participated several years ago indicated that central distribution facilities could be operated at a satisfactory profit by a third party at a cost to retailer customers of only 80% of their current costs of receiving, processing, and delivering such goods themselves.

4. Vertical Integrations

The possibilities I have discussed thus far are interorganizational alternatives to the vertical integration of logistics operations in a channel of distribution by one powerful channel member through the merger with, or acquisition of, companies with which it deals.

Vertical integration in logistics flourished during the late 1960s as industrial manufacturers

began acquiring companies offering complementary services, such as trucking and warehousing. Interestingly, transportation companies were not leaders in this trend, possibly because of the Interstate Commerce Commission's historic tendency to impose stringent controls on the acquisition of companies offering competing modes of service. Indicators point to more active participation by transport and other companies in ventures involving the vertical integration of logistics services.

However, the rate at which this takes place will depend, among other things, on (a) the level of pressure exerted on the ICC to relax its control, (b) the rate at which legal means, such as financial holding companies, are found for accomplishing vertical integration, and (c) the level of prosperity in the logistics industries themselves. In the latter regard, adversity may help rather than hinder the trend.

IMPLEMENTATION APPROACHES

Perhaps the three most important factors in implementing creative approaches to interorganizational problems and institutional change in logistics are management practices, labor attitudes, and regulatory policies.

Management Practices

Clearly, individuals and companies that can adopt the attitudes and practices necessary to foster creative approaches to interorganizational problems will have an edge on their competitors. What are these attitudes and practices? Early research in the field of interorganizational management has suggested some.[4]

Companies likely to be recognized as leaders during an era of institutional change and interorganizational problem solving will be characterized by:

A tendency to seek what bargaining theorists have termed "nonzero-sum results from negotiations."

Essentially, a nonzero-sum result is one which reduces the total cost of the negotiating organizations, regardless of how they divide the resulting benefits. Nonzero-sum results can be achieved only through a basic change in procedure, such as the design of quantity discounts to reflect efficient handling and shipping or the implementation of incentives to encourage the faster unloading and turnaround of transportation equipment.

In contrast, zero-sum results produce no such net benefits. Price changes made without accompanying changes in procedure only transfer costs and profits from one comapny's P&L statement to another's, with no net economic benefit to the channel system.

A willingness to absorb risks for the mutual benefit of participants in a channel system.

A 1968 study examined the common problem of congestion at shippers' truck docks.[5] Its authors estimated that the addition of extra truck bays in several cases would reduce truck waiting time significantly, thereby producing high rates of return on investment.

Unfortunately, to implement these programs, shippers would have to make the investment to alter their facilities, while the benefits would accrue to truckers supplying pickup and delivery services.

Presumably, such situations could be resolved if one or more truckers could reduce rates selectively to encourage the necessary investment, a practice frowned on by the Interstate Commerce Commission. Or the trucker might make the investment with some assurance that he would continue to receive business from the shipper at least over a period sufficient to pay him back for his investment. Again, this practice could be looked on with disfavor by the ICC or a state regulatory body.

Perhaps the only feasible course of action would be for the shipper to absorb the uncertainty by constructing the bay. In return, he might obtain an informal agreement that future consideration, in the form of a rate reduction based on cost improvement, would be given by the carrier. This would only work if one carrier provided all or at least a significant portion of the service.

A willingness to innovate on behalf of the channel.

Some companies are known as innovators in their respective business spheres, in the testing of new technologies, organizational relationships, or contractual relationships. A company that is first to establish a pool of pallets for the economic handling of goods in a channel of distribution is likely to be regarded as such an innovator, with resulting long-term rewards for successful experiments (and perhaps losses for unsuccessful ones).

The establishment of a mechanism for collecting and transmitting information and skills throughout a channel.

Information that provides an early warning of inventory build-ups at the retail level can be of use to all participants in a channel system. Manufacturers of such diverse products as drugs and fertilizers have not only provided their distributors with inventory-control systems, but also educated them in the use of these systems. Expectations of long-term improvements in distributor profitability and loyalty motivate such manufacturers with enlightened interorganizational practices.

The exchange of personnel with other parties to interorganizational relationships.

A factor which distinguishes management in the United States from that in most other parts of the world is executive mobility. U.S. executives expect to make frequent moves; rarely do they expect to spend a lifetime working for a single firm. The exchange of personnel between "business partner" organizations can set the stage for important interorganizational achievements by executives in cooperating organizations who understand each other's problems and economic constraints.

Labor Attitudes

Unionism is typically held up by management as the greatest obstacle to beneficial changes of the type I have discussed. And yet, in situations where managements have recognized the value of providing job (and union membership) security in return for freedom to redesign jobs and introduce technological improvements, labor's attitudes have been positive.

Perhaps the best example of labor's cooperative attitude was reflected in an agreement some years ago between the Pacific Maritime Association, representing ship operating managements, and the International Longshoremen's and Warehousemen's Union. Under the terms of the agreement, the PMA established a trust fund to protect until retirement the salaries of ILWU members expected to be displaced.

As a result of the technology introduced subsequent to the agreement, volume increases made possible by operating economies actually created jobs, leaving the union with a trust fund that it had limited immediate need for. Thus both parties found this transaction beneficial.

Regulatory Policies

The fear of undue advantage or discrimination in dealings between carriers and shippers has proved to be a deterrent to interorganizational problem solving in logistics.

For example, the proposed introduction a few years ago of "Big John" hopper cars with several times the capacity of their predecessors, significantly higher minimum shipping quantities, and rate reductions of 60% on grain transportation from the Midwest to the Southeast by the Southern Railway was delayed for months by the ICC. This period of time was necessary to investigate the effects of the proposed innovation on the traffic of competing inland waterway barge operators. The litigation involved, among other things, a dispute over the question of whether the proposal exaggerated the magnitude of cost reductions which Southern could achieve with the innovation.

In spite of regulatory deterrents, there appears to be a trend toward more creative interorganizational problem solving on the part of carriers and shippers. The trend would be accelerated if, for example, regulatory agencies would emphasize this question in their investigations of carrier rate or service proposals: To what extent will changes resulting from such proposals produce procedural changes necessary to achieve non-zero-sum benefits for negotiants? With this shift in emphasis, proposals scoring high would have a greater chance of being approved and expedited by the concerned regulatory agency.

CONCLUSION

Institutional changes will, to an increasing extent, replace technological changes as the major sources of continued productivity increases in transportation, warehousing, inventory-control, and order-processing activities in the intermediate future. They both make possible, and are being fostered by, the application of interorganizational management thinking which attempts to produce operating efficiencies for two or more cooperating institutions in a channel of distribution.

This shift in emphasis in logistics threatens to envelop a number of shippers, carriers, and companies in associated industries in problems with which they are not equipped to deal. Significant competitive advantages already have accrued to those fully aware of the favorable competitive positions to be gained by shifting responsibilities for logistics activities from one company to another, creating third-party joint ventures to facilitate the consolidation and coordination of product flows, and seeking non-zero-sum results from interorganizational negotiations.

Such changes promise to inject additional dimensions of excitement to match those provided by recent significant technological developments in logistics. They also promise continued rewards to the executive of sufficiently broad view and flexible mind who is able to change to meet the needs of his chosen field. Clearly, they offer unexplored frontiers in the redevelopment and restructuring of logistics services.

Notes

1. Results of this symposium were reported in *Urban Commodity Flow*, Special Report 120 (Washington, D.C., Highway Research Board, National Academy of Sciences, 1971).
2. Described in *Nieuwe Wegen Naar Bevoorrading* (Rotterdam, Holland, Transport Advies Groep Trag, 1971).
3. For an interesting appraisal of the trend toward joint-venture or third-party arrangements for marketing products and services, see Lee Adler, "Symbiotic Marketing," HBR November-December 1966, p. 59.
4. Much of this section is based on J. L. Heskett, Louis W. Stern, and Frederick J. Beier, "Bases and Uses of Power in Interorganization Relations," in *Vertical Marketing Systems*, edited by Louis P. Bucklin (Glenville, Illinois, Scott, Foresman and Company, 1970), p. 75.
5. Karl M. Ruppental and D. Clay Whybark, "Some Problems in Optimizing Shipping Facilities," *The Logistics Review*, Vol. 4, No. 20, 1968, p. 5.

29
THE MYTHS AND REALITIES OF CORPORATE PRICING

Gilbert Burck
Associate Editor
Fortune

Do large corporations "administer" prices? This theory, put forth by many economists, including Galbraith, is now being challenged by new evidence and new thinking.

Corporate profits may be recovering briskly this year, but resentment and suspicion of profits are rising briskly too. It is by now an article of faith in some sophisticated circles that the U.S. has become a corporate state, in which giant companies increasingly dominate markets and write their own price tickets regardless of demand by practicing "administered" and "target return" pricing. Ask ten campus economists whether prices will fall with demand in industries that are concentrated—that is, dominated by a few *large firms*— and nine of them will tell you that prices won't fall as much as they would if the industry were competitive. And almost everywhere the putative pricing power of big business is equated with the well-known monopoly power that organized labor exercises over wages.

So the pressure is mounting to police pricing practices and other "abuses" in concentrated industries. Senator George McGovern, for example, is denouncing oligopolies as responsible for most of the nation's inflation, and is sponsoring measures to break up big companies. Meanwhile, the notion that price controls should become a permanent American institution is certainly taken

From Gilbert Burck, "The Myths and Realities of Corporate Pricing," *Fortune, April 1972, pp. 85-89ff.* Reprinted by permission of the publisher.

seriously by more and more people. The Price Commission itself, which has adopted the practice of regulating prices by relating them to profit margins of the past three years, seems to be leaning toward a theory of managed prices.

Yet all these passionately cherished attitudes and opinions are based at best on half truths, and perhaps on no truth at all. The portentous fact is that the theory of administered prices is totally unproven, and is growing less and less plausible as more evidence comes in. Always very controversial, it has lately been subjected to an extended counterattack of highly critical analysis.

Some of the best work on the subject is being done by the privately funded Research Program in Competition and Business Policy at the University of California (Los Angeles) Graduate School of Management, under Professor J. Fred Weston. For nearly two years now, Weston and his group have been taking a fresh, empirical approach to subjects like industrial concentration, profits, competition, and prices. Their techniques include asking businessmen themselves how they set prices, and trying to find out why businessmen's formal statements about their price policies are usually so different from their actual practices.

The program, among other things, hopes to come up with a new theory of corporate profitability. "So far," Weston says, "we find that profit rates are not significantly higher in concentrated than in nonconcentrated industries. What we do find is that there is a relationship between efficiency and profits and nothing else." But a vast amount of work, Weston admits, needs to be done. As happens so often in the dismal science, the more economists find out about a subject, the more they realize (if they are honest) how much they still have to learn.

MR. MEANS SHOWS THE WAY

The argument about administered prices is now nearly 40 years old; one philoprogenitive professor who took sides at the start is preparing to instruct his grandson on the subject. Few controversies in all economic history, indeed, have used up so many eminent brain-hours or so much space in learned journals. Much if not most of the argument has been conducted on a macroeconomic level; that is, it has been concerned with analyzing overall statistics on industrial concentration and comparing them with figures on prices. And that is exactly what was done by the man who started the argument by coining the phrase "administered price" in the first place. He is Gardiner Means, 75, author (with the late Adolph Berle) of the celebrated book *The Modern Corporation and Private Property,* published in 1932.

Like a lot of economists in that day, Means was looking for reasons why the great depression occurred. He noticed that many prices remained stable or at least sticky, even when demand was falling. Thus demand was depressed still further, and with it production and employment. Means's figures showed that wholesale prices fluctuated less in highly concentrated industries than in others; so to distinguish these prices from classic free-market prices, which are assumed to fluctuate with demand, he called them "administered" prices, or prices set by fiat and held constant "for a period of time and a series of transactions."

As an explanation for depression, Means's theory got some devastatingly critical attention over the next few years, but it did not fade away. In the middle 1950s it was revived as a major explanation for cost-push inflation, which Means calls administrative inflation; i.e., the supposed power of big business to raise prices arbitrarily. In 1957 the theory was taken up by Senator Estes Kefauver's antitrust and monopoly subcommittee, whose chief economist was John M. Blair, one of the nation's most energetic and passionate foes of industrial concentration. Ere long, dozens of the nation's eminent economists got into the argument, and many confected novel and often persuasive arguments in behalf of the theory of administered prices. Besides Blair, the advocates included the Johnson Administration's "new economists," such as James Duesenberry, Otto Eckstein, Gardner Ackley, and Charles Schultze, with "independent" savants like Adolph Berle and J. K. Galbraith helping out from time to time.

WHY DID THEY WAIT SO LONG?

The burden of proof, of course, is on the advocates of administered-price theory. They must do more than merely nourish a prejudice, particu-

larly if their thesis is to provide a reliable guide for antitrust and other public policy (to say nothing of serving as a base for a new interpretation of the American economy, such as Galbraith vouchsafed to the world in his book, *The New Industrial State).* In other words, they must offer very convincing evidence they are right. That, it is fair to say, they have not done. In 1941 economists Willard Thorp and Walter Crowder, in a study for the Temporary National Economic Committee, used a sophisticated analysis of price, volume, and concentration to conclude that there was no significant relationship between the level of seller concentration and price behavior and volume. Shortly afterward, Alfred Neal, now president of the Committee for Economic Development, arugued that any measure of price inflexibility must consider cost changes, "a matter over which industries have little if any discretion." These and other attacks on Means's theory seemed to dispose of it as a proven cause of depression.

As a major explanation of cost-push inflation, the theory was also subjected to severe criticism. Murray N. Rothbard of the Polytechnic Institute of Brooklyn, for one, simply laughs at the theory of administered prices, and terms it a bogey. "If Big Business is causing inflation by suddenly and wickedly deciding to raise prices," he says, "one wonders why it hadn't done so many years before. Why the wait? If the answer is that now monetary and consumer demand have been increasing, then we find that we are back in a state of affairs determined by demand, and that the law of supply and demand hasn't been repealed after all."

Just two years ago the National Bureau of Economic Research printed a little book calculated to put an end to the argument. It was called *The Behavior of Industrial Prices,* and was written by George J. Stigler, a distinguished economist at the University of Chicago, and James K. Kindahl, of the University of Massachusetts. Stigler and Kindahl correctly observed that, owing to hidden discounts and concessions, a company's quoted prices are often very different from the prices it actually gets. So instead of using official figures compiled by the Bureau of Labor Statistics on sellers' quotations, as Means and others had done, Stigler and Kindahl used prices at which their surveys told them sales were made. These

"OLIGOPOLIES" AND INFLATION: A THEORY DEBUNKED

A popular belief among economists is that companies in concentrated industries (those dominated by a few big firms) have the market power to write their own price tickets, while those in unconcentrated industries do not. Household durables and automobiles are supposed to provide the worst examples of oligopolistic pricing. These charts suggest just the opposite. Between 1953 and 1958, when the consumer price index rose 8.1 per cent, the price of services rose twice as much, while the price of household durables actually declined 3.4 per cent. The price of new cars, it is true, rose 5.9 per cent, but probably because Regulation W, which limited time payments, was suspended in 1952, enabling people to buy more expensive cars. In the period 1958-66, the consumer price index rose 12.2 per cent. While the price of services soared, the price of both household durables and new cars actually dropped. In 1966-71, years of great inflation, the price index rose about 25 per cent. And while the price of services rose 37 per cent, that of household durables rose only 15 per cent and that of new cars only 13 per cent.

were then matched with figures on industry concentration. The Stigler-Kindahl findings for the period 1957-61 did not differ much from findings made with B.L.S. figures. But the findings for 1961-66 differed considerably, and Stigler and Kindahl at least showed that prices in concentrated industries were not as inflexible as some people thought. What is very important is that Stigler and Kindahl probably understated their case because their surveys did not manage to get at true selling prices. As most business journalists are well aware, companies neither record nor generally talk about all the "under the table" prices and other valuable concessions they make when the market is sluggish.

"NORMAL" PROFIT ISN'T SO NORMAL

While this macroeconomic analysis of price and concentration was going on, a few economists were beginning to take a microeconomic or close-up view of pricing. Why not ask businessmen themselves just how they really price their products? This bright idea, however, proved not so easy to apply as to state. Classic economic theory says business should set prices to balance supply and demand—i.e., "to clear the market." But in 1939 two economists at Oxford University published a survey of 38 British companies that found most of them tended to price their output pretty much on a stodgy cost-plus basis, almost as if they were accountants, or trying to behave like Gardiner Means's oligopolists.

It remained for Professor I. F. Pearce of the University of Nottingham to clear up the paradox. Pearce had been trained as a cost accountant, and understood why prices are not always what they seem. He pointed out that business almost universally bases prices on a cost figure, which in turn is based on both past cost data and future cost estimates; an economist would call this figure the long-term average cost. In most firms, moreover, a recognized profit margin remains stable over periods long enough to be significant, and is therefore considered normal. "What is less generally known, except to those who practice the art of price fixing," Pearce says, "is how often and for what a variety of reasons 'normal' profit is not in fact charged against any particular sale. . . . The informal adjustment of margins, since it is both informal and *ad hoc*, tends to be left out of any general discussion of price fixing routine, *and yet the issue really turns upon it*. Margins charged are highly sensitive to the market under normally competitive conditions, and the 'norm' is simply that figure around which they fluctuate."

To demonstrate what he meant, Pearce made an elaborate study of one medium-sized British manufacturing firm. He sent out questionnaires and conducted formal interviews, and made a record of quoted prices and actual selling prices. He found that a wide variation existed between the margins talked about in interviews and surveys and the margins actually achieved. "Normal" profit margins, in other words, were mere checkpoints in the company's planning process.

Of course, a significant minority of U.S. businesses actually do price on a cost-plus basis— the regulated monopolies like utilities, pipelines, and transportation companies, as well as a lot of military contractors. At first glance, many unregulated companies also seem to price on a cost-plus

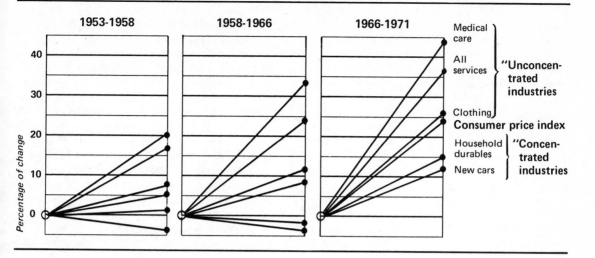

basis. This is only natural. Since they obviously cannot survive unless they take in more than they spend, the easiest way to think about a price is first to think like an accountant: price equals costs plus overhead plus a fair profit. Cost-plus, furthermore, is a useful ritual, with great public-relations advantages. A smart, prudent businessman would no more publicly brag about charging all the traffic will bear than he would publicly discourse on his wife's intimate charms. Recoiling from branding himself a "profiteer," he admits only to wanting a "fair" return. Ironically, this had made him a sitting duck for economists who accuse him of not striving to maximize his profits because he controls the market, and of changing his prices only when his planned return is threatened.

WHEN IT'S RIGHT TO CHARGE ALL YOU CAN GET

But no mechanical formula can guarantee a profit. Both cost and profit estimates depend on volume estimates; and volume, among many other things, depends on the right price, whether that price maximizes unit profit right away or not. A company with unused capacity and a growing market may well take the classical course of cutting prices and temporarily earning a smaller return on investment than it considers normal.

But it may have equally cogent reasons for not cutting prices. The theorists of administered prices have pointed accusing fingers at business' behavior in the recession of 1957-1958, when it raised prices somewhat in the face of falling demand. What happened was that costs were increasing faster than demand was falling. According to the theory of pure competition, they should have raised prices. That they did, both small firms and large.

On the other hand, many companies, particularly those with new products, do charge all the traffic will bear, and so they should. It is not going too far to attribute the innovativeness and technical progress of the Western world to this kind of profit maximizing, and the innovative backwardness of the Soviet Union and East Europe to the absence of it. The hope of realizing extraordinary profits on their innovations, at least temporarily, is what drives capitalist corporations into risking money on research. DuPont's strategy for the best part of 50 years was to develop "proprietary" products and to charge all it could get for them as long as the getting was good. So with the giants in data processing, pharmaceuticals, machine tools, and other high technologies. But these proprietary profits inevitably fire up competition, which invades the market with innovations of its own. Thus the story of Western industrial progress is the story of the progressive liquidation of proprietary positions.

THE RAZOR BLADES
WERE TOO CHEAP

This is not to say that all or even most businesses are skillful practitioners of the art of pricing. Daniel Nimer, a vice president of a large Chicago company, has made an avocation of studying pricing, and lectures and conducts surveys and seminars on the subject both here and abroad. Nimer believes that business in general is still far too inflexible in its pricing techniques, and too prone to take a merely satisfactory return. The most frequent error, Nimer says, is to fail to charge what the traffic will bear, particularly when marketing a novel product. In 1961, Wilkinson Sword Ltd. brought out its new stainless-steel razor blades at 15.8 cents apiece. Overnight Wilkinson accumulated a staggering backlog of orders, the sort of thing that usually results in delivery delays and an expensive crash expansion program. Had Wilkinson started at 20 cents a blade, Nimer believes, it would have been much better able to fortify its position. Among Nimer's pearls of wisdom:

1. A big backlog is a nearly infallible indication of an underpriced product.
2. Always make decisions today that will help you tomorrow, and remember that it is easier to cut prices tomorrow than to raise them.
3. The key to pricing is to build value into the product and price it accordingly.
4. Above all, pricing is both analytical and intuitive, a scientific art.

SETTING A TARGET

The major if not the first case study of U.S. pricing was published in 1958 by the Brookings Institution, in its book *Pricing in Big Business.* The authors were A.D.H. Kaplan (who was then a senior staff economist at Brookings and is now retired), Joel B. Dirlam of Rhode Island University, and Robert F. Lanzillotti of the University of Florida. Using questionnaires, interviews, and memos, the trio analyzed the pricing policies of 20 of the largest U.S. companies, including G.E., G.M., Alcoa, A&P, Sears, Roebuck, and U.S. Steel.

Although the actual practices of the companies were predictably hard to describe and even harder to generalize about, the authors did manage to narrow the corporations' *goals* to five. The most typical pricing objectives, the authors decided, were to achieve (1) a target return on investment, (2) stable prices and markups over costs, (3) a specified market share, (4) a competitive position. Another objective, not so frequently cited, was to compete by taking advantage of product differences. The study's conclusion, written by Kaplan, was that many big, powerful companies seem not to be overwhelmingly controlled by the market, yet even they do not dominate the market. They do not have things their own way, with steady prices and rates of return, but are constantly forced to examine and change their policies.

Manifestly this study gives scant comfort to the administered-price theorists. Professor Lanzillotti apparently felt it was too easy on big business. Granted money to do further work on the data, he came up with a more critical interpretation of them in an article in the *American Economic Review* of December, 1958. Since Lanzillotti is now a member of the Price Commission and has been described as knowing "more about prices" than anyone else on that body, his thoughts are worth attending to. Lanzillotti devoted much of his thesis to the prevalence of so-called target-return pricing, which at that time was an almost esoteric concept.

When companies use target-return pricing, he explained, they do not try to maximize short-term profits. Instead they start with a rate of return they consider satisfactory, and then set a price that will allow them to earn that return when their plant utilization is at some "standard" rate—say 80 per cent. In other words, they determine standard costs at standard volume and add the margin necessary to return the target rate of profit over the long run.

More and more companies, Lanzillotti argued, are adopting target-return pricing, either for specific products or across the board. He also concluded that the companies have the size to give them market power. Partly because of this power and partly because the companies are vulnerable to criticism and potential antitrust action, all tend to behave more and more like public utilities. Target-return pricing, with some exception in specific product lines, implies a policy of stable or rigid pricing.

Many of Lanzillotti's conclusions have already proved vulnerable to microeconomic analysis, most particularly at the hands of J. Fred Weston, who launched U.C.L.A.'s Research Program in Competition and Business Policy about two years ago. Prior to that, Weston studied finance and economics at the University of Chicago and wrote the three most popular (and profitable) textbooks on business finance. He got into pricing by a side door, having steeped himself in the literature on corporate resource allocation. He spent a considerable part of three years talking about that subject with executives—at first formally, then informally and postprandially. But he soon began to realize that he was also talking about the way prices were made. So he shifted his emphasis from financial to economic questions, and broadened considerably the scope of his work. Like others before him, he discovered that what businessmen formally say about their pricing and what they do about it are often very different. And their action is more consistent with classical theory than their talk.

In a major paper not yet published, Weston proceeds to apply his investigations to the three "popular" and related theories that were at the heart of the administered-price concept:

1. that large corporations generally try to realize a target markup or target return on investment;
2. that their prices tend to be inflexible, uncompetitive, and unresponsive to changes in demand;
3. that contrary to a fundamental postulate of classic economic theory, large, oligopolistic corporations do not maximize profits, but use their market power to achieve planned or target profit levels.

THE CONSTRAINTS OF THE MARKET

The concept of target pricing, Weston's research showed, was an arrant oversimplification of what actually happens in large companies. "The Brookings study," he explains, "focused on talking to top sales and marketing men, who take a target as given. If you talk to top executives, you find they use the target as a screening device, a reference point." Pricing decisions, he found out, cannot be (and are not) made apart from other business decisions; price lists are based on long-run demand curves. In fact, all the considerations that go to make investment and other policies also go into pricing, either deliberately or intuitively.

Neither large nor small businesses have price "policies," Weston adds; pricing is too much interwoven with other factors to be formulated independently of them. And most of the people Weston talked to kept emphasizing the constraints of the market. In short, target-return pricing is not what the critics of business think it to be. If anything, it is an interim checkpoint set up by management to specify tentatively the company's potential.

Often, Weston argues, critics of corporate pricing condemn behavior as oligopolistic that does nothing more than follow modern accounting practices. Firms of all sizes use accounting budgets, plans, and controls to formulate performance objectives. Standard volume represents the firms' best judgment of the expected volume of operations, and standard cost is the unit cost at standard volume. And a technique called variance analysis compares management's actual performance with standard performance in order to evaluate and improve the former.

Economic textbooks, says Weston, have failed to keep up with such developments in the art of management, with the result that economists often fail to understand the nature and implications of business planning. In *The New Industrial State*, for example, Galbraith argues that planning by firms, aided by government, is eliminating the market mechanism. Nonsense, says Weston. Planning and control as management uses them do not eliminate the market or its uncertainties. Planning and control are what the market forces you to do. Since they provide a way of judging performance and spotting defects, a device to shorten the reaction time to uncertainty and change, they really increase the market's efficiency.

HOW DETROIT REACTS

The administered-price theorists have pointed to the auto industry as the archetype of a disciplined oligopoly whose prices are very rigid. This characterization is largely based on the industry's practice of setting dealers' recommended prices at the beginning of a model year. Actually, the auto companies change those prices, sometimes frequently and substantially, as the year rolls on and specific models demonstrate their popularity or lack of it. The price changes take a wide variety of forms: bonuses for sales exceeding quotas, bonuses for models not doing well, and so on. As Professor Yale Brozen of the University of Chicago analyzes the industry: "Competition in the auto market actually *makes* the retail price. If the retail price is low relative to wholesale prices, the dealers can't live, and the company must give them better margins; if the retail price is high, the dealers tend to get rich, and the company raises wholesale prices and steps up production."

Now that foreign competition has become so powerful, the auto companies find it harder than ever to price arbitrarily. "Take our Vega," a G.M. man says with some feeling. "If anything is the reverse of target-return pricing, that Vega is. We did not *make* its price. We had to *take* a price that was set by our competitors. Then the only way we could make a profit was to bring our costs down."

Summing up the alleged reluctance of large corporations to compete, Weston quotes Professor Martin Bailey of Brookings, who describes the idea as "a theory in search of a phenomenon."

The third allegation dealt with by Weston—i.e., that the large corporation, in formulating its price policies, does not seek to maximize profits—is a tough one to prove either way. "Management's approach to pricing is based upon planned profits," Lanzillotti has contended. "If we are to speak of 'administered' decisions in the large firm, it is perhaps more accurate to speak of administered *prices*." To support his contention, Lanzillotti reexamined profit data on the 20 companies covered in the Brookings book. The data seemed to verify his belief that large firms are able to achieve their target returns on investment.

Weston noticed two major defects in the argument. One was that targets were specified for only 7 of the 20 firms. The other was that Lanzillotti defined return on investment as the ratio of income before preferred-stock dividends to stockholders' net worth, including preferred stock, which makes the return look artificially large. But return on investment is normally and more realistically defined as the ratio of income (before interest payments) to total operating assets. On this basis, the figures show a big discrepancy between target and actual returns. And the Lanzillotti table included results for only the years 1947-55. When the figures were extended through 1967, there was an even larger discrepancy.

"WE JUST DON'T KNOW"

Moreover, the returns above target were consistent with a lot of contradictory theses—with target pricing, with random behavior, and with profit maximization; the returns below target were also consistent with a number of alternative theses. Weston's final conclusion: Studies by Lanzillotti and by others have established neither that large firms are able to "control" or plan profits, nor that they do not want to maximize or optimize profits. Case not proved: additional evidence and analysis needed.

"The third proposition probably cannot be answered anyway," Weston adds.

> "How do you know if firms are maximizing their profits? In an early draft I made the mistake of thinking that a company earning more than target was maximizing its profits. This isn't necessarily so. We just don't know. We are, however, finding out a lot of positive facts about other related things. It has always been assumed, for example, that there will be collusion in an industry with few firms. But the fact is that we are beginning to get solid evidence that competitive efficiency is an important characteristic of such industries."

This finding, Weston points out, is consistent with the work of Professor Brozen, who has analyzed in detail the profitability of hundreds of companies. "Concentrated industries are concentrated because that, apparently, is the efficient way to organize those industries," says Brozen. "Unconcentrated industries are unconcentrated because that, apparently, is the efficient way to organize them."

THE BIG COMPANY AS COST LEADER

Standard textbook theory assumes that only "atomistic" industries—i.e., those with many companies and dominated by none—are perfectly competitive in price and highly responsive to changing tastes and technologies. But Weston contends that companies in concentrated industries can and do serve the consumer just as effectively. This view, incidentally, is persuasively set forth in a new book, *In Defense of Industrial Concentration*, by Professor John S. McGee, on leave from the University of Washington. The notion that concentration leads to the end of capitalism, McGee argues, springs from indefensibly narrow definitions of both competition and the aims of the economic system. Economic competition is best understood as an evolutionary process and not as a rigid structure or set of goals. But there is no necessary conflict between concentration and "competitiveness," even when the latter word is used in its narrow sense.

You can't explain the new competition with narrow textbook theory, Weston says. Big companies may be price leaders, but they are also cost leaders. Continually subjected to the efforts of rivals to steal business away, they deal with this uncertainty by reducing costs wherever they can. As Weston sees it, this kind of price leadership does not result in high prices and restricted output, as textbook theory says it should. What it does is to compel companies to try to strike a balance between growing as fast as possible and raising earnings per share as fast as possible.

ARE OLIGOPOLISTS MORE PROFITABLE?

Among the other provocative papers financed by the U.C.L.A. program is an unpublished dissertation on the relationship between industrial concentration and prices, by Steven H. Lustgarten, 28, who now teaches economics at the Baruch College of the City University of New York. His investigations show that during the period 1954-58, prices rose faster in concentrated industries. But the reason seems logical. Firms expanded plant and equipment at an abnormal rate. As production costs increased, prices did too. So Lustgarten could neither confirm nor reject the theory that 1954-58 was a period of profit-push inflation. For the years 1958-63, however, there was no relationship between concentration and price changes. The theory of administered prices, in other words, remained unproven.

A study of concentration and profits was done by Dr. Stanley Ornstein, 33, a consultant to the program. He examined the traditional hypothesis that, as concentration increases, the likelihood of collusion or "weak competitive pressures" also increases, and leads to higher profits in concentrated industries than in others. Not so, says Ornstein. Because stock market prices represent the discounted value of expected future earnings, Ornstein used stock market values to represent profitability over the long run. To eliminate false correlations, he also examined individual profit rates of the largest corporations in each industry, 131 companies in all, and subjected them to multiple regression analysis, a mathematical technique that is used to determine the relative influences of several variables.

"From 1947 through 1960," Ornstein observes, "the return on equity dropped from around 15 per cent to 8 or 9 per cent, and in a continuous trend. Long-term fluctuations like this shouldn't occur if there is collusion or administered bias." Like Brozen, Ornstein finds no connection between high profits and concentration. On the contrary, he finds there is vigorous competition among so-called oligopolists. His conclusion, made after much analysis, was somewhat more cautious: "This study does not disprove the traditional hypothesis [that oligopoly is characterized by high profitability], any more than previous studies proved it. It does show, however, that prior conclusions have gone far beyond those warranted by economic theory."

REMEMBER THE NEW YORK YANKEES

One of the U.C.L.A. program's most distinguished participants is Professor Harold Demsetz, 41, on leave from the University of Chicago, where he taught for eight years. Demsetz' interests at present lie mainly in identifying the true sources of corporate efficiency. He maintains that when there is no real barrier to the entry of new competitors, concentration is not an index of monopoly power. Therefore, if a concentrated industry has a high rate of return, monopoly power is not the cause of it. Concentration results from the operation of normal market forces, and from a company's ability to produce a better or cheaper product or both, and to market it efficiently. Some companies are downright lucky, and some outperform others, while some are both lucky and superior performers.

Confirming Demsetz' belief, Professor Michael Granfield, 28, has tentatively concluded that differences in efficiency may account for most differences in profit levels, and that high profits do not necessarily imply high prices but often quite the opposite—high volume and low prices. One way he accounts for efficiency is by what he calls Team Theory. "The old saw holds that the team outperforms its individual members; it may be right," says Granfield. "Although other companies are constantly hiring executives away from I.B.M., these companies never seem to do as well as I.B.M."

"Many managerial economies are not always evident," Ornstein adds.

"The only way to get them is to get the whole team. The New York Yankees were a winning team for years; the technical skills responsible for their record accounted for only about 10 to 20 per cent of the answer. What is really involved is managerial skills, and they can't be duplicated. To some extent a successful management is synergistic. By this I mean that there seem to be managerial economies of scale just as there are multiplant economies of scale. If so, the argument that you can break up big business and not hurt the consumer is wrong."

It may not be long before the program staff develops a formal theory about what really makes enterprises excel, and why the country is better off handling them with a certain amount of care instead of busting them up like freight trains in a classification yard, or subjecting them to permanent price controls.

STORED IN THE MINDS OF MILLIONS

The theory of administered prices, however, is not yet done for. Its new critics will doubtless find the going slow. Before their credo can hope to gain "popular" acceptance, it must first achieve standing in professional economic journals. And it has, for the moment, absolutely no political appeal. Thanks in large part to Ralph Nader, the big corporation is the whipping boy of the day. Indeed, George Stigler glumly predicts that the controversy will continue for another generation or more. "Administered-price theory," he says, "is like the Sacco-Vanzetti case. Whatever the jury's verdict, the defendants' innocence is stored in the minds of millions. So is the 'guilt' of administered prices, and the businessmen who practice them."

The administered-price theorists are not resting on their oars, either. Gardiner Means, who started it all nearly 40 years ago, now argues that the recent combination of inflation and recession can be explained *only* by his administered-price thesis. In the June, 1972, issue of the *American Economic Review*, he defines his theory and then tears into the Stigler-Kindahl book, which he says misrepresents his position.

What may be more important in its effect on public opinion, John Blair, he of the Kefauver committee, is publishing a monumental 832-page volume entitled *Economic Concentration—Structure, Behavior and Public Policy*. This opus contains something from almost everybody who has written about concentration, and is complete with dozens of charts, as well as an introduction by Means. The fruit of more than 30 years of fighting big business, the work is larded with quotations and chuck-full of footnotes. Blair's mind is made up, and his book is passionately partisan; but that will probably not prevent it from being given glowing reviews in the popular press.

For all this, there seems no doubt that the case against the theory of administered prices will grow stronger. Groups like Weston's are being organized elsewhere. The University of Rochester, for example, has set up the Center for Research in Government Policy and Business in its Graduate School of Management, and is looking around for private donations.

No matter what such groups find, it will be salutary. For the controversy about administered prices proves, among other things, how little Americans know about the inner workings of the big corporation, the country's most characteristic institution. And if present trends in research are any indication, the more that can be learned, the stronger will be the case for revising wrong notions about corporate behavior.

30 RISK-AVERSIVE PRICING POLICIES

Joseph P. Guiltinan
Office of Industry Affairs
and Technology Utilization
National Aeronautics and Space Administration

Pricing policy is changed more often in today's uncertain economic environment. Under these conditions, how can pricing be made less risky?

The marketing manager for a heavy-equipment manufacturing concern in northern Ohio recently suggested that before 1973 he spent no more than three days a year on pricing policy but that currently pricing dominates all marketing policy-making activities in his firm. This experience is not unusual. Decision makers are becoming increasingly aware that pricing policy changes must be made with consideration for possible major shifts in economic conditions such as the prices and availability of raw materials, aggregate demand, interest and exchange rates, and liquidity. Uncertainty regarding these economic forces leads to uncertain and fluctuating gross margins, creates difficulties in planning working capital needs, and impedes budgeting. Since price can influence cash flow and margins more quickly than other marketing variables, the development of policy regarding price levels, changes, and discounts has become of paramount concern in current marketing practice.

This article reviews some current pricing responses to economic uncertainties and identifies key problems associated with the implementation

From Joseph P. Guiltinan, "Risk-Aversive Pricing Policies: Problems and Alternatives," Journal of Marketing 40 (January 1976), pp. 10-15.

of these responses. In particular, responses that reflect risk-aversive, defensive perspectives are of primary concern. While it is often appropriate for managers to adopt policies that seek to minimize risk, this article contends that such responses may have unanticipated consequences that entail a good deal of risk. Alternative courses of action for developing pricing policies under economic uncertainty are also presented. The analysis is based on concepts, practices, and theories gleaned from marketing theory, general business periodicals, and a series of executive development pricing seminars in which the author has participated with senior pricing executives.

CURRENT PRICING RESPONSES

Most current pricing responses reported in the literature are concerned with reducing the risk of low margins, avoiding bottlenecks, and improving cash flows.[1] In general, these responses are of two types: cost based and selling related.

Cost-Based Pricing Responses

Many current pricing methods and related product decisions are primarily responses to production cost uncertainties and related pressures on margins.

Adoption of "Delayed-Quotation" Pricing In this approach, which is particularly widespread among manufacturers of custom-made products such as machine tools, the seller sets a final price only when the items have reached the stage of finished goods. This is due to a combination of long production lead times (often because of bottlenecks on key materials) and rapidly escalating prices (typically in metals and petro-chemicals). This approach (which includes the "price at time of delivery" variation) is not novel but has been practiced much more broadly the past couple of years.

Elimination of Low-Margin Products This policy has also received widespread attention by firms that are uncertain about future cost increases or their ability to pass such increases forward. In addition, the cost and unavailability

of working capital have made it unprofitable to maintain inventories of low-margin items.

Adoption of "Escalator" Clauses This policy is simply one in which price increases (frequently across-the-board increases on all items in a product line) are automatically implemented based on a previously stated formula. The objective is to alleviate the risks involved in cost increases. The bases for such escalations include simple factors such as increases in wholesale price indexes, industry-specific published indexes, listed price increases of raw material suppliers, or highly complex formulas that incorporate increased costs of labor, energy, and several material inputs. The effective use of such escalators depends on the willingness of customers to accept them, and on the firm's ability to change the formula over time as cost structures change and to measure variations in cost changes across products.

Selling-Related Pricing Responses

These responses focus on increasing margins by reducing customer incentives used by the sales force (particularly in industrial firms). While they reflect cost pressures, unlike cost-based responses they have a minimal impact on direct list prices. Rather, they reflect an attempt to redirect sales efforts to nonprice approaches.

Unbundling of Services In this response, a firm that has priced a major product (typically a large, complex piece of equipment) to include special services, peripheral equipment, or replacement parts shifts to a policy in which each element of the product-service mix is priced separately. Typically, the sum of the prices (after unbundling) will exceed the old, single price. Thus, unbundling represents the elimination of a form of product-line discount to buyers purchasing the full mix.

Reduce Cash and Quantity Discounts Because discounts represent direct reductions in the gross margins earned by sellers, there is a temptation to arbitrarily eliminate many cash and quantity discounts as a means of improving margins. Further, many firms have found that large customers (including many government agencies) often subtract the cash discount but still fail to pay invoices within the stipulated period. The incentive to maintain quantity discounts is also reduced for suppliers who experience shortages of key materials.

Elimination of Price "Shading" The concept of varying price policy, or "shading," is one in which reductions from list price are made as the result of negotiations between buyers and salesmen. The recent trend toward a "one-price" policy in many firms can be attributed to the desire to maintain gross margins (as was the case with discounts), to centralize control over pricing (by removing the sales force from this role), and to attempt to generate more sales effort in nonprice attributes of the product.

While price is generally a competitive tool for increasing demand for a firm (and often a tool for stimulating industry demand), risk-aversive policies generally do not explicitly consider competitive response and consumer demand as significant inputs to the pricing decision. This appears to result from the knowledge that similar pressures (such as the rising cost of materials) also usually plague competitors, from the expectation that competitors will adopt (or have adopted) similar policies (especially on discounts or escalators), or from limitations in the comparability of products and services among competitors.

PROBLEMS EXPERIENCED WITH CURRENT PRICING RESPONSES

For a variety of reasons, an individual enterprise may find that the foregoing responses are difficult to implement or that they lead to unintended consequences. Marketing theory and the experiences of many pricing executives are used in this section to illustrate such difficulties.

Distribution and Sales Force Problems

Distributors may react negatively to the elimination of discounts because in some cases this may eliminate part of their competitive advantage, because it typically violates traditional trade practices, and because it reduces possible bases for promoting the product to final buyers. Similarly, they will react negatively to any changes that influence the total effectiveness of a product line (such as the elimination of an important low-margin, sales-leading product). Consequently, the degree of reseller support may be influenced by such pricing policies.

It is also important to understand the nature of distributors' cost and profit structures before radically changing discount policies. For instance, one St. Louis manufacturer eliminated quantity discounts to improve margins and then learned that many of the firm's distributors relied almost exclusively on the discount for the profit they made on that company's products.

Many of the risk-aversive responses also lead to a serious alteration in the role of the company sales force, often diminishing the role of the salesman while giving him the task of smoothing over customer reactions to price increases and product shortages and backlogs. This role change is likely to lead to increased sales force dissatisfaction and turnover.

Product-Line Problems

Where arbitrary elimination of low-margin items or unbundling takes place, product-line considerations on both the production and demand sides become important. Low-margin items may significantly stimulate sales of complementary, high-margin items, especially where items are bundled. Accordingly, care must be taken to ascertain the competitiveness of each element of the mix when unbundling takes place. For instance, a small institutional services firm in Tennessee found that it was not equally competitive on all components of the product-service mix, and declining sales of part of the line more than offset the revenue gains from price changes.

When a price change significantly affects end prices, buyers' perceptions of the entire line's price/quality image may be influenced.[2] A western manufacturer of special fertilizer products recently introduced a third, middle-of-the-line product. However, pricing executives failed to price it high enough to avoid a perception of similarity in quality to the low-end product, which had just experienced a price increase. Thus, both products appealed to the same market and few new customers were obtained.

Where bottlenecks are a problem, the decision to concentrate on so-called high-margin items may backfire. To the extent that high-margin items require materials, labor, or equipment in short supply, production capacity will be underutilized and total dollar margins may not be maximized.

Escalator Clauses and Cost-Forecasting Problems

Probably no pricing problems are as pervasive as those associated with escalators. Most firms can readily appreciate the problem of spiraling costs and, consequently, industrial buyers appear more willing to accept some sort of escalator provision today.

Problems related to escalators fall into categories typified by the following:

A California aircraft supplier must bid now on products to be delivered in 1983.

An Indiana automotive parts manufacturer has had a bid for a large order rejected until the company indicates what percentage of a cost increase it will absorb itself and what portion of its escalator clause is attributable to labor and each of various materials.

A New England manufacturer in the electronics industry developed a cost escalator based heavily on the price of copper. When copper prices fell, his customers demanded sharp price decreases; yet other cost elements that were not incorporated into the escalator formula had recently increased significantly.

These considerations demonstrate the need for improved and realistic costing. This is true whether a firm is developing an escalator clause for direct use in a contract or for setting a fixed future price.

Problems Related to Demand Curve Assumptions

A fundamental problem with all cost-based pricing strategies is the implicit assumption that demand is inelastic. Such assumptions gain credence if recent price increases have not resulted in any major loss of sales. Even where demand curve estimates are developed, however, three factors must be considered:[3]

Cumulative Price Increase Effects and Confounding Real Income Effects   The presence of either or both of these effects often results in the invalidation of historical price/quantity relationships.

Illustrative of this is the plight of a Texas manufacturer of metal home improvement products. Normally, sales in this industry are booming and demand is inelastic when new construction is down. As the recession began to take shape in mid-1974, however, this firm's home improvement sales began to slide when prices were raised to reflect steel and aluminum cost increases, even though new housing starts remained low.

This situation probably resulted from both of the effects suggested above. As price increases become more frequent, historical relationships become less applicable because the historical range of price/quantity observations is increasingly remote from current price levels. The firm may well have moved into a range where demand elasticity is higher.

Demand estimates may also be confounded when economic forces (such as recessions) result in a downward shift in the demand curve. Smaller quantities are demanded at all (or most) price levels as either the rate of use or number of users diminishes.

In both cases, the failure of historical relationships to hold reduces the usefulness of simple statistical demand curve models and of untempered executive judgments that rely on recent sales history. More complex forecasting models that incorporate economic conditions as well as price variables may reduce confounding effects. Where feasible, the use of experimentation or surveys may provide some information for updating judgments.

Poor Sales Force Estimates of Demand   Sales force estimates of the effect of price changes are considered inadequate by many pricing executives. The tendency to rely on price selling and the desire to be more competitive have generally made subjective sales force estimates of the effects of a price reduction very optimistic and their estimates of the effects of increases very pessimistic. The controller of an Ohio-based equipment manufacturer suggested that his sales force typically overestimates actual sales increases by about one-fourth of unit volume when queried about the effects of prospective price decreases. Consequently, sales force estimates may be ignored if not accompanied by supportive value analysis comparisons, data on customer revenue trends, or other specific customer purchasing constraints.

Limitations of the Demand Curve Concept Elasticity and demand curve estimates reflect the impact of price on total revenue only. While revenue may increase as a result of a price increase, reduced unit volume may result in sharply increased average unit costs when fixed costs are a major portion of total costs.

Problems with Cost Orientation in General

In the long run, perhaps the most serious problem facing firms that adopt cost-oriented approaches to pricing is the self-perpetuating nature of the price squeeze that often results—particularly in periods of reduced consumer and industrial demand. Automatic and continual escalation of prices merely to preserve target gross margins is a fundamental culprit in prolonging recessions. When such increases occur in the elastic zone of a demand curve, reductions in demand in response to these changes often lead to increased average unit costs. This, in turn, leads to increased prices by those firms that rely on target margins as a pricing device (even in the absence of further increases in labor, energy, and materials costs).

The foregoing problems in demand curve estimation notwithstanding, pricing executives must consider the unit-sales implications of average-cost pricing. When the pricing objective is to maximize profit, then it is appropriate to use marginal analysis of the incremental costs and expected incremental revenue associated with either a price cut or the attempt to avoid a price increase.

In short, many firms are now realizing that pricing to maintain a given gross margin may not really be a low-risk strategy. In an economy where demand may be increasingly elastic and where fixed costs are very high for most industries,

lower margins may be required to maintain adequate demand. Stated alternatively, it will generally prove counterproductive to rely solely on higher prices and margins to deal with problems of cost control and cost forecasting. Since risk-aversive policies may not achieve the objectives for which they were designed, perhaps more positive approaches are needed.

DEVELOPING SOME ALTERNATIVE RESPONSES

Given that many of the current pricing responses will not be appropriate for a given firm due to the problems outlined above, some alternative responses do exist that may be more consistent with the actual decision environment. Further, some guidelines are available to help pricing executives evaluate and implement alternative policies.

Developing Price Objectives

Price responses are always made with some objective in mind, at least implicitly. As suggested earlier, objectives such as improving margins, avoiding bottlenecks, and improving cash flow seem to be the dominant forces behind current price responses. However, such objectives may not be mutually consistent. Focusing on high-margin products may lead to increased bottlenecks due to the materials or labor required, or it may lead to reduced total cash flow as a result of reduced sales of items complementary to low-margin items. Accordingly, a clear statement of the objectives of pricing policy is a fundamental requirement for selecting alternatives. Also, the impact of short-term policies and objectives on long-term profit must be clarified. As Kotler suggests, the identification of weak products should consider potential sales growth and annual cash flow generated per dollar of asset tied up in the product.[4]

Positive Pricing Perspective

While most current price responses are risk-aversive, organizations that have clearly defined price objectives, that have carefully analyzed the pricing and cost environment, and that are organized to absorb and act on all appropriate information should be in a position to act positively and opportunistically in creating pricing policy. The following policies illustrate this posture.

Balance pricing policy on a major product with policy on related items. For instance, by restricting large price increases to replacement parts, services, and complementary items, a West Coast firm was able to hold the line on price increases for the major item.

Employ a varying price policy (where injurious price discrimination is not a problem) as a tool that permits the sales force to orient demand toward those products that the firm wishes to promote and to obtain a foothold in new accounts for the long run. Maintaining this policy may be especially effective in softening the blow of price increases or reduced cash discounts.

Rather than reduce quantity discounts and promotional allowances, use them creatively to stimulate demand for products not requiring critical resources, or to partly offset price-level increases. Further, as costs change, frequent review of the quantity discount structure becomes imperative and may lead to the discovery of more marketable and more competitive quantity discount policies. (Interestingly, many firms are not even aware of competitors' quantity discount structures.)

Where cash discounts are under review, be sure to consider both the marketing and financial issues involved (including changes in short-term interest rates). A period of tight money and inflation may present opportunities to obtain new customers and build long-term goodwill. Many firms have countered the trend toward eliminating cash discounts by initiating or expanding them. One California manufacturer reported that the average age of accounts receivable was reduced by over 40 days with the initiation of a 1½% cash discount, thus dramatically

reducing working capital binds. (Note that paying 1½% for getting payment 40 days earlier is tantamount to paying:

$$\frac{360 \text{ days/year}}{40 \text{ days}} \times 1\tfrac{1}{2}\% = 13.5\% \text{ annual interest for that money.})$$

Where buyers fail to pay invoices on time, several firms have invoked penalty charges at 1% to 1½% per month with some success.

To spread the financing costs of large-scale capital projects, a Pennsylvania construction firm began to write contracts that included progress payments—with the first payment made at the start of construction.

Discounts may also serve as an alternative to escalator clauses. An Ohio manufacturer with a large product line has begun to print price lists that are expected to last six months. However, at the start of the period, all products are discounted to all buyers; as cost increases occur, discounts are reduced. This practice reduces the number of price increases and eliminates the problem of delays in buyer notification of changes.

Cash or merchandise rebates (promotion allowances) may be useful for industrial manufacturers as well as for consumer products manufacturers. As in the case of across-the-board discounting, this avoids a complete overhaul of price lists (and related notification) for short-term pricing policies.

Conduct periodic audits of the cost structures of all major products or (where joint costs are difficult to separate) major product groups before developing escalator clauses. Such audits would examine possible savings in labor, energy, or distribution costs that might offset cost increases in materials. This approach frequently makes escalators more palatable to buyers by demonstrating the seller's good faith in holding down controllable costs and by developing an up-to-date data base for constructing realistic escalator indexes. Several firms have uncovered previously undetected productivity improvements on some items (often due to learning curve effects) which enabled them to set more competitive prices on those products.

Exploit the product life cycle.[5] As products go through growth, maturity, and decline, price levels and promotional policy change to meet consumer, competitive, and technological changes. Typically, one would expect practices such as discounts, shading, and product-service bundles to be fundamental aspects of marketing strategy in the maturity/saturation stages, where price level and technological parity tend to exist.

Where demand conditions permit, increase the use of long-term contracts to guarantee transactions, in part to reduce costs, but also to guard against multiple ordering by buyers who are attempting to hedge against further inflation and who will likely cancel out at a later time. This is particularly important for products where material shortages and long production backlogs formerly existed.[6]

Employ new sales force incentives to meet production, cash flow, and margin objectives, to reduce reliance on price shading, and to stimulate more sales force concern with accurate demand estimation.

Promote distributor cooperation by: expanding cooperative promotions on key items, emphasizing any product improvement associated with price increases, contrasting price increases with either industry averages or the Industrial Wholesale Price Index, and noting that distributors selling on commission or fixed percentage discount will increase their gross income.[7]

CONCLUSION

Each firm faces a unique set of cost, supply, customer demand, and competitive forces at a given point in time, and each must select its price objectives and policies accordingly. This article has suggested some considerations for making policy selection. Pricing executives should avoid adopting current practices used by other firms without considering the problems that may hinder their implementation or that may lead to unintended consequences. Pricing responses should be developed on the basis of clearly defined price objectives, incorporating research on the anticipated effects of price changes. Further, pricing policy under uncertainty need not consist solely of defensive, risk-aversive alternatives, but can be positive and opportunistic in perspective.

Price has long been one of the most ignored dimensions of marketing policy in both academia and industry.[8] The cost-oriented, risk-aversive trends that are so prominent in current business practice seem to bear this out. Firms are defensive about pricing, probably because its ramifications are not well understood. Improved knowledge of this aspect of marketing may be an unforeseen benefit of attempts to deal with the current problems.

Notes

1. This section was developed based particularly on Daniel Nimer, "Pricing Capital Goods," *Industrial Marketing*, March 1971, pp. 53-55; "Profitless Boom in Machine Tools," *Business Week*, July 6, 1974, pp. 52-54; "Pricing Strategy in an Inflation Economy," *Business Week*, April 6, 1974, pp. 43-49; and "The Squeeze on Product Mix," *Business Week*, January 5, 1974, pp. 50-55; as well as from discussions with pricing executives.
2. This is treated in detail in Kent B. Monroe, "Buyers' Subjective Perceptions of Price," *Journal of Marketing Research*, Vol. 10 (February 1973), pp. 70-80.
3. For a more extensive discussion of demand curve estimation problems and approaches, see Mark Alpert, "Demand Curve Estimation and Psychological Pricing," in *Managerial Analysis in Marketing*, Frederick D. Sturdivant et al. (Glenview, Ill.: Scott, Foresman & Co., 1970), Chap. 10.
4. Philip Kotler, "Marketing During Periods of Shortage," *Journal of Marketing*, Vol. 38 (July 1974), pp. 20-29.
5. See Chester Wasson, *Product Management* (St. Charles, Ill.: Challenge Books, 1971), for a thorough treatment of pricing over the product life cycle.
6. "A Reducing Diet for Inventories," *Business Week*, August 3, 1974.
7. "Is There a 'Best Way' to Tell Distributors of Price Hike?" *Industrial Marketing*, June 1967, pp. 27-32.
8. See Alfred Oxenfeldt, "A Decision-Making Structure for Price Decisions," *Journal of Marketing*, Vol. 37 (January 1973), pp. 48-49, for an excellent discussion of this problem.

31 PROFITABILITY ANALYSIS BY MARKET SEGMENTS

Leland L. Beik
Professor of Marketing
Pennsylvania State University

Stephen L. Buzby
Assistant Professor of Accounting
University of Indiana

Costing by market segments may result in better planning of expenditures and more control of costs. This approach is based on a contribution approach to cost accounting.

By tracing sales revenues to market segments and relating these revenues to marketing costs, the marketing manager can improve and control his decision making with respect to the firm's profit objective.

First expressed by Smith in 1956, the concept of market segmentation has since been elaborated in many different ways.[1] It has recently been defined by Kotler as ". . . the subdividing of a market into homogeneous subsets of customers, where any subset may conceivably be selected as a market target to be reached with a distinct marketing mix."[2] The underlying logic is based on the assumption that:

> . . . the market for a product is made up of customers who differ either in their own characteristics or in the nature of their environment in such a way that some aspect of their demand for the product in question also differs. The strategy of market segmen-

From Leland L. Beik and Stephen L. Buzby, "Profitability Analysis by Market Segments," Journal of Marketing (July 1973), pp. 48-53. Reprinted by permission of Journal of Marketing.

tation involves the tailoring of the firm's product and/or marketing program to these differences. By modifying either of these, the firm is attempting to increase profits by converting a market with heterogeneous demand characteristics into a set of markets that although they differ from one another, are internally more homogeneous than before.[3]

The concept of market segmentation may be used for strategic alignment of the firm's productive capacities with its existing and potential markets. By analyzing market needs and the firm's ability to serve those needs, the basic long-run policies of the firm can be developed. Through choice of target segments, competition may be minimized; through selective cultivation, the firm's competitive posture may be greatly improved.

For both strategic and tactical decisions, marketing managers may profit by knowing the impact of the marketing mix upon the target segments at which marketing efforts are aimed. If the programs are to be responsive to environmental change, a monitoring system is needed to locate problems and guide adjustments in marketing decisions. Tracing the profitability of segments permits improved pricing, selling, advertising, channel, and product management decisions. The success of marketing policies and programs may be appraised by a dollar and cents measure of profitability by segment.

Managerial accounting techniques have dealt with the profitability of products, territories, and some customer classes; but a literature search has revealed not one serious attempt to assess the relative profitability of market segments.[4] Although the term "segment" has a history of use in accounting, this use implies a segment of the business rather than a special partitioning of consumers or industrial users for marketing analysis. Even when classifying customers, accounting classes are formed by frequency and size of order, location, credit rating, and other factors, most of which are related to controlling internal costs or to assessing financial profit.[5]

After indicating the value for marketing decision making, this article will delineate a framework for cost accounting by market segments. An industrial product example is constructed to demonstrate the process and to spell out the features of the contribution approach to cost accounting as applied to accounting for segment profitability. Further discussion extends the concept to a consumer situation and specifies difficulties that may attend full-scale application of the technique. The expectation is that the technique will better control marketing costs and improve marketing decisions.

MARKET SEGMENTATION AND ITS UTILITY

To have value for managerial judgments, Bell notes that market segments should: (1) be readily identified and measured, (2) contain adequate potential, (3) demonstrate effective demand, (4) be economically accessible, and (5) react uniquely to marketing effort.[6] For present purposes, the key criterion for choosing the bases for segmenting a given market is the ability to trace sales and costs to the segments defined. Allocating sales and costs is the most stringent requirement and limitation of profitability accounting as used to support marketing decisions.

Among the many possible bases for market segmentation, the analysis can be accomplished using widely recognized geographic, demographic, and socioeconomic variables.[7] Many of these, such as geographic units and population or income figures, provide known universe classifications against which to compare company sales and cost performance. Other bases of segmentation such as buyer usage rate, expected benefits, or psychological or sociological characteristics of consumers typically require research to match their distribution, directly or indirectly, with company sales and costs.

Given proper segmentation, separate products (or channels or other elements of the marketing mix) can serve as the primary basis for cost and revenue allocation. Knowledge of profit by segments then contributes directly to decisions concerning the product line and adjustment of sales, advertising, and other decision variables. The process is illustrated in the following industrial example.

A matrix system can be developed as part of

marketing planning to partition segments for profitability analysis.[8] A company with lines of computers, calculators, and adding machines might first divide its market into territories as in the upper section of Figure 1. The cell representing adding machines in the eastern market might next be sorted by product items and customer classes. The chief product preference of each company class is noted by an important benefit segmentation within the cells of the lower section of Figure 1.

Since the segments react differently to product variations and other marketing activities, it is advantageous to isolate profit by product for each market segment. Using this information, the marketing manager can specifically tailor product policies to particular market segments and judge the reaction of segments to increased or decreased marketing efforts over time. Decision adjustments and control of marketing costs interact to improve product line management directly and other decisions indirectly.

In theory, segment profitability analysis is worthwhile only where decisions adjusting the marketing mix add incremental profits that exceed the costs of the extra analysis. In practice,

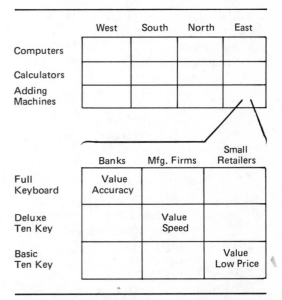

Figure 1. Matrix Breakdown by Products and Segments.

information concerning the profitability of marketing decisions has been so sparse that the analysis is likely to be profitable where allocations to market segments are approximate and fail to approach theoretical perfection.

MARKETING COST ANALYSIS

In its simplest form, marketing cost analysis relates the cost of marketing activities to sales revenues in order to measure profits. A profit and loss statement must be constructed for any marketing component (e.g., product, channel) being analyzed. The approach consists of dividing the firm's basic costs (e.g., salaries, rent) into their functional categories (e.g., selling, advertising). The functional category amounts are then assigned within the appropriate marketing classifications.

The actual form of the profit and loss statements will depend upon the nature of the company being analyzed, the purpose of the marketing analysis, and the records available. The form of statement will also depend upon the accounting technique used to assign costs to the marketing components under study. One might use a full-cost approach, assigning both direct and indirect costs across the marketing classifications on the best available bases. Alternatively, one might use a direct-cost approach and assing direct costs only, avoiding arbitrary assignment of fixed or overhead costs. Most marketing sources have utilized the full- and direct-cost approaches.

A third costing approach is better suited to the needs of the marketing manager and the requirements of analysis by market segments. Essentially, it is an adaptation of the contribution approach to preparing financial statements.[9] Table 1 presents a simplified illustration of how

Table 1. Product Productivity Analysis—Contribution Approach.

	Company Total	Full Keyboard	Deluxe Ten Key	Basic Ten Key
Net Sales	$10,000	$5,000	$3,000	$2,000
Variable Manufacturing Costs	5,100	2,500	1,375	1,225
Mfg. Contribution	$ 4,900	$2,500	$1,625	$ 775
Marketing Costs				
Variable:				
Sales Commissions	450	225	135	90
Variable Contribution	$ 4,450	$2,275	$1,490	$ 685
Assignable:				
Salaries—Salesmen	1,600	770	630	200
Salary—Marketing Manager	100	50	25	25
Product Advertising	1,000	670	200	130
Total	$ 2,700	$1,490	$ 855	$ 355
Product Contribution	$ 1,750	$ 785	$ 635	$ 330
Nonassignable				
Institutional Advertising	150			
Marketing Contribution	$ 1,600			
Fixed-joint Costs				
General Administration	300			
Manufacturing	900			
Total	$ 1,200			
Net Profits	$ 400			

the contribution approach can be adapted to break out product profitability for adding machines in the eastern market.

First, all of the variable nonmarketing costs have been assigned to products. These costs represent nonmarketing dollar expenditures which fluctuate, in total, directly in proportion to short-run changes in the sales volume of a given product. Similarly, variable marketing costs have been deducted to produce variable product contribution margins identical to those which would result from a direct costing approach.

The remaining marketing costs have been broken down into two categories—assignable and nonassignable. The assignable costs represent dollar expenditures of a fixed or discretionary nature for which reasonably valid bases exist for allocating them to specific products. For example, the assignment of salesmen's salaries in Table 1 might be based on Sevin's recommendation to use "selling time devoted to each product, as shown by special sales-call reports or special studies."[10] The marketing manager's salary could be assigned on the basis of personal records indicating the amount of time devoted to the management of each product. Product advertising would be assigned by reference to the actual amount spent on advertising each product.

The use of the actual dollar level of sales was purposely avoided in choosing the allocation bases for the assignable costs in Table 1. Horngren, among others, has stated that when dealing with fixed or discretionary costs, "The costs of efforts are independent of the results actually obtained, in the sense that the costs are programmed by management, not determined by sales."[11]

The nonassignable marketing costs represent dollar expenditures of a fixed or discretionary nature for which there are no valid bases for assignment to products. Consequently, institutional advertising has not been assigned to the products to avoid confounding the product profitability margins which would result from the arbitrary allocation of this cost. Since the primary purpose is calculating marketing related product contribution margins, the remaining nonmarketing costs can be taken as a deduction from the total marketing contribution margin to produce a net profit figure for the firm.

Although the preceding example was purposely simplified, the framework is sufficiently flexible to handle different objectives and more complex problems. If the firm in Table 1 were a single product firm, for example, the three customer classes (banks, manufacturers, and retailers) could easily be substituted for primary emphasis in place of the products. The analysis would differ only through variations in the treatment of fixed, variable, and assignable costs required by the new objective. That assignability changes with objective may be illustrated by the fact that product advertising costs can often be assigned to products but rarely to customer classes.

To aid in handling more complex problems, a discussion of common bases for assigning a wide range of marketing costs may be found in Sevin.[12] In some instances, the approach can be further improved by application of mathematical programming to assign costs to the marketing components.[13] Budgetary data and marketing lags could also be introduced to upgrade the analysis.[14]

COSTING BY SEGMENTS

In particular, the framework of the contribution approach may be applied to costing by segments. Table 2 extends the product analysis of Table 1. Recall that the segments are partitioned by territorial, customer class, and product benefit criteria although the primary customer class names are used to identify segments in the table. Instead of tracing the sales of each product to all three customer classes, one simplifying device is to identify the primary benefit sought by a customer class as segment sales and to combine sales of the given product to the other customer classes as nonsegment sales. For example, sales of the full-keyboard adding machine to banks become segment sales, while sales to large manufacturing firms or to retailers are nonsegment sales. This device is appropriate where nontarget sales are expected to be minimal; otherwise more columns can be added to the table.

Where sales revenues can be traced directly to customers, customer classes, and territories and where marketing costs can be similarly traced, the analysis is straightforward. Where the less tangible benefit segmentation is used, sales analysis or marketing research must measure the degree to

Table 2. Segment Productivity Analysis—Contribution Approach.

	Company Total	Full Keyboard		Deluxe 10-Key		Basic 10-Key Retail Seg.
		Bank Seg.	Nonseg.	Mfg. Seg.	Nonseg.	
Net Sales	$10,000	$3,750	$1,250	$2,550	$450	$2,000
Variable Manufacturing Costs	5,100	1,875	625	1,169	206	1,225
Mfg. Contribution	$ 4,900	$1,875	$ 625	$1,381	$244	$ 775
Marketing Costs						
Variable:						
Sales Commissions	450	169	56	115	20	90
Variable Contribution	$ 4,450	$1,706	$ 569	$1,266	$224	$ 685
Assignable						
Salaries—Salesmen	1,600	630	140	420	210	200
Salary—Marketing Manager	100	38	12	19	6	25
Product Advertising	1,000	670	-0-	200	-0-	130
Total	$ 2,700	$1,338	$ 152	$ 639	$216	$ 355
Segment Contribution	$ 1,750	$ 368	$ 417	$ 627	$ 8	$ 330
Nonassignable						
Institutional Advertising	150					
Marketing Contribution	$ 1,600					
Fixed-joint Costs						
General Administration	300					
Manufacturing	900					
Total	$ 1,200					
Net Profits	$ 400					

which benefits are related to each customer class. If sales analysis shows that banks purchase 75% of the full-keyboard sales because they value accuracy while manufacturers and retailers account for the remaining 25%, both revenues and sales commissions may be prorated accordingly. This allocation is employed in Table 2.

To illustrate a few marketing implications, it might be noted that over one-half of the full-keyboard profit contribution actually comes from nonsegment sales rather than from the primary target segment. The nonsegment profitability results in part from low personal selling and absence of advertising costs. An opportunity possibly exists in further promotion, perhaps to large manufacturing firms. Had the table completed the analysis for purchases of full-keyboard machines by manufacturers and retailers, the actual segment of opportunity could be pinpointed. If institutional

or other possible sales proved substantial during further classification, a new segment of opportunity might be identified.

Quite obviously, the eastern banking segment has a low profit contribution considering the level of marketing effort expended. Table 2 deals with one sample area and product class, and a comparison with other area banking segments might prove enlightening. Perhaps marketing costs could be reduced in the eastern segment if sales were up to par. Or if sales were comparatively low, marketing effort (price, personal selling, advertising) could be reallocated to meet competition more effectively.

Similar analysis can be applied to the manufacturing and retailing segments of Table 2, and to the territories and products not incorporated in the present illustration. The advantage over standard sales analysis is that a profit rather than a volume measure is applied and that variations in marketing costs and sales response are taken into account.

MARKETING PRODUCTIVITY: CONSUMER SEGMENTS

The previous example has been simplified so that minimum tables serve to explain the technique. Segment analysis becomes complex as more than two or three criteria are used for partitioning and as additional criteria are considered for different classes of marketing decisions. A further example adds realism and extends the concept to a consumer situation.

A company that sells snowmobiles is likely to have some special channel problems. To control channel management, meteorological data permit primary and secondary snow belts to be mapped across the U.S. and Canada. Sales analysis or research could show how to allocate purchases among consumers in major metropolitan, city, town, and rural areas. Further analysis could determine patronage among department stores, automotive dealers, farm equipment dealers, marinas, and other classes of outlets. Sales to resorts for rentals might be included as a segment or analyzed separately. Finally, the several analyses could map sales into geographical units. Segmenting by snow conditions, population density, outlets patronized, and dwelling area and then allocating revenues and costs to the segments would point outlet selection and channel adjustments toward the more profitable outlets in favorable population and snow-belt locations.

By collecting and analyzing warranty card information, snowmobile purchasers could be classified as to family life cycle, social status, or other variables. This data would probe the profit potential of appealing to young families, selected social classes, or possibly even to hunters, sailing enthusiasts, and other outdoors people. Dates on the warranty cards would help adjust the timing of promotions in advance of the snow season or to balance the pre-Christmas advertising in line with purchase habits of its customer segments. Having targeted promotion on the basis of past data, current warranty card information, and revenue and cost information, the profitability of each target segment could be determined.

Analyzing the profitability of advertising or price decisions involves special problems in tracing sales and costs. If segments have been defined on tangible bases, say area and dealer patronage, the difficulty might be overcome by setting up an experiment.[15] Variations of advertising messages, local media, and possibly price would serve as treatments in segments matched to control other variables. Recording segment revenues and treatment costs would constitute a profit measure of selected advertising and/or price decisions. Experiments may thus be used with segment cost analysis to plan corporate marketing programs.

MANAGERIAL IMPLICATIONS

Given responsible means of partitioning market segments, major elements of the marketing mix may be segregated for analysis using the contribution approach to cost accounting. An example has been employed to show how segment profitability can be measured for items in a product line thereby contributing directly to product management decisions. By analyzing the profit and loss statements for the costs of other marketing efforts, additional adjustments can be made in other decisions such as personal selling and advertising. A further example has indicated how channel and other marketing management problems can be similarly gauged by a profit measure for a consumer product and consumer segments.

Several major problems have to be met in applying costing techniques to market segments. One difficulty is choosing productive bases for segmentation, and limiting analysis to a manageable number of bases is another. Although some bases are obvious from experience, they remain product specific, and criteria for choice are not fully developed. Another major problem is obtaining data for the less tangible modes of segmentation, particularly data that permit assignment of sales revenues and costs in accord with each base used for segment definition.

Recognizing and solving problems, however, often leads to further improvements. For example, many of the behavioral applications to marketing imply use in segment analysis but are difficult to relate to other marketing variables on any basis other than judgment. As limitations of source data are overcome, profit accounting by segments may add to the marketing utility of behavioral advances.

Costing by market segments promises improvement in marketing efficiency by way of better planning of expenditures and control of costs. Upon documenting reasons for today's soaring marketing costs, Weiss comments over and over that marketing costs are resistant to sophisticated cost analysis and that marketing cost controls are inadequate in modern corporations.[16] Although not calculated to stem such pressures as inflation, cost accounting by market segments can control selling, advertising, packaging, and other marketing costs in relation to profit potentials. Perhaps even greater value stems from the potential ability to fine-tune product offerings and other marketing decisions to the requirements of well-defined consumer segments. As part of the material regularly supplied to marketing managers, market segment profitability analysis could easily become a key component of marketing information systems of the future.

Notes

1. Wendell R. Smith, "Product Differentiation and Market Segmentation as Alternative Marketing Strategies," *Journal of Marketing*, Vol. 21 (July 1956), pp. 3-8; and James F. Engel, Henry F. Fiorillo, and Murray A. Cayley, eds., *Market Segmentation: Concepts and Applications* (New York: Holt, Rinehart and Winston, Inc., 1972).
2. Philip Kotler, *Marketing Management*, Second Edition (Englewood Cliffs, New Jersey: Prentice-Hall, Inc., 1972), p. 166.
3. Ronald E. Frank, "Market Segmentation Research: Findings and Implications," in *Applications of the Sciences in Marketing Management*, Frank M. Bass, Charles W. King, and Edgar A. Pessemier, eds. (New York: John Wiley & Sons, Inc., 1968), p. 39.
4. Closest to the present analysis and perhaps the best summary of the state of the art is Charles H. Sevin, *Marketing Productivity Analysis* (New York: McGraw-Hill Book Company, 1965).
5. Robert B. Miner, "Distribution Costs," in *Marketing Handbook*, Albert W. Frey, ed. (New York: The Ronald Press Company, 1965); see especially pp. 23·17 and 23·32.
6. Martin L. Bell, *Marketing: Concepts and Strategy*, Second Edition (Boston: Houghton Mifflin Company, 1972), p. 185.
7. See William M. Weilbacher, "Standard Classification of Consumer Characteristics," *Journal of Marketing*, Vol. 31 (January 1967), p. 27.
8. See William J. E. Crissy and Robert M. Kaplan, "Matrix Models for Marketing Planning," *MSU Business Topics*, Vol. 11 (Summer 1963), p. 48. The matrix "targeting" treatment is also familiar to readers of basic marketing texts by E. J. McCarthy or G. D. Downing.
9. See Charles R. Horngren, *Cost Accounting: A Managerial Emphasis*, 2nd ed. (Englewood Cliffs, New Jersey: Prentice-Hall, Inc., 1967); and Ralph L. Day and Peter D. Bennett, "Should Salesmen's Compensation be Geared to Profits?" *Journal of Marketing*, Vol. 26 (October 1962), pp. 6-9.
10. Same reference as footnote 4, p. 13.
11. Same reference as footnote 9, p. 381.
12. Same reference as footnote 4, chapter 2.
13. William J. Baumol and Charles H. Sevin, "Marketing Costs and Mathematical Programming," in *Management Information: A Quantitative Accent*, Thomas Williams and Charles Griffin, eds. (Homewood, Illinois: Richard D. Irwin, Inc., 1967), pp. 176-190.
14. Richard A. Feder, "How to Measure Marketing Performance," in *Readings in Cost Accounting, Budgeting, and Control*, 3rd ed., W. Thomas Jr., ed. (Cincinnati, Ohio: South-Western Publishing Co., 1968), pp. 650-668.
15. Same reference as footnote 4, chapters 6, 7, and 8.
16. E. B. Weiss, "Pooled Marketing: Antidote for Soaring Marketing Costs," *Advertising Age*, Vol. 43 (November 13, 1972), pp. 63-64.

5 INSIGHTS INTO: THE CHALLENGE TO MARKETING

The previous sections of this book have probed the importance of marketing in our society, and how marketers work.

Underlying many of the concepts already presented is the belief that marketing is more than selling goods. It can be a system of communication, maintain the coauthors of the first article in this section, that can guide the overall practices of the firm. What happens when this system breaks down is covered in the second article.

The final article comprises no less than a forecast of the future of the world. We believe it is of interest to our readers because every marketing man is, in a sense, a futurist.

32 MANAGING WITH THE CONSUMER'S HELP

Betsy D. Gelb
Assistant Professor of Marketing
University of Houston

Gabriel M. Gelb
Certified Management Consultant
Gelb Marketing Research

Ricky W. Griffin
Instructor in Organizational Behavior
University of Houston

Market-focused management calls for the customer, not the chairman of the board, to be placed at the top of the organizational chart. This model also affects such areas as public policy and organizational goals.

From Betsy D. Gelb, Gabriel M. Gelb, and Ricky W. Griffin, "Managing with the Consumer's Help," Business Horizons *(April 1976), pp. 69-74. Reprinted by permission of* Business Horizons.

What would happen to an organization if its board of directors or chairman or president disappeared? Nothing necessarily fatal. What would happen to the organization if its customers disappeared? Most organizations would answer: "Disaster." The power lies not with the organization's supposed power structure, but with its customers.

The realistic manager may well conclude that the customer belongs figuratively at the top of the organizational chart, and literally should be a prime source of direction for managerial decisions. This conclusion, which can be called market-focused management, attempts to unify organizational policies by recognizing who really controls the survival of the firm.

Is this reasoning a rehash of the familiar marketing concept, that marketing decisions ought to flow from customer needs as customers perceive them? No, it can be more: the marketing concept goes exactly half way. It says that marketing decisions on pricing, promotion strategies, distribution channels and product features should recognize consumer sovereignty. But it says nothing about *management* decisions on planning, staffing, implementing and controlling.

One result of the marketing concept is an organizational mismatch of two "bosses." On one hand, the customer is in charge when marketing decisions are made. For instance, if industrial customers choose to buy a product from a knowledgeable sales representative who can adjust credit and billing procedures, then that's the marketing mix; the firms selling to those buyers spend the marketing budget on sales reps and credit extensions. A marketing manager may believe that he controls the department's budget, but his authority is limited by customer preferences. His sales eventually drop to zero if he ignores the customer's position as the ultimate decision maker.

On the other hand, a second group of decision makers often determines how much will be spent on pollution control, how many sales representatives will be women, how long they will be trained and how much of their pay will reflect commissions. These decisions exemplify management functions of public policy or personnel or government relations. No customers or potential customers direct them as a matter of course. These decisions are instead left exclusively to the organization's owners (or in a publicly held company to their elected representative on the board of directors), and to the management they hire. Laws and government agencies place constraints on decision making, of course, but these restrictions are as likely to spring from the preference of an industry trade association as they are from the preferences of buyers.

Not surprisingly, activities attuned to the customer-oriented marketing concept can be severely diluted by this division of sovereignty. But if managers acted as though the organization chart showed the customer on top, then both marketing and other management decisions would be made with the same set of bosses in mind.

THE CUSTOMER ON TOP

Marketing-focused management is a philosophy that attempts to unify the direction of organizational decision making by utilizing customer viewpoints in all management areas. Market-focused management can be illustrated by examining the actual power relationships of a steel company. A large amount of power over a steel company rests with its major customers, automobile companies, construction firms and other large buyers of steel. But power over these customers lies, in turn, with groupings of auto buyers, or the potential major tenants of the office buildings under construction. These tenants are dependent on their customers—one step up the ladder. Looking at the world this way, managers in a steel company would be ultimately subject to the will of a tremendous number of individuals whom they now virtually ignore, unless these individuals happen to be stockholders as well as automobile buyers.

In general, these buyers are particularly ignored when policies are set. Customers' needs and preferences may be considered in marketing decision making because they would otherwise be lost to competition. But customers do not appear to be shopping for the company with the most acceptable policies on resource depletion, environmental protection or employee retirement. Thus, it requires some sophistication for managers to recognize that such policies project company image, which in turn influences individual buying decisions.

The market-focused management approach builds on what has been advocated by writers and consultants in marketing. Mack Hanan has supported the structuring of organizations around their markets, noting with approval that "IBM's data-processing operations are segmented organizationally according to key markets, such as . . . hospitals and retail establishments like supermarkets." Xerox is another firm which fits Hanan's pattern. He points out that its Information Systems Group, which sells copiers and duplicators, "has converted from geographic selling to vertical selling by industry."[1]

Similarly, Benson Shapiro has spoken out for managing "the customer, not just the sales force." He suggests that when superhuman efforts must be directed at the sales force to move a particular product out of the warehouse, the problem actually lies with a customer farther along the channel: retailers or consumers who have not been consulted about the marketing mix of product, price, promotion or distribution.[2]

Further support comes from William Davidson's writing in the retailing area. Davidson sees the manufacturer at the top of the channel and the consumer at the bottom, but then notes that "in the long run, the nature of channels is determined from the 'bottom up' rather than from the 'top down.'"[3] Turning Davidson's idea upside down is the whole market-focused management idea.

Customer Relations Training

To see how the idea works, one area to examine is training of personnel who meet customers. Recently, one of the authors was asked to develop a customer relations training module for field engineers of an industrial company. "We will train 150 young engineers next year in our learning center," said the training director. "They sometimes get into trouble at the customer's location and we need to sensitize them to the gamut of interpersonal problems."

A proposal was then written that started by identifying the specific problems, and then setting up an educational sequence to identify the psychological principles involved with case histories, followed by role-playing by the trainees. First, interviews with customers were proposed, to learn how the field engineers interacted with them.

The training director told the consultant that management was pleased with the reality-anchored approach. "But," he added, "my boss (the personnel director) wants to know why you have to interview any customers. He says our people can tell you all about our customer relations problems." The consultant cheerfully collected the personnel director's list, then persuaded him to let the customers speak for themselves in telephone interviews. As a result, the list of possible problem areas rose from three to fifteen, and the training process differed dramatically from what the internal boss would have proposed.

Market-focused management may also be used in merger decisions. By recognizing that all corporations are ultimately funded by the purchases of their customers, this approach offers a way to measure a proposed acquisition. For example, if a company is thinking of acquiring a new product line or another company, the traditional yardstick is its addition to the company's earnings based on "projection of past data" or "industry-wide experience." As has been proven time and time again, this is an illusory measurement. There are no additional earnings unless the new function or company adds value to customer satisfaction, and to the extent that customers are willing to pay for it. Only if the end result is more satisfied customers will the acquisition mean a better deal for the company.

Workers as Buyers

Public policy decisions affecting unemployment, minimum wage and similar considerations are another area in which a market focus applies, because the customer population ultimately includes the employee population. In the case of the steel company discussed earlier, its workers buy cars, and also buy the products which enable office building tenants to prosper. Therefore, steel company employees indirectly support their own firm. The recognition of customer sovereignty leads to recognition of worker sovereignty: workers are the buyers whose power—and dollars—activate the system.

Any organization that has opposed public policies which "put dollars in workers' pockets at corporate expense" now should realize that support of such proposals will help it to survive. Even an industrial marketer depends in the long run upon mass consumption, and employees are those masses.

It's Already Here

All of this may sound like anarchy. The implications boggle the mind: customers on the board of directors, workers involved in goal setting, buyers dictating organizational priorities. It may be soothing to realize that all these things are already happening in many successful organizations. A company evaluating the shift to a four-day week, for instance, considers the potential problems if customers cannot reach key people on Mondays or Fridays. A multinational firm planning to promote a promising foreign national to vice-president anticipates enthusiastic reaction from customers abroad, even though the individual's responsibilities will include little direct customer contact. A local school committee deposits funds in several banks, although centralizing them would be simpler, so it will not antagonize anybody. Payroll checks take precedence over any payment to creditors, in a realistic assessment of employee reaction if the checks were late.

Furthermore, industrial democracy, or worker involvement with company management, is already part of the industrial scene in several European countries. One American observer, Jaroslav Vanek of Cornell University's Center for International Studies, calls self-management a viable option for U.S. industry. In self-management, voting shares are transferred from the company's stockholders to its workers. The employees establish working conditions, hours, their own salaries and even company policy. Vanek says, "In a small company, decisions can be made by consensus or by direct vote. In larger organizations, it may be necessary to elect workers' councils, like we elect representatives to Congress."[4]

Consumer Views and Management Wisdom

In fairness, it must be noted that putting the customer on top does not eliminate divided leadership; customers, of course, vary greatly. Their degree of sophistication in economics is one example. Some understand that a business must earn a certain level of profit; and that as the price of raw materials increases, so must the price of the final product. Further, these customers understand that stock-outs may be the result of decisions to hold down inventory costs, and thus prices. The market-focused manager making decisions for this type of customer is similar to many business leaders today. All that is required is his verification that consumer beliefs, feelings and expectations match his own.

By contrast, other customers expect perfection and sometimes are unhappy with that. This group desires low prices which will never be increased. They expect lifetime guarantees, top quality and performance, and magnificent service facilities. These customers expect to find every product on the shelf in all sizes, colors, styles and flavors. Faced with this consumer, the market-focused manager will probably throw up his hands in despair.

Obviously these two groups of customers are extremes. A realistic approach to market-focused management must assume a certain level of rationality on the part of most constituents.

Decentralization is an issue on which customers will have different views that will have to be weighed along with conventional management wisdom on the subject. Convention appears to favor decentralization for reasons ranging from improving decision timeliness to reduction of red tape. However, consumer viewpoints may add the following considerations.

> Decentralization is perceived as an aid in the development of managers. The consumer might favor this approach on the assumption that better management means lower costs and lower prices.

> Decisions in a decentralized organization can be made at a lower level, perhaps at a branch plant or office. The individual making the decision is closer to the consumer and better prepared to meet the customer's needs.

> More managers must now be trained for higher-level decision making, and this suggests expensive training programs.

> Decentralization may result in a duplication of service throughout the company. This drawback may increase costs, and therefore raise prices, in contrast to the assumptions stated earlier.

The issue may boil down to a simple comparison of benefits versus costs for the most rational consumers. They are not the whole consumer population, however. Others may see additional benefits. Decentralization may enable a firm to contribute more money to local charitable organizations, previously a decision made on the national level by the central authority. And the community may feel it has gained prestige because now a division manager, not just a plant manager, lives there.

GETTING STARTED

Organizations which are considering market-focused management must understand that implementation is a gradual process. First, the organization should already be practicing the marketing concept of consumer direction for decisions that are obviously consumer-related; packaging, for example. Some industries have yet to reach this point: A *Sales Management* study reported in 1970 that consumer wanted ingredients included on over-the-counter drug labels, but today they are still either missing or printed in miniscule type.

Many companies which have not shown excessive interest in the marketing concept have actually moved in a similar direction under differently perceived pressures. Because of consumerism and its legal implications, a number of companies have set up consumer affairs advisors at varying levels of the hierarchy.

Shell Oil Company has combined its retail and commercial advertising, credit card merchandising, consumer affairs and marketing research functions into a newly established consumer relations department. It is not unreasonable to expect that the manager of this department has a primary allegiance to consumer relations, as the former manager did to the advertising field.

Consumer Research

The next step for organizations already responding to consumer guidance of their marketing effort is the expansion of consumer research to encompass the kinds of policy issues it probably now ignores. Clearly, the techniques of marketing research and opinion research can also offer customer input to all areas of organizational policy making. Customer feedback should influence not just conventional marketing activities, but all of the organization's activities. These may include promotion to influence the price of its stock, corporate reaction to political contributions by employees, the firm's labor relations, or the archi-

tecture of its office buildings. Customers have opinions on all these matters, and the organization has the means to discover what they are. These customer attitudes can form the basis for setting priorities if the organization wants to respond to customer preferences.

One major petrochemical company, for example, has retitled its market research group "opinion research." Instead of focusing on consumers and dealers, the opinion research expertise now extends to the seeking of communities receptive to refinery construction. Similarly, opinion research efforts should provide support for public and governmental relations programs, and logically, could then move into providing assistance to a much broader range of corporate activity.

For example, staff reports on future profit centers should consider both the economic impact and reactions throughout the company to the proposal. The shutdown of distribution centers or regional offices may be interpreted as a sign that the company is not growing, and may lead to lowered morale, and, perhaps, subsequent resignations of key personnel.

In a former era, a company thinking of relocating an important plant would make a straight financial decision. Today, that decision is more complex. Once the staff person studying this issue reports back to management that there are two new locations possible, management may decide to consult two key groups: the employees and major customers of the plant. The company's research director may then survey a sample of customers and employees on a direct basis, asking their views on the issue.

Another more subtle and less disruptive approach would be to conduct the opinion research on an indirect basis, calling in an outside consultant who will gather data without revealing the nature of the issue under consideration. The consultant can ascertain the problems and advantages of the present plant's location and help employees and customers explore several alternatives, only one of which is a change in location.

Whatever the research method, the gathering of information from those most affected, outside of management, will certainly lead to a better decision by management. It can also reduce the opposition after the decision is announced.

Table 1. Standards for Evaluation Set by Market-Focused Management.

Industry	Department	Prior Measurement	New Measurement
Bank	Security	Dollars lost to robbery	Percent of customers who rate security force as "exceptionally courteous"
Airline	Scheduling	Percent of time planes are in the air	Percent of flights scheduled within thirty minutes of a time reqested by customers
University	Placement Office	Percent of graduates placed within thirty days	Percent of graduates who rate placement service as "helpful"
Industrial equipment	Production	Cost savings	Percent of potential customers who specify our brand in bid requests
Automobiles	Finish/paint specifications	Number of years before 5% of paint chips off	Number of compliments on new car received in one month by average buyer
Milk cartons	Quality	Percent of cartons that leak before shipping from dairy	Percent of cartons that leak before consumer has used up milk
Coal	Mining	Number of tons/day	Decrease in number of complaints to EPA about mining operations

What are the practical consequences of market-focused management? One basic result is a reevaluation of criteria for performance measurement; as shown in Table 1, previous standards may shift for workers in a wide range of jobs. Certainly there will be economic costs associated with the new requirements, but whether benefits outweigh these costs depends upon the customer. If a bank's management has accurately judged that its customer expects friendliness from a security guard, not just safety, then new screening and training expenses will flow back through increased deposits.

Market-focused management is proposed for an era in which private enterprise is under severe scrutiny. Its implementation can produce an immediate return in customer patronage, but that is not its only impact. As the public becomes aware of its crucial role in any business organiza-tion, it may move from an adversary posture toward business into a more realistic stance of responsibility commensurate with its power.

Notes

1. Mack Hanan, "Reorganize Your Company around Its Markets," *Harvard Business Review* (November-December 1974), p. 63.
2. Benson P. Shapiro, "Manage the Customer, Not Just the Sales Force," *Harvard Business Review* (September-October 1974), pp. 127-136.
3. William Davidson, "Distribution Break-through," in *Plotting Marketing Strategy*, ed. Lee Adler (New York: Simon and Schuster, 1967), p. 283.
4. "Self-Management Called Key to Liberate Workingman," *Houston Chronicle*, 27 July 1975.

33
THE DIALOG THAT NEVER HAPPENS

Raymond A. Bauer
Professor of Business Administration
Harvard University

Stephen A. Greyser
Associate Professor
Harvard University

Businessmen and their critics have two different views of the consumer world. The authors stress how important it is that both sides understand why the two views exist and what can be done to resolve this crucial problem.

In recent years government and business spokesmen alike have advocated a "dialogue" between their two groups for the reduction of friction and the advancement of the general good. Yet, all too often, this is a dialogue that never happens. Rather, what passes for dialogue *in form* is often a sequence of monologues *in fact*, wherein each spokesman merely grants "equal time" to the other and pretends to listen while preparing his own next set of comments. Obviously, this is not always the case; and, if taken literally, it tends to minimize some real progress being made.

Our aim here is to try to facilitate and stimulate that progress by exploring what lies behind the dialogue that never happens and by suggesting what can be done—on both sides—to develop more meaningful and effective business-government interactions.

Authors' note: This article is based on a speech given by Professor Bauer to the 1967 National Conference of the American Marketing Association in Toronto in June. We gratefully acknowledge the assistance of Robert D. Moran, Harvard Business School Doctoral Candidate, in the development of and research for the article.

In this context, we link "government spokesmen" with "critics." Naturally, not all in government are critics of business, and vice versa. However, almost all critics seek redress of their grievances via government action and seek government spokesmen to present their views "in behalf of the public."

Our primary focus will be in the field of marketing—particularly selling and advertising—which is perhaps the most controversial and most frequently criticized single zone of business. Marketing seems to be the area where achieving true dialogue is most difficult and where business and government spokesmen most seem to talk past each other.

Before examining why this takes place, let us look at two comments on advertising that illustrate the lack of dialogue. The first comment is that of Donald F. Turner, Assistant Attorney General in charge of the Antitrust Division of the Justice Department:

> There are three steps to informed choice: (1) the consumer must know the product exists; (2) the consumer must know how the product performs; and (3) he must know how it performs compared to other products. If advertising only performs step one and appeals on other than a performance basis, informed choice cannot be made.[1]

The other comment is that of Charles L. Gould, Publisher, the San Francisco *Examiner:*

> No government agency, no do-gooders in private life can possibly have as much interest in pleasing the consuming public as do . . . successful companies. For, in our economy, their lives literally depend on keeping their customers happy.[2]

DOUBLE ENTENDRES

Why do business and government spokesmen talk past each other in discussing ostensibly the same marketplace? We think it is because each has a basically different model of the consumer world in which marketing operates. This misunderstanding grows from different perceptions about a number of key words.

The first word is *competition.* The critics of

business think of competition tacitly as strictly price differentiation. Modern businessmen, however, as marketing experts frequently point out, think of competition primarily in terms of product differentiation, sometimes via physical product developments and sometimes via promotional themes. The important thing is that price competition plays a relatively minor role in today's marketplace.

Some of the perplexity between these two views of competition has to do with confusion over a second word, *product*. In the critic's view, a product is the notion of some entity which has a primary identifiable function only. For example, an automobile is a device for transporting bodies, animate or inanimate; it ordinarily has four wheels and a driver, and is powered by gasoline. There are variants on this formula (three-wheeled automobiles) which are legitimate, provided the variants serve the same function. Intuitively the businessman knows there is something wrong with this notion of the product because the product's secondary function may be his major means of providing differentiation (an auto's looks, horsepower, and so on).

Then there is the term *consumer needs*, which the business critic sees as corresponding to a product's primary function—for example, needs for transportation, nutrition, recreation (presumably for health purposes), and other things. The businessman, on the other hand, sees needs as virtually *any* consumer lever he can use to differentiate his product.

Next, there is the notion of *rationality*. The critic, with a fixed notion of "needs" and "product," sees any decision that results in an efficient matching of product to needs as rational. The businessman, taking no set position on what a person's needs should be, contends that any decision the customer makes to serve his own perceived self-interest is rational.

The last addition to our pro tem vocabulary is *information*. The critic fits information neatly into his view that a rational decision is one which matches product function and consumer needs, rather circularly defined as the individual's requirement for the function the product serves. Any information that serves that need is "good" information. To the businessman, information is basically any data or argument that will (truth-

fully) put forth the attractiveness of a product in the context of the consumer's own buying criteria.

Exhibit I summarizes our views of these two different models of the consumer world. We realize that we may have presented a somewhat exaggerated dichotomy. But we think the models are best demonstrated by this delineation of the pure views of contrasting positions, recognizing that both sides modify them to some extent.

VIEWS OF HUMAN NATURE

A review of our "vocabulary with a double meaning" and the two models of the consumer world shows that the critic's view is based on a conviction that he knows what "should be." In contrast, the businessman's view is based on militant agnosticism with regard to "good" or "bad" value judgments which might be made (by anyone) about individual marketplace transactions.

The businessman's view of human nature may be the more flattering, perhaps excessively so. Certainly, the marketer's notion of "consumer sovereignty" compliments the consumer in attributing to him the capacity to decide what he needs and to make his choice competently even under exceedingly complex circumstances. It also sometimes challenges him to do so. This perhaps undeserved flattery glosses over some obvious flaws in the market mechanism. It is rooted in the belief that this mechanism, even though imperfect in specific instances, is better than administrative procedures for regulating the market.

The critic takes a far less optimistic view of human nature—both the consumer's and the seller's. He thinks that the seller often (sometimes intentionally) confuses consumers with a welter of one-sided argumentation. Such information, in the critic's eye, not only lacks impartiality, but usually focuses on secondary product functions and is not geared to consumer needs.

Both sets of assumptions are, we think, at least partially justified. Customers do have limited information and limited capacity to process it. This is the way of the world. Furthermore, there is no reason to believe that every seller has every customer's interest as his own primary concern in every transaction, even though in the long

Key Words	Critic's View	Businessman's view
Competition	Price competition.	Product differentiation.
Product	Primary function only.	Differentiation through secondary function.
Consumer needs	Correspond point-for-point to primary functions.	Any customer desire on which the product can be differentiated.
Rationality	Efficient matching of product to customer needs.	Any customer decision that serves the customer's own perceived self-interest.
Information	Any data that facilitate the fit of a product's proper function with the customer's needs.	Any data that will (truthfully) put forth the attractiveness of the product in the eyes of the customer.

Exhibit I. Two different models of the consumer world.

run it probably is in the seller's own best interest to serve every customer well.

All of this disagreement comes to focus on a point where both business and government are in agreement; namely, modern products are sufficiently complex that the individual consumer is in a rather poor position to judge their merits quickly and easily. The businessman says that the customer should be, and often is, guided in his judgment by knowledge of brand reputation and manufacturer integrity, both of which are enhanced by advertising. The critic argues that the customer should be, but too seldom is, aided by impartial information sources primarily evaluating product attributes.

These conflicting views of vocabulary and human nature are reflected in several specific topic areas.

BRANDS AND RATING SERVICES

One of these areas is the relationship of national branding to consumer rating services, the latter being a traditional source of "impartial information" for consumers. Somehow the crux of this relationship seems to have escaped most people's attention: consumer rating services are possible *only because of* the existence of a limited number of brands for a given product. In order for a rating to be meaningful, two conditions are necessary:

1.   *Identifiability*—the consumer must be able to recognize the products and brands rated.

2.   *Uniformity*—manufacturers must habitually produce products of sufficiently uniform quality that consumer and rating service alike can learn enough from a sample of the product to say or think something meaningful about another sample of the same product which may be bought in some other part of the country at some later time. This is a seldom-realized aspect of national branding.

It is generally assumed by both groups that the "consumer movement" is basically opposed to heavily advertised branded goods. The stereotype of *Consumer Reports* is that it regularly aims at shunting trade away from national brands to Sears, to Montgomery Ward, or to minor brands. Yet the one study made of this issue showed that, contrary to the stereotype, *Consumer Reports* had consistently given higher ratings to the heavily advertised national brands than to their competitors.[3]

Ideological Blindness What we have here is an instance of the consumer movement and brand-name manufacturers being ideologically blinded by different models of the market world. The consumer movement concentrates on the notion of a product having a definable primary function that should take precedence over virtually all other attributes of the product. True, some concessions have recently been made to aesthetics. But, on the whole, the consumer movement is suspicious of the marketing world that strives to sell products on the basis of secondary attributes which the consumer movement itself regards with a jaundiced eye.

The evidence available to the consumer movement is that, in general, national advertising is *not* accompanied by poorer performance on primary criteria. But the consumer movement fails to realize that it *takes for granted* the central claim for advertised branded products—namely, that by being identifiable and uniform in quality, they offer the customer an opportunity to make his choice on the basis of his confidence in a particular manufacturer.

But the manufacturers of nationally branded products and their spokesmen have been equally blind. First of all, we know of none who has pointed out the extent to which any form of consumer rating must be based on the identifiability and uniformity of branded products. The only situation where this does not apply is when the rating service can instruct the consumer in how to evaluate the product—for example, looking for marbelizing in beef. However, this is limited to products of such a nature that the customer can, with but little help, evaluate them for himself; it cannot apply to products for which he has to rely on the technical services of an independent evaluator or on the reputation of the manufacturer.

Moreover, except for such big-ticket items as automobiles, consumer rating services usually test products only once in several years. In other words, they rate not only a *sample* of a manufacturer's products, but also a sample of his performance *over time.* Thus, if one "follows the ratings" and buys an air conditioner or a toaster this year, he may buy it on the rating of a product made one, two, or three years ago. Similarly, if one buys a new automobile, he depends in part on the repair record (reported by at least one rating service) for previous models of that brand.

In large part, then, consumer rating services are devices for rating *manufacturers!* This is not to say they do not rate specific products. Sometimes they even draw fine distinctions between different models from the same company. But in the course of rating products, they also rate manufacturers. What more could the manufacturer ask for? Is this not what he claims he strives for?

Basic Dichotomy   More to the point, what is it that has kept the consumer movement and

brand-name manufacturers from paying attention to this area of shared overlapping interests? Neither will quarrel with the exposure either of factual deception or of product weaknesses on dimensions that both agree are essential to the product. This is not where the problem is. The problem is that the manufacturer *sells* one thing and the rating service *rates* another.

The concept of a "product" that dominates the thinking of rating services and the thought processes of those who suggest more "impartial evaluation information" for consumers (e.g., Donald Turner of the Department of Justice and Congressman Benjamin Rosenthal of New York) is that a product is an entity with a single, primary, specifiable function—or, in the case of some products such as food, perhaps a limited number of functions, e.g., being nutritious, tasty, and visually appealing. The specific goal of many proposed ratings—with their emphasis on the physical and technical characteristics of products—is to free the customer from the influence of many needs to which the marketer addresses himself, most particularly the desire for ego-enhancement, social acceptance, and status.

The marketer, oddly enough, tends to accept a little of the critic's view of what a product is. Marketing texts, too, speak of primary and secondary functions of a product as though it were self-evident that the aesthetic ego-gratifying, and status-enhancing aspects of the product were hung on as an afterthought. If this is true, why are Grecian vases preserved to be admired for their beauty? And why did nations of yore pass sumptuary laws to prevent people from wearing clothes inappropriate to their status?

We shall shortly explore what may lie behind this confusion about the nature of products. First, however, let us examine another topical area in which similar confusion exists.

"Materialist Society"

The selling function in business is regularly evaluated by social commentators in relationship to the circumstance that ours is a "materialist society." We could say we do not understand what people are talking about when they refer to a materialist society, beyond the fact that our society does possess a lot of material goods. But, in point of fact, we think *they* do not understand what they are talking about. Let us elucidate.

At first hearing, one might conclude that criticism of a materialist society is a criticism of the extent to which people spend their resources of time, energy, and wealth on the acquisition of material things. One of the notions that gets expressed is that people should be more interested in pursuing nonmaterial goals.

The perplexing matter is, however, that the criticism becomes strongest on the circumstance that people *do* pursue nonmaterial goals—such as ego enhancement, psychic security, social status, and so on—but use material goods as a means of achieving them. Perhaps the distinctive feature of our society is the extent to which *material* goods are used to attain *nonmaterial* goals.

Now there are many ways in which societies satisfy such needs. For example, there are ways of attaining status that do not involve material goods of any substance. Most societies grant status to warriors and other heroes, to wise men who have served the society, and so on. Often the external manifestation of this status is rigidly prescribed and involves signs whose material worth is insignificant: a hero wears a medal, a ribbon in his lapel, or a certain type of headdress, or he may be addressed by an honorific title.

However, in societies that value economic performance, it is not uncommon for material goods to be used as status symbols. Indians of the Southwest, for example, favor sheep as a symbol even to the extent of overtaxing the grazing lands and lowering the economic status of the tribe. As a practical matter, this might be more damaging to the welfare of the Navaho than is the damage that many low-income Negroes do to their own individual welfares when, as research shows, they insist on serving a premium-priced brand of Scotch.

Many of the things about which there is complaint are not self-evidently bad. Art collecting is generally considered a "good thing." But take the worst instance of a person who neurotically seeks self-assurance by buying art objects. Clinically, one might argue that he would do himself a lot more long-run good with psychotherapy even though, when one considers the resale value of the art objects, he may have taken the more economical course of action. Similarly, it is not self-evident

that the promotion of toiletries to the youth as a symbol of transition to manhood is inherently cruel—unless the commercials are especially bad! It is clear, however, that there is no societal consensus that the transition to manhood should be symbolized by the use of toiletries.

What seems to be the nub of the criticism of our society as a materialist one is that simultaneously a great number of nonmaterial goals are served by material goods, and there is no consensus that this should be so. Behind this is our old friend (or enemy): the concept of a product as serving solely a primary function. In the perspective of history and of other societies, this is a rather peculiar notion. Who in a primitive society would contend that a canoe paddle should not be carved artistically, or that a chief should not have a more elaborate paddle than a commoner?

Much of the confusion over the words on our list seems to be a residue of the early age of mass production. The production engineer, faced with the task of devising ways to turn out standardized products at low cost, had to ask himself, "What are the irreducible elements of this product?" This was probably best epitomized in Henry Ford's concept of the automobile, and his comment that people could have any color they wanted so long as it was black. Clearly, Ford thought it was immoral even to nourish the thought that a product ought to look good, let alone that it should serve various psychic and social functions.

But all this was closely related to the mass producer's effort to find the irreducible essence of what he manufactured. This effort broke up the natural organic integrity of products, which, at almost all times in all societies, have served multiple functions.

Many writers have called attention to the fact that in recent times our society has passed from the period of simpleminded mass production to that of product differentiation on attributes beyond the irreducible primary function. As yet, however, we do not think there is adequate appreciation of the impact of the residue of the early period of mass production on thinking about what a product is. In that period even very complex products were converted into commodities. Since each performed essentially the same primary function, the chief means of competiton was pricing.

Products as Commodities

At this point, we shall argue that the thinking of those who criticize the selling function is based on a model for the marketing of commodities. This factor does not exhaust the criticisms, but we believe it is at the core of present misunderstandings over the concepts on which we have focused our discussion.

On the one hand, to the extent that products are commodities, it is possible to specify the function or functions which all products in that category should serve. It follows that a person who buys and uses such a commodity for some purpose other than for what it was intended has indeed done something odd, although perhaps useful to him (for example, baseball catchers who use foam-rubber "falsies" to pad their mitts). In any event, it is possible both to specify the basis on which the commodity should be evaluated and the information a person is entitled to have in order to judge that product. A person searching for a commodity ought first to find out whether it serves this function and then to ask its price.

On the other hand, to the extent that products are *not* commodities, it is impossible to expect that price competition will necessarily be the main basis of competition. Likewise, it is impossible to specify what information is needed or what constitutes rational behavior. Is it rational for a person to buy toothpaste because its advertiser claims it has "sex appeal"? Presumably people would rather look at clean than dingy teeth, and presumably people also like to have sex appeal—at least up to the point where it gets to be a hazard or a nuisance.

But it does not follow, insofar as we can see, that ratings—or grade labeling—should discourage product differentiation or the promotion of products on a noncommodity basis. If the consumer were assured that all products in a given rating category performed their primary functions about equally well, could it not be argued that those attributes which differentiate the products on other functions would then become increasingly interesting and important? Or, to be more specific, what makes it possible for "instant-on" TV tuning to be promoted—other than a presumed agreement, by both manufacturer and consumers, that the TV set performs its primary function little better or worse than its competition?

This is a facet of competition not appreciated by the opponents of grade-labeling, who have argued that it would reduce competition. Perhaps it would be more helpful if the opponents of grade labeling first gathered some evidence on what has actually happened to competition in countries where grade labeling has been introduced. (The head of one major relevant trade association recently told one of us that he knew of no such research.)

Toward More Information

Readers will note that we have indulged in considerable speculation in this article. But most of the issues on which we have speculated are researchable. Relatively little, for example, is really known about how businesses actually see themselves carrying out "the practice of competition," or even about the actual competitive mechanisms of setting prices. Furthermore, in all of this, there is no mention of the *consumer's* view of these various concepts or of his model of the marketing process. To be sure, we can be reasonably certain of some things. For example, we know that consumers do regard products as serving needs beyond the bare essentials. Yet it would be helpful to know far more about their views of the overall marketing process.

What we propose as a worthwhile endeavor is an independent assessment of the consumer's view of the marketing process, focusing on information needs from his point of view. Thus, rather than businessmen lamenting the critics' proposals for product-rating systems and the critics bemoaning what seem to be obvious abuses of marketing tools, both sides ought to move toward proposing an information system for the consumer that takes into account *his* needs and *his* information-handling capacities while still adhering to the realities of the marketing process.

For those who have the reading habit, it will be obvious that this proposal is but an extension of the conclusions reached by members of the American Marketing Association's Task Force on "Basic Problems in Marketing" for the improvement of relations between marketing and government.[4] In brief, along with suggested studies on the influence of government policies and programs on corporate marketing decisions, a special study was recommended in the area of consumer-buyer decision making and behavior:

> It is of the highest importance to investigate the impacts of the host of governmental regulations, facilities, aids, and interventions upon the quality and efficiency of consumer-buyer decision making.[5]

The report went on to state that, particularly in light of the generally recognized drift from *caveat emptor* toward *caveat venditor*, "abundant basic research opportunities and needs exist" in the area of government impact and consumer-buyer behavior.

What Can Businessmen Do?

Certainly there is a crying need for more information and, as we have tried to illustrate, for fresh analytic thinking on almost all of the issues on which government and business are butting heads. We have elaborated on the different models of how the marketplace does, and should, work because we think their existence explains the largest part of why marketers and their critics often talk past each other, even when they have the best intentions of engaging in a dialogue. The other part is explained by the relative absence of facts. As we have noted, the consumer's view of the market-advertising process and his informational needs represent an important (and relatively unprobed) research area.

Returning to the "dialogue," we should add a further problem beyond that of business and government spokesmen talking past one another. Inasmuch as many on both sides see themselves as representing their colleagues' views, partisanship becomes mixed with the aforementioned misunderstanding. Since such partisanship is likely to address itself to stereotyped views of "the other side," the comments become irrelevant. That many well-qualified first-hand commentators are regarded as self-serving by their critics is a point aptly made by Denis Thomas. Equally apt is his corrolary observation that those "who view business . . . from a suitably hygienic distance lose no marks for partiality even if their facts are wrong."[6]

How then can effective interactions take place? Obviously, the key parts will be played by:

1. Thoughtful business and government leaders.
2. Marketers and their critics who take the time to consider and to understand (even if they do not agree with) each others' premises and assumptions.
3. Those who engage in meaningful dialogue oriented to fact finding rather than fault finding.
4. Those on both sides who address themselves to solving the problems of the real, rather than the presumed, public.

These constructive parts are not easy to play, but there are many who are trying, and succeeding, as these three examples illustrate:

The Department of Commerce has taken a series of measures, including the formation of a National Marketing Committee, to play a positive "activist" role in business-government relations; marketers are involved in what goes on rather than, as has occurred in many previous government situations, being informed after the fact.

William Colihan, Executive Vice President of Young & Rubicam, Inc., proposed at the University of Missouri's Freedom of Information Conference that marketing undertake a major consumer education job to "make the marketing system benefit the nonaffluent, the undereducated."[7] This 20 per cent of adult consumers represents, he feels, both a public responsibility and a marketing opportunity.

John N. Milne of Toronto's MacLaren Advertising Company Limited spelled out 11 specific major economic, social, ethical, and communications research projects to provide a "factual basis for an objective assessment of advertising, to replace emotional pleas." Business, government, universities, and projects in other nations would serve as sources and beneficiaries of data "so that advertising's usefulness to all segments of society can be assessed and improved."[8]

Beyond the parts played by thoughtful business and government people, we see a distinctive role for schools of business in bringing about meaningful interaction. Business schools are a unique resource both in their understanding of the business system and in their capability to conduct relevant research. Other faculties, at least equally competent and objective in research, generally do not have the depth of understanding of why things are the way they are—a necessary precursor to relevant study. We hasten to add that grasping how something *does* operate implies no consent that this is how it *should* operate, now or in the future.

Both in research and as participants (or moderators) in dialogue, business school faculties can play a significant role.

Business and government should sponsor the necessary research. The particular need for business is to recognize that the era of exclusively partisan pleading must end. In our judgment, the American Association of Advertising Agencies' sponsorship of research on consumer reactions to advertising and advertisements is a splendid model.[9] The findings are by no means exclusively favorable to advertising. But they make more clear where problems do, and do not, lie. And academic "insurance" of the objective conduct of the research and presentation of findings should bring about a degree of governmental acceptance and set the standard for any subsequent research.

We can use more of this, and more of it is beginning to take place. A dialogue is always most profitable when the parties have something to talk about.

Notes

1. Statement made at the Ninth Annual American Federation of Advertising Conference on Governmental Relations held in Washington, D.C., February 1967.
2. Ibid.
3. Eugene R. Beem and John S. Ewing. "Business Appraises Consumer Testing Agencies," HBR, March-April 1954, pp. 113-126, especially p. 121.
4. See E. T. Grether and Robert J. Holloway, "Impact of Government upon the Market System," *Journal of Marketing*, April 1967, pp. 1-5; and Seymour Banks, "Commentary on 'Impact of Government upon the Market System,' " ibid., pp. 5-7.
5. Grether and Holloway, ibid., p. 5.
6. *The Visible Persuaders* (London, Hutchinson & Co., 1967), p. 11.
7. *Freedom of Information in the Market Place* (FOI Center, Columbus, Missouri, 1967), pp. 140-148.
8. Speech given at the Annual Conference of the Federation of Canadian Advertising and Sales Clubs, Montreal, June 1967.
9. For a description of the research and a review of the major results, see Stephen A. Greyser, editor, *The AAAA Study on Consumer Judgment of Advertising—An Analysis of the Principal Findings* (New York, American Association of Advertising Agencies, 1965), and Opinion Research Corporation, *The AAAA Study on Consumer Judgment of Advertising* (Princeton, 1965); the findings and their interpretation are the subject of the authors' forthcoming book, *Advertising in America: The Consumer View* (Boston, Division of Research, Harvard Business School, on press).

34
A WORLD TURNING POINT— AND A BETTER PROSPECT FOR THE FUTURE

Herman Kahn
Founding Director
The Hudson Institute

William Brown
Research Staff
The Hudson Institute

Despite its many problems, the world now enjoys a higher standard of living and its future is bright, say two researchers at a noted policy analysis center. In this article, they explain the reasons for their optimism.

The 1975-1985 decade now appears destined —in certain ways—to mark one of the most important turning points in world history. The world's population is estimated with reasonable accuracy to grow about 2% a year while the gross world product, which is more difficult to assess, seems to have increased on the average about 5% a year since 1950. This means that the GWP per capita grows at a rate of about 3% a year. If these rates were to continue, world population would double every 35 years, gross world product in 14 years, and GWP per capita in 23. But all three growth rates, on the average, already have or soon are likely to start a more or less slow but long-term

From Herman Kahn and William Brown, "A World Turning Point, and A Better Prospect for the Future," The Futurist (December 1975), pp. 284-334. Reprinted by permission of The Futurist.

decline, peaking almost certainly by 1990 if not before. Their postulated decline is basically separate from the current recession. In fact, the rate of increase of GWP and GWP/capita will probably make a full recovery from the current recession, perhaps even increasing before entering a long-term decline.

If this decline actually occurs, then the scholars and publicists who have extrapolated trends on the basis of recent all-time high rates will have suggested incorrect expectations about the world's future and the underlying mechanisms at work. The popular metaphor of explosive or exponential growth will become increasingly misleading the longer is the range of the projection under study.

Undoubtedly many readers have found persuasive many current arguments which claim that the world cannot sustain recent growth rates because many mineral resources would rapidly approach exhaustion while pollutants increase to levels which would deteriorate our lungs, dim our vision, poison our water, and cause irreparable structural or climate damage. Even if the above tragedies were not likely to occur, would not the very complexity and rapidity associated with this unrelenting exponential growth overwhelm our capacity for adjustment? Would not the implied international independence increasingly demand a world government, a development which seems clearly unlikely in the absence of war or major calamity, and which may not even be desirable? What about problems associated with the increasing income gaps both within and between countries which so many believe will soon lead to high levels of violence?

What about changing priorities among our values and even changes in the values themselves? Of all the ways to express these fashionable problems, changing priorities and values appear to be the most relevant, in a casual sense, to the more or less gradual decrease in average growth rates which we should expect and, initially, changing priorities probably will be more important than changing values. This kind of preference is manifested, for example, when death rates decrease. Children are thus less needed to provide security for old age. Furthermore, the expense and difficulty of raising children are greater, especially if there is urbanization and/or the supply of domestic help decreases in developed countries. All this tends to make larger numbers of children a less welcome choice, even if the basic values have not changed. And these tend to change also, if a bit later.

It should be pointed out that, at least in the short and medium run, direct government programs intended to reduce population growth rates are remarkably ineffective, especially when compared to "spontaneous" corrective measures which arise out of the basic trends, which in turn affect first the changing priorities and then the changing values. About the only exception is government programs which disseminate family planning information. These are very likely to be more important than exhortations for public cooperation or other official policies which try to restrain population growth rates. We believe that the restraint of population growth is very likely to occur, but mostly for a variety of personal reasons, not because of lurid imaginative descriptions of future starvation, resource limitation, and pollution, or the actual occurrence of these events. Moreover, the pace of change will be determined by these individual decisions and on the whole will not be hurried, unless the basic trends are hurried.

We have heard much recently about exponential growth, especially from those who contend that such growth, or perhaps any growth, cannot be tolerated much longer. Yet it is little more than a commonplace observation that few growth curves in nature can be exponential or "geometric" for very long; rather they tend instead to follow the so-called "logistic" or (slightly mislabeled) 'S' shape. It is at the unique inflection point of any such an 'S' curve that a continuously increasing rate of growth changes to a continuously decreasing rate of growth. Such curves have been forecast by the U.N. as well as at the Hudson Institute and others, and provide, we believe, a reasonable representation of future trends in world population.

These changes in population growth rates are basically self-evident and, if correct, illustrate quite dramatically the special character of today's issues and the dramatic change likely to occur in the very near future. The Hudson Institute's analysis concludes that world population growth is more uncertain than the U.N. projections would

indicate. But in either case the point is the same: we expect within this decade or so to enter a new phase of history, one with declining rates of growth, first for world population and then GWP.

We have suggested that dramatic reduction of population growth rates will result not from physical limitations but from changing priorities and, later, changing values which occur as a consequence of the intensification of such long-term trends as urbanization, literacy, affluence, personal and national safety, birth control technology, and family planning programs. Under current conditions in most countries, growing world-wide affluence and *embourgeoisement* tend to encourage smaller families. Although these trends are strongest in affluent societies, they are evident to some extent almost everywhere. In each of the advanced societies—Western and Eastern Europe, the Soviet Union, Japan, North America, Australia, and New Zealand—as the bulk of the population became healthier, more industrialized, and wealthier, the birthrate dropped substantially. All of these countries seem to be rapidly approaching population equilibrium; that is, the age specific birthrates of various age cohorts are such that, if continued, they would gradually lead to zero or negative population growth in the next fifty years or so.

Furthermore, many members of the upper middle class in these countries are beginning to lose their taste for economic growth. Just as this bellwether group led the movement toward fewer children, it is not unlikely that their values will be encompassed by the rest of the population when they reach similar levels of affluence or soon thereafter. In general, as affluence becomes more customary or normal, an increase in affluence often seems less desirable, at least if it requires sacrificing other desires (e.g., the children of affluent people today tend to choose more leisure and travel over greater savings and increased effort at work).

To put this matter into yet another perspective, we believe that mankind is now moving into an historic period with unusual economic prospects. For the past 10,000 years most people have lived or subsisted at a very low material standard—roughly between $50 and $300 per capita—approximately equivalent to those of Indonesia or China today. In this dawning phase of a new era, a new plateau of relative material abundance can be predicted as the common lot of mankind: within the next century current U.S. and European standards could become almost a world norm in underdeveloped countries, give or take a factor or two.

We at the Hudson Institute are well aware that such a prospect for mankind directly contradicts most current projections which have, on the basis of differing postulates, "calculated" severe resource shortages and growing environmental horrors. Serious though some of these concerns certainly are, the plausible and, we believe, realistic scenarios that have been studied at the Institute suggest overall optimism about the chances for a better future for the world, at least materialistically. Our analysis leads to projections which tend to focus upon a world population leveling out near the end of the 21st century at about 10 to 28 billion people, with an average per capita from $10,000 to $20,000 derived from a GWP of $100 to $300 trillion. Such figures are of course rough estimates for futures without enormous calamities (such as large scale nuclear warfare); they do not encompass the full range of the serious possibilities. That is, we attempt to bracket the reasonably possible but relatively unlikely (which would increase the uncertainty in the range of expected results, perhaps 2 to 10 times).

Of course, no iron law of history ordains that growth rates must start to decline before we reach 1980 or 1990 or that we will be able to deal competently with some of the very real problems of growth which remain when the rates are declining. Any reading of the future must be based on the evidence of the past and present and on as careful an analysis of likely future problems and issues as can be made. From such studies we have concluded that beyond this decade the world will rarely, if ever, witness economic growth rates as high as those experienced during the first seventy-five years of this century, except as small or sporadic deviations from a gradual trend toward increased comfort and abundance, unless there are some key basic changes from current trends. There probably will be many tragedies of supply and adjustment and other problems, but all of them seem resolvable eventually or tolerable when seen in historic perspective, at least as judged by likely *middle class criteria* or proven by the actual course of events. Indeed, it seems likely that 21st century history will find, ironically, that our generation became most concerned about exponential growth just when this growth began losing its explosive character through natural processes and the gradual adjustment to a new, unprecedented abundance had just begun.

Specifically, what are some of the principal points of contention that are of such concern that many citizens now choose or claim to cast their choice for zero or much reduced growth? The list would certainly include the physical problems related to environmental pollution, food, energy, and non-renewable metal resources. Let us consider each in turn.

ENVIRONMENTAL COMPROMISES FORESEEN

It may be realized in only a few quarters today that the great surge in the worldwide environmental movement of the sixties has produced much more than a new national conscience about environmental quality. This new conscience has combined with normal processes leading to increased quality of life to achieve a major victory in Japan, North America, and Northwest Europe, and to a lesser but quite significant degree in most of the other affluent nations of the world and even in some of the less affluent ones. The victory may not yet be completely apparent because it is still in process. And in some of the less affluent nations it may quite properly be delayed somewhat or even partially reversed, at least until the costs in slower economic development become acceptable. Even in the three most dedicated areas —Japan, North America, and Northwest Europe— it may take from five to ten years before the full impact of recent trends to environmental cleanliness is clearly seen by most observers.

This period will not, however, be one of repose. There will be a constant battle between the more militant environmentalists and those who feel the financial "oppression" of the clamor for rapid solutions, especially those expenses for retrofitting existing installations to rectify past "carelessness" or for "too early" adoption of costly and unreliable interim environmental technologies. Generally, however, the majority will opt for compromise, protection of the environment where it is practical and useful, encouragement of economic growth when it is most productive and the environment is believed less important (e.g., oil from Alaska). The battles will be fought continually and openly with many "setbacks," as there will be thousands of specific skirmishes (progress in the Trans-Alaska Pipeline, continental offshore oil drilling, and perhaps some strip mining of coal will be called setbacks by some, victories or reasonable compromises by others). Generally the "victories" will be won by the moderate majority who are willing to pay reasonable costs, both directly and indirectly, to achieve clean air and clean water without carrying a policy to an extreme. In particular they will tolerate a small amount of aesthetic and environmental damage in some areas where such damage is justified for economic stability or further growth, as long as most populated or recreational areas are steadily improved and enlarged. Their environmental objective is not that of *zero* damage or *no* change but to improve the overall quality of life by reasonable standards, including economic stability and economic growth where feasible.

It is important to realize that most of the conflict will not be over life and death issues, but over aesthetic and quality of life issues, and often about relatively marginal matters. All will agree the environment cannot everywhere be left completely in its original pristine purity if the nation is to operate normally. A house, a motor, a factory, a port, or an oil well—all disturb the environment, all create some pollution. The problem we will always face is one of where and how much. How much environmental disturbance shall we allow in the future and for how long? How much shall we correct the abuses of the past and how soon? In making the determination and the later redeterminations of these compromises, we can expect a continuing struggle between the opposing forces. Only the fanatics will feel a personal defeat or a defeat for mankind each time a power plant is built, an oil tract leased, or a pipeline built. The majority will gradually learn that new power plants are cleaner and safer than ever before, that oil can be found with new protection against danger of spillage, and that pipelines can be built with only temporary scarring over small areas. This is indeed progress, progress for which the environmentalists who fought the early battles

deserve much credit. But a full victory will require a decade or more, an interval which will seem an eternity to the fanatic, until it is completed.

Let us remember the major gains already achieved in Pittsburgh and London, where choking emanations no longer offend the senses. Or the cleaning up of the Willamette River and the improving aquatic life in Lake Erie, which was sometimes written off in the last decade. But the Hudson River and the Thames River now have many species of fish in them which have not been seen for decades. Who but fanatics would question the profound impact which the expenditure of $200-$300 billion during the next decade in the U.S. will have on pollutants from motor vehicles, industries, urban waste, and farms? Many mistakes and setbacks will certainly occur. But 10 or 15 years from now, almost certainly by the year 2000, it is very likely that we will look back with great pride on our accomplishments. We will breathe the clean air, drink directly from the rivers, and smile with pleasure at the aesthetic landscape, undoubtedly while we haggle over whether or when some of the restrictions should be changed by another 5%. In any reasonable historical perspective, that outcome will be termed a clear win for environmental protection and improvement which will be obvious to all except the extremists.

At the moment, the more extreme environmentalists seem to have an unusually great influence, although one which probably has recently diminished. For example, during the November 1974 elections, voters defeated two California referendums, one for a mass transit system and one to prevent dams on wild and scenic rivers. A reasonable guess, barring unexpected environmental or economic surprises, is that during the next several years the political balance will move toward decisions which give greater weight to the economic impact of environmental protection. Part of the motivation would arise from the strains of the current stagflation and energy issues, and part from the growing realization that the costs for immediate and total implementation appear to be much larger than those previously estimated and publicized (e.g., by the Council on Environmental Quality). Consequently, over the next few years, we expect to see greater leniency toward requests for stretching out compliance with some of the more difficult or costly changes (e.g., auto exhausts, sulfur dioxide removal, thermal effluents), although such a stretch-out would not change our conclusion that within a decade the overall environment will experience profound improvements in quality.

It should be noted that such congressional actions as forcing some relatively arbitrary deadlines and decisions on the automobile industry were not a bad strategy to get action started. If the legislators had tried to be more reasonable from the very beginning, the resultant stretch-outs and compromises would have almost unquestionably been excessive. It was only by creating arbitrary and artificial deadlines and changes in the rules (that may result in inflicting more or less unjust punishment on various industries and groups) that it became possible to get the programs moving as rapidly as they have. At this point, however, we should remember that these deadlines and changes in the rules were arbitrary and artificial. At the present time relatively minor compromises often have extraordinary economic effects and slow down the total environmental program relatively little.

It might, with respect to political decisions, be reasonable for policymakers to envisage three major categories in the relationship between environmental control and land use. One would be that the most protected regions such as special wilderness areas, including mountains, national parks, lakes, and deserts, would by common consent be kept in a state of nearly pristine purity and in which any noticeable polluting activity would be forbidden or severely controlled. The second category would involve the areas in which people spend most of their time, the residential, industrial, commercial, and farming districts. This category is the one in which the major struggle to define an optimum environment would be part of the political scene for at least the next decade. The third category would be defined as one in which "junkpiles" of one kind or another, for economic of technological reasons, can be tolerated for greater or lesser periods of time. For example, strip mining operations until the land is restored; oil fields until they are depleted; pipelines or transmission lines until they are obsolete.

Indeed, in some cases there may never be

complete or satisfactory restoration. With respect to this third category, we would encourage the current trend: to set legal standards to assure that any major disturbances which are not self-healing would be restored, if practical, more or less gradually and in reasonable consonance with the economics of the local situation. The time periods involved could vary from months to decades, but rarely centuries. It may be particularly galling for a neo-Malthusian or an environmental extremist to accept this third category as necessary. Yet we would assert that it is a normal and necessary consequence of any industrial society, past, present and future, and will remain so. The time requirements for restoration, however, or the degree thereof, may be appropriate subjects for continuing debates, but not the principle that this is a big country where certain limited areas are expendable.

In retrospect, to return to a previous example, it seems strange that the environmental movement fought with such tremendous vehemence against the Trans-Alaska pipeline. How could they have failed to notice the fact that this venture, one of such obviously great economic impact, required the use of only about 15 square miles of very remote land out of a total of more than 600,000 square miles, or much less than .01% of the Alaskan area, located in regions so remote that, except for the workers, it could be seen only by a few of the most adventurous tourists? Moreover, it can be argued that for most tourists it would constitute an impressive and even desirable sight. Furthermore, once the pipeline was properly designed, its impact on wildlife could hardly be anything but negligible, or possibly even of some small benefit, for example, as an occasional refuge from the arctic wind. But the main point we wish to emphasize is how easily the opposition to the Trans-Alaska pipeline avoids noticing that, during the pipeline's brief existence of perhaps a few decades, there would still be the remaining 599,985 square miles of Alaska wilderness to be admired in its undisturbed state? Why do they struggle so hard to concentrate upon the mere 15 square miles and, in advance, find the image is distasteful? How easily they ignore, even today, that the unfortunate delay in starting the pipeline has not only added billions to its original cost, but for about the next three years in addition to the last one, also will require the U.S. to pay about $5 billion annually to foreign producers for U.S. fuel requirements—the total bill in extra costs and foreign exchange will be in excess of $25 billion. The delay may thus make necessary some very unfortunate foreign policy compromises. Historicallly the 15 square miles may yet be placed near the pinnacle of the most costly bits of real estate in the world—$2 million per acre. We cannot avoid the thought that some of the environmentalists pressed as hard as they did in the Trans-Alaska pipeline case for an ulterior ideological motive of their own, that of blocking industrial growth with little attention given to economics.

Perhaps there are some lessons in this example that can set the stage for more reasonable decisions in the future. Consider the strip mining of coal which now seems to be urgently needed to achieve our goal of energy independence. Where the land and the environment can readily be restored to approximately their original condition, we would contend that there should be little argument about whether or not the strip mining should be approved. Where the restoration to the original condition is not feasible but a reasonably aesthetic substitution can be designed, then, again, it should not create much of a decision problem, perhaps a debate to choose which form of restoration would be most desirable. A more difficult case would be one, for example, in which a particularly arid climate prevents either a restoration to nearly original conditions or a pleasing alternative. When desirable re-landscaping appears impossible or uneconomic, under what circumstances might either a partial restoration or a less-than-desirable aesthetic substitute be acceptable? Such instances, if in fact they occur at all, would seem to be the ones over which any major environmental struggles properly should be fought. The eventual decisions, presumably, would result from a combination of (1) the effective arguments about the environmental consequences, (2) the importance of the project to the country, (3) the cost to the country of "expending" the area (i.e., we would like to emphasize that not all areas are worth "saving"), and (4) as always, the most political clout.

We are not asserting here that no subtle, complex, and difficult environmental issues will arise which will be terribly difficult to solve. We doubt very seriously that any will appear which cannot be solved if international cooperation is forthcoming. We are thinking here of such issues as reduction of the ozone layer, heating or cooling of the earth, and contamination of the seas. It should be noted that most of the environmental issues that are taken seriously can be handled by purely national programs; a few need regional programs; none really need a world government, though a few require worldwide programs. One of the reasons why we need affluence, industrial growth, and advanced technology is that without them it may be impossible to deal with many of these esoteric issues. For example, a poor country may feel it absolutely necessary to use DDT, while a richer country can use more expensive insecticides. Indeed, in the long run we will have to use various kinds of low pollution agriculture or other low pollution techniques to produce food. Whether it will be possible to do this will depend very much on the standard of living of the countries concerned. It wouldn't bother the developed world very much if the controlled environment or other low pollution agriculture resulted in grain prices of $300-$400 per ton, but this would be disastrous for the poor countries.

FOOD PROBLEMS CAN BE EASED

Food now is, for many millions, an issue not so much of quality of life at the margin, but serious economic deprivation, perhaps even hunger and starvation. The problem of food is basically economic: Who pays for it and with what predictability and reliability? But this does not make the short run problem any easier. Indeed, solutions to the problems of an adequate supply of food for every country of the growing world will not be easily found or, if found, may take longer and be less reliable than those for the "principal" pollution problems. This conclusion does not result from the lack of land, resources, technology, or capital, but mainly because of government policies, poor management, and, on occasion, just plain bad luck.

Aside from the general economic problem, the trouble seems to arise, especially among the

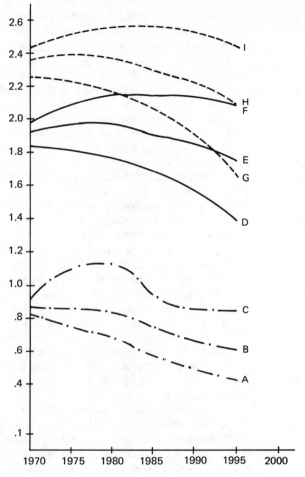

MORE DEVELOPED REGIONS (− : − · −)
A = LOW
B = MEDIUM
C = HIGH

WORLD (———)
D = LOW
E = MEDIUM
F = HIGH

LESS DEVELOPED REGIONS (− − − −)
G = LOW
H = MEDIUM
I = HIGH

Source: U.N. World Population Projections, 1973

Growth curves: a theoretical comparison. A steadily increasing growth rate eventually becomes "impossible" because the conditions necessary for growth disappear. For example, the growth rate of a population must eventually decline because all available food is used up. Demographers thinking about the future world population foresee several possibilities: the growth rate may level off as shown by the upper unbroken-line, or it may level off and abruptly decline as shown by the lower broken-line curve. This is a "population crash"—a phenomenon frequently reported in rodent and other animal populations, which may suddenly die off when the food supply is exhausted. Authors Kahn and Brown note that few growth curves can remain exponential for long; eventually the growth rate must decrease, and this will happen to the human population in the years ahead

Percent Annual Rate of Growth as Assessed in 1973 (But Based on Pre-1970 Data)

less developed countries (LDCs), from a combination of (a) cultures which have traditionally lived on the brink of starvation and tolerated some malnutrition; (b) the sporadic and haphazard nature of such natural calamities as drought, plant disease, insect plagues, frost, and excessive untimely rains; (c) the unfortunate rapid growth of population in some LDCs which have benefit-

ted from high leverage health care easily transmitted in the form of cheap medicines and
vaccines; and (d) the great political and technical
difficulties in transferring modern agricultural
technologies to some of the LDCs with large
population which need assistance the most,
countries which have resisted or which only very
slowly have been receptive to even relatively
obvious agricultural needs, such as increases in
irrigation and fertilizer use.

Yet many LDCs have made astonishing
progress (Mexico, Philippines, Brazil, Taiwan,
Korea). Also, there are increasing efforts to assist
those who still need help by furnishing aid through
technology, supplies, and equipment as well as by
direct shipments of grain after natural calamities.
For the least advantaged countries, we must hope
that a slowing of population growth, coupled with
the gradual infusion of improved agriculture,
eventually will result in abundance. Hopefully, the
combined efforts of all countries will produce a
sufficient supply to circumvent malnutrition or
starvation threats within the next few years and,
by the end of the century, an amount of progress
which would clearly point to improving nutrition
for all.

Almost nowhere on the Asian subcontinent,
where the great threats of inadequate food supplies
have existed and now exist, is there such a shortage of land or water that food production could
not be more than doubled with modern techniques.
India, the classic example, has as much arable land
as the United States, much greater ability for
multiple cropping, and a potentially bountiful
supply of water from Himalayan rivers, from
aquifers, and from monsoon rains. It is not beyond reason to expect that, if an effective approach to self-help could be devised, India could
become a food exporting country. But the effort
has to be made in India by Indians; the U.S. can
help, but not as much as is usually believed.
Actually, India did become self-sufficient in agriculture for a few years in the late sixties, during
which time the Indian government, perhaps because of unusually good weather and a premature
optimism about the expected harvests from the
green revolution, regrettably changed its policies
from an emphasis on agriculture to an emphasis
on industry.

Although it is currently popular to speak of
the *world* problem, it is nevertheless quite clear
that a severe problem exists only in certain countries, where shortages have occurred sporadically
if not chronically for centuries. Despite this fact,
it has recently become politically acceptable, or
even laudatory, to claim that the developed
countries, especially the United States, are the
cause of these problems, and even to accuse them
of having robbed the LDCs of their wealth over
the years. Yet the very countries in which the
bulk of the severe food shortages chronically
exists, the nations of South Asia, are those which
have for decades consistently received aid, often
in the form of massive food shipments, for which
they have seldom paid and are unlikely to do so.
A more valid charge that the South Asians could
reasonably level at the United States and other
developed countries is that some of our aid has
been *too effective*, in that it has removed formerly fatal diseases to such an extent that the
population growth rate has doubled in recent
years, in turn causing a rapid increase in the
demand for food. Of this offense the U.S. and
other developed countries unquestionably are
guilty, though strangely no accusers come forth.
And of course no one would now advocate the
ancient remedy to the burgeoning demand for
food, by recommending a return to poor health
and premature death.

It should be noticed and emphasized that
no particular food problem exists among most
LDCs, including the Asian communist countries,
barring an occasional temporary problem such as
a severe drought. Indeed, within the last few
decades the list of LDCs which regularly cope
reasonably well with their food needs has grown
far larger; it is now greater in population than
those which do not. The group of traditionist
countries which still have a questionable ability
to supply their own nutritional needs is composed
of the poorest third of the LDCs, by population.
Perhaps 85% of the 900 million people involved
are the South Asians of India, Bangladesh,
Pakistan, and neighboring small countries. Most
of the others are in sub-Saharan Africa and in
scattered regions of South and Central America.
Clearly the major problem to be solved is that of
helping the peoples of South Asia to become as
self-sufficient in food production as most other
developing nations. Unfortunately, this is not

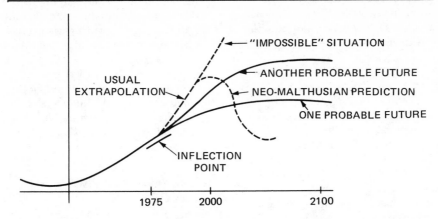

Both Hudson Institute and United Nations experts have suggested that the growth rate of the world's population will soon stop increasing and begin decreasing. The time when this happens will show on a graph as the "point of inflection," that is, the point where a growth curve shifts direction. Depending on how rapidly the change occurs, world population could vary between 10 and 20 billion by the year 2250, according to this projection.

too hopeful a counclusion because the desired results seem to depend upon appropriate and timely political changes in policy occurring within these countries. Yet the attempts to find an appropriate solution through national and international action, as well as through private efforts, generally are increasing.

For the balance of this century, the prognosis is quite favorable for two-thirds of humanity, those who live in these areas: the richest, the more dynamic, the "coping" countries, and Communist Asia, but quite ambiguous for the poorest third of the world. We cannot be confident that hunger and malnutrition will disappear. On the contrary, unhappily, much suffering and great problems are likely to be witnessed. Our assertion, however, is that these can be greatly mitigated and possibly solved by creating sensible programs within and outside the troubled areas. On the other hand, the suffering might be further aggravated through unwarranted beliefs that solutions through economics and technology are impossible, or by wide acceptance of the currently popular poetic image that Malthus is being resurrected and is coming to claim the long-awaited vindication of his prophecy.

None of the above discussion about food production has considered the more novel technical approaches to the future production of calories and proteins by advanced food factories. Some of the techniques now under development that could produce almost limitless amounts of edible, perhaps very palatable, foods include the conversion of cellulose by enzymes, of petroleum or petroleum wastes by the growth of single-cell high-protein organisms, and the intensive growth of plants in scientifically controlled pollution-free environments of various kinds that can offer annual yields from 10 to 100 times that available through conventional modern farming and yet use less inputs of water than current techniques. This last technique is unusually suitable for arid climates and has been commercially developed in several countries. Each new scientific advance in food production can be expected to be phased in more or less rapidly in accordance with its competitiveness and the growing demand, and to contribute its share to human abundance and eventually to general affluence. At a minimum, various food factories can be expected to be of great value in preventing future malnutrition.

With the 1974 World Food Conference in

Rome, the discussion of the potential for hunger and malnutrition in the world probably reached new heights. It left a widespread impression that such problems could be with us eternally. Perhaps they will. If so, this outcome seems more likely to occur if the no-growth segment of public opinion wins out over that of continued economic growth. Only the latter can substantially increase the world's wealth and technology, and wealth and technology are the major tangible assets which can overcome the threat of hunger. To develop this theme a bit further, let us consider, for example, a particular hypothetical world two hundred years from now, one which has, during that period, on average, increased its GNP/capita, at least for the less developed countries, at a modest rate of 2.3% annually, a rate quite small compared to many recent examples. The arithmetic is simple but compelling. On the average, each person in the LDCs would have an annual income 100 times greater than that of today. Even the poor will have become rich—by today's standards. The "untouchable" Indian could have by then an income equivalent to that of a middle class American today. But would there be enough food, we may still ask, if, after that two hundred years, the world population reached, say, 20 billion, about five times the current population? The answer to that question, we assert, is a simple yes!, if we are referring to what is economically and technically feasible. For example, it has been shown in *present* commercial practice that, by use of plastic greenhouse or other types of controlled-growth chambers, the annual production per acre of many edible plants can be increased from ten- to more than a hundred-fold, while requiring only minimum amounts of water and nutrients, due to very little waste. High yields occur in part because several crops annually may be scientifically grown in an optimum environment free of disease and pests! This approach is capital intensive, and even if it resulted in relatively high production costs, as much as $500 per ton of grain, or equivalent (an almost impossibly high figure), it would still be feasible for the wealthy world which we have visualized. About 15-20% of the average income could be spent for food at these high prices and at current American standards of consumption. This form of agriculture could reduce the required farm acreage to less than that in cultivation today,

freeing land for other useful purposes. Of course, this argument does not imply that this agricultural practice would be widely used in that rich hypothetical world of the future. But it does imply that if such a solution does *not* evolve, it is only because superior alternatives are adopted, resulting in better or cheaper nutrition, or both. In two hundred years, we would certainly expect to find solutions much better than those which can be adapted from today's technology.

ENERGY PROSPECTS: FAVORABLE

The problem of energy sufficiency in the world, which today may be characterized as more of a transient socioeconomic problem than one of technology or resources, is without doubt in process of solution. The resolution will probably require no more than one or two decades at most, and possibly only a few years. Undoubtedly the near term solution will combine (a) the conservation of energy to alleviate the present economic strains through the many ways already made popular: better insulation, smaller vehicles, mass transit, etc.; (b) relatively small changes in life-styles induced by higher energy costs, as long as these are expected to prevail, expressed in new energy-efficient designs for homes, industries, transport, and commerce; and (c) the vigorous development of new sources of energy both through exploratory mining for conventional fuels and through application of advanced technology for improving efficiency and harnessing new energy sources.

All these are familiar except perhaps for new sources of energy from advanced technology, now being pursued through research, some of which may be commercially feasible before the end of this century. So many promising techniques exist that are independent of fossil fuels that it is now almost inconceivable that an abundance of new energy from these sources will not be phased into extensive commercial exploitation early during the 21st century, and perhaps sooner. We list some of the possibilities:

Solar electrical power: both through the use of relatively inexpensive arrays of solar cells and through large-area radiant reflectors. The supply is "unlimited" in abundance, clean, and possibly can be furnished cheaply, eventually.

Nuclear power: though uranium reactors may always involve a residual worry about leaks, disasters, or effective waste control, the technology is here and, undoubtedly, the safety can be improved steadily over time. If necessary, we could live with current problems and uncertainties. Moreover, nuclear energy without such safety problems, through fusion, has never appeared more promising, and we well might witness the first commercial installation this century. The fusion reactor is nearly free of radioactive threats in any of its present designs, and, if successful, offers hope for almost complete safety through more advanced designs now being studied. In the advanced concepts the reactions would not leave any radioactive waste to be disposed of directly or indirectly. In addition, the power potential is eventually unlimited.

Ocean gradient power: theoretical designs and current pilot plant operations are underway. If and when they are successful, a clean renewable source, effectively unlimited in its potential, will become available—in addition to potential side benefits in the form of pure water and of nutrients for aquaculture.

Cellulose conversion: A pilot plant is now being designed to convert cellulose into glucose from which alcohol can be readily synthesized. The process offers good hope for conversion of billions of tons annually of a renewable resource, cellulose, into a clean fuel, alcohol, with a potential energy yield several times that obtained currently from all the world's fossil fuel sources.

Geothermal energy: The interior of the earth contains enough energy to supply the needs of a profligate world for billions of years. The problem is to develop this source economically. Technical solutions are being sought to overcome the problems of reaching, tapping, and conveying this energy rapidly to the earth's surface at a cost competitive with other techniques. Nature has demonstrated one approach by showing that water properly delivered into deep crustal fractures will return as great geysers of steam. If we can economically create by engineering what nature has done by chance, then clean, unlimited power from the earth's interior is in mankind's

grasp. The prospects appear good in many areas of the world.

Clearly, although we may feel the pinch of high-priced energy today, the long-run prospects offered by a few of the more promising possibilities offer potentially inexpensive and enormous, perhaps inexhaustible, supplies of non-polluting energy, a sound basis for developing worldwide affluence during the next century.

METAL RESOURCES: AMPLE

Finally, we would like to make a few remarks about the "non-renewable" resources most often discussed—namely the industrial metals. This subject is more easily examined by grouping the metals into three appropriate categories.

First, we mention five important metals in such abundant supply that they are essentially inexhaustible. These are iron, aluminum, magnesium, titanium, and silicon. A second category is a group of four metals—copper, cobalt, manganese, and nickel—which are found accreting in nodules located on the ocean floor and for which explorations and new ocean mining techniques are currently being developed by about twenty large industries or consortiums. The nodules have been found to exist in such huge quantities and in so many areas that they are believed to be forming faster than they can be mined and processed for human use. Few experts doubt that one or more of the many possible mining techniques will soon, within ten to twenty years, be commercially successful, certainly well before any exhaustion of standard mine sources can occur.

What of the other principal industrial metals? These are mainly chromium, zinc, lead, tin, gold, silver, and mercury. Although none is on the verge of exhaustion, if the demand for any of these metals increases, then we can expect their price to rise to the point where it is in reasonable balance with supply. The price would affect and be affected, of course, by (a) successful exploration for new sources; (b) improved technology for mining residual ores of lower concentration; (c) improved recycling; (d) substitution of the other minerals in adequate supply or of plastics which are becoming increasingly effective each year as metal substitutes (DuPont now has in commercial production a new plastic (trade name, KELVAR) which is much stronger and much lighter than high tensile steel, and astonishingly resistant to corrosion); and (e) new engineering designs which can circumvent or reduce the need for high priced metals. Also, and a matter of potentially huge importance, the ocean contains every industrial metal in dissolved or suspended particles, in quantities which are enormous compared to any foreseeable demand. Even at present, there are certain indications of new approaches which might soon lead to commercial mining of the ocean water for the desirable mineral content. However, even if the ocean continues to resist such commercial extraction, there seems to be little reason for any major concern about appropriate metals for the world's economy. None of the metals in this last group is indispensable, only convenient to man's current needs and styles.

We have avoided the inclination to make this essay a technical one. Rather, we have chosen to illustrate, conceptually, some of the ways in which international problems, considered today to be among the more difficult ones, can be understood and approached in order to find satisfactory solutions. During subsequent years increasing time and attention, worldwide, will be given to these problems; this should result in an even greater likelihood that they will be successfully resolved. All in all, we remain optimistic about the potential of man's future. We can only hope that he does not throw away this potential through foolish political behavior or misplaced concern about non-existent or badly formulated growth issues.

INDEX